Unredeemed Land

Unredeemed Land

An Environmental History of Civil War
and Emancipation in the Cotton South

ERIN STEWART MAULDIN

OXFORD
UNIVERSITY PRESS

OXFORD
UNIVERSITY PRESS

Oxford University Press is a department of the University of Oxford. It furthers
the University's objective of excellence in research, scholarship, and education
by publishing worldwide. Oxford is a registered trade mark of Oxford University
Press in the UK and certain other countries.

Published in the United States of America by Oxford University Press
198 Madison Avenue, New York, NY 10016, United States of America.

© Oxford University Press 2018

First issued as an Oxford University Press paperback, 2021

Library of Congress Cataloging-in-Publication Data
Names: Mauldin, Erin Stewart, author.
Title: Unredeemed land : an environmental history of Civil War and
emancipation in the cotton South / Erin Stewart Mauldin.
Description: New York, NY : Oxford University Press, [2018] |
Includes bibliographical references and index.
Identifiers: LCCN 2018012959 (print) | LCCN 2018013388 (ebook) |
ISBN 9780190865184 (Updf) | ISBN 9780190865191 (Epub) |
ISBN 9780190865177 (hardcover : alk. paper) | ISBN 9780197563441 (paperback : alk. paper)
Subjects: LCSH: Cotton trade—Environmental aspects—Southern States. |
Agriculture—Environmental aspects—Southern States. |
Southern States—Environmental conditions—19th century. |
Southern States—Economic conditions—19th century. | United States—History—
Civil War, 1861–1865—Environmental aspects.
Classification: LCC HD9077.A13 (ebook) | LCC HD9077.A13 M38 2018 (print) |
DDC 338.10975/09034—dc23
LC record available at https://lccn.loc.gov/2018012959

For my family

CONTENTS

ACKNOWLEDGMENTS

From its conception during graduate research seminars at Georgetown University to my first glimpse of the cover image, many kind, wonderful, supportive people contributed to the completion of this project. I must first thank my dissertation committee, for without them, there would be no dissertation, and no book. Adam Rothman enriched my work with his valuable criticism, and Chandra Manning, a deeply gifted teacher and scholar, always knew what I was *trying* to say and why it was important, even if I didn't. And since I showed up in his office as a terrified first-year grad student, John McNeill has been a better adviser and mentor than I could wish for, someone who sacrificed his time to skillfully guide me through coursework, read seminar papers, promptly respond to the most trivial of emails, and comment on drafts of this project long after I had left Georgetown. For that, I am indescribably thankful.

Of course, the comments and ideas of fellow historians helped shape my thinking over the years. Megan Kate Nelson, Mart Stewart, Paul Sutter, and Judkin Browning gave helpful comments and suggestions on my work at various conferences, and I am especially grateful to Mark Hersey for providing so many opportunities to present pieces of this project to a range of audiences in the CHASES and Agricultural History circles. In the final stages of the manuscript, I greatly benefited from the support and detailed guidance of Susan Ferber at OUP, and I appreciate the challenging questions and gracious suggestions of the two anonymous readers of the manuscript.

I was very lucky to work with a group of talented scholars at Samford University while writing this book. I would like to thank my colleagues Ginger Frost, Carlos Alemán, Jason Wallace, and particularly John Mayfield and Jonathan Bass for their support and encouragement, whether in the form of words, emails, offers to babysit, or help with classes. John Mitcham, with whom I was lucky enough to teach with at Samford before he joined the faculty at Duquesne University, deserves special thanks. His careful editing and words of guidance shaped every chapter of this book, and I am so appreciative of his selfless collaboration.

Research is a time- and money-intensive process, even though I was lucky to be doing archival work in the geographic region where I live. I received generous financial assistance for my research, first from the Georgetown University Department of History and Graduate School and, later, the Andrew C. Mellon Foundation. Samford University provided me not only with a teaching position but also funds for conference travel and presentations related to this project. I would also like to extend my gratitude to the librarians and archivists at the Library of Congress Manuscript Division, the University of Alabama, Auburn University, the University of North Carolina at Chapel Hill, the North Carolina State Library, the National Archives and Records Administration, the Atlanta History Center, Emory University, Duke University, the Birmingham Public Library, the Tennessee State Library, and Samford University who pulled boxes, pointed to additional resources, filled Inter-Library Loan requests, and offered encouragement during long days in overly air-conditioned reading rooms. Finally, I would like to acknowledge my family. I am indebted to my parents, Dickie and Leslie Stewart, and my in-laws, Don and Glenda Mauldin, for the years of blind faith that I would finish whatever it was that I was working on, and for caring for my son while I wrote or traveled. But it is to my boys—my husband, Daniel, and our son, Jack—that I dedicate this book. They have shared my burdens and my dreams, and no words can express my gratitude for their presences in my life.

Unredeemed Land

Introduction

Thick, cloying smoke perfumed by gunpowder and carrying with it the tang of hot metal shrouded the battlefield of Nimrod Porter's nightmare. The commotion of suffering punctured his subconscious, leaving impressions of "the clashing of arms, the groans of the wounded and dying, the awful and uncommon loud peals of the cannon," a din he found both horrifying and sublime. Stretching upward from the landscape of slain men and wounded horses rose a stately oak tree. He dreamt that its beautiful emerald leaves remained untouched by the slaughter around it, its branches flapping as gently in the wake of cannon fire as they might in a spring breeze. Yet the tree's presence on the field troubled him more than the blood coursing across the grass. Fearing the oak's inevitable destruction, he awoke, startled by his own cries to God. "Stop this dreadful battle!" Hours passed and still the idea of the tree haunted him. Nimrod Porter recorded his strange imaginings on the paper nearest to him—his farm diary for September 20, 1863. "I shall never forget this dream."[1]

At first, the inclusion of a nightmare in the journals of a Tennessee farmer seems out of place among the decades of mundane entries detailing barley planting, hog killing, weather watching, and other agricultural activities. December 18, 1861: "We fed all the long field to the hogs except 5 loads." November 7, 1862: "We halled 19 loads of corn from the Glade lot." Still, over four volumes chronicling the writer's loss of his daughter, the deaths of his closest contemporaries, the uncertainty of farming amid springtime storms or late summer droughts, Porter's angry response at Republicans' election to local office and the passivity with which he recorded the actions of the Ku Klux Klan, the dream's entanglement of nature, violence, and human action foreshadows how war and emancipation upended Porter's life. The environment is the centerpiece of the dream, constantly threatened but not yet destroyed, the chaos of human change playing out in, on, and around it.[2]

Nimrod Porter was not a "typical" southern farmer. A wealthy man, he owned at least thirty-one slaves in 1850 and four hundred acres of fields and woodlands near the Duck River in Maury County, Tennessee.[3] He grew a mix of crops and raised livestock, an approach that exemplified the practices of many farmers of the time. Throughout the antebellum period, large-scale cotton planting flourished in a few areas, and the lure of rising cotton prices caused rampant land speculation on the western frontier, but the spatial boundaries of the Cotton Kingdom remained fairly limited on the eve of the Civil War. Like Porter, the majority of southerners prized self-sufficiency over risky ventures in capital-intensive staple production. The primary cultivar on Porter's farm was corn (of which he planted three varieties), but he also produced oats and barley, a range of truck crops, nursed apple and peach orchards, and kept relatively large herds of cattle and hogs in the forested lots along the edges of his land. His slaves, rarely named in the antebellum journal entries, maintained the repairs on his corn cribs and wagons, hauled poles across his acreage to fence new fields, and cleared fresh ground to plant as old fields lost their fertility. It was a productive and profitable regime, despite the gradual disappearance of woodland on the property and decreasing corn yields by 1860.[4]

And then the war came. Soldiers in both blue and gray camped on Porter's land during the latter half of the Civil War. They impressed his slaves, often without his knowledge or permission, and removed tens of thousands of dollars in timber to build tents, make fires, and construct defenses. On January 13, 1863, Porter complained that Confederate troops from General Nathan Bedford Forrest's brigade had uprooted his fences and left his wood lot "vary much destroyed." He felt distressed to see it, but decided that "it must be borne." The Confederate commissary prowled for horses, mules, and cattle to send to camps in nearby Giles County, and men with alleged "government contracts" pilfered corn and bacon. After Federal forces chased the Confederates from the area, the farmer suffered the same depredations under the Union Army's presence: soldiers required slaves to work, firewood to burn, and animals to eat. On November 26, 1864, Porter fumed, "The soldiers are camped in every piece of woods they can find on the plantation, burning up the fences, cutting down the trees all over the plantation. Killed nearly all of our fat hogs." With Union occupation eventually came abolition. In the summer of 1865, slaves began to leave, act out, or simply refuse to work. Porter celebrated the end of the war, but he lamented the conditions of the peace and dreaded the process of recovery.[5]

Over the subsequent years, Porter recorded a number of changes to the business of farming in middle Tennessee. The physical damage to his plantation proved temporary, but the disappearance of agricultural resources, introduction of new animal diseases, clearance of his woodland, and, most importantly, the new system of arranging wages or shares to compensate his laborers gradually altered how Porter (and others like him) farmed. Before the war, he had slaughtered eleven to fifteen hogs every December; now he only had three. The animals no longer roamed the woods, for he sold off his cedars to pay his promissory notes. At least in a pen the animals were less likely to be pilfered by his less fortunate neighbors and, he hoped, less susceptible to disease. Since he did not provide rations, Porter's farmhands—some of whom were ex-slaves who had returned after the surrender—required his signature as security when they purchased bacon from merchants on credit. The farm gradually fragmented into individual plots for each laborer. Some rented enough land that they needed daily wage laborers to help with the harvests. Others only possessed a "patch" of land and paid for their food by doing piecemeal tasks for Porter: felling trees, fixing fences, or hauling corn to feed the hogs. Most importantly, Porter no longer hewed to the principle of self-sufficiency. He, and all his renters, grew cotton. He still planted corn, albeit only one variety, as well as several garden crops. But it was cotton that dictated the rhythms of the farm and daily life.[6]

As Nimrod Porter's farm journals show, the American Civil War marked a watershed moment in the history of agriculture in the US South. For four years, competing armies traversed the various crop regions of the South, marshalling, foraging, and impressing the resources of the home front for use on the battlefield. In 1865, the states of the former Confederacy emerged from the war defeated, physically scarred, and economically handicapped. Their four million slaves enjoyed newfound legal freedom, but faced significant obstacles to the acquisition of capital, land, or agricultural resources. A series of constraints complicated farmers' efforts to resurrect crop production during the Reconstruction era, including a lack of capital, the war's alterations to credit and debt structures, reduced access to livestock and farm machinery, changing labor arrangements, and a series of droughts. Still, many planters hoped for a quick return to prosperity amid high cotton prices at the end of the conflict.

Between 1865 and 1875, the economic allure of King Cotton enticed landowners such as Porter, as well as yeoman farmers and recently freed slaves in all areas of the South, to eschew a "safety first" approach in favor of heavy investments in staple production. Within fifteen years of the Confederate surrender, the region's cotton output surpassed prewar benchmarks. Gone was the relative agricultural diversity of the antebellum period. As Reconstruction ended and the "New South" dawned, the ever-expanding Cotton Kingdom and the coercive crop arrangements it engendered formed the basis of a stagnating regional agricultural system that existed well into the twentieth century. Until the Second World War, Dixie was a land of cotton, and little else.[7]

Why did so many postwar southern farmers rely on continuous cotton cultivation? What caused such a shift in attitudes toward self-sufficiency in farming areas that had been known for their relative crop diversity before the war? And if cotton was famously the only crop that would "pay," why did it leave its cultivators so poor? In contrast to histories that answer these questions by examining the free operation of market forces or the persistence of racial and class conflict,

Unredeemed Land connects these postwar agricultural shifts to the ecological legacies of the Civil War and emancipation. The conflict was a profoundly environmental event, rather than a purely military or political occurrence. As historian Stephen Berry writes, the Civil War was "a massive stir of the biotic soup," and it fundamentally changed the relationships between people, plants, and animals.[8] The war and the subsequent rise of the contract labor system destroyed traditional land-use practices and intensified environmental change in ways that altered both the land itself and how farmers conceived of its use—encouraging, and sometimes necessitating, continuous cotton cultivation, despite shrinking financial incentives.

This book provides both a narrative and an environmental analysis of southern agriculture from the antebellum period through Reconstruction. After all, farms are merely ecosystems shaped by human attempts to harness biotic productivity for food or profit. Agriculture is thus the interaction of human beings and other species within a dynamic, ever-changing physical environment. As historian Jack Temple Kirby writes, "Landscapes have the power to invite, constrain, and occasionally prohibit human occupance .... Humans nonetheless have ever shaped landscapes as best (or worst) they could."[9] Farmers deliberately cultivate the parts of the environment best suited for human use—and try to eliminate those that are not—but they are never successful in exerting mastery over the natural communities they "own." "For all the power farmers have to reorganize biotic communities," environmental historian Lynn Nelson explains, "they still 'negotiate' with crops, livestock, soils, and weather to determine the shape of agricultural ecosystems." Before the advent of industrialized agriculture, it took massive amounts of labor to protect a crop field, which is simply a highly simplified, artificial ecosystem, from the rest of nature. Nevertheless, farmers across time and space have adapted to the ecological constraints with which they are presented.[10]

During the antebellum period, farmers in the American South adapted to environmental limitations on agriculture by utilizing a set of extensive agricultural techniques that worked only as long as the region and its slave-based system were able to expand onto fresh soil. The southern landscape, though often praised for its suitability for agricultural pursuits, presented natural obstacles to long-term, profitable agricultural production. Its weathered soils lacked key nutrients and eroded easily. Hot, humid summers and frequent and often heavy rainfall prevented the growth of pasture grasses and accelerated the leaching of nutrients from the soils.[11] This led to a set of land-use practices that were drastically different from those of northern farms, which were typically characterized by the intensive cultivation of a small plot of land for many generations. Grain production formed the basis of crop regimes in the North, and livestock-raising using pens and permanent pasture was widespread. These practices made little economic and ecological sense in the South. Neither the grains that supported mixed-crop planting schedules nor the grasses required to feed penned livestock fared well in the acidic soils of the region.[12] Instead of intensively planting small pieces of land, southerners extensively farmed larger acreages. They cultivated a fraction of the land they owned and cleared additional ground when yields began to fall. Farmers allowed their animals to graze in woodland and old fields most of the year, and in the absence of a significant livestock industry to produce manure, agriculturalists burned vegetation to mitigate soil nutrient deficiencies. Most white farmers used family, hired, or slave labor to perform a set of "land maintenance" tasks that helped alleviate problems of soil erosion and flooding.[13]

These extensive cultivation methods allowed southerners to circumvent some of the environmental limitations on long-term crop production and stock-raising, at least temporarily. The "sustainability" of southern agriculture, its ability to replicate itself in a profitable way over time, depended on practices such as shifting cultivation and free-range animal husbandry to keep erosion at bay, soil nutrients in balance without investment in fertilizers, livestock fed with little capital, and crop yields high. As long as the South and its system of slavery had access to new lands and fresh soil, this particular set of land use practices masked the environmental impacts of farmers' actions.

The war abruptly tore off that mask. For four years, military operations ripped up fences, reduced open range or made roaming stock more vulnerable to soldiers, stopped the flow of fertilizers and other agricultural goods, and interfered with crop production. Indeed, the environmental conditions under which antebellum southern agriculture developed made the region particularly vulnerable to these standard military practices. Although in many ways the conflict provided the natural resources of the South with a respite from human use, it also accelerated the pace and extent of environmental constraints, such as erosion, soil nutrient imbalances, woodland clearance, and the presence of animal diseases. Meanwhile, emancipation had created a new class of mostly landless farmers who could not be supported without widespread changes in land use. Emancipation's subsequent entanglement of agricultural techniques with race and labor relations complicated poor southerners' access to vital subsistence resources and chained them to increasingly intensive cultivation techniques that were too expensive to be profitable. Thus, the region felt the Civil War's environmental impacts for decades after Sherman marched through Georgia.

In the years after the Confederate surrender, the subsistence economy of the antebellum South—in which poor whites and (to some extent) slaves utilized common lands to raise livestock, grow food crops, and hunt—gradually disappeared. The pressure to maximize space for the cultivation of staple crops and the increasing impracticality of free-range animal husbandry and shifting cultivation amid the dramatic environmental changes of the Civil War era weakened the economic logic of maintaining common lands. Social and racial constraints contributed as well, for the reorganization of plantations, contentious labor contract negotiations, and the desire for planters to reassert their authority converged in the debates over the open range and the use of tenant plots for crops other than cotton or tobacco. Key subsistence practices and agricultural reform efforts fell by the wayside, making market integration the only way for poor farmers to provide for their families. The loss of autonomy due to debt, the ecological conflicts it created, and those conflicts' exacerbation of social divides led to the gradual but unrelenting impoverishment of southern farms and farmers beyond the end of the nineteenth century.

In short, the Civil War and emancipation forced southerners to face the "reconstruction" of their agricultural landscape with the four cornerstones of the antebellum agricultural regime—shifting cultivation, free-range animal husbandry, slavery, and continuous territorial expansion—either eliminated or significantly less practical. Changes in land use, combined with ecological factors, meant that many farmers' land required too many inputs to remain profitable, constraining their choices and encouraging the cultivation of cotton at the expense of self-sufficiency. They had to plant cotton to pay for the fertilizer, seed, implements, and provisions they needed to plant cotton. Had the subsistence economy existed as it had before the war, southern farmers might have used common spaces to raise provisions or livestock. Instead, sharecropping and tenancy had very real effects on the land, creating an ecological feedback loop that kept cotton farmers shackled to that crop despite diminishing returns. The "cotton burden" and the loss of self-sufficiency among farmers, so often characterized as the result of market forces or landholder and merchant greed, was a complex interplay between ecological shifts, land-use changes, and broader socioeconomic structures. The southern environment could not support the widespread intensive cultivation of cotton without expensive outlays many agriculturalists could not afford.

As lands around the South degraded, both white farmers and black farmers sought a way to "redeem" their exhausted soils. A concept as old as southern farming itself, to "redeem" one's lands meant to restore, reclaim, or revitalize fields worn out by cash-crop cultivation, and return to a more balanced, profitable approach to land use. Almost every nineteenth-century agricultural magazine regularly highlighted stories of "redemption," with contributors spinning tales of irresponsible farmers who had nearly ruined their lands suddenly converting to the methods promoted by reformers: crop rotation, terracing, ditching, growing pasture grasses, penning stock, and using animal manure to fertilize the soil. Invariably, the lesson was that by improving the health of their land and ensuring the permanence of their operations, these reformed agriculturalists had saved their farms. During the postwar years, however, it was no longer practical or feasible to pursue this course of action.[14] The dramatic and irreversible changes to the landscape during the war made the negotiation between farmer and nature more difficult than ever, and because of the ecological legacies of the Civil War and emancipation, the southern environment remained unredeemed.

To ask how the Civil War and emancipation transformed southern agriculture engages a historical narrative over a century in the making, one that traveled along the well-worn paths of slavery and emancipation, the devastation of wartime, and the vain search for prosperity after defeat. To answer this question is to get at the most profound transformation of the nineteenth-century South, one that defined and continues to define the region, and to comment on the central themes of its history: continuity versus change, an abiding perception of economic and social "backwardness," and the persistence of racial oppression.

In a vast and dynamic literature, scholars have detailed how the Civil War reshaped the rural South. This work first charted the war's physical and economic devastation—the ruination of the land through military operations and the large-scale loss of currency, agricultural implements, and cottonseed. Above all, it focused on the economic consequences of emancipation. The freeing of four million slaves cost white southerners billions of dollars in investments and encumbered farmers at all socioeconomic levels in their efforts to resurrect agricultural operations after the war.[15] A second body of work drew on quantitative analysis to show how the war changed market structures: it created new lending protocols, gave rise to predatory postwar credit systems, and shuffled trade patterns by making the railroad boom of the 1870s possible. In this view, "the world the war made" was more intensively capitalistic than its antebellum predecessor.[16] Other scholars employed sociocultural perspectives on the South's transformation from its antebellum agricultural halcyon to its postbellum crisis. In previous decades, this work centered on planters' continuing monopoly of resources and the destruction of the rural white yeomanry amid the expansion of cotton production and the rise of sharecropping.[17] More recently, historians have elevated the experiences and agency of black southerners. Illuminating the role of freedpeople in altering plantation operations during Reconstruction, while under the constant threat of violence, they uncovered ways in which the actions of blacks affected the processes described in the older, more quantitative literature.[18]

All these works frame the relationship of land and labor during the post–Civil War period in either social or economic terms. But what happens if the discussion of southern agriculture begins with the land itself? The widely recognized hallmarks of nineteenth-century southern agriculture—expanded cotton production, the rise of sharecropping, and evolving labor relations—took place in an environmental context that shaped both individual actions and broader structural forces. Although the contention that natural elements, such as climate and soils, both respond to and shape human actions may no longer be novel, it has rarely been applied to the rural South during the Reconstruction era.[19]

The story told here begins in the late antebellum period, as the slave-based cotton plantation complex reached its prewar apogee. Land-hungry southerners had largely settled the "Old Southwest" and established the broad outlines of the kinds of agricultural operations that became common to the era. Scattered railroads had increased market access for some, but those limited track lines had not yet transformed regional commerce. The book ends roughly around 1880, by which time the region seemed certain to become a "solid South" based on cotton production. Even the more isolated upland areas of the Appalachians exhibited symptoms of cotton contagion: the production of tobacco, grains, and livestock succumbed to the pursuit of "white gold," and postwar hierarchies of agriculture tenure, such as sharecropping, weakened local labor relations. This period allows for analysis of southern agriculture at the dawn of the New South, before the boll weevil's rampage caused environmental disaster and reset conditions in the region at the opening of the twentieth century.[20]

Geographically, the book examines the "cotton South" as it existed in the 1880s, meaning that it covers parts of most southern states but largely excludes Kentucky, some of Virginia, and Florida. Although it is difficult to construct environmental change across a space as large and diverse as the American South, the book surveys the region using aggregate data and historical studies of regional processes, and then draws from individual and local stories gathered from sixteen archives in ten states for more detailed illustration of general trends. Notwithstanding an abundance of evidence, the result is hardly comprehensive. In justifying his own approach to a regionwide environmental survey of the South, Albert Cowdrey wrote, "The landscape of the essay, like that of its subject, is a patchwork of well-worn fields and fallow."[21]

In 1930, one of Frederick Jackson Turner's students, A. B. Hulbert, observed that "history has numerous handmaidens," which include geology, soil science, botany, and climatology. "Every one of them must come into range of the student's vision if we are to give a proper weight to all the factors which will aid us in arriving at correct solutions of historical problems and processes."[22] Following Hulbert's plea, this work employs an interdisciplinary methodological approach. On the one hand, it relies on traditional manuscript sources, such as farmers' letters and journals, soldiers' remembrances and records, census data, and a range of agricultural periodicals and government records. On the other hand, this project draws on a wealth of current scientific and agronomic literature from human geography, crop science, ecology, geomorphology, botany, dendrochronology, and hydrology to provide an overlooked window into the past.

Using insights of environmental history and the natural sciences to re-examine the crucial decades between 1840 and 1880 reveals new ways to conceive of the war's place in the trajectory of southern agriculture. The four-year conflict and its emancipation of slaves dramatically transformed how farmers thought about, manipulated, and organized their land. These gradual revolutions in agricultural practices initiated a series of ecological disruptions that went hand-in-hand with the economic displacement of sharecroppers and tenants, poor whites, and poor blacks. In other words, environmental changes acted as a "threat multiplier," a term used when ecological instability accelerates violence, political division, and economic hardship—problems compounding problems.[23] Altered methods of land use and rapidly shifting natural processes amplified the well-known dislocations of the postbellum era: shortages of capital, racial prejudice, and repressive crop legislation. All these elements are essential to understanding postwar developments and, ultimately, the outlines of the New South. Restoring the land to the study of land and labor recovers an important piece of a large and complicated narrative.

Bridging the antebellum, wartime, and Reconstruction eras also brings the first wave of environmental histories of the Civil War into conversation with the rich literature on Reconstruction and New South agriculture, connecting the ecological legacies of the war with postwar issues of racial conflict, economic shifts, and social upheaval.[24] Too many histories of Reconstruction effectively divorce the postwar narrative from its earlier origins; looking at the evolution of southern agricultural systems over the course of the entire nineteenth century helps clarify the paradoxes of post–Civil War developments. The failure of Reconstruction policies to alleviate the plight of landless white and black farmers was not inevitable; rather, it was the result of thousands of individual decisions interacting with ongoing ecological processes in the context of a long-standing system of land use.

Revisiting the records of farmers like Nimrod Porter through an environmental lens puts them back in conversation with the subject they were most concerned with: the land. And doing this on a regional scale demonstrates that the impoverishing nature of postwar cotton expansion was not merely the result of slave emancipation, or predatory lending practices, or falling cotton prices. The Civil War revealed environmental limits and constraints that were already in place, whose effects had long been delayed by territorial expansion and the use of slave labor to create and maintain agricultural landscapes. Accelerated soil erosion, woodland clearance, and land abandonment, as well as the war's exacerbation of the antebellum system's ecological weaknesses, helped to shape the postwar economy from the ground up. Even without the war, white southern farmers would likely have eventually exhausted the ability of the landscape to support extensive agriculture. However, the conflict guaranteed that outcome sooner rather than later. Just as extensive land use and ecological conditions united the Old South, so, too, did the economic and environmental dislocation of the postwar agricultural system create and then bring together the New South.

Deferring Crisis

The history of this South . . . is mainly the history of the roll of frontier
upon frontier—and on to the frontier beyond.
—W. J. Cash, *The Mind of the South* (1941)

The clay soils along the creek bed remained swollen after an unusually rainy
January, forming a slick morass that pulled at Big George's feet and slowed his
pace. One of thirty-six slaves owned by Joseph Macafee Jayne Sr., Big George
was twenty-eight years old in 1854 and worth $1200. He was not the best cotton
picker—that was usually Adams or Amon—but he always took the lead in the
laborious tasks of the lay-by season, between December and March. This was his
third straight week working in the Gin Field, a knotted mass of hardwood trees
and blackberry briars a few hundred yards from the cotton gin. The trees had
been girdled during previous winters and their trunks left to weaken, making
them easier to fell. Along with fellow slaves Hank, Jim, and Tad, Big George set
about "cutting along the creek." The men sheared through brush in the partially
cleared bottomland and removed deadened beeches from the embankment.
Once they finished ridding the ground of any obstacles to future plowing, they
rolled the logs toward the house yard, where they would be split into rails. Jayne
meticulously kept track of each man's output: Harris, 117 rails; Little George,
150 rails; Dan and Jess, 280 rails; and Big George, 300 rails. The slaves shaped
the logs into boards and poles, and later that month, toted them back to the Gin
Field to build a fence. The size of the plot made the job a daunting one, but without a fence, the hogs and cattle ranging in the plantation's woodland could feast
on any crops they planted there come spring.[1]

The tasks Big George, Hank, Jim, and Tad performed on Jayne's Mississippi
plantation were essential components of an extensive land-use regime commonly employed by cotton farmers during the antebellum period. When the
slaves "cleared new ground" in the Gin Field, they were engaging in shifting
cultivation, a modified form of long fallow in which the boundaries of agricultural operations moved regularly around a planter's landholding. Jayne's slaves

burned trees, brush, and cotton stalks over the fields, new or old, to improve the nutrient content of the topsoil. It is clear from Jayne's plantation journals that he also engaged in free-range animal husbandry, a popular method of raising livestock in the South in which farmers fenced in their crops and allowed animals to forage in the woods for large portions of the year. Finally, Jayne's slaves carried out land-maintenance work, such as ditching, which helped to control erosion or protect crops from damage. Extensive land-use techniques allowed antebellum farmers to maintain profitable operations without making significant capital outlays for fertilizers, mechanization, new breeds of livestock, and other agricultural resources used to maintain more intensive operations.

This chapter shows how common ecological constraints engendered a set of agricultural techniques used by farmers, rich and poor, across the antebellum cotton South. Travel writers and land speculators of the time waxed enthusiastic about the South's seemingly inexhaustible fertility. In reality, the southern environment presented farmers with a range of difficulties. Its soils lacked key nutrients; the topsoil eroded easily; the climate accelerated the weathering of soils; and the region's hot summers prevented the growth of pasture grasses necessary for livestock. The continuous cultivation practiced in northern-style commercial agriculture was not economically or ecologically rational in the South. Whether they farmed the prairie bottomlands, as Joseph Jayne did, lived on the sandier coastal plain, or mined the soils of hilly upland regions, southern cotton farmers made use of shifting cultivation, free-range animal husbandry, and a particular set of erosion control and farm-maintenance techniques, many of which relied on the work of centrally commanded labor forces.

These practices temporarily restored some of the land's fertility and thus helped to offset the effects of farmers' rapacious consumption of natural resources. But in many areas of the cotton South, the pace of environmental change was unsustainable given the conversion and exhaustion of flora, fauna, soil, and water for agricultural purposes. The land simply could not keep up with the world's voracious hunger for cotton. "Agricultural reformers" talked seriously throughout the antebellum period about the impoverishment of the South's landscape under the influence of plantation-based agriculture. They lamented the exhaustion of the soil, disappearance of old-growth trees, proliferation of "wastelands," and presence of almost-feral livestock ranging freely in uncultivated spaces. They believed the South was on the brink of an ecological—and thus an economic—crisis.

Before the Civil War, their fears were never realized because extensive land use masked the ecological implications of cotton cultivation. It provided a cheap way to restore nutrients to the soil and mitigate erosion; it also acted a kind of safety valve for farmers who had overused their land. It did not solve the problems of the southern agroecological system but merely deferred any impending threats to the economic stability of the largely agrarian region. Of course, this agricultural regime was only feasible as long as southerners could depend on continuous territorial expansion and, so the planters believed, slave labor. When all these elements were in place, as they were in the 1840s and 1850s, extensive land use kept the South's regional development from collapsing under the weight of environmental degradation. If conditions changed—as they did after 1861—the balance was disturbed. And the disconnect between natural limitations and land use would have dire consequences for southern farmers.

Proponents and critics of southern farming alike recognized the centrality and limitations of the antebellum land-use regime, and political rhetoric over westward expansion and secession argued that continuing (or increasing) the geographic reach of the South's slave-based agrarianism was essential to the region's prosperity. As the nation carved up newly seized territories into "slave" and "free" areas, both slaveholding and nonslaveholding southerners saw a very real threat to their way of life. The debate over whether to expand slavery into new territories was more than a virulent political issue: constraining slave territories threatened the profitability and long-term sustainability of the southern agricultural economy. In this way, the national schism over the future of the Mexican Cession and the growing support for abolitionism in certain circles challenged southerners' environmental understandings of their lives and livelihoods. Both political and ecological crises loomed in the 1850s, and extensive land use by cotton farmers was at the center of it all.

The plantation of Big George's owner, Joseph M. Jayne, stretched across 960 acres of cotton-growing land in central Mississippi, a thickly timbered but generally fertile area that others called the "black prairie." Its irregular plains and high, narrow ridges transected by creeks and rivers contained a calcareous, dark-colored soil coveted for its fine texture and cropping potential. Although Jayne recognized the limitations of his land—the topsoil was highly erosive; the clay dirt supporting his plants visibly expanded and contracted in response to rain; his bottomlands flooded too often to reliably make a crop—he had to admit that his purchase had been a good one. In 1855, at the age of twenty-eight, Jayne's property holdings included not only his acreage but also thirty-six slaves and decent herds of cattle and hogs. The profits his slaves coaxed from the soil provided Jayne with the money to pay for luxuries, such as pleasure carriages and a grand piano, as well as the time and leisure to reflect on his farm's operations in a daily journal. His father had not done nearly so well. Drawn down the eastern seaboard from Long Island, New York, by the promise of riches in the newly acquired Creek and Choctaw cessions, Jayne's father, Anselm, landed in the pine lands of Mississippi's coastal plain in 1828. There, he married the daughter of a displaced upland farmer from South Carolina and struggled to carve out a living from his acidic, sandy ground. Not until his oldest son, Joseph, moved to Rankin County did the Jayne family begin to realize the prosperity Anselm had dreamed of when he abandoned the North for a place in the Cotton Kingdom.[2]

The antebellum cotton boom that had lured Anselm Jayne from New York in the 1820s and ensured the financial stability of his son in the 1850s was part of a multidecadal shift that forged the socioeconomic basis of the Old South. At the opening of the nineteenth century, cotton production prudently clung to its coastal confines, where plantations on the Sea Islands grew the environmentally discriminating long-staple variety. Short-staple cotton, in contrast, grew well away from the coast. This variety only needed two hundred frost-free days and twenty inches of rain annually, climatic benchmarks met in much of the southeast. After the invention of the cotton gin, farmers turned to the production of short-staple cotton in droves.[3] Southerners raised 750,000 bales of short-staple cotton in 1820, and by the eve of the Civil War, census records tallied a regional total of 4.6 million bales. Farmers adopted new seed varieties with larger bolls, which, together with improvements in ginning and packing equipment and the ever-increasing picking quotas forced on slaves, buoyed production numbers over time.[4] Demand on the world market and general profitability affected cotton's expansion as well, because the crop hitched the South's agricultural future to booming European centers of textile manufacturing. In 1840, cotton accounted for half the value of all US exports, and the South supplied well over half the world's cotton. The prices farmers received for their crops reflected the centrality of cotton in the global market: prices rose steeply between 1830 and 1835 and then steadily through the 1850s. By 1855, a newspaper could boast, "Cotton–Cotton–Cotton—that is the great staple!" Although poor-quality cotton never sold for "anything but a sacrifice," the general stability of cotton prices during this period encouraged many farmers, in a range of landscapes, to try their hand at the crop. In 1820, most cotton production occurred in the central region of South Carolina; by 1840, east-central Georgia, the Mississippi Delta, middle Tennessee, and southern Alabama were also participating in the burgeoning cotton economy.[5]

However, cotton was not then the all-consuming crop it later became. Even as the cotton boom matured, the geography of the South's staple production remained concentrated in discrete subregions that specialized in tobacco, rice, sugar, or cotton, but rarely in more than one of those cultivars.[6] Rice planters and their slaves perfected a carefully engineered and intensely managed plantation landscape extending from the Altamaha River near the border of Georgia and Florida up through the Cape Fear River in North Carolina. Wetland rice fields used tidal irrigation, which allowed the ebb and flow of ocean tides to flood and drain the fields, but which also required elaborate, labor-intensive systems of water control.[7] Sugar was similarly capital- and labor-intensive, and production was localized to the southernmost portion of Louisiana. The intermingling of terrestrial and aquatic ecosystems in the low elevations of the Mississippi floodplain suited the perennial grass that grew there, and Louisiana slaves planted, harvested, cut, transported, and processed 96 percent of the nation's cane crop amid levees and ditches carved from the river.[8] Unlike rice or sugar cultivation, which required grueling and often dangerous slave labor, the fieldwork for tobacco slaves was simply tedious. Production of *Nicotiana tobacum* covered hundreds of thousands of acres in the Piedmont of Maryland, Virginia, and North Carolina; by 1860, the Black Patch of Tennessee and Kentucky was also a center of tobacco cultivation. Tobacco was notorious for stripping the soil of nutrients, or "exhausting" the land, faster than other crops, and its profitability was uncertain during this period. Between the financial crisis of the Panic of 1819 and 1850, many farmers abandoned tobacco for mixed-use agriculture, and many more decided to head west for the Cotton Kingdom.[9]

At the outbreak of the Civil War, "cotton fever" was most closely associated with the Old Southwest, the millions of acres of land the United States had appropriated from the Creek Nation after the War of 1812, plus later cessions from the adjoining Cherokee and Chickasaw tribes.[10] These territorial acquisitions opened up a vast area to white American settlement, and between 1840 and 1860 the spread of cotton cultivation from its origins in the seaboard states metamorphosed the socioeconomic makeup of Mississippi and Alabama. The influx of cotton growers to the Black Belt and the surrounding areas forced out the small farmers and herdsmen living along the Gulf Coastal Plain, where commercial stock-raising had previously thrived. Average farm size and slaveholding grew disproportionately larger in this section compared to other areas in the South. The cattle populations of several southern "cow counties" decreased by 30 percent, as cotton production jumped between 200 percent and 500 percent. Even in eastern Texas, where herdsmen did so well they didn't have "to slave themselves looking after niggers" on a cotton plantation, the number of drovers declined as cotton gripped the Deep South. By 1860, the Mississippi River Valley, the Black Belt of Alabama and Mississippi, Piedmont Georgia, most of South Carolina, and significant portions of east Texas, west Tennessee, west Arkansas, and northeastern North Carolina were producing cotton for the global market.[11]

Cotton's suitability for such a range of geographies meant that it failed to create an easily defined plantation belt. But it also meant that the cotton South acted as a unit, rather than a collection of subregions joined together only because they later became the Confederacy. The combined influences of a humid subtropical climate and relatively old and acidic soils—the "elemental South," as environmental historian Albert Cowdrey calls it—promoted agricultural techniques that persisted over time despite the range of landscapes cotton farmers engaged as they spread along the continuum of the southern frontier.[12]

The climatic and soil conditions of the cotton South presented a set of both opportunities and limitations that influenced the way white southerners used their land during the antebellum period. The long summers there are character-ized by masses of maritime tropical air that hang heavily over the region, produc-ing the heat and humidity that typify summer days. Temperatures during the summer often reach 90 degrees to 100 degrees Fahrenheit, and the humidity magnifies the heat's effects, making the air feel thick and sticky as it settles on the skin.[13] Summer days are frequently interrupted by "gully-washers"—brief, scattered, and often violent downpours caused by the clashing of tropical air masses with colder, drier air circulating from the north or west. Winter in the humid subtropical zone can be just as unpredictable. Southern winters are usu-ally described as "brief and quickly forgotten," and except at high elevations, no winter month has an average temperature below 32 degrees Fahrenheit. But cir-culating polar continental air injects an element of changeability into southern winters; warm spells may alternate with brutally cold frosts to punctuate the sea-son as far south as the coast of Texas. Levels of precipitation can vary consider-ably, too. Most areas receive between twenty and forty inches of rain per year; in some, it is closer to sixty inches. Some places are prone to drought—the upland areas of South Carolina and central Georgia, for instance, regularly experience brief periods of drought during both the summer and winter months.[14]

Because the South escaped the last glaciation, states in the humid subtropical zone have particularly old soils that contain relatively low levels of fertility even in their "virgin" state. Except for alluvial material, continually refreshed by sedi-ment from bodies of water, millions of years of weathering and leaching by rain-fall, heat, and natural chemical processes have made most southern soils, in the words of one historian, "mediocre." The geological parent material of much of the South is not particularly rich in the base elements needed for plant growth, and the long exposure to weathering means that essential nutrients, such as calcium and phosphorous, have drained away over time. More resistant minerals, such as clay and aluminum, remain in the topsoil, but these break down too slowly to release an abundance of nutrients available for plant uptake every year. So southern soils are limited in their nutrient content and suffer accelerated weath-ering, and both characteristics retard plant growth by pushing the pH of the soil toward the acidic. While the heat of the South's longer summers accelerates the wearing away of soils' parent material and nutrients, the precipitation patterns of the humid subtropical zone are also influential. Due to their structure and inabil-ity to absorb water rapidly, clay soils are highly erosive. In the region's frequent, often intense, rains, these red or mottled clay soils can wash away in trickles or in sheets, filling lowlands and waterways with their sediment. In fact, when soil scientists calculate the natural erosivity of various regions of the United States, the South usually ranks near the top of the list because of the combination of the terrain, climate, and soil content.[15]

These environmental factors converged to ensure that, on the whole, cotton growers did not have nutrient-rich, geologically young loamy soils to farm. Combined with the region's climate, southern soil types acted as a significant natural limit on production in most of the areas that were attracting cotton growers during this period. In the Piedmont, erosion plagued agriculturalists regardless of the crop they were growing. Stretching nine hundred miles from New Jersey into central Alabama, the Piedmont was a rolling landscape of gentle hills and small valleys, and rivers and their tributaries crossed the region's hardwood forests like veins. Soils in the Piedmont were almost all residual soils formed from underlying beds of granites, gneisses, schists, and diorites as they broke down through the processes of physical and chemical weathering. Unlike sedimentary materials, where the building blocks of the soils are added and compacted over time, residual soils remain highly granular because they are simply very small pieces of rock from below mixed with decomposing plant material from above. Such soils are looser, lack long-term stability, and are usually erosive. This proved a boon to Piedmont farmers at first, because the dominant soil types were well-drained silt or clay loams, as demonstrated by the forest they supported: a mixed-hardwood and pine forest, where hardwoods like oak and hickory were more plentiful than the acid-loving, scattered longleaf pines.[16] However, once farmers removed vegetation and placed the land under cultivation, Piedmont soils proved to be easily exhausted and prone to "washing" or eroding. As early as 1800, observers reported that the soil of Amelia County, Virginia, had completely eroded away, leaving only a thick, sticky layer of red clay. The James River was a "torrent of blood" during heavy rains as the upland soils washed down its banks. One farmer in 1859 complained, "Every county in Virginia . . . is a wilderness of piney old fields and gullied hill-sides," the fruits of agriculture in the Piedmont.[17]

The most coveted soils were on land often refreshed by new infusions of sediment. Bottomlands throughout the region contained alluvial material—the soils left behind when rivers wash over the land—but the largest concentrations of soils rich in base elements could be found in subregions of the Gulf Coastal Plain, such as the Black Belt and the Mississippi River Valley. These were the antebellum seats of King Cotton. Running from the southwest corner of Tennessee southeast through the top of Mississippi and across central Alabama into southwestern Georgia, the Black Belt was a crescent-shaped region of dark-colored soils. During the nineteenth century, it was sometimes referred to as the "prairie lands" because of the black, calcareous soil. Manuals and handbooks praised the rich Black Belt soils, which sat atop an ancient bed of chalk deposits and marine clay, and touted their indestructible fertility, stating with confidence that no fertilizers were needed to cultivate a profitable crop of cotton.[18] It was the Mississippi River, however, that became the South's "premier" area for growing cotton toward the end of the antebellum period. Made up of materials deposited by the waters of the Mississippi River and its tributaries, the soil profile of the Mississippi River Valley changed more frequently than that of the inland soils. To farmers, these were "made" lands. The muddy waters of the Mississippi River deposited heavy silt along its riverbanks during seasonal flooding, creating a fertile sandy loam known as "frontlands." The river also carried a lighter silt into the "backlands," the areas beyond the riverbanks, laying down a bed of rich clay loam for future farmers. Farmers initially preferred the frontlands, however, because they only had to be cleared before planting could commence; backlands soils had to be drained and cleared before they could be planted.[19]

Southern farmers seeking to make it rich in cotton instinctively sought out alluvial soils and bottomlands. Cotton's potential to create wealth may have pulled the Jaynes and others to the South, but once they arrived, it was wide recognition of the South's natural limitations that helped push farmers into particular regions. The wealthiest cotton planters of the 1850s were transplants from Virginia, North Carolina, and Georgia; some had been successful tobacco or rice plantation owners, others came from the margins of society to find a new start on the more fertile ground of the Old Southwest. They intended to make their fortune in the west, not expand it. "The new country seemed to be a reservoir," an early historian of Alabama wrote, "and every road leading to it a vagrant stream of enterprise and adventure."[20] One North Carolina planter lamented, "The Alabama *fever* rages here with great violence and has *carried* off vast numbers of our citizens." But it is no coincidence that so many of the pioneer planters of the Mississippi River Valley and Alabama Black Belt hailed from upland or Piedmont farms in the seaboard areas, whose thinner, acidic, and highly erosive soils had noticeably declined in productivity by 1840. In the Piedmont, cotton farmers owned one-fifth of the cotton-producing land in the country, but they only marketed one-tenth of the total crop. Thus, farmers seeking to take advantage of better ecological conditions reshaped the South's spatial and demographic makeup between 1820 and 1860, as thousands of farmers moved into Alabama, Mississippi, Arkansas, Texas, and upper Louisiana.[21]

With cotton came slavery. Although most southerners did not own slaves, the "peculiar institution" was almost universal in the region. The slave population increased from 1.5 million in 1820 to 3.2 million in 1850 and nearly 4 million in 1860, even without significant importations. The global demand for crops such as tobacco, rice, sugar, and cotton ensured that forced labor remained relevant in the face of an emerging free-labor ideology in the North.[22] About four hundred thousand southerners owned slaves in 1860, but the trading, outfitting,

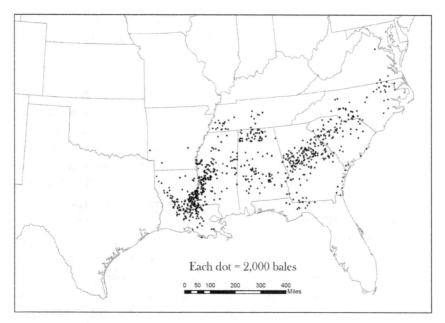

Figure 1.1 Cotton production, 1840. Map prepared by Michael Austin Mohlenbrok and Jennifer Rahn, Department of Geography, Samford University. Data courtesy of IPUMS National Historical Geographic Information System: Version 12.0 [Database]. University of Minnesota, 2017.

transporting, and medical treatment of slaves involved an estimated 30 percent of the white population.[23] This brutal form of organizing labor used violence and coercion to dictate human interactions with the land. Slaves cut wood and cleared forests, built fences and dug ditches, planted crops and hoed weeds, and fed and butchered livestock. These tasks put African Americans into contact with the southern environment from sunrise until well after sundown, as they helped to gradually simplify ecosystems for the purposes of agriculture. Slavery shaped planters' investment priorities and decisions regarding crops and permitted or prevented the implementation of agricultural reform.[24]

Indeed, the institution of slavery is often blamed for suppressing agricultural diversification on cotton farms and plantations and fostering a reliance on imported goods and foodstuffs at the expense of local industry. As one Mississippi planter quipped, "[The cotton planter] is generally scarce of everything but cotton." "We are confident that American cotton planters have not produced any too much cotton," a contributor to the *American Cotton Planter* wrote, "but we are *equally confident* that American cotton planters produce too *little grain*, and consequently *too little bacon*, too *few mules*, and *no wool!*" The profits from cotton southerners expended annually to procure basic foodstuffs that could have been produced on a plantation with well-kept livestock were seen as a waste. J. L. Whitten, observing the farms of central Georgia, complained, "To think one million is expended annually in Georgia for stock and provisions that [planters] can raise as cheap, or nearly so, as where they are brought from, and cotton hawked in the market, at four or five cents, to raise the money!"[25]

In this view, John Gray Allen of Alabama was a typical cotton planter. His farm, worked by over fifty slaves, grew mostly cotton but also corn and peas. Letters from his overseer show that Allen followed the practice of planting cotton and then buying the other provisions he needed. He secured the provisions for his slaves' subsistence by purchase or trade, rather than growing them himself. A letter from his overseer William Watkins reads: "I embrace the first opportunity to . . . [ask] when to send to the river for the provisions you spoke of sending. We have nothing to feed on except green meat which is not so very healthy for negroes. We need some salt, you know better what to send for than I do, we have borrowed 2 sacks from Mr. Devan, which you will have to return . . . . I am looking for a boat up Turkey Creek thinking perhaps it will bring us flour and sugar and coffee plenty for we have none." An official of the Statistical Bureau of Louisiana noted that in his state, "Our butter and cheese, pork, lard, etc., are brought to us from the western States; we import thence also cattle, horses, mules, etc."[26]

However, slaveholding cotton growers were more subsistence-oriented than has previously been thought. They usually divided their land between cotton and corn, but they also regularly grew wheat, oats, peas, sweet potatoes, and potatoes. In the upcountry, especially, cotton was a secondary or even tertiary crop. Farmers used one or two bales to barter for luxury goods but maintained grain as the focus of their operations.[27] Alabamian Hugh Davis, for instance, hated the doctrine of planting cotton to buy provisions. At the beginning of the war, he owned seventy-eight slaves and a range of stock, such as mules, horses, cows, hogs, bulls, oxen, sheep, and goats. His farm journal entry entitled "System of Farming" for 1861 asserted that "the object of the proprietor is to buy neither bread nor meat nor any thing that can be made on the place . . . all plow stocks, ax handles, hoe helves, harnesses, horse collars, and well ropes." He aimed to plant enough vegetables to supply his slaves three times a day and to raise a half acre of wheat for every slave. Edwin W. King, another Alabama cotton planter, also produced a wide variety of food crops for the 152 slaves on his four plantations, from turnips and peanuts to grapes and figs. In fact, his diary indicates that maintaining an adequate supply of meat on his plantations was of great concern to him.[28] It is true that many planters relied on the national and international markets to provide them with provisions and some basic agricultural necessities; however, their crop mixes often reflected a more agriculturally responsible approach than is apparent at first glance.

Not only planters relied on imported meat and foodstuffs. Small farmers, or yeoman, sometimes engaged in similar patterns of market integration. This is particularly important because cotton planters constituted a minority of farmers. In Georgia, one of the wealthiest and most densely populated cotton states, planters only accounted for 6 percent of the white population. Over 75 percent of the white populaton were small slaveholders, yeomen, or poorer whites who grew a mix of grains and foodstuffs, raised livestock, let their herds range the woods for food, and produced a bale or two of cotton or sold bushels of corn and wheat.[29] In the late antebellum period, when railroads opened regions that had been isolated from markets by overland or water routes, some nonslaveholders abandoned the subsistence model and began to participate, albeit in a limited way, in the market economy. In the piney woods region of Mississippi, for instance, farmers did not produce enough grain to feed their households, and they depended on the market to make up the difference.[30]

Thus the majority of "plain folk" existed in a dual economy that mixed subsistence farming with limited market participation. David Golightly Harris was a successful uplands Georgia farmer who owned slaves and planted cotton but placed his family's subsistence before cash-crop production. In 1850, he owned five slaves and almost two hundred acres; he planted fifty of those acres in corn, wheat, and food crops, such as peas, beans, and potatoes, and his hogs and cattle ranged on the remaining "unimproved" acreage. In most years, he planted a small amount of cotton and produced enough to make a bale. His surplus grain crops supplied most of his disposable income. In 1860, he sold enough wheat and corn to make a profit of $310.26, more than many other farmers in his area could ever boast. Although the encroachment of large-scale cotton planting and railroad access made states like Mississippi and Alabama agricultural El Dorados, most southerners—even slaveholders—preferred not being completely beholden to a single crop. They grew corn in large quantities because it was used by both humans and livestock, and they cultivated a variety of grains and vegetables, including wheat, rye, oats, beans, barley, peas, beans, squash, pumpkins, sorghum, and buckwheat. Indeed, during the unprecedented boom in cotton prices of the 1850s, most cotton farmers were growing more corn and foodstuffs than they had the previous decade.[31]

Farmers' recognition of the precariousness of cotton cultivation included their assessments of both economic and ecological risk. After all, what was cotton's geographic expansion but a search for better soil? The cumulative effects of the region's climate, soils, terrain, and geology increased the financial hazards of planting a single crop year after year. The cotton plant required certain nutrients to flourish, nutrients the South's soils did not possess in abundance. Furthermore, the multigenerational farming of cotton demanded a more self-sustaining farming regime. As historian Julius Rubin explains, the length and extreme heat of summers in the South parched shallow-rooted plants, such as grains or hay crops, especially in clay-heavy soils that retained moisture poorly. Frequent precipitation reduced the protein and carbohydrate content of fodder crops, making them less nutritious as animal feed. Finally, the hot, humid weather negatively impacted milk production, growth rates, and reproduction among cattle. In other words, natural conditions in the cotton South worked against the long-term profitable production of cotton.[32]

Farmers made the South the country's wealthiest region per capita by developing systems of production that were adapted to these environmental constraints. Anglo-American settlers in the early colonial period had created these practices when they had first experienced the peculiarities of the southern environment. One of the most widely reproduced accounts of seventeenth-century South Carolina, written by Samuel Wilson in 1682, described how the long summers and mild winters—as well as the type of soil available for planting—affected farmers' choices. How easily cattle and hogs thrived by grazing freely in the woods, he wrote, eating mast, nuts, grass, and roots until they were quite fat, never requiring any fodder or shelter. "The Soyle is generally fertile," he continued, and produced good crops of corn, oats, and peas, although he noted that tobacco, cotton, and other more profitable cultivars were increasingly popular. Wilson's near-contemporaries offered similar descriptions of agriculture as it evolved in the southern half of the North American British colonies. Some focused on the use of slaves in agriculture, characterizing the region as a transition zone between the economy and ecologies of the global plantation South and the American North. A German immigrant living in what is now North Carolina described his amazement at how cheap livestock-raising was in his new home. "It costs almost nothing" to keep them, he said, for they "pasture" in the woods all year long. Not every observer appreciated the agricultural methods of the southern colonists, however. A Scottish woman who traveled to the West Indies and then to Carolina in 1774 decried the way farmers neglected the "uncommon advantages" of the landscape by rudely cultivating the soil with only a hoe, preferring to burn new woodland after a field had been exhausted than to use animal manure on their crops.[33]

During the seventeenth and eighteenth centuries, the practices these observers detailed, including slave-based plantation agriculture that raised a combination of cash crops and grains, livestock that ranged freely in unenclosed woodland, and the method of land clearance and fallow called shifting cultivation, had formed the core of the southern agricultural system. At the same time, territorial conflicts with Native Americans and a daunting line of ridges, valleys, and mountains that lay to the west of the British colonies had confined the "South" and its methods for manipulating the landscape. By the end of the antebellum period, those barriers to expansion had long since crumbled. "The

South" and its agricultural system had spread across a vast expanse of territory, maturing into the set of practices recognizable in the plantation journals of Joseph M. Jayne.

While Big George carved "new ground" from the Mississippi prairie, other slaves prepared older fields for planting. Of the 960 acres Jayne owned, slaves cultivated only a fraction at a time. They spent their spring, summer, and autumn days on sixty- and hundred-acre plots, first sowing oats and corn, and then cotton and peas, and, finally, truck crops, such as watermelons and Irish potatoes. Corn required little attention once it was planted unless the rows needed to be purged of weeds or storms flattened the stalks, forcing slaves to start anew. Cotton required considerably more care and attention. From the preparation of the soil for seeding to the chopping of the crop during the summer months and the picking of the lint, fieldwork was grueling and tedious. Between ginning the cotton in late autumn and planting again in early spring, however, slaves labored to "maintain the general upkeep of the farm." The overseer ordered the female slaves to "hack" or "knock" cotton stalks from the freshly picked rows so they could burn them over the field; feebler slaves did the same to the brush and deadened logs Big George moved from the Gin Field to older ground. Other slaves cleaned out ditches dug around the cotton plots to keep flooding at a minimum or scraped up manure from the Horn Lot (the pen where cows were fattened for slaughter) to line furrows waiting for seed. These jobs kept the plantation profitable, and they had to be completed every winter as fields rotated in and out of production.[34]

The rhythms of slave life on Jayne's plantation responded to the demands of extensive land use. An amalgamation of European, Indian, and African farming techniques, the antebellum agricultural regime was a productive, profitable system adapted to its environment. Although the practices ate away at the resource frontier of the South—they required that new woodland be cleared semiannually, for either new cultivable land or large fences for the crop fields—shifting cultivation and free-range husbandry persisted much longer in the South than elsewhere for a reason. Understanding the interplay between the environmental context of the South and the antebellum agricultural regime reveals how crucial extensive land use was to the profitability of cotton production.[35] The practices were both a response to and an active force in the southern landscape, simultaneously extending and exhausting the region's natural resource base.

The foundation of extensive land use was the technique of shifting cultivation, which meant that farmers cultivated only about a third of the land they owned at a time. They kept the remainder of the land in reserve; sections of it would be cleared and burned periodically to create new fields when the old ones were exhausted. A variation on "slash-and-burn" agriculture, shifting cultivation was common in both the northern and southern colonies through the eighteenth century as European settlers (selectively) borrowed Native American land-use methods to "hack out" temporary fields in the dense woodland forest of the Atlantic Coastal Plain. A former slave named I. E. Lowery described clearing new ground in Sumter County, South Carolina. First, "the undergrowth was grubbed up and burned"; slaves then felled, split, and hauled away any hardwoods that could be used for firewood or fence building and girdled the rest, leaving them to die in the field. When the girdled trees were decayed enough to be felled easily, slaves or laborers removed them from the field in a process called called "rolling logs," and burned the smaller ones.[36] The routine was roughly the same for both slaveholding and nonslaveholding farmers across the South, and it was completed every one to five years between January and April, depending on existing vegetation to be cleared, the type of crop to be grown, and the availability of labor.

The widespread use of shifting cultivation created a patchwork of farmlands that possessed an agricultural logic, but often clashed with antebellum ideas of "improvement." Southern plantations and farms were sprawling, unkempt, and included not only cultivated fields but also woodland, newly cleared ground marred by stumps or girdled trees, and overgrown plots lying fallow. They were, as one historian writes, "temporary, in process, abandoned, repossessed, and so on, seldom pretentious, manicured, or lovely." Whereas northern farmers stressed permanence and the improvement of farms within relatively static boundaries, southern farmers lived and worked in an agricultural landscape in various states of cultivation. For instance, an 1850 land inventory for Newberry County, South Carolina, showed a hundred thousand acres of forest, 168,000 acres of cultivated land, and another hundred thousand acres of "waste" and "regrowth."[37] Wastelands, or "old fields," were a necessary by-product of extensive land use, and thus the practice of shifting cultivation complicated the northern dichotomy of "improved" and "unimproved" land in ways often viewed as evidence of southerners' improvidence.

Although anecdotal evidence for shifting cultivation abounds, it is difficult to quantify these observances with hard data. Census categories are frustratingly vague, for "unimproved land" could include swamp, stony areas, brush, old fields, or forested areas. The census considered any old field to be "brush," so it is almost impossible to reconstruct the state of vegetative cover in agricultural areas from the census data during this period. Nevertheless, when one looks at the percentage of "improved" land recorded on individual farms, it is clear that southerners did not cultivate large swaths of the acreage they owned.[38] Farmers in the border states improved much larger portions of their

Table 1.1 **Type of Land in Farms, 1860**

State	Acres of Improved Land in Farms	Acres of Unimproved Land in Farms	Percent of Land in Farms Improved
Alabama	6,385,724	12,718,821	33%
Arkansas	1,983,313	7,590,393	21%
Florida	654,213	2,266,015	22%
Georgia	8,062,758	18,587,732	30%
Kentucky	7,644,208	11,519,053	40%
Louisiana	2,707,108	6,591,468	29%
Maryland	3,002,267	1,833,304	62%
Mississippi	5,065,755	10,773,929	32%
North Carolina	6,527,284	17,245,685	27%
South Carolina	4,572,060	11,623,859	28%
Tennessee	6,795,337	13,873,828	33%
Texas	2,650,781	22,693,247	10%
Virginia	11,437,821	19,679,215	37%

Note: Figures compiled and percentages calculated by the author using the US Census for 1860, Minnesota Population Center, University of Minnesota, National Historical Geographic Information System: Version 12.0, http://www.nhgis.org.

land, and the pattern of land use in their census data approximates that of northern states.[39]

Although shifting cultivation was a practical and necessary adaptation to the constraints of the southern environment, it was widely criticized. Contemporaries viewed the technique and the landscape it created as the physical manifestation of the backwardness of the slave South. Of his tour of the "cotton states," Frederick Law Olmsted remarked that for every mile of farmland in cultivation, there were a hundred of forest or waste land, "with only now and then an acre or two of poor corn half smothered in weeds." Echoing these nineteenth-century critiques, historians describe cotton planters' never-ending quest for fresh soil as the product of greed and a lack of concern for the rabid consumption of natural resources.[40] This was no doubt true in many cases, but environmental factors were at play. Primarily, shifting cultivation periodically helped to restore the fertility of southern soils without the need for costly fertilizers. Temporarily abandoning old fields allowed secondary vegetation, such as species of brush, pine, or grasses, to reclaim the soil, so when farmers put an old field back into cultivation, the initial burning injected substantial quantities of soil-reviving material into the ground. Especially before the introduction of commercial fertilizers after the Civil War, the low, steady burn of forest and plant biomass was an inexpensive way to add the nitrogen, phosphorous, potassium, and sulfur necessary to make the depauperate soils in many parts of the South more productive.[41]

Widespread use of the technique not only kept lands in reserve for future plantings but also produced networks of uncultivated, unfenced lands that served as open range for livestock. Since the seventeenth century, southern stock-raisers had allowed their animals to graze in the interstices of farmland, particularly in reserve woodland or on old fields. The oak-hickory-pine forest complex of the region provided mast and forage, such as chestnuts, acorns, hickory nuts, pea vines, hog peanuts, and a variety of grasses during the spring and summer, for hogs and cattle, though this did not provide the high-quality nutrition that hay or cultivated meadow grasses did. During autumn, farmers "called in" their animals and penned them for fattening. A cotton planter in Louisiana, for instance, always had his slaves "hunt up" the hogs in early November, so that he could feed them

Figure 1.2 "American Farm Yard," 1857. This Currier & Ives lithograph depicts the antebellum farm "ideal," with a fenced garden next to a spacious home, penned livestock, and well-maintained barns. Prints and Photographs Division, Library of Congress. LC-DIG-pga-00592.

fodder for a few weeks before killing time.[42] A brutal winter might require supple-menting a herd's food with grain. But antebellum farmers often did not provide shelter or fodder during the winter because of the "mildness of the weather."[43]

Practicing free-range animal husbandry meant that southerners fenced in their crop fields to keep grazing stock out, rather than fencing the livestock in a pen or pasture. A crop field without a fence was legally not a field at all, and if a farmer failed to provide an adequate fence, he bore responsibility for the damage done by invading stock. A case reached the Supreme Court of Alabama involving the trespass of livestock in the crop fields of Joel Sandiford, who had sued Cientat Jean for allowing his cattle to break down Sandiford's fence on multiple occasions, enter the garden, and destroy entire crops of vegetables. The jury awarded Sandiford $200 in damages, because "his said fence, or inclosure, was in all respects a law-ful one."[44] Since a Virginia rail fence, the most commonly used design, required approximately 6,500 rails per mile, farmers expended a considerable amount of time, labor, money, and materials on crop enclosures each year. As we have seen, Big George's job involved cutting and hauling timber for fence building on Jaynes's plantation during the winter months. Jesse Rice, a former slave from South Carolina, recalled that some of his fellow slaves were called "rail splitters," and that their sole task, year-round, was to procure and prepare timber to make fences.[45]

Figure 1.3 A "rural homestead" in Rogersville, Alabama, 1862. Adolph Metzner sketched this scene as he passed through Alabama during the Civil War. It shows how northern eyes took in the rougher appearance of a southern farm. The Virginia rail fence sits askew, and the yard looks overgrown and unmanicured. The buildings are a mixture of slave cabins, a main house, and a kitchen or storehouse—none are fenced or used to shelter the stock, which roam freely. Adolph Metzner American Civil War Collection, Prints and Photographs Division, Library of Congress. LC-DIG-ppmsca-51239.

The debate over the merits of the land-use practices of free-range husbandry and shifting cultivation occupied a considerable number of pages in agricultural publications of the time. The *Southern Planter* included this exchange in an issue from 1848:

> Mr. Bradley was walking through his field of corn, evidently in search of something or somebody, and presently was met by his head-man.
>
> "Well, Jake, have you found the hogs?"
>
> "Yes, masser—we found thirteen shoats and three ole sows, an we got em out arter so long a time—they blong to Mr. Glasby, sir—theys the same ones we got out last Friday."
>
> "Did you find out how they got in?"
>
> "Yes, sir; the dogs run em to the low end of the field and thare at the plum nusry they had a hole in the fence big enough for your ole boar to git through. I looked at the rails and seed where one was chawed most in two and then broke, and I spose the old sows kep a pushin and a workin till they got the hole big as they wanted to."
>
> "Why, that part of the fence was done up last spring—I ordered you to do it well."
>
> "Yes, masser, and so I did. Most all the rails was good as new, and the whole fence was one rail higher than the measure you giv me— but them ole sows could git through creation when they hongry, an Mr. Glasby's man tole me he done stop feedin em—his corn done giv out."[46]

The fact that Mr. Glasby's "corn done giv out" is revealing, for it points to the difficulties southern farmers faced trying to feed their stock. Although most southern farmers grew corn, the resulting meal either went to the family or the slaves, not the cows and hogs. Maintaining penned stock was expensive compared to allowing them the freedom to find their own food. Many of the nutrient-rich grasses that were common on northern farms did not grow well in the humid subtropical climate of many southern states, so pasturage was less viable for southern farmers.[47] Wastelands or marginal lands may have created an unattractive and unimproved landscape, but they were essential spaces that allowed farmers to feed their livestock affordably year-round. Even foreign observers recognized their economic importance. An 1843 pamphlet advertising "improved" farms for sale in Tennessee to British immigrants emphasized the benefits of free-range animal husbandry. These were farms that had been reclaimed by banks after the Panic of 1837, and the writer tells potential buyers that the labor of penning and feeding stock will disappear if they move. "Cows and hogs will almost support themselves in the woods; and the sheep will do so entirely."[48] So for nonslaveholders or those with poor lands and small acreages, these practices allowed for the inexpensive, piecemeal clearance of land and a supply of meat that required little investment in fodder or feed. Fences were often built a little at a time, perhaps whenever a farmer brought on additional labor. Sometimes the only way poor farmers could afford the grain to fatten their stock for slaughter was to let them feast on others' cultivated land.

Extensive land use was extremely important to yeoman and upland farmers, and the practices they used on their small acreages and roughly cleared forest plots shared many characteristics with those used by the few residing on grand plantations. However, slavery's absence on these farms made a difference in the way agriculturalists marshaled labor for tasks such as shifting cultivation or fence building. In North Carolina, white sharecropping and tenure arrangements were common before the war, and these landless farmers provided labor for large-scale agricultural projects such as land clearance. Hiring slaves was another option, of course, but as historian Steven Nash writes, "Whereas yeomen living in the plantation districts were often bound to local planters for economic assistance, the independent small farmers outside the Black Belt relied on one another." Thus, labor-intensive tasks such as rolling logs or clearing ground were "community functions" where many farmers came together.[49] Even those southerners isolated from slavery, then, utilized the approaches to cultivation most frequently associated with cotton planters.

The final pillar of extensive land use was a series of land-maintenance jobs that included crop cultivation, erosion-control measures, and jobs to improve soil nutrient content. Growing cotton, a relatively delicate crop, required punishing levels of care and attention to produce lint of any quality. The remembrances of a former cotton slave in Mississippi describe the very particular work he and his fellow field hands performed during the spring planting season:

> The land was deeply plowed, long enough before . . . planting to allow the spring rains to settle it. Then it was thrown into beds or ridges by turning furrows both ways toward a given center. The seed was planted at the rate of one hundred pounds per acre. The plant made its appearance in about ten days after planting, if the weather was favorable . . . . As soon as the third leaf appeared the process of scraping commenced, which consisted of cleaning the ridge with hoes of all superfluous plants and all weeds and grass. After this a narrow plow known as a "bull tongue," was used to turn the loose earth around the plant and cover up any grass not totally destroyed by the hoes . . . . Subsequent plowing, alternating with hoeing, usually occurred once in twenty days.[50]

Picking began in late August or early September and continued through November or December. Several farm journals include descriptions of multiple rounds of picking, the first one dedicated to making that "first bale" to go to market in places such as Memphis, New Orleans, Mobile, or Savannah. Once slaves had picked and collected the cotton bolls, they fed the lint through a cotton gin, usually located a short distance from the main house, which separated the seeds from the lint; then the lint was collected and baled.[51]

However, farmers, laborers, and particularly slaves often devoted long hours to arduous but necessary work that went beyond crop cultivation. Land-maintenance tasks, such as ditching fields, filling gullies, hauling manure, draining waterways, burning brush, felling trees, and hoeing down cotton stalks were essential to render the land productive and profitable within the constraints of southern climate and soil conditions. Ditching, for instance, slowed the loss of topsoil in cultivated fields. Even gentle rains slowly eroded the topsoil once farmers removed vegetation from the land in preparation for planting. One way to help alleviate soil erosion was to cut trenches in the ground to collect the topsoil displaced by precipitation, thus preventing the loose dirt from running into and slowly damaging waterways. But ditches had other utilitarian purposes. Cotton was very sensitive to water levels, and when temporary ponds developed in plant rows after a violent rain storm, the water weakened the stalks and stunted plant growth. Ditches funneled excess water away from the crop rows, protecting the valuable cotton crops.[52]

Although smaller landowners and nonslaveholders implemented these measures, they proved particularly integral on farms worked by slaves. Indeed, planters used these techniques not only to maintain the profitability of their soils, but also to keep slaves busy during the lay-by season between harvest time and spring planting, as well as in midsummer when crop work was slack. In the farm journal of John Horry Dent of Alabama, an entry from November 1855 enumerated what he called "upkeep jobs," including "two branches to ditch and reclaim in Cox fields" and "manure collected." Setting up a newly purchased plantation in Arkansas, Francis Terry Leak's slaves spent February and March clearing out an "old deadening" (previously cultivated land allowed to fallow), running ditches along four different fields, and repairing fences in addition to the work of preparing the soil for planting. These chores were often divided by gender. On one plantation, for example, female slaves cleaned out the ditches around the cotton fields, and male slaves dug new six- to nine-foot ditches around the corn plots.[53]

Slaves' labor in "upkeep jobs" and land management was obviously of paramount importance in ensuring the profitability of cotton production. A settler who moved to Perry County, Alabama, in 1832 recalled that everyone in the county was talking about picking cotton and clearing land. So naturally, "every man we met, either wanted to buy a 'nigger' or take a drink." Take the application of fertilizer, for example. Agricultural publications often touted the uses of manures, but the practice often proved to be impractical for those who had large acreages—unless they had slaves—since it was difficult to collect in a region where stock ranged freely. Even if southern farmers had penned their stock and collected the manure, it would never be enough to fertilize more than a few acres. An overseer's letter illustrates this point: "We have plenty manure to hall and its nearly time we were beginning. You do not mention whether you wished the house field planted in corn or cotton. We can't hall manure to any other place."[54] The average farm size in most of the cotton states was between three hundred and four hundred acres, and even in such places as the hills of North Carolina, yeoman farmers sometimes had between fifty and one hundred acres in cultivation. Animal manure alone was not enough, especially to "reclaim" or "redeem" exhausted lands. Instead, farmers used compost (usually leaf or vegetable matter), the remains of a previous crop (such as cane trash, pea vines, corn stalks, or cottonseed), or minerals—usually lime, bones, marl, potash, or others.[55] Possessing a concentrated labor force allowed some slave owners to apply the beneficial mixtures more efficiently than other farmers who perhaps lacked the help.

Farmers often called ditching, manuring, and fence repair "slack-time tasks" because they were typically performed during slow points on the agricultural calendar or during the evening, but the label obscures the time-consuming, back-breaking, and labor-intensive nature of the work. And yet the integrity of the antebellum plantation system absolutely depended on them. Shifting cultivation, free-range animal husbandry, and land maintenance formed an agricultural regime that was adapted to slave-based labor. Even small slaveholders tailored these agricultural techniques to suit, and indeed justify, their brutal exploitation of human lives. James Washington Matthews, a corn farmer in middle Tennessee who turned to cotton during and after the Civil War, owned only one slave and her two children. He and his son, Gilbert, worked alongside them in the fields and hired additional help during certain parts of the year. Matthews did not have the acreage or the labor force of Joseph Jayne, yet his farm journal is remarkably similar. Cherry and Isham, two of Matthews's slaves, hauled wood, made rail timber, cleared land, rolled logs, repaired fences, applied manure, and cut ditches. Diary entries note that Matthews had all his "white family" at the fair in Bigbyville, while Isham, it recorded, was making rails. Cotton planters and other farmers admitted in their journals that it took large work forces and the constant attention of slaves to keep fences, ditches, and other repairs current on plantations.[56] If slaves such as Big George, Cherry, or Isham did not provide the labor, who would?

This question stalked the political debates of the 1840s and 1850s. It was clear that the long-term viability of the slave-based system relied on having access to new lands and fresh soil. "Our farmers trust too much to their rich, fresh lands," a Georgia farmer wrote in 1853, "the idea never entering their heads that theirs is an exhausting system." Edmund Ruffin, a tobacco planter from Virginia and gentleman agricultural scientist, speaking in Charleston in 1852, explained, "The loss of [the South's] both political and military strength would be the certain consequences of the impoverishment of [the South's] soil."[57] In other words, the rate at which southern farms consumed soil and old-growth forests was unsustainable, and the South was headed for an ecological crisis.

On May 30, 1860, Joseph M. Jayne called the Democratic Convention of Mississippi to order. As chairman of the Central Committee, as well as one of the eleven delegates to the convention from Rankin County, Jayne spent forty-eight hours in the elegant hall of the House of Representatives debating "the question." Could Mississippi Democrats support a national party platform that, as a planter from Hinds County angrily claimed, failed to give "adequate protection to the rights of the citizens in the slaveholding States"? Or would Mississippi follow the example of South Carolina, whose convention had met the previous month, and vote to separate from the national Democratic Party? One after another, the delegates voiced their fears that the national Democratic Party was too wedded to the "Northwestern Democracy" of Stephen Douglas and had no intention of upholding "Southern Rights and Southern Equality." The Constitution of the United States granted the right to buy, sell, and hold slaves as property, these delegates ardently maintained, and that right was sacred. Some pointed to other states, such as South Carolina, Virginia, and even Tennessee, which were said to be "waiting in line" to secede if their demands were not met. Jayne's position, however, was one of moderation. His voting record throughout the convention demonstrated that he desired Mississippi to pursue as many avenues of compromise as possible. He counseled against making any dramatic gestures simply for the sake of principle. He voted in favor of resolutions that forced Mississippi Democrats to wait until northern Democrats had convened, to be more "considerate" of the evolution of national political opinion. But on the question of slavery and, indeed, the continual expansion of slavery into new territories, Jayne adamantly agreed with his fellow planters: he could not be a part of Union that robbed him of his constitutional right to possess slaves and to take those slaves westward.[58]

The reasons given for the South's vehement protests against closing off any territory from slavery include the wish of southerners to maintain parity in the US Senate between the "free" and "slave" states, the vested financial interest most southerners had in the continuance of slavery (whether or not they owned any slaves), and the fear that restricting slavery in new territories would mean eventually restricting slavery in existing territories.[59] The minutes of the southern conventions that took place in cities such as Savannah, Georgia; Knoxville, Tennessee; and Montgomery, Alabama, during the late 1850s—days-long meetings during which prominent southerners dissected the political crisis of disunion and weighed the costs and benefits of secession—show the role these issues played. At the Savannah convention, in 1857, the attendees agreed that the "free soil scheme" to settle Kansas with foreign immigrants jeopardized southern political power and imperiled the prosperity of what they called the South's "domestic institutions," a common euphemism for slavery. "The security and honor of the South demands that she should maintain her equal rights in the Territories of the United States," the convention members resolved, "and she should resist at every cost any attempt, wherever made, to exclude her from those Territories."[60]

The debates over slavery and secession revealed two additional truths: one, that extensive land use was central to southerners' ideas about future regional development, and, two, that many southerners believed expansion and slavery were the keys to the profitability of their farms. Shifting cultivation, when practiced correctly, was a sustainable, albeit continuously moving, form of long fallow. Southern cotton farmers, however, often "picked up stakes" once they had exhausted all the new ground they could clear. A popular refrain was "Gone to Texas." If moving westward was no longer an option, how was King Cotton to survive? Indeed, very practical concerns about continuing the southern land-use regime undergirded the words and actions of prominent southerners, such as Edmund Ruffin, who were not just secessionists but agricultural reformers. Furthermore, the ability of slaveholders to command a group of laborers who worked the land in service of crop cultivation in addition to performing maintenance tasks was, in their minds, crucial to the continuance of labor-intensive, land-extensive agricultural techniques. Slaveholders such as Jayne could be expected to defend their substantial monetary investments in human flesh, and they did. But the actions of that man and so many others during the tumultuous summer of 1860 cannot be separated from their experiences as cotton farmers.

Regardless of their suitability to both the landscape and socioeconomic makeup of the antebellum cotton South, shifting cultivation and free-range animal husbandry had very real ecological consequences, including rampant soil erosion, sedimentation build-up in rivers, and timber shortages. Northern observers often provided vivid descriptions of environmental degradation on southern farms; one, for example, was "forcibly struck" by the "dreary and uncultivated wastes, barren and exhausted soil, half cloathed negroes, lean and hungry stock . . . scarcity of provender . . . and fences wind shaken and dilapidating" that greeted his eye on plantations.[61] Reporting from the densely populated Piedmont belt, where cotton plantations abounded, a US patent agent lamented that Georgia farmers "cut down and cripple forests" to cultivate the land, "with the sole view of the largest annual profits," until the land will produce no more.[62] Even in Jacksonborough (now Jacksboro), Tennessee, tucked into the western foothills of the Appalachians with very few slaveholders and almost no plantations, "in nine cases in ten a field is worked . . . without being once manured, until the richness of the soil is exhausted, when it is abandoned, and a new clearing is made which undergoes a like treatment."[63]

Northerners assumed that their way of farming was the best way and never considered how well extensive land use fit the specific environmental context in which southern farmers operated. This does not mean that antebellum agriculture was an environmentally friendly system. Shifting cultivation, for instance, resulted in significant forest clearance in parts of the South, particularly the Atlantic coastal region, the Piedmont, and the bottomlands of the Mississippi River Valley. One contributor to a southern farming magazine explained, "The system of agriculture practiced by [slave-holders] . . . necessitated the destruction of vast areas of valuable timber . . . . Indeed, the rule was to cut down and destroy the timber, to exhaust, either wholly or partially, the land, and then move farther West in quest of other land, to be treated in the same way." A writer for *De Bow's Review* lamented the loss of valuable saleable timber to the "wanton and prodigal" planters. "Where, twenty years since, there was an unbroken pine forest," the author stated, "now in places there is a scarcity of timber for fencing . . . not unfrequently will one planter deaden and destroy a thousand acres in one season."[64] Given the gradual elimination of vegetative cover, it is no coincidence that rates of soil erosion for extensively farmed areas of the South increased between 1820 and 1860. "Trees were the great obstacle to cultivation," and farmers' first object upon obtaining land was to get rid of them. The use of fire and girdling was common, but in places with high concentrations of slaves, one could hear the "axes cutting until midnight" to fell trees in the month leading up to spring planting.[65] Because many farmers planted newly cleared lands in Alabama and Mississippi almost immediately in cotton, rates of soil erosion reached critical levels sooner there than in the states that were settled during the colonial period. As early as the 1840s, land clearance by white farmers had scarred the woodlands of even the most remote corners of the Old Southwest. One observer noted that along the lower Mississippi River, "the more recent plantations are invariably indicated by masses of dead trees, presenting an abrupt and disagreeable transition from the rich verdure of the living forest, to the dreary aspect of decay and ruin."[66]

The removal of vegetation, combined with the practice of planting of cotton in rows, further endangered precious topsoil during the region's regular downpours. Cotton was a "clean-cultivated" crop; slaves and field hands kept the plant rows free of weeds and other vegetative cover during the summer so they would not compete with the staple for soil nutrients, water, or sunlight. This method encouraged the rapid loss of topsoil, for the straight-row crops offered no impediment to water that dislodged the soil and funneled it down hillsides and ridges.

Describing how quickly topsoil disappeared from newly plowed fields after a southern rain storm, one traveler wrote, "Every plough furrow becomes the bed of a rivulet after heavy rains—these uniting are increased into torrents before which the impalpable soil dissolves like ice under a summer's sun." The washing of soil, especially in upland or bottomland areas, then led to the buildup of sedimentation in rivers and streams all around the South. In South Carolina, for instance, the Enoree River was, as of 1859, "a turbid stream, discolored by the dissolving clay of wasted soil."[67] If farmers allowed the topsoil to wash, further cultivation exposed the stiff clay or alkaline subsoils beneath, materials bereft of organic material and unable to absorb water.

The practice of grazing animals on the open range also encouraged abuse of the southern landscape. The fencing of croplands to keep out ranging stock required millions of wood rails every year as farmers cleared new land and planted new fields. One local farmer's club calculated that fencing 100 acres cost $179, plus twenty-two days of labor: eleven days to haul the wood and eleven days to put it up. If the average size of a farm was a hundred acres, they stated, then their state alone had $22 million invested in "perishable" fences. As a result, many accused southerners of clinging to a method of stock-raising that wastefully depleted their timber resources. One newspaper editorial lamented that fences in the South had led to "the gradual and ceaseless prostration of our forests." Another editorial pointed out that if all the time and labor spent on fencing went into improving the land by collecting manure, building drainage ditches, and reclaiming old fields, then southern farms might actually turn a profit.[68]

Ironically, the removal of timber for fencing eventually diminished the capacity of a farmer's woodland to support his livestock. Settlers' use and abuse of the woodland in areas along the eastern seaboard removed vital forage for ranging livestock. Secondary succession species such as broomsedge, scrub brush, and pine replaced mast-producing hardwoods such as oak, chestnuts, and hickory. One traveler in the antebellum South described a tobacco planter's land, observing that an oak forest had originally covered the place, "but this having been cleared and the soil worn out . . . pine woods now surrounded it in every direction."[69] Eventually, the land could not support the stock, and the farmers who depended on that income moved on. John Frank and David Headrick were small farmers from central North Carolina who planted corn and wheat but made most of their money from butchering stock they raised on common land. In 1857, Frank and Headrick uprooted their families and moved west to Dent County, Missouri. Writing back home to relatives who remained in North Carolina, Headrick bragged that he could do "a grate deal better in the west then I could in that old poor brier country . . . . It is the best plaise to rais [sic] cattle that I ever saw an horses an sheep if you can keep the wolfs from killing them." Frank also praised his new home, writing, "There is good range all over the woods," so his hogs were doing much better there.[70]

Shifting cultivation and free-range animal husbandry required southerners to own much more land than they cultivated so that there were reserves for clearing new ground and for feeding livestock. Once timber or soil resources had been depleted, they had to push into new areas to continue cultivating. "Expansion became the normal condition," then, and "growth from small to large units [landholdings] and from old to new regions" became a regular part of southern agriculture. Historians mapping the "geographic persistence" of planters and farmers found that between 1850 and 1860, almost 60 percent of slaveholders in the Cotton Belt had moved, presumably to areas with better soil or cheaper land. Historian James Oakes concludes, "If such rates of persistence and change were typical, it is likely that between 80 and 90 percent of the slaveholders [of the Cotton Belt] did not stay in one place for more than two decades."[71]

The frequency with which slaveholders migrated fits nicely with the assumption that the practice of slavery was responsible for environmental decline across the region. "There is ample reason to believe that the use of negro slaves in southern agriculture made it extremely difficult, if not impossible, to engage in profitable agriculture and at the same time, avoid wearing out the soil," early twentieth-century historian William Chandler Bagley observed. "To the extent that this was true, the farmers who made use of slaves found soil exhaustion a permanent problem and not a temporary one." When farmers devoted as much acreage as possible to profitable staple crops in order to maximize the return on their investment in slaves, they were less likely to keep stock, rotate crops, use fertilizers, or "improve" their land. Treating the land as if it were only a vessel for cotton reinforced its value as a temporary, expendable possession.[72]

Slaves were crucial to keeping the plantation ecologically viable in several ways. The maintenance tasks they performed kept land in cultivation much longer than it would have been under continuous monoculture. Furthermore, their labor—and the profits planters gained by that labor—allowed planters the luxury of experimenting with fertilization, intercropping, and various manuring techniques. One of the more important innovations in land management was a product of slave-owning cotton planters. During the 1840s and 1850s, planters began a new approach to crop rotation: they alternated cotton with corn and cowpeas. When cotton yields declined in a field, planters replaced it with corn and, during late June or early July, sowed peas among the corn stalks. Although corn takes up more nutrients from the soil than cotton, modern agronomists have shown that cotton bolls are larger and the stalks taller after a two-year corn rotation. The pea vines climbed the corn stalks, and the microorganisms in their roots fixed nitrogen from the air into the soil, restoring an essential component of soil fertility to the field. As summer and autumn rains set in, the intercropped peas kept the soil from washing down the rows of corn, and they later provided excellent forage for hogs, which would be put in the fields once the corn was harvested to "mow down" the vines and stalks.[73] It was not a crop mix that ensured self-sufficiency in food production, but it helped improve yields. Planters' journals from cotton-growing areas often list peas as one of the crops they produced annually; the number of acres planted fluctuated according to a field's soil fertility and rate of exhaustion.

More recent work on antebellum expansion and migration shows that small slaveholders and poorer whites moved more often than wealthy planters. Large landowners already monopolized the best lands (which had the most potential for long-term use) and had the capital to intensify use or ameliorate environmental damage by using slaves in soil conservation and land maintenance. Some planters had the wealth to purchase other estates to maintain planting on a large scale and make up for reduced yields on their original land. As one observer noted, those with their "very handsome houses, gardens, and improvements about them" were "fixed to one spot." Poorer farmers or those on more marginal lands usually found it more attractive and cost-efficient to migrate. Historian William Barney found that in Jefferson County, Mississippi, 87 percent of nonslaveholders moved during the 1850s compared to 17 percent of wealthy slave owners. One contemporary observer called poor southern farmers "almost nomadic."[74] Like John Frank and Daniel Headrick, who moved from North Carolina to Missouri in the 1850s to escape the "barrenness" of their original lands, it was the small farmers who most heavily relied on the benefits of expansion. This helps to explain why reduced opportunities to migrate mattered for such a large segment of the southern population—both white and black. Intensification was expensive, and extensive agriculture better suited those who had little capital to invest in farm improvement.

This also helps explain why so many southerners, even those who had never owned a slave, were so enraged during the 1840s and 1850s by the limitations placed on the movement of slavery into newly acquired territory. The debate over the westward movement of southern farmers was also about expanding the extensive agricultural system reinforced by slavery—a slight, but very important difference. Historian Adam Wesley Dean has recently shown how ideas about proper land use infused the rhetoric of Free Soil and Republican Parties in the 1850s and tied northern agrarian ideals to larger questions of national development. In his telling, the Republican enmity toward the Slave Power stemmed largely from the belief "that civilization and loyalty in the West could only be secured by societies of small farmers practicing scientific land management." Antebellum northerners equated multigenerational farming and intensive continuous cultivation with progress and democracy. They believed that slavery, and the extensive land-use practices it supported, fostered barbarism and oligarchy.[75]

It should be no surprise, then, that nineteenth-century southerners viewed the future development of their agricultural economy in similarly agrarian terms.

The rhetoric espoused in the southern press during the political crisis of the late 1850s reveals that southerners believed that the North's efforts to "wall up the South within her present limits" and exclude slavery from new territories would lead to the decay of the agricultural landscape and the collapse of their system of land use.[76] "The adoption of the expansive principle," a resident of Leon County, Texas, wrote to *De Bow's Review*, was the South's way of shaping "the world to her own terms" and protecting her history and policy of agriculture. "The system of slave labor requires more *space*," Edmund Ruffin declared, to secure the population from "extreme privation." Expansion was necessary to keep agriculturalists from becoming destitute. In 1942, William Chandler Bagley Jr. posited that soil exhaustion, not population growth or land greed, could have caused an urgent feeling to press westward, thus reinforcing, if not creating, the conflicts between the free states and the slave states in the years before the Civil War. Bagley actually blames the soil-exhaustion problem in the South on slaves' carelessness and inability to use implements properly, though he does point to the role of environmental limits in fueling southerners' opposition to the creation of nonslave states.[77]

A group of wealthy slave owners pushed agricultural reform for decades precisely to reduce southern agriculture's dependence on continual expansion. Men such as Edmund Ruffin, his fellow Virginian planter Willoughby Newton, and the president of the South Carolina Agricultural Society, Whitemarsh Seabrook, argued that the ecological degradation and irresponsible land use associated with antebellum southern agriculture threatened the future of slavery by destroying the other pillar of their economy—the land.[78] "The institute of slavery is a fixed fact," Newton declared in an address to the Virginia Agricultural Society in 1852. "We have a class of laborers, tractable, efficient, and profitable. Without them, Virginia would be a wilderness." Southerners had a responsibility to marry their system of labor with scientific knowledge, so that the South could "defy the competition of the world." In another speech to the society later that year, Ruffin warned that if southern farmers did not take better care of their farms, the same social evils wrought upon the North by free labor—wages wasted on an inferior race, hordes of immigrants snatching up resources—would visit the South.[79] They decried the short-sightedness of planters who thought that if they exhausted the soil, they could always move west.

One of the reformers' most prominent causes was to put an end to free-range husbandry, which seemed a root cause of southerners' wasteful use of space. Requiring farmers to pen their stock would reduce the pressure on timber resources, especially in areas such as Tidewater Virginia, where decades of shifting cultivation had removed most of the trees suitable for fencing. Repealing the existing fence laws would also increase the amount of manure available for crop fields. The *American Cotton Planter and Soil of the South* put it this way: the manure made by penned stock would more than pay for the expense of feeding them in the extra bushels of corn or bales of cotton produced from its application. "It is much cheaper and far more satisfactory," the editors stated, "to remain here at home, and [by applying manure from the barnyard] make rich and productive already cleared lands, than it is to break up and remove to the inhospitable 'far West.'" Most importantly, enclosing the open range would decrease the need for vast expanses of unimproved land on which stock could forage. "Lands are only of value when used," an anonymous Cotton Belt planter wrote to an agricultural magazine. "See what an immense amount of capital is locked up in unused lands" kept in reserve for future cropping or woodland forage.[80]

Agricultural reformers also pushed the use of commercial fertilizers, hoping this would eliminate the need to constantly clear land. Guano was the first practical commercial fertilizer, and its introduction served as a flashpoint for the debate over southerners' extensive agricultural techniques. First imported into Baltimore in 1843 from Peru, guano comprised seabird droppings and contained a considerable amount of nitrogen and phosphates. It was the most concentrated, most complete fertilizer on the market for decades. Because of its ability to greatly improve crop yields, the demand for guano skyrocketed in the late 1840s and 1850s. James McCormick, the "Inspector of Guano," reported 3,728,621 pounds of guano inspected and weighed at his office in 1848. Just one year later, this figure rose to 9,052,081.[81] A contributor to the *American Cotton Planter* stated, "We do know it is more economical to buy and use guano than it is to dig and haul marl; and much more so than it is to haul street manure, even if it could be had within a mile of the place using it, for nothing."[82]

But before the Civil War, guano was a luxury good. "Genuine, unadulterated" guano cost from $40 to $50 per ton (2,000 pounds), and farmers sowed anywhere from 200 to 800 pounds of guano per acre, depending on the land, supply of fertilizer, and crop being grown. Although many planters' daybooks, farm journals, and diaries mention it, the use of the fertilizer was not as widespread as these records make it seem. It was simply too expensive. A survey of planters' journals indicates that the largest plantation owners in every state regularly applied it to their fields, but many of the smaller farmers, whose papers have either been kept or printed in edited collections, mention buying guano only every now and then. Those who relied on it to solve problems with their yields were destined to be disappointed, however. Guano was an unbalanced fertilizer: it injected a great deal of limiting nutrients into the soil, but it lacked potassium salts. Famed chemist Justus von Liebig understood that fields fertilized with guano would gradually lose their fertility. If guano was misapplied, its nutrients could (and sometimes did) end up in local waterways instead of plant beds.[83] Because of its prohibitive price and its mixed ecological effects, guano failed to make the intensification of land use practical at a time when shifting cultivation was still possible.

Although extensive land use and the ability of southerners to move westward masked the true extent of the problem, the pace of environmental change was one of the primary vulnerabilities of the southern agricultural system, precisely because very few southern farmers had to face the consequences of that change. If conditions were altered, not only would the environmental constraints of the region harm agricultural production, but southern farmers would also have no precedent for dealing with them. Expansion and reliable access to labor was the key to southern agriculture and, as the antebellum period progressed, southerners experienced a real and urgent threat to their ability to export this particular set of land use practices into new territory. The Cotton Kingdom had to expand its borders or eventually face the reality of its environmental constraints.

Despite the impressions created by agricultural publications and travel writing of the late antebellum period, northern and southern farms were not completely dissimilar. A majority of both northerners and southerners made their livelihoods in agriculture, and during this period, farmers of both regions became increasingly specialized in the types of crops they grew. Tobacco, cotton, rice, and sugar may have prevailed in the South, but northern farmers planted wheat year after year. A substantial number of New York and Pennsylvania farmers, for instance, feared the failure of their land-management techniques and similarly turned to the doctrines of "improvement." The continuous-cultivation methods of northern farmers may have been made possible by the more regular use of manure and, to some extent, better erosion-prevention practices, but northerners were just as interested in maintaining a profit as southerners, even if the "long-range needs of the soil" had to suffer.[84]

Yet regional differences grew increasingly obvious in the late antebellum period. Northern farmers continuously cultivated most of the land they held, but southerners often planted only a fraction of their landholdings so that they could clear new fields when the old ones gave out. Northern farmers penned their stock, but free-range husbandry made sense in the South because of the soil makeup, climate conditions, and native vegetation. These land-use practices were highly rational approaches when they were predicated on the certainty of the territorial expansion that had begun in the South after the American Revolution and continued through the Civil War. The combination of extensive land use and expansion, then, helped to mask the vulnerabilities and prevented the economic and ecological crisis that Joseph M. Jayne, Edmund Ruffin, and others so clearly feared.

These environmental conditions and land-use practices made the region particularly vulnerable to military operations when the war came. Troop movements, forage raids, a blockade of debatable efficacy, and the severe reduction in the labor force—all commonplace in wartime—accelerated soil erosion, woodland clearance, and land abandonment around the South. At the same time, the mobilization of natural and agricultural resources on the Confederate home front to support the operations of both armies initiated a cycle of intensive use not seen before the war and prevented southerners from engaging in extensive agricultural techniques. The magnitude of the environmental disturbance caused by the Civil War did not match, say, that on the near-stationary fronts of World War I in France and Belgium, but even in places where evidence of military activities disappears quickly, war operations accelerate changes in the land. Because of how the antebellum land-use regime had shaped both the cultural and natural landscapes of the South, the Civil War proved devastating to the Cotton Kingdom.

2

Revealing Vulnerabilities

Behold the havoc we have spread
Through all your fair and broad domain
Behold the myriads of your dead
In the unequal contest slain.
We pillage, ravage, lay waste, burn
Your cities, houses, mills, barns, fields;
Your food and raiment. Yet you spurn
(scorn) Submission and the peace it yields.

—Walter Waightsill Lenoir,
"Yankee Blessing" (1865)

To Jasper George, or "Jap" for short, the Mississippi River, its waters blackened with the sediment of smaller streams, swamps, and farms, moved so sluggishly that only the broken limbs drifting past the boat indicated a current. The deadness of the water muffled sounds and choked the breezes, and Jap wondered if the river's malaise might be to blame for his own sense of boredom with army life. Jap and his best friend, Alonzo "Lonnie" Miller, had been eager to travel the Father of Waters, as the Mississippi was called, with the rest of the 12th Wisconsin Volunteer Regiment, but this particular journey had been "rather long for comfort, to say the least."[1] Too green as Union recruits to participate in the recent Meridian campaign, the two privates' experiences in "the South" in April 1864 were largely limited to what they could see as they embarked and debarked along the river. At Vicksburg, George and Miller witnessed the destruction wrought by siege warfare; the lands surrounding what "had been a nice city once" were riven with trenches and blotched by rifle pits. In Tennessee, they touched newly grown cotton plants and visited camps where ex-slaves cut wood to fuel government boats for a dollar a cord. At every stop, they "jayhawked," or foraged, while their boat took on fuel wood, distracting their commanding officer. Unguarded cattle, chickens, peaches, and barrels of molasses enlivened their rations and alleviated the tedium of travel.[2]

Neither the mighty river nor the landscape along its banks impressed the pair of farmers from Wisconsin. Lonnie Miller, in particular, disparaged the Confederacy's famed plantations. Unlike on the farms in the North, flocks of nearly feral hogs roamed the woods and levees. The land appeared unkempt, marred by fields left to grow over and cut-over forests, making it "such a rough looking country." Private Miller wrote to his father that he "had not seen but one plantation that [he] liked the looks of."[3] Of course, neither soldier complained when the South's agricultural bounty supplied them with fields of corn, or cattle to shoot. One letter marveled at how quickly the 12th Wisconsin had spoiled a planter's crops and orchards. "The Rebs may as well give up," Lonnie wrote, "for we will clean them out." By the time their unit joined General William T. Sherman's Atlanta Campaign, Jap and Lonnie agreed: "[They] do not think much of the south so far [and] Wisconsin is [their] preference."[4]

The letters of Privates Jasper George and Alonzo Miller are typical in their descriptions of the lived experience of soldiers during the Civil War. Between 1861 and 1865, Federal and Confederate troops crisscrossed the South, from the tobacco counties of eastern Virginia to the sugar plantations of southern Louisiana, from the shores of Gulf Coast to the Ohio River. As they moved from place to place, soldiers regularly bought, confiscated, or stole livestock, fodder, and foodstuffs from civilians and their farms. Troop movements and military operations dramatically reshaped the physical landscape around cities and plantations by necessitating both the construction of defensive works, of which the immense network of trenches seen by Jap and Lonnie around Vicksburg is only one example. Impressment of men and materiel, such as the swaths of woodland cut down by ex-slaves to fuel transport boats like the one carrying the 12th Wisconsin upriver, also left the "marks of Mars" on the southern environment.[5] Jap and Lonnie's experiences, then, reveal the variety of ways hundreds of thousands of soldiers interacted with and altered the South's environment during military movements. Yet the same letters also hint at how southern agriculture proved to be particularly vulnerable to them.

Military operations unmasked and exacerbated the conditions created by antebellum farming practices. At the start of the Civil War, the South was characterized by a wide range of agricultural systems and crop regimes, although cotton was certainly ascendant. Climate and soil conditions helped unite this disparate region to some degree, as did extensive land-use practices. This set of agricultural methods worked for many southern farmers during the antebellum period, but it fostered and simultaneously concealed a series of liabilities. As a result, the region's farmers were ill-prepared for the abrupt changes made to their agricultural system by the Civil War. As noted in Miller's letters, free-range animal husbandry rendered livestock more vulnerable to foraging. The reliance on expansion into new forest lands for shifting cultivation provided timber resources for soldiers' use, but that use endangered yields. The utilization of long fallows or burning to return nutrients to the soil, as well as the need for slave labor to maintain land, made farmers ill-equipped to handle more intensive cultivation methods necessitated by the war's consumption of men, land, and fertilizer. Ultimately, the region's natural conditions, as well as common land-use practices, primed the environment to be damaged by wartime operations and troop movements.

As a result, Federal and Confederate military practices, commonplace in a global context, impacted the southern environment long after 1865. For decades, scholars have debated the degree to which the South was left "prostrate" at the time of the Confederate surrender. Environmental historians have subscribed to the idea that the war was a "rough, no-holds-barred affair, a bloody and brutal struggle" that utterly devastated the South.[6] Yet the damage wrought was not particularly destructive, nor unique, in the tactics and strategies employed by militaries toward civilians in wars before and since. So why was the South affected for so long by the physical damage of war?

This chapter argues that antebellum land use ensured that the alterations to southern agriculture caused by the war went beyond the geographically restricted scars of battles or sieges. Military operations precipitated the breakdown of southerners' extensive land use by removing vital agricultural resources and accelerating ongoing environmental damage, such as soil erosion and woodland clearance. Troop movements cut many parts of the region off from the markets they relied upon for agricultural necessities. Prewar methods of dealing with poor soils—shifting cultivation, the felling and burning of trees, or simply moving somewhere else—were no longer an option because of troops' consumption of woodland. Soldiers put additional pressure on soil and timber resources through the widespread construction of breastworks, trenches, ditches, rifle pits, and batteries across farmland. Finally, crop regime changes due to Confederate policies, combined with the halt of guano importations, altered the mineral content of the topsoil on many farms, affecting future yields. While in some ways, war proved an ecological boon to the land as more fields lay fallow and southerners shifted reluctantly toward field peas and other subsistence crops, the heavy tread of armies significantly reduced southerners' ability to engage in extensive land use. The outcome reset parameters for southern farmers long after Appomattox.

The ferocity of the fighting on Kennesaw Mountain surprised Lonnie Miller, even though he and Jap had been in skirmishes since arriving in Georgia weeks before. The 12th Wisconsin marched through Tennessee and Alabama to join General Sherman's Atlanta Campaign in June of 1864. Immediately, the two friends experienced a new kind of soldiering, punctuated by onslaughts of shells and bullets that landed "like hailstones." "The heavy guns are speaking all around us," Jap scribbled on the bottom half of one of Lonnie's letters, "enough so as to make the ground tremble whenever they are discharged."[7] Both sides fired continuously in an effort to reduce the number of men hiding in the opposing breastworks, and only the pouring rain hanging over the mountain dampened the sounds of combatants' volleys. "I go to sleep hearing shell and bullets and wake up in the morning the same," Lonnie confessed. "I am getting so used to noise I think no more of it than I would of the flies buzzing." But the rain was also a problem. It had rained every day since they set foot in Georgia, and the water sometimes blinded Lonnie as he loaded and fired. More frustratingly, it weakened the hastily erected walls of Union defenses. Battle lines shifted, sometimes hourly, and Lonnie and Jap quickly learned that making "good works," or defenses, mattered as much as their aim. The weather, however, transformed their rifle pits into little more than craters of mottled clay, and worse, it funneled blood, soil, and human filth into their works. As Sherman's men battled their way southward toward Atlanta, Jap "got lousy" in the soggy environment of the trenches and removed himself to the hospital. Lonnie stayed on the line. The fighting he described was neither glorious nor exciting. "It was awful."[8]

The military campaigns in which Alonzo Miller, Jasper George, and thousands of other Confederate and Union soldiers participated throughout the war required vast networks of breastworks, trenches, rifle pits, and other defenses to protect their positions against enemy artillery. Beginning in the 1830s, the US Military Academy at West Point emphasized the use of defensive field fortifications as the counterpoint to the "Napoleonic lust for the offensive" so often taught in military strategy. Accordingly, cadets received intensive training in the construction of major fortifications and temporary fieldworks on the battlefield. Jacob Dolson Cox remembered his education at West Point by saying that it was "essentially the same . . . as that of any polytechnic school, the peculiarly military part of it being in the line of engineering."[9] The creation of defensive works could take weeks or months, or they could be hastily built as battle lines changed and armies retreated. "Such fighting and digging, such winning and relinquishing of lines won," one Union soldier wrote, "simply to advance, to gain ground and throw up new works again to be abandoned . . . all this was repeated again and again."[10]

Because of its removal of woodland, damage to vegetation, and displacement of large quantities of soil, the building of defenses also proved to be the source of multifaceted environmental damage that was seldom confined to the battlefield.[11] The area affected in the Civil War was limited, but in several of the economically important regions of the once and future cotton South—Mississippi, Tennessee, Georgia—military engagements were agents of obvious environmental change. Trench digging and compaction not only altered the soil structure but reshaped the contours of farmland and fields and changed the soil's nutrient content, its capacity to absorb water, and the way it responded to cultivation. The removal of a patch of woodland during a battle led to increased soil erosion, loss of species habitat, and destruction of open range land for livestock. If the woodland was part of a farm, it left the owner with fewer resources for building fences and outbuildings and in need of imported products. These were not unusual or particularly destructive tactics, but in this particular environmental context these military operations intensified preexisting vulnerabilities in the southern agricultural system.

Breastworks, in their most sophisticated form, were low, earthen walls, lined by rails of wood—a trench. Depending on the line of battle, breastworks (or earthworks) could be tightly clustered, running in a variety of directions and angles, or constitute a linear series of trenches stretching for miles.[12] Commonly used in conjunction with breastworks, chevaux-de-frise were portable anticavalry obstructions made by attaching wooden spikes to a simple frame, also constructed of wood. In later wars, wooden chevaux-de-frise would be replaced with barbed-wire constructions. Armies placed these and abatis, piles of sharpened logs sometimes topped with glass or jagged items, in front of breastworks to prevent the enemy from getting into the trenches. Lonnie Miller described the Confederates' use of chevaux-de-frise in Georgia, writing that they "have a strong fort . . . in front they have driven down sticks and sharpened them, so close together that no man can get through all around it."[13]

As the correspondence, diaries, and remembrances of soldiers show, by the final year of the war, a significant portion of a soldier's work consisted of building defensive works. Daniel Chisholm, a private in the Union Army, kept a detailed account of the defense building his regiment did. If they expected an attack, the soldiers often worked through the night digging rifle pits, sending groups out to "slash timber" from the adjoining woodland. Chisholm marked in his diary that he and other men "went to the woods to cut abattoes to put in front of the works to jab the Johnnies if they should want to pay us a night visit. We took things moderate and sent back several wagon loads of trees." Often, soldiers took material from nearby farms. They tore down fence rails, cotton gins, and sometimes homes to secure wood. A surgeon in the Union Army noted that soldiers "stripped every board" from the structures on the plantation unlucky enough to host them. "An unoccupied house or barn dissolves in an hour," he wrote. "One after another takes a board, and it is soon gone." The experiences of the Confederate soldiers experiences mirrored those of their Union counterparts. Charles Walden of Alabama noted in his diary, "We moved to the front this morning . . . went into position about twelve o'clock on a high hill. Had to cut down some trees before we could have food."[14]

Figure 2.1 Chevaux-de-frise and breastworks outside Petersburg, Virginia.
The earthworks transect the scene, spiked by sharpened logs used as anticavalry
defenses. Erosion is rampant, and the tree line has been thinned by soldiers' efforts
to build fortifications. Prints and Photographs Division, Library of Congress.
LC-DIG-cwpb-02604.

Often, however, soldiers did not plan the defensive works in advance.
Trenches looked more like shallow ditches, and cheveaux-de-frise were simply
piles of branches thrown up as a battle approached. In campaigns in which one
army closely pursued another, soldiers had to build a temporary fortification
every time their unit halted. James A. Congleton, a corporal in the Union Army
serving under General Sherman, noted in his diary that his company had to "dig
in" every night: "We have dug pits piling the dirt on the outside. Also have a log
on top of the dirt raised enough to let a gun between the log and the dirt. The log
is to protect the head." Any time the men bivouacked, they collected logs, fence
rails, anything to stop a bullet. He later added that "old soldiers know . . . that
a little protection is much better than no protection. We commence to dig as
soon as we come in front of the enemy—often we use fence rails or timber—
anything that will stop balls." During a fight, the lines of battle could shift significantly, and a group of soldiers could have abandoned their breastworks only to

build other defenses a few feet away using bayonets, tin pans, old canteens, and even their hands to dig trenches.[15] One Confederate soldier laughed at Yankees who desperately "threw up earth" to protect their men who were hauling the guns. As General Nathan Bedford Forrest attempted a last-ditch effort to protect Selma, Alabama, from advancing Union raiders in April 1865, his men hurriedly slashed all the pine they could from the surrounding woodland and pulled down the fences from around the fields, piling up trunks, branches, and rails to protect their flank. General Joseph Wheeler, another Confederate cavalry leader, gained a reputation for slowing the enemy by filling the road with piles of felled trees; by the time the opposing soldiers had gone around them, Wheeler's men were in place for a skirmish.[16]

The strategically important cities of the Confederacy, those with arsenals or rolling works or ports, merited the largest and most sophisticated fortifications. Massive and elaborately layered sets of defenses that used a combination of breastworks, rifle pits, parapets, and trenches protected Vicksburg, Richmond, Petersburg, Atlanta, and Charleston.[17] Even Selma, a relatively small trading post for Black Belt planters across the southern half of Alabama, required extensive fortification because it housed a valuable arsenal—a site of munitions production vital to the largely agrarian Confederacy. The Confederate government impressed or hired thousands of slaves to erect a continuous line of parapets around the city, eight feet tall and eight feet wide. They built several forts to buttress the most vulnerable parts of the line and dug ditches five or six feet deep and ten to fifteen feet wide in front of it. General James H. Wilson, the commander of the Union cavalry units tasked with capturing the city, commented on the "strongly constructed" and "well defended" works. Tellingly, his reports indicate the natural landscape around the city gave his men as much trouble as the breastworks. The Confederate authorities ordered slaves to clear all the plantations around the city of trees, crops, and any other vegetation that might provide cover to an enemy combatant. In his official report, Wilson testified to the effectiveness of these tactics: Union troops lacked the natural cover of trees, the felling of woodland prevented the proper drainage of the soil and allowed the land to become marshy, and the resulting soggy terrain slowed the horses down and provided an easy target for Confederate artillery.[18]

Though Wilson was chiefly concerned with life and death on the battlefield, his report alludes to possible ecological impacts of wartime fortification building. Yet there have been almost no scientific studies of the soil depletion or changes in forest composition that resulted from the military operations of the American Civil War, partly because the areas that require study are now privately held or, in many cases, have been turned into shopping centers or parking lots. Another reason is the focus on exploring the ecological consequences of explosive ordnance in the literature on warfare.[19] Soldiers' descriptions of battles often provide little definitive source material on the environmental damage their defenses caused. Even Lonnie Miller's contain only vague indications of the extent or complexity of the Union fortification, whereas he devotes entire passages to the terror of artillery.

In the absence of such literature, defensive works provide a valuable case study for how fortifications might act as ecological agents in places where large-scale battles occurred, such as Atlanta. Located amid the rolling and sometimes steep hills on the northwest edge of central Georgia, farms in the immediate vicinity of the town grew a diverse mix of crops; cotton was the important cash crop, but truck crops, especially fruit, were also common. North of Atlanta, farm sizes were smaller because of the increased elevation and steepness of the slopes, whereas south of Atlanta, cotton plantations were more common and slave density was higher. However, because it was located in the Piedmont, the city and the surrounding farms sat on highly weathered and very erosive soils that already lacked sufficient quantities of key nutrients for staple crop growth. Furthermore, this area received some of the most erosive rainfall, which caused significant soil erosion even without human alteration to the soils or vegetative cover. Euro-American extensive agricultural practices had been acting on the natural environment in this section of the South for at least a century by the time of the Civil War.[20]

The environmental context of the city and the surrounding farms helped determine the relative significance of Georgia campaigns for postwar agriculture. In 1861, Atlanta was a relatively small town, simply the terminus of several railroads. As the war progressed, it gained enormous importance to the Confederacy because of its armament factories, and the government erected a series of ringed defensive works around the town.[21] Henry Stanley, a second lieutenant in the 20th Connecticut Volunteers, described them as "certainly the most remarkable constructions for combined defense and offence that I have seen.... About 60 yards in front of the works a line of heavy trees had been placed the branches pointing outward, which being sharpened made death almost certain by being impalled on them." Stanley assumed they had been built by slaves impressed by the Confederate government, but if so, he wrote, "they were laid out and built under the supervision of a most skillful engineer." Unfortunately for the Confederates, General Sherman refused to storm these works. His army dug their own trenches and chose instead to bombard the city.[22]

These elaborate defenses displaced enormous amounts of soil. A map produced for the *Memoirs of General William T. Sherman* depicts over fifty miles of defensive works constructed during the Atlanta Campaign of 1864, including ten or so miles of fortification ringing the city. One soldier poetically described the effect on the landscape, writing that the "soil which formerly was devoted to the peaceful labors of the agriculturist has leaped up, as it were, into frowning parapets." It seemed as if "some giant plowshare" had passed through, digging "gigantic and unsightly furrows" into the rolling plains.[23] Unlike the records associated with postwar railroad building, where foremen accounted for labor-ers' work by documenting the cubic feet of soil they dug, the maps, letters, and diaries describing breastworks and trench digging do not attempt estimates of displaced soil.[24] But the impact of the fortifications was not necessarily about the number of cubic feet displaced but, rather, about where those cubic feet were located, what types of soil were displaced, and how well the land was able to heal itself afterward.

In maps created for the *Official Records of the War of the Rebellion*, lines of entrenchments zig-zag through privately held woodland and agricultural fields. Such constructions immediately affected farmers' lands and incomes. Rain stripped away valuable topsoil—no longer covered by vegetation or even crops—and funneled it into trenches and surrounding waterways. A Union soldier noted how the ground they used during the battle was being "washed by the rent rains," the rivulets opening up gullies and ditches in the earth. A Confederate soldier described how the rains had made the banks of his trench wash downward, filling the bottom with a stiff blue clay that held fast to their feet.[25] The presence of clay in the soldier's trench suggests that the soldiers who constructed the trench had dug through the first two or three soil horizons and had reached the subsoil or that past land use had already removed the topsoil. The first scenario meant the land could still be farmed, but only with intensive fertilization or the acceptance of low yields. The sec-ond, however, meant that the particular piece of land would not support farm-ing on any scale after the war.

Photographs taken around Atlanta toward the end of the war provide visual evidence for some of the environmental changes that occurred in the wake of soldiers' movements. One photograph, titled "Confederate fortifications with Potter house in the distance," shows how the Confederate army has clear-cut several acres of woodland, leaving behind only stumps and a few standing trees. The dense woodland on the horizon suggests that before the army arrived, the area may have been thickly forested with common hardwoods, such as maple, oak, and hickory trees. Whether from the removal of the woodland or the foot traffic of soldiers, it is clear that military operations promoted soil erosion. Rills and gullies have formed in the right of the photo and the breastwork walls required the displacement and removal of large quantities of soil. The woodland opposite the house, perhaps once held in reserve by the owners for future use or designated as range land for livestock, had been cut down, the timber used to build abattis. Soldiers also constructed wood and sandbag-lined trenches, and the work required to de-construct those trenches would be considerable for the Potters or their laborers.

Figure 2.2 "Confederate fortifications with Potter house in the distance." An undated Civil War photograph showing land owned by the Potter family marred by denuded soil and irregular breastworks. Civil War Glass Negative Collection, Prints and Photographs Division, Library of Congress. LC-DIG-cwpb-03414.

The combination of vegetative removal and soil erosion severely reduced the productive capacity of the land and sometimes rendered it completely useless.[26] Additional timber would be needed to replace the fences, but the nearby woodland had been stripped. Without vegetation, the land could not absorb moisture, feed people, or support open range for grazing livestock during and after the war. One farmer could not use his largest field because a set of entrenchments, described as "a titanic furrow," ran through the middle of it. After the army had passed through, in December 1864, a woman in the county south of Atlanta wrote to her brother, informing him that soldiers "almost destroyed our place . . . breastworks dug through the yard—filled up our well—tore down the house, the smoke house and the crib to build the breastworks." Her uncle had examined the property and said she would not be able to plant in the fields where the soldiers had plowed their trenches.[27] Replacing the farm buildings and improving the fields would require money and labor, and both were in short supply during and after the war. The land would thus be less productive and less suited to intensive cultivation during a time when so many farmers pursued cash-crop cultivation.

The wounds these military operations inflicted directly on the landscape sometimes lasted for decades. In 1879, almost fifteen years after the end of hostilities, *Harper's Magazine* reported on the "marks of Mars" that still greeted visitors to Atlanta. The wartime breastworks closest to the city had yet to sprout grass because of the damage to the topsoil done by soldiers "throwing up earth." The reporter noted that riding out of Atlanta, one would see the "half-filled trenches" that had once protected Confederate sharpshooters, line after line of earthen works, woods still scarred by bullets, and fields "sown with leaden seed." Even in places where the evidence of military activities quickly disappeared from the surface, war operations subtly shifted the places of crop production and planting. The reporter from *Harper's Magazine* concluded, "The red soil upturned by the soldier's spade contains no dormant seeds, and takes so slowly to new planting that for fifteen years compassionate Nature has tried in vain to hide these marks under her mantle of herbage and wild shrubbery."[28] With such intensive changes to the land, the South could not conceal its scars.

By the time the rains ceased on Kennesaw Mountain, the iron bite of shells had savaged the denuded landscape around Lonnie Miller's camp. Jagged stumps of hastily felled trees dotted the space between breastworks. Rifle pits pockmarked fields once covered in crops. Each time the boys needed firewood or rails to strengthen trench walls they had to go further and further afield. The picked-over ground around Atlanta, and the paltriness of his rations, made Lonnie nostalgic for the days he and Jap had spent marching through Alabama. It was there, he wrote, "we began to live." Every time the five-mile column of troops stopped on their progress through that state, they foraged.[29] Men in his regiment jayhawked chickens and sheep from farms they passed. They hunted geese and ducks. Miller's letters spoke of flocks of hogs crowding the woods, and Lonnie reveled in the way "the boys pitched into them," killing at their leisure. Soldiers often dispelled the "melancholy" of marching and camping by chasing free-range cattle with their mules. Because it was "the largest farming Country [he] had been in," with corn fields five hundred acres or more in size, Lonnie always had plenty of fence rails to use for firewood or make camp. The young private delighted in remembering how in May of 1864, he and six other soldiers encountered a two-year-old heifer grazing in the woods. He bragged in a letter to his sister how easily he penned it and cut her throat. The jubilant soldiers dragged her back to camp and lived off of her "splendid beef" for days.[30] But those days were over. Until Sherman captured Atlanta on September 2, 1864, there weren't even squirrels left for Lonnie's regiment to hunt. "I hope this war will end before long," he wrote, "... for I have seen enough of it."[31]

Lonnie Miller's descriptions of his regiment's brutal radius of destruction underscore the degree to which Civil War armies absorbed natural resources over a vast area. A soldier camped in Tennessee explained, "You can not well imagine how destructive the march of an army through a country is.... Hungry men seize stock. Cold men burn fences." The act of moving and supplying them required enormous reserves of water, wood, livestock, and food, and was an often a violent process recorded by soldiers and civilians. Describing Sherman's infamous "March to the Sea," a resident wrote, "Like a huge octopus, [Sherman] stretched out his long arms and gathered everything in, leaving only ruin and desolation behind him."[32] Sherman himself bragged to his wife, "Enough horses, mules, and beef cattle were taken for the army to have more of all these animals when it reached Savannah than it had when it left Atlanta." "You can hardly realize how much it takes to supply an army as large as ours with rations and forage," one Union soldier wrote to his wife in Ohio. "If you could pass over the country where our army has marched and see the marks of desolation on every side, you would have some idea of what [war] is."[33] While the chaos of the battlefield was restricted to a few areas, the ecological impact of livestock foraging matched the more visible effects of fortification building.

Decades of extensive land use had made the cotton South particularly vulnerable to wartime military operations. The proliferation of free-range animal husbandry meant that southern livestock were easier for hungry soldiers to capture without fear of reprisal or official reprimand. Once a field's fences were destroyed, livestock had full access to a farmer's cropland. Woodland clearance by troops—and sometimes just the army's presence in an area—was enough to keep farmers tethered to rapidly eroding or nutrient-deficient soils. The ecological regime of slavery began to collapse, leaving some planters without concentrated labor forces to sustain their agricultural operations. As a result, fairly standard military practices, such as foraging, impressment, conscription, or simply moving soldiers from one place to another facilitated the disintegration of long-time extensive land-use practices. Discussions about the Civil War's "destruction," then, must include how battles, campaigns, and military transport created new ecological constraints on cotton farmers, even as armies' actions closed off possibilities for circumventing them.

Livestock were a frequent target of both armies. The Confederacy fashioned an internal market by which quartermasters and subsistence-bureau agents obtained, or "impressed," foodstuffs and other goods from southern civilians to distribute among soldiers. Although the policy did not become official until 1863, the Confederate government used impressment from the beginning of the war to marshal livestock, as well as cash crops, provisions, preserved meat, fodder, hay, timber, and slaves.[34] The Union Army simply seized animals such as horses and mules to replace aging or sick animals of their own or to use to haul army wagons. Hogs and cattle could be easily herded, and soldiers confiscated them in larger numbers. "The men have all had plenty to eat," one soldier wrote to his wife, "although no rations have been issued to them for several days."[35] For a farmer, the end result of impressment and foraging were the same: fewer animals for home consumption.

Long marches led to heavy foraging along major roads, railways, and rivers because armies did not want to carry all their rations with them. The citizens of Covington, Georgia, pleaded with their governor to do something about the "large bodies of the enemy engaged in foraging the county in various directions . . . along the course of the South river." The troops, numbering in the thousands, were "stripping the citizens of their corn, wheat, fodder, bacon, hogs, cattle, and poultry," leaving most families destitute. As army personnel appropriated larger numbers of livestock, marching or camped troops required additional forage to keep the confiscated animals alive. Troops took grains such as corn and oats from inhabitants' stores and allowed their animals to graze in fields of unharvested crops. One farmer in Jones County, Georgia, lamented that after Union cattle were driven through his corn fields, "there was no more corn in there than there is on the back of my hand."[36] Foraging policies thus initiated a cycle of increasing demand on the southern populace: the more food and supplies taken, the more animals and wagons needed to haul them, and the more food needed to feed the increasing number of animals in the train.

Although free-range animal husbandry made it harder for hungry soldiers to find a particular farmer's stock, the fenced-in crops generally made for virtually risk-free livestock pilfering.[37] Union soldiers were often shocked by the appearance of the animals they encountered roaming the countryside. Accustomed to fatter breeds of pigs and cattle that stayed penned for most of the year, Union soldiers sometimes remarked on the almost feral animals southerners raised. For instance, Major General Lovell Rousseau, raiding northern Alabama for provisions in late 1862, complained of the "inferior cattle, small and thin." An Ohio soldier stationed in western Virginia declared that the local hogs were the "longest, lankiest, boniest animals in creation," while northerners in Georgia wrote that swine there were "mainly long-headed. Long legged, fleetfooted 'piney woods rooters' used to depending on Providence for food."[38]

After 1862, commanders in the US Army increasingly saw the destruction of the South's agricultural economy as the key to defeating the Confederacy. The earlier, pragmatic approach to foraging gave way to what has been dubbed a "hard war" phase, during which foraging became less of a means to an end and more of an end unto itself. "Hard war" began in fits and starts during small-scale, everyday confrontations where Union soldiers killed livestock, burned mills, tore down fences, flattened fields or crops, or emptied corn cribs simply to prevent their future use by Confederate soldiers or civilians.[39] Lemuel Foote, a chaplain in the 151st Regiment of the New York State Volunteers, witnessed a confrontation like this between his general and a farmer during an 1863 campaign. The farmer refused to take an oath of allegiance to the United States, and Foote's commanding general simply said, "Starve then." Foote wrote that "the boys" walked into the man's cornfield, whose crop was "just right to roast," and stripped the stalks of their corn and let the troops' livestock graze on the remainders. By the time the regiment moved on, the field was as clean as one in summer fallow. Foote concluded that though he felt sorry for the farmer's family, at least the crop would not fall into the hands of the rebels. During 1864 and 1865, the hard-war approach included several infamous "scorched earth" campaigns.[40] Commanders such as William Tecumseh Sherman, David Hunter, and Philip Sheridan perfected and refined the massive forage raid during the last year of the war.

Both soldiers and civilians reveled in dramatic descriptions of the "terror and atrocities" visited upon the South during the Civil War by armies.[41] Northern politicians boasted about "making the South a desert," and those who toured the region often referred to the devastation of its economic and physical landscapes. Southern newspapers circulated reports of Yankees' acts of destruction, stating that the "despots" of Washington "boldly avow the purpose of destroying our industrial system and bringing on famine and starvation."[42] A Mrs. Ashley of Bowling Green, Kentucky, wrote a friend that her farm had been "*most* shamefully abused" by Federal soldiers and lamented that it would take years of hard labor to make it recognizable again. A planter in Virginia cursed the "barbarious and cruel system of warfare, pillaging, burning, destroying, and stealing private property and warring on defenceless non-combatants" practiced by the Union Army, estimating there was "not a dollars worth of anything left" on his land.[43]

However, the hard-war campaigns did not destroy the foundations of the southern agricultural landscape as completely as these contemporary descriptions made it seem, and oftentimes, it was the indirect effects of these campaigns that mattered in the long term. In his report of the Shenandoah Valley campaign in 1864, Sheridan estimated that he had burned 435,802 bushels of wheat, 77,176 bushels of corn, and 20,397 tons of hay, in addition to killing or consuming 10,918 beef cattle, 12,000 sheep, and 15,000 hogs.[44] The numbers are impressive, but it is difficult to say how many bushels of wheat or tons of hay there had been in the Shenandoah Valley before Sheridan came through. Furthermore, only the leaders of campaigns in which large-scale foraging was the objective kept such careful accounts. Overall, there is a general lack of figures regarding the number of livestock impressed, confiscated, stolen, or foraged, but some scholars have estimated that the South as a whole experienced between a 30 percent to 40 percent reduction in its livestock population. Census records corroborate those figures, albeit in a general way. They do not take into account how those animals were lost—whether due to foraging, impressment, overwork, livestock diseases, migration patterns after the war, or other factors.[45]

The true importance of hard war is that some of these operations brought the conflict to sections of the cotton South previously untouched by large-scale military action.[46] Benjamin Kenney of Shelby County, Tennessee (Memphis), claimed the US Army took 2 mules, 1 hog, 45 bushels of corn, 2 tons of hay and 1 ton of fodder. In Dallas County, Alabama, Mary Saffold listed 12 mules, 2 horses, 250 bushels of corn, and 2½ tons of fodder among her losses. And William Albright of Alamance County, North Carolina professed to have lost 15 hogs, 1 mule, 100 bushels of corn, 100 bushels of oats, and 2 tons of hay to the US Army.[47] "Scorched earth" operations placed intense pressure on the resources of certain parts of the South when livestock, feed, and manure were already in short supply. The massive forage raids, such as Sherman's March in Georgia, occurred in places where manure was needed to continue profitable cultivation or in places where livestock were an integral part of an already-diversified agricultural regime. The consumption of livestock, then, was not just about the numbers: the integrity of the southern agricultural system relied on livestock, and thus foraging and impressment had an impact on the region's self-sufficiency that extended beyond the end of the war.

Besides animals, other agricultural resources disappeared as armies traversed the cotton South. Timber, especially, suffered intense pressure as a result of military movements. One southern newspaper praised the way soldiers ingeniously constructed their shelters from materials around them, stating that "the forest is fast disappearing before the axe of the stalwart soldier," who, lacking tents, must "provide himself with bivouacs either of brush, boards, corn stalks or broom straw."[48] Troops required wood for fuel and to build camps, winter quarters, and plank roads, among other uses, and soldiers often devoured all the sources around encampments almost immediately after stopping. Captain Edward E. Dickerson noticed that even a small band of men had denuded their surroundings. He wrote, "I was in the edge of the timber when we first stopped. But there is not a bush, stump, rail, or anything of wood kind on the ground at present. Everything has been burned . . . to cook with." The notations of agents from the Bureau of Refugees, Freedmen, and Abandoned Lands (Freedmen's Bureau) who surveyed plantations at the end of the war often indicate "timber cut by troops" or "much timber has been cut during war" or list the approximate number of cords of wood removed from the woodland. This was true in every state the agency monitored, even those that had been largely spared from the fighting.[49] Of course, timber supplies would eventually rebound. But for farmers who relied on extensive land use, the disappearance of forests foreclosed the possibility of employing shifting cultivation and free-range animal husbandry for years.

Table 2.1 Livestock in the Confederate States

	Horses		Mules		Cattle		Swine	
	1860	1870	1860	1870	1860	1870	1860	1870
Alabama	127,063	80,770	111,687	76,675	685,080	427,987	1,748,321	719,757
Arkansas	140,198	92,013	57,358	36,202	489,092	322,548	202,753	841,129
Florida	13,446	11,902	10,901	8,835	380,699	384,623	271,742	158,908
Georgia	130,771	81,777	101,069	87,426	931,395	693,571	2,036,116	988,566
Louisiana	78,703	59,738	91,762	61,338	456,449	302,665	634,525	338,326
Mississippi	117,571	90,221	110,725	85,886	381,545	442,929	1,532,708	814,381
North Carolina	150,661	102,763	51,368	50,684	645,299	475,754	1,883,214	1,075,215
South Carolina	81,125	44,105	56,456	41,327	484,187	231,018	965,779	305,999
Tennessee	290,882	247,254	126,345	102,983	492,711	579,726	2,347,321	1,898,600
Texas	325,698	424,504	63,334	61,322	3,363,276	3,361,636	1,371,532	1,202,445
Virginia	287,579	152,899	41,015	26,903	946,595	465,756	1,599,912	674,670
TOTAL	1,743,697	1,387,946	822,020	639,581	9,256,328	7,688,213	14,593,923	10,220,441

Soldiers often did not take the time to fell trees for tent poles or firewood and instead seized existing sources of wood. Fortunately for them, southerners' practice of fencing crops put millions of miles of cut rails at their disposal. One farmer complained that General Lee's men took over ten thousand panels of his fences (eighty thousand rails). Lucy Buck, a wealthy debutante, wrote that a Union regiment "encamped [on the] south end of [the] wheat field and destroyed the third rail fence within sixty days from that end of the field, trampling and destroying the wheat and using much of it from the shocks for bedding."[50] By the last year of the war, marauding armies had destroyed so much fencing that one report from Virginia stated, "With the exception of small enclosures of one or two acres, here and there, there is scarcely a fence worthy of the name . . . and the fields, once the pride of the farmers' hearts, and shut in by 'ten rails and a rider,' are now broad commons."[51]

The construction of winter quarters consumed enormous quantities of wood for semipermanent structures, usually timber huts of varying sizes and sturdiness. Some soldiers describe them as miserable, leaky constructions; others note that their huts were quite large. J. B. Merritt wrote home that he had to stay in a hut about ten-feet long and thirty-feet wide with a partition running down the middle. Massachusetts soldier Mason Whiting Tyler noted that each year his winter quarters became more elaborate. The first year he had lived in a "miserable" log hut. The next winter, he enjoyed a hut with a chimney made of wood, "thickly plastered with mud on the inside, and with a wooden barrel on top." In his final year in the army, Tyler built a log hut with a stone chimney, which he described as being "a real palace, so to speak." Housing two men, it was fifteen-feet long and six-and-half-feet wide. "It grieves me very much," he wrote, "that we cannot have a fireplace, because wood is so scarce in this neighborhood that it is impossible to get enough to supply a fireplace."[52] Diaries and letters complain often of the inability of soldiers to procure wood from either felled trees or foraged civilian property; Tyler wrote that trying to build huts during the winter of 1864 was "like making bricks without straw."[53]

Quartermasters and impressment agents of the Confederate government also targeted timber and cut rails. A family who lived near Greensboro, Alabama, became furious when Mr. Smith, the local impressment agent, had his (impressed or rented) slaves cut down seventeen trees on their plantation. Smith's slaves then hauled the logs off in wagons without making a payment or providing a receipt. When the agent returned later that month, the family refused to let him touch their woodland, fearing they would have "no timber to spare." For the remainder of the war, they counted their trees regularly. But despite this family's outrage, timber impressment was fairly standard. Nimrod Porter of Tennessee estimated that a Mr. Moore, an agent of the Confederate government, had removed $60,000 worth of cedars from his land. In fact, by the

Figure 2.3 Winter quarters at Centreville, Virginia. This 1861 photograph shows the typical levels of timber consumption for building and maintaining winter quarters, as well as plank for the "roads" through the camp. Prints and Photographs Division, Library of Congress. LC-DIG-ppmsca-32991.

spring of 1864, the state of Virginia needed so much timber to repair railroads, erect defenses, and manufacture salt that it issued a special legislative order allowing agents to take up to four-fifths of the "standing wood" on a farm.[54]

The common military practice of "railroad wrecking" and bridge-burning constituted a significant drain on old-growth species on an equally large scale. Cutting off an enemy's supply lines is a crucial military strategy, so both armies ripped up railroads and burned down bridges all over the South. General Sherman, for instance, made the destruction of Confederate infrastructure one of his highest priorities. When Lonnie Miller and Jap George were traveling to join their regiment in Mississippi in 1864 as part of a group of recruits, veterans already serving in their company were spending their time destroying railroads in Enterprise and Canton, Mississippi, at Sherman's orders. When the 12th Wisconsin participated in the infamous "March to the Sea" through Georgia ten months later, they engaged in similar operations. Sherman boasted that his men had severed Confederates' railroads for a hundred miles in several directions from their corridor. The engineer corps, under the command of Captain Orlando M. Poe, was responsible for the destruction of the railroad tracks. In fact, Poe's personal diary of the march lays out the number of miles of railroad destroyed or depots burned scrawled in pencil under the date and the name of the nearest town. The rails could be literally ripped up, bent, or when the army was in a hurry, the ties simply burned. Confederate forces engaged in "railroad wrecking" as often as the Union soldiers did. Lemuel Foote, a chaplain in the New York Volunteer Regiment, noted the ability of Confederate forces to destroy their own infrastructure, writing that for hundreds of miles through southern Virginia, "every tie and every rail was torn up and the bridges annihilated."[55]

It was not the wrecking that constituted a drain on timber resources but the repairing of that wreckage. Both sides ensured these structures' replacement required large amounts of fresh timber, often right away. The "field engineers" of both armies handled much of the work of replacing railroads, bridges, and roads across the South. Foote stated that the Federal Government had sent a force of 4,300 men to repair the Virginia railroad, work that might take a month. To get across the Chattahoochee River in Georgia, Union soldiers rebuilt a bridge that had been demolished by retreating Confederate forces. "Nothing was left of the old bridge except the piers," one soldier wrote. Its reconstruction constituted "one of the curiosities of 'military energy,'" for the finished product measured 900 feet long with an average height of 70 feet and, according to this soldier's account, was completed in a matter of days.[56]

The supply and resupply of railroad crossties placed intense pressure on the timber resources of the region. During and immediately after the war, armies and railroad companies relied on "along-the-line" farmers and landowners to supply them with cut wood. These men (and sometimes women) allowed railroad workers and soldiers to clear woodland on their farms; oaks (especially white and post oaks) were singled out as the best material for crossties in the upcountry, with the bald cypress of the bottomlands a decent substitute. Workers indiscriminately cleared land on either side of the proposed track, and these key old-growth species became exceedingly rare in some spots. What looked like "progress" or the quick recovery of transportation infrastructure was disastrous for the ability of farmers to continue free-range husbandry, and it simultaneously lessened the opportunity to shift cultivation into unimproved woodland.[57]

The peculiarities of southern agriculture meant soldiers' appropriation of timber had more widespread and enduring impacts than the removal of trees might under different circumstances. Even in areas with relatively dense rural populations, soldiers noted that southern farms typically contained large acreages of "unimproved" land.[58] But military operations made farmers' use of these spaces less feasible. Expansion, on any scale, from state to state or field to field, became more difficult, and when forest lands became inaccessible because of

occupation or consumption, more-continuous, intensive agriculture prolifer-
ated. The repair of railroads targeted the exact same trees that farmers relied
on to provide natural forage for their free-ranging animals. Many farmers complained that key hardwood species had disappeared from the woods by 1860
because they were particularly suited to fence- and house-building. This put significant pressure on livestock, because it made them vulnerable to impressment
or foraging and replaced the underbrush with vegetation that could not support
cattle or hogs. It also added another pressure to cropland—foodstuffs were vulnerable to impressment, foraging, and now, hooved animals. P. E. Beauvais, an
agent for the Federal Government's Plantation Bureau, reported to his superior
that the operations on one of the plantations he supervised in Louisiana were
rapidly disintegrating because of free-ranging livestock. "I think it my duty to
let you know," Beauvais wrote, "that the cattles have had full sway for more than
one month on the part of the plantation." What was left of the provisions planted
there would be destroyed by hogs, he continued, "if they are allowed free scope
all over the plantation as they are now, the fences are down in many places and
no body to repair them."[59] Armies' appropriation of the cotton South's timber,
then, is an excellent example of how extensive land use proved to be an ally to
passing armies and an enemy to farmers.

Estimating the radius of resource appropriation is even more difficult for
felled trees or burned fence rails than for livestock. These items often proved
too commonplace to record, but they were vital for southern crops and soils.
Personal accounts by soldiers are spotty in their coverage of timber usage, and a
truly representative sample is hard to obtain due to variations in rank (and thus
responsibilities), location, and commanding general. Furthermore, the records
of an army's geographical location are often unreliable. A report might state that
an army was camped "at" Nashville, Tennessee, for instance, but be referring
only to the headquarters. The various commands could be scattered for up to
twenty miles. Contemporary accounts of the damage, too, contain only general
descriptions of how military transport or movements might have altered the surrounding landscape. One observer in southern Georgia claimed that "few in the
country . . . were so completely reduced as were those of Savannah, owing principally to the fact that the army was at the city, and subsisting itself upon what it
could get from plantations and counties in the immediate vicinity."[60] The source
does not say what the army seized, or how much, or from where.

Works of urban ecology and economic geography, however, allow historians to estimate the implications of Civil War armies' resource consumption in
the agricultural context of the cotton South. Historian Lisa Brady argues that
armies are essentially mobile cities that "could not help but consume everything
in their path." Brady's comparison of armies to cities is a helpful one, for scholars
of urban ecology and land use have much to say about the dynamics of resource

accumulation. Urban areas have a variety of environmental impacts both in their immediate vicinity and farther afield that constitute their "ecological footprint," and even small concentrations of city dwellers appropriate millions of acres of productive land.[61] William Rees, one of the earliest scholars to draw attention to how ecology influences urban economics, estimates that Vancouver, Canada, uses the productive output of land over 174 times larger than the size of the city. So while historians cannot definitively calculate the ecological footprint of the armies of Grant, Lee, or Sherman, the literature on urban ecology suggests that at least 110,000 acres of land were needed per year to support an army of 65,000 men with food, fuel, and materials for infrastructure—if they were living at the lowest levels of consumption.[62] Even the roughest calculations demonstrate how the movements of soldiers through the southern landscape affected a vast area. The absorption of the cotton South's resources to support the transport and operations of both armies had widespread effects, even in regions largely isolated from battles.

Thinking about armies as cities also opens up new ways to conceive of the more intangible impacts of military supply and movement.[63] Civil War armies not only served as sites of resource accumulation—gorging on livestock, fuel-wood, water, and wild game—they also reordered the agricultural economy. Military forces dismantled or, at least, made riskier the networks of exchange that supported antebellum cotton farming. Upland areas generally contributed foodstuffs to slave-dense areas; the upper South supported the lower South with infusions of horses, mules, and grain; farm implements along with some grains and foodstuffs came from the North; and items such as salt came from international trade.[64] Southern farmers typically looked to woodland for sources of soil nutrients and supplemented shifting cultivation with manure or guano. However, secession stopped the flow of goods from the North and, especially, the Midwest, and military operations in the first two years of the war cut off the upper South from the lower South. The presence of armies necessitated crop regime changes and drained labor from farms. Planters' conversion from rais-ing cash crops to cultivating low-maintenance food crops changed the pressures humans put on the land for two or three years. This often had positive results. For instance, cotton lands that grew corn during the war experienced a reduc-tion in pests and toxins in the soil, as well as an increase in available nitrogen. Conscription and slave emancipation, however, led to a breakdown in land maintenance and increased land abandonment—issues that would continue to plague farmers well after the surrender.[65]

On the outbreak of hostilities in 1861, Confederate leaders began urging cot-ton farmers to grow more food crops—corn, peas, and garden vegetables—and severely reduce the acreage devoted to cotton. "A change in our pursuits must be promptly made," the *Southern Cultivator* proclaimed. "We have no time for

delay!" Newspapers around the South trumpeted, "Plant Corn and Be Free, or
Plant Cotton and Be Whipped!" A paper out of Savannah, Georgia, went so
far as to declare that anyone who planted cotton "deserves to be destroyed, or
to have all his plantations and negroes ravaged and desolated, and himself fed
upon corn cobs as long as he lives."[66] Because the war had begun after the planting season of 1861, there was a delay in the conversion of crop regimes from
cash crops to foodstuffs, but once the first war year's crop was harvested, the
appeals to farmers seemed to take effect. The South harvested four-and-a-half-
million bales of cotton in the first autumn of the war; the next year, it produced
only one-and-a-half-million bales.[67] Although plenty of farmers resisted making
crop changes, travelers through places such as the Black Belt of Alabama and
Mississippi noted that vast fields formerly devoted to cotton were now mostly
planted in corn. A Black Belt planter named John Parrish wrote to his brother
in Germany: "Nearly all our lands are planted in corn, peas, potatoes, etc. Little
or no cotton was planted. I made a visit to Mr. Hagan a day or two ago. He has
planted about 85 acres in cotton [but] he has a world of corn." Most states
reported only a tenth of their usual cotton crop. Only Texas continued to cultivate cotton at antebellum levels.[68] A merchant from Mobile, Alabama, wrote
that the "disposition" of most planters was to plant more grain and raise stock
because "there seems to be no question about the bad policy of adding another
crop to the present unless this is sold or saleable." Unless sales prospects bright-
ened, cotton planters would more than likely grow what he called "army supplies." Regardless of the motivation, by 1864 the land between John Parrish's
plantation in the Black Belt and the merchant in Mobile was reportedly "one
vast cornfield."[69]

The self-sufficiency campaign was crucial to the survival of the Confederacy
because after 1862, the "granary" of the South, the states of Kentucky, Tennessee,
and Virginia, could no longer provide their share of supplies due to an unfortu-
nate mix of Federal occupation and heavy military operations. The Confederacy
usually produced enough corn to offset the losses in those states, but it could
not make up the deficiency in meat production. The cotton planters of the lower
South had traditionally relied on the upper South or the Midwest for horses,
mules, and even hogs and cattle. When the flow of livestock into the lower South
slowed, both soldiers and civilians suffered. This was particularly true for pork.
Before the war, hog meat was abundant and the consumption of bacon or salt
pork was considered "indispensable, especially to a laboring man." Yet the pork
southerners consumed was not necessarily raised in the South. Of the three million hogs slaughtered and packed domestically during 1860, only twenty thousand were packed in the South.[70] Once the war broke out and access to provisions
from the Midwest and the upper South withered, the Confederacy suffered
from intense shortages of pork products. Planters complained that they could

not procure meat for their families or their slaves, and soldiers began to count bacon as one of the most prized foodstuffs they could acquire. Furthermore, the abundant herds of beef cattle in the South were concentrated in Texas. By 1862, Texas was the primary supplier of beef for the Confederacy, but Union military operations the following year effectively prevented those herds from reaching states on the east side of the Mississippi River.[71]

The intensification of food-centered agriculture successfully increased the percentage of food crops being raised, but military operations ensured that in many areas, it was not enough.[72] The Confederacy had always imported many products from elsewhere, especially meat, salt, fertilizer, and hoes. When the war began, leaders of the South assumed they would be able to continue, and even expand, international trading to secure these products. However, just as the Federal occupation of the upper South prevented the collection of meats and grains, so, too, did the arrival of Union troops in important cash-crop areas undermine the cultivation of agricultural commodities that could have been exported in exchange for consumer goods.

The Union's blockade of southern ports also prevented necessary items such as guano and salt from reaching cotton farmers. Blockade runners concentrated on luxury goods over the utilitarian items essential to southerners' everyday lives. The South's supply of necessary metals, such as iron, zinc, copper, and steel, for the creation and repair of machinery, railroads, bridges, and farm implements dried up. Although southern women worked to create replacements for items that were no longer available because of the blockade, several items vital to the continuation of southern food production did not have adequate substitutes. Guano could only be imported from Peru. The blockade halted those importations, and though merchants sold adulterated versions of the fertilizer, none were as successful in returning nitrogenous compounds to the soil. The sudden scarcity of guano meant smaller corn yields in the cotton belt.

Because the guano shortage affected only relatively wealthy planters, its consequences for agriculture went largely unnoticed at the time, whereas the salt shortage affected everyone and presented a significant obstacle to the southern push for agricultural self-sufficiency. Before the war, southerners used and consumed 450 million pounds of salt every year, most of which came from Wales. Once the blockade reduced shipments of salt, farmers could not preserve the meat of the animals they slaughtered, contributing to the shortage of saltmeat (salt-cured pork) rations for soldiers. An ex-slave who grew up near Ridgeway, South Carolina later recalled that after the second year of the war, "most everything to eat and wear got scarce. Sometimes you couldn't git salt to go in the vegetables and meat that was cooked. People dug up the salty earth under their smoke houses, put water with it, drained it off and used it to salt rations." Salt was also essential to the diets of both cattle and horses: without it, cattle did not fatten and horses lacked a necessary electrolyte.[73] The blockade's efficacy as a military tactic may be in doubt, but insofar as the North sought to starve the South, the absence of guano and salt helped weaken the South during the war and afterward.

The presence of armies also siphoned free and slave labor from southern farms.[74] Conscription, impressment, and, ultimately, emancipation made it substantially harder for planters and farmers to muster the human energy required to clear new lands or repair fences. Without the work force to perform the tasks needed to keep cultivation and land maintenance going, the South's agricultural regime began to break down. It was no coincidence that the move to grains and food crops coincided with an enormous loss of labor in the agricultural sector due to military service. Between 750,000 and 1,227,890 white men served in the Confederate Army (out of a population of roughly 5.5 million free southerners). Over 483,000 of those men died or were wounded during the conflict; the dead alone accounted for almost 20 percent of the South's population of white males.[75] On smaller farms, the loss of even one or two men from the available labor pool meant the difference between planting or abandoning cultivation entirely. On plantations, the loss of labor had less to do with the white men (an overseer or planter's son leaving for military service would not usually halt crop production) and more to do with the emancipation of slaves.[76]

Passing armies or impending military occupation inspired many slaves to flee to Federal lines or join the columns and wagon trains on campaigns—to "self-emancipate." Henry Hitchcock, who accompanied Sherman, wrote of an "immense train" of refugees and wondered at how many able-bodied men the Confederacy had lost as armies moved through. One Georgia farmer wrote that though he had not been disturbed by the "yankees when they were all over the country," his "negroes left about that time," and he had since had no help cultivating his land.[77] A planter's son in Louisiana described "a perfect stampede of negroes" fleeing the plantations. J. C. Norwood of North Carolina observed that as Sherman's forces approached in the spring of 1865, "a considerable number of negro men left for Tennessee— & have not been heard from since," in addition to several of his own slaves, who "went with the cavalry." Newspapers all over the country ran cartoons showing long lines of "contrabands" following the army, carrying their worldly belongings in packs slung over their shoulders.[78]

Further reducing the number of slaves on farms and plantations was their impressment by the Confederacy as a source of "noncombatant labor" to build defenses, cut roads, and repair railroads. Individual states passed laws calling for and regulating the impressment of slaves beginning in 1862, and each state set rates of compensation to slaveowners and limits on the period of time slaves could be retained. South Carolina, for instance, asked for 750 slaves a month from each of its four districts and offered $11 per slave per month to their owners; Virginia impressed ten thousand slaves at a time but at a rate of $16 per slave per month including rations; and Mississippi offered $30 a month, rations, and clothing for each impressed slave.[79] As the war dragged on and the numbers of healthy Confederate troops dwindled, the government requisitioned slaves in larger numbers and with little concern for their well-being. The Confederate government, in desperation, actually passed a law in March 1865 to enlist slaves as soldiers.[80] As one tobacco planter-turned-soldier vented, "Our wise President wants 200,000 negro's drafted . . . . Two hundred thousand laborers taken from our fields, where they are absolutely needed and placed in the army which we now cannot feed. 200,000 fewer workers and 200,000 more eaters."[81]

Because of the transfer or loss of labor, on many farms only a fraction of improved acreage was being tilled, if any. Although grains typically require less attention than cash crops—for instance, corn grows taller and harvests are larger when the beds are regularly weeded, but it will usually yield something regardless of care—farm journals trace the gradual decline of production as either farmers or their slaves disappeared from the land to serve in the army as soldiers or laborers. Without labor to clear new land, combined with the shortage of fertilizers, the intensive cultivation of even food crops was not sustainable on worn-out or exhausted fields. John Horry Dent of Barbour County, Alabama, suffered steady declines in his corn yields during the war despite retaining at least two-thirds of his slaves through the planting of 1864. His farm journal points to several reasons for the decline: reduced labor, less "new ground" cleared, erosion, and a lack of fertilizer. [82] He complained that both cotton and corn looked "sickly" because it was being choked out by weeds and grass due to heavy rains and a lack of labor (he does not say why his labor is reduced). The signs of a "backwards" corn crop for Dent, however, such as wilting leaves and a "shriveled" appearance to the grain, suggest that there was a potassium deficiency in the soil as well, which would not be unusual for soils in the Black Belt that had been growing cotton before being planted in corn.[83]

Dent noted that the ground of the older fields was alternately "flooded" and "baked," suggesting that the soil was eroded to the point where the clayey subhorizons could not absorb normal precipitation. They flooded when it rained and cracked open when it did not. The "fix" for this problem before the war— plowing deeper, fertilizing with guano, and clearing new ground—was not as easy to do by 1863 or 1864. Dent's journal indicates that he was still able to clear "new ground," but that he cleared 40 percent fewer acres in 1863 than in 1861. Dent could not acquire guano, and because impressment took all of his fodder, he had fed his cottonseed to his hogs. Cottonseed, a waste product of cotton production, was one of the most common fertilizers of the day. As a result, his grain production fell far below expectations. "War or no war," he wearily lamented, "a new place must be had." Like many of his southern contemporaries, his exhausted lands could no longer support even subsistence agriculture.[84]

Labor shortages also led to widespread land abandonment. After 1861, hundreds of thousands of acres went uncultivated, rice canals and ditches fell into disrepair, and sugar mills lay quiet. Land abandonment caused widespread ecological shifts in the southern landscape and can be considered one of the environmental impacts of an army's presence. As southerners vacated their land, severe soil erosion occurred on farms or fields that had been intensively cultivated before the war, especially in areas with highly erosive clay loam soils or a particularly hilly topography. An example of this is found in the old tobacco regions of the Piedmont of Virginia and North Carolina, where, geographer Stanley Trimble notes, the rates of erosion increased during the war because of the rising trend of land abandonment.[85] Normally hardy secondary succession species, such as pine, could not grow on lands already damaged by soil erosion. The lack of vegetative cover simply led to more erosion, eliminating any possibility of ever coaxing the land back into cultivation.

A more common result was reforestation, an ecological silver lining amid wartime changes. If land was still suitable for agriculture at the time it was abandoned, then within weeks, a shallow-rooted herbaceous community dominated by broom-sedge invaded, and other early succession species such as blackberry and sumac bushes swiftly followed. After a year, shortleaf, loblolly, or slash pine seedlings sprang up, often in great numbers.[86] During the war, many observers noted the reclamation of abandoned land by flora; soldiers often found pine seedlings to be convenient sources of tinder, though others felt brambles and weeds to be unsightly. One Union captain recorded in his diary that he had built a fire, "back in the thick jack pines where they have spring up on an old plantation and are thick and bushy." Journalist John Trowbridge noted the phenomenon of "old fields," or abandoned cropland, throughout the South: "The more recent of these are usually found covered with briars, weeds, and broom-sedge (a tall grass often called blue stem)—often with a thick growth of infant pines coming up like grass."[87]

The antebellum practice of shifting cultivation meant that even at the beginning of the war, many southern states were a patchwork of cultivated fields, "waste fields" or "old fields" lying fallow, woodland used for livestock ranging, and fields no longer suitable for cultivation. Thus, it is difficult to distinguish between prewar "old fields" that had been left to fallow and "old fields" that had been abandoned because of military operations. In 1863, the US Government set up a special bureau in the Treasury Department to deal with abandoned plantations in occupied parts of Mississippi. After the war, these plantations, as well as all other abandoned or confiscated lands, were transferred to the Freedmen's Bureau. Each bureau district submitted reports on abandoned lands to the assistant commissioner for the state; these records range from cursory entries that only list the name of the former owner to detailed descriptions of the location, lands in cultivation, soil types, and available timber. In a small region of North Carolina that had been "invaded" during Sherman's Carolina campaign, only 1,800 of over eighteen thousand "abandoned" acres were in cultivation as of the 1865 harvest. The reports for St. Bartholomew's Parish in South Carolina for August 1865 listed 27 plantations as abandoned, 11 of which were under no cultivation whatsoever. On the other 16 plantations, no more than 5 percent of the cleared acreage was being cultivated; on 2 plantations consisting of 1,200 and 5,000 acres, respectively, only 40 were being cultivated on the first and 120 on the second. As far as it can be calculated, 20 percent of the "improved acreage" of the entire South fell out of cultivation during the war, although it is possible that labor shortages, military occupation, and the loss of fencing, buildings, and implements caused much wider abandonment.[88]

The results of the rising trend of land abandonment were mixed. Clearly, whether it was a field neglected for a year or a farm unoccupied for a decade, abandonment provided a respite from the pressures of human resource consumption. It was, at its core, a continuation of the long fallow that had occurred with more-stable shifting cultivation regimes during the antebellum period. It allowed the land to rest. In the Mississippi Delta, forest and cane had reclaimed significant portions of previously cleared land by the end of the war. However, the benefits of secondary vegetative growth often had subtle consequences for the long-term use of that land and, more specifically, for the continued practicality of the extensive land-use practices that were common in the antebellum era. The spread of pine forests across the South in the wake of abandonment exacerbated the region's already acidic soils. Over time, fallen pine needles become a part of the topsoil; they do not add as many nutrients as the leaves of maples or oaks and the needles increase the acidity of the soil. This shift in nutrient content and pH subtly undermined yields after farmers cleared a secondary pine forest to put the land into cultivation.[89] So the acceleration of land abandonment by military operations and labor shortages led to a net increase in the available topsoil in places that had been isolated from battles, but ironically, it created the preconditions for an entirely new and more destructive type of land abandonment after the war.

The ecological transformations taking place across the cotton South between 1861 and 1865 reflected the complicated relationship between the battlefield and the home front. In places made quiet by the din of battle elsewhere, bottomland forests recovered to some extent, and though land abandonment could lead to extreme soil erosion and gullying, it could also result in the growth of secondary vegetation. Furthermore, the pull of the Confederate war effort caused a brief florescence of subsistence agriculture—after all, cash crops did farmers little good amid Federal occupation and the inflation of Confederate currency. The dissolution of the national and international markets for southern products, reduced numbers of laborers in the fields, and high prices of provisions and basic agricultural goods meant that truck crops were more popular than ever, and grains were favored heavily over cotton and tobacco. But the respite for the ecologies of fields and farms on the home front was only made possible by the multiplication of environmental threats on the battlefield. Where soil had once washed away during summer rains because of the planting of clean-cut rows of cotton, it was now dislodged by soldiers digging breastworks and trenches around forts and camps. Areas of the southern forest previously under pressure due to the expansion of cultivated land were transformed, not by farmers, but by battles and artillery fire. Foraging and impressment drained vital resources from fields and farms. Between 1861 and 1865, the most significant force acting on the southern landscape was no longer agriculture, but human conflict.

Scholars have spilled considerable amounts of ink trying to gauge how much or how little defense building, railroad wrecking, foraging, and impressment truly meant after 1865. The numbers of heifers taken or cotton gins burned are often lumped in with the tallies of "destruction," "devastation," or "desolation" caused by the war. Union commanders such as Sheridan or Sherman take much of the blame—their hard-war campaigns are typically described as having spared no buildings, fences, herds of stock, or fields of crops that would denote the existence of widespread or organized farming. Of course, Union troops were not the only ones who raided the South. Historian Paul Gates calls the areas where Confederates foraged heavily a "belt of desolation." The Piedmont section of North Carolina, for instance, where Lee's troops foraged to support their operations in Virginia, was so exhausted by raids that 50 percent of the land previously in cultivation lay idle owing to the lack of animals, fences, forage, and foodstuffs.[90]

The focus on "destruction" fails to explain why the South was so adversely affected by damage that should have been ephemeral. Part of the answer is that southerners' antebellum system had forged the preconditions for the so-called devastation so many contemporaries described. Soldiers' removal of livestock, provisions, fences, and woodland, as well as the exacerbation of soil erosion by fortification building, were all more damaging because of the region's reliance on extensive land-use practices. If viewed as an acceleration, or exacerbation, of preexisting vulnerabilities of southern land use, then soldiers' removal of livestock, provisions, and fences, as well as the quickened pace of soil erosion and woodland clearance, matter in the long term. White farmers and planters had to operate under the environmental limitations they had previously been able to circumvent while also dealing with the pressures of prewar and wartime debt and a shortage of credit and currency.[91] The loss of just one crop could mean bankruptcy or the forfeiture of lands and property.

Some in the South viewed the war and the defeat of the "southern way of life" as an opportunity to rebuild the region's agriculture in the image of the ideal: small, diversified operations with penned, well-cared for animals, ample manuring of grounds continuously used rather than abandoned, and, most importantly, an approach to farming characterized by a commitment to place rather than profit. Indeed, what reformers and northern officials wanted gradually became more common on southern plantations: continuous cultivation, fenced livestock, and the widespread use of "improvement" techniques, such as fertilization. Unfortunately, the intensification of cotton cultivation was hardly an upgrade to southern farms, at least in ecological terms. Environmental changes that occurred as a result of the war and emancipation undermined any efforts to reorganize southern agriculture, worsening environmental conditions and restricting economic opportunities for white and black farmers alike.

3

Intensifying Production

Let me picture to you the footsore Confederate soldier. . . . What does
he find when, having followed the battle-stained cross against overwhelming odds . . . he reaches the home he left so prosperous and beautiful? He finds his house in ruins, his farm devastated, his slaves free, his
stock killed, his barns empty, his trade destroyed, his money worthless,
his social system, feudal in its magnificence, swept away. As ruin was
never before so overwhelming, never was restoration swifter.
                           —Henry Grady, "The New South" (1886)

When the war ended, and the fear and uncertainty of those four years slipped
back into the familiar routines of plantings and harvests, James Washington
Matthews was relieved to find his children alive and home, and his small farm
intact. A year later, however, the sixty-six-year-old Tennessean felt anxious, for
survival was not a guarantor of recovery.[1] An unusually cruel drought in 1865
seared the farm's already friable soils, and the winter rains failed to restore them.
Matthews had not been able to replace the livestock the Yankees had taken as
they pursued General Hood's men at Columbia in 1864, and he had managed to
repair only a few of his burned fences. It seemed ironic that a farm in what was
advertised as Tennessee's finest stock-raising country would be short of meat,
and the farmer feared that a neighbor's hogs might eat his already reduced corn
crop.[2] Matthews also worried that his son, Gilbert Dooley, would not be able to
halt the family's slide into poverty. Gilbert had not been the same since his capture at Chickamauga, and though he seemed physically whole again, he insisted
that profits might be made by subdividing the farm. He boasted that a man need
only plant cotton and corn: one for money and one for fodder. What would
they do for labor? Matthews asked. Gilbert assumed they would hire someone.
"There were boys to be had" was the refrain of the county's farmers. Men who
had lost their land were looking for work, ex-slaves needed to avoid vagrancy
charges. No farmer had money, James Washington included, but at least he had
land.[3] The war had not taken that—yet.

It is difficult to determine the true "cost" of the Civil War for white agriculturalists like James Washington Matthews who existed outside the planter class.
Slave emancipation and the subsequent evaporation of credit and collateral may
have precipitated a wave of bankruptcies among planters, but slaveholding elites
proved much more insulated from hardship than "plain folk."[4] For large populations in Matthews's home state of Tennessee, as well as in northern Alabama,
central North Carolina, the hills or pine lands of Georgia, and upland South
Carolina, the loss of a son or a few hogs to military operations was the difference
between getting by and suffering. Over a quarter of the Confederate soldiers
who had marched away never returned, and not all who survived could work.
Even the undocumented effects of war, such as psychological trauma, had the
potential to alter individuals' economic fortunes.

"Blood is the first cost," writer Robert Penn Warren argued, but not the last.
"Not only men, with their debatable cash value, are expended in war; property,
with its more clear-cut price tag, is destroyed."[5] The South's landscape may not
have been physically ravaged in areas outside battle lines, but roving armies had
removed livestock, timber, and implements from all areas of the Confederacy.
The absorption, neglect, depreciation, or loss of agricultural resources during
the war cost the region an estimated 1.5 billion dollars (in 1860 currency).
Robert Philip Howell, a farmer from North Carolina, echoed the sentiments of
many ex-Confederate soldiers when he stated, "Of course, I was glad that my
life had been spared with whole bones, but I was in a tight place."[6] His stock was
gone, his currency was worthless, and the bit of corn he eked out of his land in
1865 was not enough to provide for his family. The conflict, often characterized
as a rich man's war and a poor man's fight, continued to disproportionately affect
the plain folk of the South long after the surrender.

Yet many within agricultural reform circles viewed the plight of small farmers such as James Washington Matthews as an opportunity for change. The consensus in publications such as the *Southern Planter, De Bow's Review*, and the
Southern Cultivator was that the failure of the Confederacy and the slave-based
cash-crop system it had fought to retain was a pivotal moment for the rehabilitation of southern agriculture. Hardship on the home front had demonstrated
the unsoundness of cash-crop agriculture and the importance of a diversified,
food-centered approach. The conflict freed farmers to construct a new base of
prosperity patterned on northern-style agriculture. The recently formed US
Department of Agriculture (USDA) echoed these sentiments, declaring, "The
whole country is desirous of knowing the present and prospective condition of
agriculture [in the South]," so that "unremitting efforts" could be made to "initi-
ate a new era in the history of its productive industry."[7] One USDA employee
claimed that only a more "enlightened system of husbandry" was needed for the
southern landscape to support any crop desired, including those typically grown

in the North. What reformers and northern officials wanted was intensive agriculture rather than extensive, and they called on yeomen to fence their livestock, abandon shifting cultivation in favor of continuous planting, and use modern improvement techniques such as fertilization.[8] By intensifying production, the argument went, small farmers could not only recover their fortunes, but also restore the health of their lands after decades of "wasteful" agriculture.

James Washington Matthews and other southern farmers gradually adopted some intensive agricultural techniques, but not out of admiration for "Yankee" methods. The environmental consequences of the war—including soldiers' removal of woodland, farmers' abandonment of fields because of occupation or labor shortages, and armies' impressment or foraging of livestock—encouraged intensification. In many places, shifting cultivation became less frequent. The assault on free-range husbandry was renewed, and all states either considered or passed a series of "stock laws." As livestock numbers dipped, more farmers began to apply fertilizers such as guano, superphosphates, and, eventually, chemical fertilizers to their land. Although the changes mirrored the desires of reformers and officials, these developments failed to transform the region's farms into the "ideal" homestead of the early nineteenth century. Indeed, intensification actually tightened ecological constraints and actively undermined farmers' chances of economic recovery.[9]

This chapter on the immediate postwar period through the 1870s examines the results of wartime environmental change on smaller farms owned by whites. There were many ironies associated with intensive agriculture for white landholders, even those outside nontraditional cotton-growing areas. Wartime "self-sufficiency" campaigns and land abandonment owing to the loss of labor or military occupation reinvigorated the land through crop rotation and vegetative regrowth during the mid- and late 1860s, but this also created false hopes for cotton yields at a time when preexisting debt created enormous economic risk for farmers and severe drought marred several harvests. Because of these wartime environmental changes, then, cotton production was initially more successful on some land than perhaps it might have been considering the unforgiving weather in the South and the well-documented difficulties farmers had accessing seed, credit, or currency. By the 1870s, however, this intensive production method came to a crashing halt, for much of the land being put into cotton was not suitable for continuous production without the use of fertilizers. Although advocates of agricultural reform advocates celebrated the expansion of fertilizer use, those purchases became a major source of debt for farmers during this period and did little to improve the long-term prospects for agriculture.

For farmers whose self-sufficiency had once included the use of livestock for food and fertilizer, the war's effects on livestock populations was significant. Foraging and disease had wiped out considerable numbers of cattle and hogs in the region, and with fewer animals, the logic of self-sufficiency fell apart. Aiding the decline of stock-raising in upland regions was the war's destruction of fences, forests, and railroads. The replacement of fences and railroads put pressure on old-growth trees needed for range, and the accelerated woodland clearance during the war threatened the existence of common lands. Railroad companies expanded their lines, opening more isolated, subsistence-oriented areas to logging companies. The removal of woodland through extraction, when combined with the shortage of animals, made the twin practices of free-range animal husbandry and shifting cultivation less viable. Southern farmers more often penned their remaining animals along the lines of northern-style farms and, in another irony, exacerbated the recurrence of infectious animal diseases introduced by the war, such as hog cholera. Ultimately, by intensifying production, smaller farmers not only increased their integration with the market, but also unwittingly accelerated a cycle of ecological change the war had initiated.

During the 1850s, patches of oats, millet, corn, wheat, and garden crops dotted the ridges of James Washington Matthews's holdings, on plots he burned out amid oaks and hickories that were too large to fell. When he planted cotton for the first time during the war, it took him and his slave exactly two days to pick the clouds of lint clinging to the bolls. After the surrender, Matthews continued to grow a range of food crops, and his son surveyed an additional plot for cotton. Gilbert took on a hired hand, and then Matthews rented out several fields. By 1868, a growing number of renters and hired hands cycled on and off the farm, and additional workers meant more cotton. Gilbert paid Nathan and Wat, young freedmen, $10 a month to work on his cotton field and employed at least two more freedmen during picking season that year. It took the group two months to harvest Gib's "patch." By the close of the decade, the farm also supported three renters and their own work forces. Sandy, Silas, and Bill all grew corn on "stubble ground" around their tenant plots, and every January, they handed their cotton over to Gilbert. The elder Matthews, his health declining, spent most of his days in his garden and frequently noted "done nothing as usual" in his diary. But he watched as the farm stopped growing food in favor of cotton. It was not an intentional decision, but small choices made in response to the war or changing circumstances, modifications that seemed reasonable or responsible at the time, which agglomerated into a path away from self-sufficiency. His entries ceased to mention burning new land and only remarked on fence repair every two years. The number of hogs they killed each year declined, and stock-raising gave way to fertilizer-buying. While the types of crops sprouting from the fields continued in their variety for a few postwar years, by the 1870s, the transformation of his mixed-crop farm to a cotton-only operation was complete.[10]

These changes on James Washington Matthews's farm echoed those occurring across the South. The Civil War's financial implications for yeoman farmers caused a wave of postwar market integration and the conversion of farms once known for their self-sufficiency toward cotton production, although the timing differed from place to place. Indeed, Matthews's farm diaries helpfully provide a window into several reasons for cotton's spread among yeomen: the loss of property during the war, the specter of drought and floods, the changing nature of labor as sons and husbands did not return or returned injured, the ripple effects of emancipation, and the anxieties of operating in an uncertain market with little access to currency. Landholding whites in many areas now found cotton growing a more attractive prospect. Gilbert Dooley Matthews certainly argued for greater cotton production on his father's Tennessee farm, despite decades of a mixed-crop approach and the area's reputation as having "indifferent" soils for cotton growing. The supposed advantage of cotton for small farmers was that the profits would help alleviate the burdens of their material losses and make up for a less-productive workforce.[11]

Another reading of Matthews's diary, however, reveals that ecological processes, specifically wartime environmental change, also affected farmers' transition into continuous cotton production. The expansion of food-centered agriculture during and immediately after the war had provided just enough respite for fields, so that if a farmer decided to plant cotton in 1866, the yields were deceivingly robust.[12] In this case, the Matthews family grew a range of food crops, including oats and millet, through the war. Once they converted those fields to cotton, the reduced pest load or replenished levels of nutrients in the soil from the food crops might allow the cotton crops of 1866 and 1867 to exceed expectations. After that, the same land required ash, marl, manure, or fertilizer to replenish the substances in the soil. If Gilbert's or Matthews's renters used forested or reforested lands for cotton, that, too, had temporarily positive effect on yields. However, shifting cultivation broke down as the family subdivided the farm, and the loss of stock or provisions or other agricultural resources during the war created additional economic and environmental challenges. In conjunction with the very real problem of debt, the removal of livestock, implements, timber, and provisions prevented Gilbert Dooley Matthews and other planters or farmers from spreading out their risk over multiple harvests. In short, the changes wrought by and during the Civil War gave false hope to farmers looking to "get rich" planting cotton. A broader context that considers both the land's past and how nature helps shape agricultural outcomes is necessary for understanding what cotton production during the late 1860s meant for yeoman farmers.

During the war, white farmers, whether responding to the siren song of Confederate nationalism or simply endeavoring to cultivate their land with

minimal labor, favored grain or truck-crop production. John Nick Barker of
Clarksville, Tennessee, maintained a decidedly diverse approach to farming
during the 1850s, but supplemented grains and garden crops with both tobacco
and cotton. His wartime diaries, however, indicate that he raised oats, beets,
parsnips, corn, sweet potatoes, okra, Irish potatoes, and cowpeas. An entry for
December 1865 illustrates the importance of food crops during waves of military occupation and impressment, stating simply, "finished gathering corn [;]
thank God for bread."[13] Although large-scale planters continued to raise cotton
during the conflict, they, too, adjusted their crop schedules. A chaplain traveling with the US Army described the remarkable fields of grain and food crops
planted in Mississippi at the end of the war. "The breadth of corn planted this
year is very great and will suffice for the subsistence of the people," he wrote.
"Cotton has not been planted this year to any considerable extent . . . in Madison
County, not one bale to a thousand of their former large crops will probably be
raised this year." The elimination of slavery in some areas of the South during the
war also contributed to an increase in food production. Some planters allowed
their slaves more time and latitude in the gardens traditionally allotted to them.
Discussing his master's policy toward slave-directed agriculture toward the end
of the conflict, ex-slave Henry Ryan of South Carolina remembered, "Over in
old Edgefield . . . we had plenty to eat; plenty of peas, corn bread, turnips and
other things."[14]

The emphasis on food crops during the war was most evident in places where
slaves had the freedom to work in whatever ways they desired. In some instances,
the US government commanded slave labor on occupied plantations or transferred control of the land to them.[15] On an abandoned plantation in Coahoma
County, Mississippi, for instance, a US Plantation Bureau agent reported in 1864
that freedperson David Thomas planted and controlled 20 acres, 8 of them in
corn and the rest in garden vegetables, whereas Albert Barley had only cultivated
10 acres, 5 in corn and 5 in vegetables. Curtis Pollard, who enjoyed the help of
his family, managed over 40 acres, with 25 in corn in "good and promising condition," and 15 acres of garden vegetables in "fine order." In fact, the Honorable
John Covode, sent to the Mississippi Valley by the US secretary of war at the time
of the surrender, stated that "negroes would work at raising corn . . . while they
were unwilling to work at raising cotton or sugar." When asked why, he replied
that freedpeople could not eat cotton or sugar—they preferred to grow food that
would provide subsistence and eschewed in particular the cultivars used to justify their former bondage. Although whites eventually reclaimed a great deal of
the land parceled out to ex-slaves during the war, even the temporary acquisition
of these plantation lands by freedpeople served the same role as wartime crop
rotation by whites who supported the Confederate war effort. Cash crops such
as cotton, sugar, and rice gave way to food production.[16]

Figure 3.1 St. Helena Island, South Carolina, 1863. Plantation supervisor David Franklin Thorpe overseeing freedpeople on a confiscated farm. Many of the largest plantations in occupied portions of Louisiana, Mississippi, Georgia, and South Carolina were given over to ex-slaves so that they could farm for themselves, or were put back into cotton or food production by the US Military, as shown here. Prints and Photographs Division, Library of Congress. LC-DIG-stereo-1s03961.

Emancipation and the collapse of the Confederacy did not end the South's focus on food production. In fact, several public figures argued that one of the primary lessons of the military conflict was that it showed the danger of staple monoculture. The blockade and military operations hadcaused cotton farmers to "resort to home productions," and one prominent Alabamian wrote, "War has now put an end" to the mentality of planting cotton to buy provisions. Self-sufficiency and crop diversity were "necessit[ies]" to make southerners "a self-reliant people." James Lawrence Orr, the newly elected provisional governor of South Carolina, declared in 1865 that though the war had brought hardship and privation, growing food at home would give southerners "independence." Orr stressed that South Carolina should henceforth "raise, grow, and make everything themselves" that they had once imported from western or northern states. Orr was not only referring to finished goods, such as furniture, but also horses, mules, cattle, hogs, bacon, lard, beef, and implements. Slavery had been the driver of the South's fealty to King Cotton, he said; with this "dishonorable" form of labor abolished, it was time to make better use of the southern landscape's natural endowment.[17]

Evidence suggests that whites continued to produce a variety of subsistence crops for several years after the Confederate surrender. The records of factors and merchants indicate food-centered agriculture among all economic classes, even in the period between 1865 and 1867, when cotton prices were at their peak. In the ledgers of southern Georgia factorage L. J. Guilmartin and Co., farmers and planters traded tobacco, wool, rice, wax, hemp, potatoes, oats, corn, melons, and animal hides for provisions confiscated during the war or taken from their homes during raids, such as bacon or barrels of flour. Cotton was always mentioned, but as one crop of many.[18] Farm diary entries and financial receipts for 1865, 1866, and 1867 also reveal the extent to which landlords still relied on a diverse set of crops. In Newton County, Georgia, Gustavus Orr contracted with his former slaves to grow corn, sorghum, fodder, and sweet potatoes—the agreement mentioned no staple crops. In neighboring Alabama, planters contracted with laborers to grow cotton, but it was a tertiary crop. The acreage devoted to a mix of corn, potatoes, peas, oats, rye, and wheat was larger.[19] In Crawfordsville, Georgia, accounts of local farms sent to Alexander Stephens, the former vice president of the Confederacy, mentioned no cotton in 1865 or 1866 but rather corn, oats, wheat, and several types of fruit. George Bristow wrote to Stephens that "the corn crop in this section will be larger than for several years."[20] The hardships of the home front had caused a surge in food-centered agriculture, and the uncertainty of the immediate postwar days ensured that in pockets of the South, raising provisions would still be the goal.

Ironically, the florescence of food production during and after the war would eventually push farmers into cotton monoculture by skewing expectations for yields. When they did plant cotton, the previous years' crop rotations or vegetative growth caused a temporary surge in productivity or quality. William O. Nixon of Lowndes County, Alabama, provides a good example of this process. Located on the Gulf Coastal Plain west of Montgomery and characterized by rolling prairies and scattered pine and oak forests, Nixon's land largely escaped the physical scars of the Civil War, and agricultural operations had continued there uninterrupted during the war, albeit on a smaller scale due to slave impressment. After 1861, corn, oats, and peas occupied more field space than cotton. General Wilson's men did burn Nixon's home in 1865, and over the course of the war, Confederate tax-in-kind policies reduced his stock and provisions. Following emancipation, Nixon had little currency with which to purchase new livestock or provisions, so he took out loans on future cotton crops. He worried that his first postwar cotton crop would fail because of a drought, but ultimately, the cotton harvest of 1866 was a decent (and profitable) one. His yields were so great that after the 1866 harvest he wrote, "I begin almost to feel as if I am rich again."[21]

Planting cotton on land previously used for food crops temporarily boosted Nixon's yields (and profits). Corn and oats are cultivars high in biomass, and legumes such as cowpeas fix nitrogen. Once Nixon switched to cotton on those fields, the *Gossypium* stalks grew taller, the bolls increased in size, and the lint was heavier. Rotated with corn for one year, a continuous cotton field will produce stalks that grow 10 percent taller than they would without rotation. After a two-year corn rotation, a continuous cotton field sprouts stalks 13 percent taller, and each boll has 13 percent more lint.[22] In addition, the gradual siphoning of labor and livestock from Nixon's farm due to impressment, emancipation, and raids had led to smaller cultivated acreages. The land allowed to fallow would have produced better yields after the war, at least for a time. After two years, however, Nixon's crop yields plummeted. By 1868, his letters hint that it became harder to coax high yields out of his lands and that the outlay for fertilizers and provisions meant that in some years he could barely pay his hands for their work. Nixon wrote, "With all my economy, management, and industry this year I do not know that I shall be able to put aside $5." Determined to make a profit, Nixon devoted most of his land to cotton. By 1870, planting cotton cost too much in labor, provisions, and fertilizers to make it worth his while. Still, he continued to plant it, because cotton was the only crop that could guarantee a quick sale and a decent profit.[23] Thus the resulting yields in districts outside battle-scarred Virginia following years of less predatory agriculture mirrored the temporarily high cotton prices on the international market: while they held, there was a fortune to be made.

The role of previous land use in shaping postwar yields for small farmers can be clearly seen in the Piedmont and the Atlantic coastal plain. Individual landholdings in this region averaged only a third of the acreage common to Nixon's corner of the Black Belt. The soils are highly erosive, as well as deficient in nitrogen or phosphorous. Agriculture in both places tended to expose what ecologists call "chemically and physically unfavorable subsoil horizons" that severely restricted crop productivity. The only way to rejuvenate these soils was to add the organic matter and soil nutrients that come from rotating crops or to allow reforestation to occur.[24] During the war, military clashes and army occupation caused waves of land abandonment or lapses in cultivation, enabling a long fallow. Weeds carpeted former crop rows and, after a few months, gave way to herbaceous or woody plants that protected the soil from washing away during rainfall. Organic matter from that vegetation's decomposition replenished pools of carbon and nitrogen in the topsoil. The roots of the secondary grasses or trees also improved the ability of the land to absorb water by churning up the topsoil, loosening the texture. When farmers complained that the breakdown in labor during the conflict allowed crop rows to grow over in grass, they were remarking on a development that, though unsightly, restored a measure of fertility to the earth.[25]

Once farmers returned to that land, the soils of the Piedmont and Atlantic plain responded more favorably to cotton production than expected. Edward Foneville, a self-described "poor" or "one-horse" farmer from Duck Creek, North Carolina, challenged his neighbors in the fall of 1873 to see who could grow the most cotton on six acres of the Atlantic coastal plain soil from which they "scratched" their livelihood. Foneville won the contest, managing to raise fourteen bales of cotton at the next harvest in a region that had averaged only a half bale of cotton per acre after the Civil War. His success attracted considerable attention in his area, and the following year, the *Southern Cultivator* published his advice for profitable farming.[26]

Foneville's success was directly related to how previous land use had increased the capacity of the soil to produce cotton. In his account, Foneville mentioned that his land had first been put under cultivation in 1856, relatively late by coastal North Carolina standards and, until the war, had only been used to plant potatoes. Between 1861 and 1872, he did not cultivate that field, which reforested rather than eroded. In 1872, he cleared it of the pines and wire grass covering it, leaving 326 stumps and planting it in cowpeas until he was ready to plant cotton. The stumps from the pine trees continued to act as a brake on erosion until they were removed in the spring of 1874. The cowpeas he planted on the plot between 1872 and 1874 fixed nitrogen, loading the naturally deficient soil with an essential nutrient for cotton fruitage.[27] The startling results, he stated, were well within the reach of any farmer who adopted his "intensive" system, but it is doubtful whether Foneville's land would still be producing such spectacular yields after three additional years in continuous cotton without commercial fertilizers.

If Foneville's story illustrates how the temporarily rejuvenated Piedmont and Atlantic coastal plain soils enticed farmers into the postwar cotton market, reduced cultivation and wartime crop rotation also boosted the profits of planters already firmly enmeshed in cotton production. John Horry Dent, for instance, made significant sums of money during these years thanks to changes in land use, despite several years of low rainfall and pre-existing pockets of "exhaustion" on his lands. Between 1861 and 1865, Dent planted over cotton fields in corn and converted over 370 acres of corn fields to cowpeas in 1864. His descriptions of the grain crops and the effect of climatic conditions on his soils suggest a range of obstacles to plant growth: a degree of compaction, meaning the soil failed to absorb and release water properly; the loss of nutrients because of erosion so that plants had less to draw from in the topsoil; and a potassium deficiency in the soil that impacted the quality of the boll.[28] Dent's grain experiment ultimately failed to produce decent yields, but the three or four years of crop rotation had positive consequences for his subsequent cotton crops.

Most importantly, rotation reduced the effects of soil-borne diseases and pests. Pathogens and parasites that affect plant life act much in the same way as those circulating in human populations. Compared with uncultivated landscapes, agricultural fields are dangerously simplified—human actions eliminate any sort of natural "immunity" those plants might have by putting them all in the same place. Writer James C. Scott describes arable fields planted in the same crop every year as essentially "permanent feedlots" for insects and plant diseases.[29] Blights such as Verticillium wilt, Fusarium wilt, and Texas root rot (Phymatotrichum root rot) infect cotton seedlings and cause yellowing and wilting of the leaves, stunted growth, premature defoliation, and malformed cotton bolls; rotation interrupts the pathogens' reproductive cycles and lessens the severity of crop losses. The cotton plant is also susceptible to pests, and rotation is the quickest way to rid the field of an infestation. Nematodes, for instance, are microscopic worm-like animals that feed on roots of cotton plants, severely stunting growth and causing a 10–50 percent crop-yield loss per year.[30] If cotton is planted every year, the nematode population explodes. When a different plant, such as corn, roots in the same soil, the nematode population is starved out of existence. If the farmer reintroduces cotton to that ground after a year or three of corn harvests, the cotton will grow for a time without the interference of nematodes. So even on microscopic levels, wartime crop changes boosted subsequent yields or, at the very least, the quality of the cotton.

Rotation also reduced soil-nutrient deficiencies by demanding different types and amounts of nutrients. The elements that corn needs to grow are slightly different than those that most benefit cotton, and each plant requires contrasting levels of each. Corn needs more phosphorous than potassium, and cotton needs more potassium than phosphorous (depending on soil conditions). This is true for macronutrients—the ones in modern fertilizers such as nitrogen, potassium, and phosphorous—as well as micronutrients such as calcium, sulphur, and zinc. Since peas were often grown in conjunction with corn, that would actually add more nitrogen to the soil to be later used by the cotton plant. Rotations with corn also increase soil porosity and root depth—the roots of the corn plant stretch deeper and farther into the topsoil, helping to increase its potential to absorb water. If cotton follows corn, the cotton plant's roots can reach farther into the soil, too, gaining access to additional organic matter in the lower depths of soil. In 1866, Dent reversed his cotton-to-corn ratio, putting 350 acres in cotton and 150 in corn, and hired about thirty laborers to plant cotton on the fields that had been "sowed down" in peas or corn during the previous two seasons. His diary entries for this harvest focus primarily on the unreliability of free labor and the irresponsible plowing practices of his freedmen. But despite their only "half-tending" the cotton crop, Dent made an enormous profit because of the high price of cotton and the high quality of his lint.[31]

Finding descriptions of a healthy crop during the immediate postwar years, however, is complicated. Most farmers complained of a terrible drought that stunted all of their cotton and scorched their corn. One farmer wrote to Alexander Stephens: "Mr. Stevans I rite you a few times—stating to you my distress cituation. We lived last year in Grean County and the drout was so sever on us." Indeed, the South did suffer reduced rainfall from 1856 to 1865, but the fragility of most residents' economic situations led to some exaggeration in claims of damage when short-term droughts struck after that date. William Landers of Greensboro, Alabama, admitted to a friend that though crops were "spotted" throughout the county, most planters had not "suffered at all" from the drought of 1868 despite what many claimed. A similar observation was made by a Freedmen's Bureau agent in Alabama, who wrote, "The general drought which appears to have visited this section for such an unusual length of time has caused some dissatisfaction in a few instances among hands upon one or two plantations only." In fact, cotton yields were only marginally less in Alabama in 1866 and 1867 than the average for the period between 1866 and 1875: planters averaged 120 pounds per acre in 1866 versus 137 pounds per acre over the decade.[32] Yields would likely have been a lot worse under the circumstances if not for wartime crop rotations or land abandonment.

More robust production as a result of these wartime decisions encouraged continuous cotton planting among some farmers. But when their yields began to decrease, farmers underestimated the cost of sustaining cotton crops in the altered circumstances of the postwar agricultural system. Thus cotton begat more cotton. Factor correspondence, labor contracts, and farmers' diaries all hint that the moment of opportunity for food-centered agriculture or crop diversification gradually disappeared as more farmers experimented with expanded cotton acreage because of high prices. An 1868 contract between Alfred Austell and J. A. Stubbs, a white tenant farmer, is typical: Austell required Stubbs to "put all in cotton which will do for cotton."[33] Not all lands were suited to cotton production, so postwar cotton experiments sometimes failed completely. This was especially true in the Piedmont of Virginia, where tobacco planters such as Edmund Ruffin Jr. tried their hands at cotton in 1865 and 1866 to help restore their fortunes. Ruffin does not mention cotton again after 1867, so assumedly, the crop proved to be unprofitable for him. Letters to factors or family are generally hopeful for a quick return to prosperity in the postwar cotton market. Historian Michael Wayne points to this sense of hope when he writes that more planters would have emigrated to Latin America after the war "had they thought it impossible to repair 'broken fortunes' in the South." The *Montgomery Weekly*

Advertiser regularly published pleas to the "destitute" whites of Alabama in 1867 and 1868 to plant their land in half cotton, half corn, so as to remove themselves from government support.[34]

Abandonment or crop rotation between 1861 and 1865 emboldened farmers to invest in cotton. On grounds that had been cultivated in cotton before the war, these processes helped restore a measure of fertility; on land not previously planted in cotton, soil organic matter and nutrient balance would produce quality cotton temporarily, encouraging farmers to keep planting it. Despite complaints of drought, a labor shortage, or the "devilish" policies of Radical Republicans, the *Southern Planter* suggests that, on the whole, cotton harvests were financially rewarding during these years.[35] The optimism proved short-lived. Farmers were aware of the benefits of crop rotation and fallows, but the problems of the antebellum period—erosion, soil-nutrient depletion, widespread woodland clearance—had not disappeared, and some had been accelerated by the war. Furthermore, military operations and the Confederate war effort hampered farmers' economic recovery by removing agricultural resources such as livestock. With fewer livestock to produce manure, fertilizers became the only viable response to reduced yields. Farmers who wished to continue cotton production had to make a serious monetary investment in "improvement."

There was a remarkable sense of continuity in the ideas for reforming agriculture over the course of James Washington Matthews's lifetime. Amid the rampant speculation on cotton before the war; the turmoil of military occupation; the unpredictability of Reconstruction; and the halting, uncertain beginnings of regionwide emancipation, the agricultural publications Matthews came across still advocated the same practices to ensure "profitable farming." Magazines, circulars, and journals such as the *Southern Planter* or the *Southern Farm and Home* insisted that farmers grow a range of crops centered on subsistence, raise enough livestock to feed their families and laborers, graze livestock on pasture and house them in barns to protect them from the elements, use livestock manure to replenish the soil, buy better machinery to plow the ground more deeply, and, above all, to imbue operations with a sense of "permanence." In other words, treat a few acres well over a long period of time rather than scratching out a quick profit and then abandoning the land to grow over in weeds.[36] A June 1873 issue of the *Rural Sun*, produced in Nashville, suggested that all the Tennessee farmer had to do to reverse the depreciation of his lands was to put them in grass and fill the resulting pastures with good stock. After two years, the lands would be "in good condition as they ever were," and the wise farmer would clear thousands of dollars in profit.[37] In Matthews's case, raising stock would do little to help. Choleras and fevers were on the rise, and besides, the family would make more money by renting out land for cotton or corn than they would putting it in pasture. Pasture needed a fence, and timber was too dear. So Matthews ignored the *Rural Sun*.[38]

One of the most obvious problems with intensive land use in the postwar South was the general absence of livestock. Every "scientific farming" journal since the early nineteenth century had urged southern farmers to collect manure to use as a natural fertilizer. The *Southern Planter* declared, "No industrious, economical farmer, who has enough to manure freely . . . has failed to secure his independence."[39] Stock also provided food for the family and laborers, increasing self-sufficiency, and provided an extra source of income through the sale of an animal, its meat, or any number of by-products. However, southerners had historically allowed their livestock to range freely, which limited the use of "home-grown fertilizer." There were exceptions, of course. Some agriculturalists, such as David Golightly Harris of upland South Carolina, penned livestock over land he wanted to plant later, so that the manure would already be on the field. But as "M. B.," a contributor to the *Southern Planter* remarked, the Civil War altered the possibilities of stock-raising and manure production. "Is there any country," he asked, "which could be expected to yield profitable returns to a population of farmers who make one of the distinctive features of their land its nakedness of livestock?"[40] Indeed, the South's sudden "nakedness of livestock" through foraging, as well as newly introduced animal diseases such as hog cholera, significantly impacted small farmers' ability to remain self-sufficient, and contributed to a decline in shifting cultivation and free-range animal husbandry.

Foraging, impressment, and other wartime processes significantly reduced livestock populations across the South. On average, the states of the Confederacy lost 20 percent of their horses, 20 percent of their cattle, and 30 percent of their swine, although there was considerable variation from state to state and animal to animal. Georgia, for instance, recorded a 37 percent decrease in the number of horses, 26 percent fewer cattle, and a 51 percent decline in the number of hogs. North Carolina lost 43 percent of its swine, 25 percent of its cattle, and 31 percent of its horses, but the number of mules remained stable.[41] At the end of the war, Charles Douglas Gray, of Augusta County, Virginia, reported, "From Harper's Ferry to New Market, which is about eighty miles . . . we could cultivate grain without fences, as we had no cattle, hogs, sheep or horses, or anything else" to harm the crops. The *Southern Planter* announced that "the country is literally drained of hogs. In those parts of the South where hogs were once so abundant, there is now very great scarcity . . . . The war left few of these immense droves, and most of these few, the farmers who were without the means to buy meat from abroad were obliged to slaughter for immediate consumption."[42] A cotton planter named G. P. Collins hinted at this trend, writing that he planned to kill ten or twelve of his fattest shoats immediately; he did not want to "keep more

Figure 3.2 "Beef for the army—on the march," 1864. Artist Edwin Forbes's pencil drawing depicts Union soldiers around Rappahannock Station, Virginia, corralling cattle for Army use. Morgan Collection of Civil War Drawings, Prints and Photographs Division, Library of Congress. LC-DIG-ppmsca-20663.

[hogs] on hand due to the scarcity of meat on the place." Slaughtering the young pigs before adulthood would "make meat and save corn."[43]

One of the more immediate consequences of the livestock shortage was the reduced availability of meat for "home consumption" and rations for laborers. Farmers described the prices of provisions as "unprecedented" and "exorbitant," especially of pork products. One Freedmen's Bureau agent reported in 1868 that "good crops were gleaned in many districts; but . . . did not pay for the subsistence . . . necessarily consumed in their production." [44] Of course, a lack of self-sufficiency in meat production was a long-standing problem in some regions. The war's reduction of livestock through raiding, impressment, and disease transformed the South's reliance on outside sources for agricultural necessities into an impoverishing, oppressive arrangement, especially for those whose subsistence relied on rations provided by or purchased from landlords. A. J. Youngblood, a farmer in Georgia, wrote to his factor: "You will please send me (300) lbs of bacon sides please send clear sides. . . . I [need] bacon or stop feeding my Freedmen." A Freedmen's Bureau report from the same area stated that suffering among ex-slaves laboring on plantations was "greatly increased by the inability of the planters to supply provisions." Even in the upcountry, where ex-slaves were fewer in number, farmers understood that the consequences of livestock shortages would fall on their tenants or laborers. David Golightly Harris's journal entries for 1866 contain a thinly disguised sense of relief at the changed labor situation—the number of hogs Harris had on hand to slaughter in 1866 meant his totals for the winter were far short of what his family and laborers needed to survive. Luckily, Harris wrote, he was no longer legally bound to provide rations, and his freedmen could buy food on the open market.[45]

Several legacies of the war conspired to keep livestock herds in the South small. Changes to farmers' material circumstances sometimes prevented them from replacing their stock or, in some cases, forced them to sell their horses, mules, hogs, or cows for cash. Ann Hairston, a member of Virginia's planter elite, remarked that many of her neighbors were holding huge sales of all their property, including livestock, to raise the funds to keep their land. As farmers' circumstances improved and the region's agricultural outputs rebounded, it would be reasonable to assume that the numbers of livestock in the South would return to their prewar levels. Instead, populations of cattle and hogs continued to decline. Cost may have been a factor, although the prices of livestock, especially hogs, remained low throughout the 1870s, and some farmers had the money to invest in other stock-raising enterprises. In fact, sheep-raising increased in the ridges and valleys of the mountain South, particularly as northern investors brought mills into those regions.[46]

Another possible reason for the persistence of livestock shortages, particularly in the late 1860s, might be plunder and pillage. Political, social, and racial tensions across the region ran high after the surrender. There were acts of violence visited upon civilians by occupying troops, alleged attacks on landowners' property by freedmen, and removal of freedmen's animals by disaffected whites. In North Carolina, for instance, there were reports of soldiers "riding all over the county by day and night," taking animals and food from both white and black residents. A Tennessee farmer found several of his missing swine in a makeshift pen belonging to a local freedman's son, who kept and altered the marks on animals that "wandered" into his possession. Ex-slaves on a plantation near Greensboro appropriated livestock and then sold them to a local merchant. Indeed, newspapers across the region mentioned "outrages," such as mules and horses being stolen from barns or hogs being "thieved."[47] It is impossible to calculate the losses of livestock from isolated robberies, and in many cases, the reports of such losses may have been driven by racial concerns. Nevertheless, many southerners lost a hog here and a cow there to theft as postwar food insecurity pressed freedpeople and whites alike.

Certainly, in some areas, a major contributor to the decline in livestock numbers was the disappearance of common land on which animals could range, which hindered farmers' use of several key practices of the extensive land-use regime. Troops' clearance of woodland during the war had removed old-growth trees. Oaks, hickories, beeches, and other species needed to produce mast disappeared rapidly under the soldier's ax. Secondary growth, which included a range of grasses, brambles, and pines, produced little of nutritive value for hogs and cattle to forage. Those localized impacts became more widespread as armies, and later railroad companies, consumed forests as they repaired and expanded the region's tracks. The combined numbers of track in the thirteen states of the South rose from slightly over 9,000 miles in 1865 to nearly 39,000 miles in 1910.[48] This growth required constant infusions of timber and soil, all of which came from land that might once have provided spaces for subsistence: workers needed wood for crossties and their own shelters, and they displaced millions of cubic feet of soil to grade the roads.[49] The record books of the Alabama and Chattanooga Railroad demonstrate the enormity of the resources consumed in the making of a railroad track. For just 9.25 miles of track, the company bought or cut 37,282 wooden crossties, "excavated" 84,241 cubic yards of soil, cleared and grubbed six acres of woodland (for camps), and cut down one square mile of forest land on either side of the road. The railroads' destruction of timber resources was so conspicuous that residents began to link the rail companies' widespread deforestation to changes in local climates or incidences of disease. M. J. Kenan of Milledgeville, Georgia, blamed the spread of the railroads for the harsher, colder winters of the late 1860s: "[T]he climate of Georgia, if not the whole Southern States, has materially altered . . . ever since Railroads have cut through the country from all points and to all quarters with their almost interminable link of avenues that run parallel north to south, east to west and nor'west!"[50]

The increasing number of rail lines made the vast pine forests of the South more accessible to logging companies, which acquired and then picked clean the land used as commons. The pine belts of Alabama and Georgia, as well as the great hardwoods forests in Appalachia and the bottomlands of Mississippi, were the most desirable and most isolated timber regions—and the most important stock-raising areas through the 1880s. Subsistence agriculture persisted on a large scale, especially on the steep slopes and highly erosive soils of the southern Appalachians, and farmers depended on the forest for wild game, rangeland for their stock, forage plants, and the occasional log that could be sold for cash.[51] Historian Ronald Lewis describes the introduction of the railroad and its merchants, mill towns, and lumber camps as a second "market revolution," writing that promoters of industry in Appalachia were interested in the forest for its cash value, and little else. But when the forest had been "skinned," the external capital disappeared, the mill towns fell silent, and the farmers were left without rangeland for their livestock or habitats for the wild game they depended on. In the piney woods of Georgia, Mark Wetherington reports, "lumber companies' engrossment of 300,000 acres of timberland increasingly destabilized the open range as railroading, timber cutting, and naval stores widened out. Traditional hunting grounds and 'sheep ranges' were altered in subtle ways . . . inescapable to plain folk dependent on the grazing lands."[52]

The restriction of common lands by market forces and the South's growing interest in extractive industries fostered new support for the repeal of fence laws. In regions where "plain folk" predominated and fewer slaves had lived before the war, extensive land-use practices remained viable, and free-range animal husbandry and shifting cultivation continued to be an important part of agricultural life. As late as 1871, an agricultural journal censured the people of North Carolina for employing shifting cultivation and letting their animals run wild: "Their idea of rotating crops . . . is corn the first year, corn the second year, and corn till the land is worn out; then they enclose more wood-land, girdle the trees, and corn it . . . till it will corn no longer."[53] But as timber scarcities resulting from the war made fencing less viable or the number of miles of railroad track multiplied, even areas where large populations of whites depended on free-range animal husbandry considered overturning the practice.

Contemporaries often cited wartime fence destruction as one of the reasons free-range animal husbandry was no longer suited to these areas of the South. Indeed, troop movements during the conflict necessitated a huge surge in rail cutting after the Battle of Appomattox, and it was harder to find suitable "fencing timber" because soldiers had felled the old growth trees. De Bow's Review announced, "The march of invading armies and the havoc of war have made sad work among the plantations of the South . . . the necessity for fences and buildings is felt everywhere, and a great practical drawback results from the scarcity of lumber."[54] In areas where the conflict accelerated decades of woodland clearance, such as North Carolina, the price of rail timber soared to twice its prewar levels. In southern Alabama, solid rail timber became more expensive simply because the prairie landscape had fewer suitable tree species to support the postwar rush for rails as planters re-fenced cotton plantations.[55] The rising cost of fencing material meant that crop fences were worth considerably more than the stock they were intended to keep out. "School Boy," a contributor to the Carroll County Times in Georgia, stated, "The fences of Carroll county [Georgia] are worth three times more than all the hogs, cows and sheep in the county, and I . . . ask . . . if it is economy for a man to have one dollar invested in a business and it takes three to keep that one dollar up."[56] As fencing timber became harder to find or too expensive, farmers who might not have supported stock laws before the war found the practice of penning stock (and not large fields) more attractive.

Railroads also proved to be powerful actors in the fight over the open range that peaked during late nineteenth century. The rail companies were liable for

Figure 3.3 "[Soldiers] stripping a rail fence for fires." Artist Alfred Waud sketched a group of Civil War soldiers tearing apart a fence to use the wood for fuel. Wartime fence destruction was a commonly cited factor in the postbellum reduction of southern range land. Morgan Collection of Civil War Drawings, Prints and Photographs Division, Library of Congress. LC-DIG-ppmsca-21020.

damages to stock that got in the way of an oncoming train. In disputes over ani-mals' deaths on farms, the liability for damages lay with the fence builder, not the stock owner. The same rule applied to railroads: since all unenclosed lands were treated as common pasture, the death of stock on a track placed the railroad at fault. Legal cases over railroad companies' "right of way" versus stock own-ers' ability to allow their animals to graze unrestricted exploded in the 1850s. As states, such as Alabama, grappled with the ramifications of their free-range animal practices, most decided that even "care or diligence" on the part of the railroad would not relieve it of any liability for damages to stock. In the 1870s and 1880s, the laws remained the same regarding railroads and injuries to stock, but the railroad companies were more plentiful and more powerful and the pres-sure to keep common lands common had diminished considerably. As a result, legal codes regarding such cases were modified to better accommodate railroads, although the process was piecemeal and proceeded at a very slow rate.[57] The loss of woodlands and range as a result of railroad expansion, logging, and legislative changes encouraged farmers to pen their livestock.

A critical yet underexplored legacy of the war that shaped the debate over open range is the introduction of new livestock diseases. The best-known war-time epizootic was glanders, a bacterial disease that affected horses and mules. Known since antiquity, glanders first appeared in North America at the end of the eighteenth century and caused noticeable numbers of animal deaths in the Seminole Wars of the 1830s. The herculean efforts by Civil War armies to corral, forage, or impress horses and mules into depots, camps, wagon trains, and rail-road cars gave the bacterium easy access to hundreds of thousands of potential hosts. At the depot at Giesboro, near Washington, DC, an estimated one in ten animals died of disease in army stables. Between January 1864 and April 1865 alone, the depot lost 17,000 horses. Given the centrality of horses and mules to both military operations and farming, the disease proved crippling. The glanders epizootic continued to impact farming through the end of the century. Since equine infection could be either chronic or acute, horses could act as carriers without necessarily appearing ill. Both armies sold sick horses to civilians, and returning soldiers brought infected horses home with them, and so the cycle of contagion continued.[58] Glanders may have inhibited farmers' efforts to plow their fields and transport their crops, but it contributed little to the discussion over fencing livestock. However, another more insidious animal disease, which became endemic in the South as a result of the war, dramatically influenced the debate over the open range: hog cholera.

Hog cholera, now known as classical swine fever, caused millions of dollars in losses every year until it was eradicated in 1978. In the early 1900s, for instance, Alabama reported the loss of over a hundred thousand hogs per year to the infec-tion. In 1914, 1928, and 1958, the state suffered full-blown epidemics.[59] Between 1865 and the development of germ theory in the 1880s, however, hog cholera kept swine populations low in the region and caused a debate among agricultural "scientists" over the best way to keep animals healthy. Furthermore, efforts to treat and prevent the disease played a role in advancing the cause of agricultural reformers who decried the traditional practice of free-range husbandry. By pro-viding a "medical" reason for penning stock, hog cholera gave stock-law advo-cates a language and logic for their actions free of class- or race-based concerns.[60] In yet another ecological irony, however, enclosing animals provided vectors for a number of diseases introduced during the war.

A highly contagious hemorrhagic fever, hog cholera affects many different types of tissues at once, including the skin, lungs, kidneys, larynx, intestines, and lymph nodes. The incubation period of the virus ranges from a few days to two or three weeks depending on the age and condition of the animal, but once the disease has been contracted, the mortality rate often reaches 70 percent. Survival confers lifelong immunity against the disease, although the pigs seldom return to full health.[61] Hog cholera first appeared in the United States in the Ohio Valley in the 1830s, and because a wide range of symptoms are associated with the disease, it was frequently confused with other ailments, such as anthrax, tuberculosis, pneumonia, swine plague, and lung worms.[62] Before the Civil War, it was not generally known in most parts of the southeastern United States. There were scattered reports of outbreaks in the border states of Kentucky and Tennessee, but the lower South and the coastal South remained relatively untouched.

The increased mobility of animals during the war created ideal conditions for the transmission of hog cholera. The most common channels for its spread were healthy hogs coming into contact with those from infected farms; hogs occupying the same grounds as diseased swine up to three months after the infected animals had been removed; and the transmission of the virus through feed, implements, or on the feet or clothing of persons who had contact with diseased herds.[63] Crowded pens, railroad cars, and supply depot stockyards were common sites for the eruption of the virus due to the accumulation of manure, the short intervals between successive herds of swine, and the congregation of large herds from multiple locations with varying levels of immunity. In Arkansas, an 1862 outbreak was enough to wipe out much of the state's meat supply. In November of 1863, Major P. W. White of the Office of the Chief Commissary reported that the ravages of hog cholera meant the Confederacy's supply of bacon—on the verge of "exhaustion"—would not be replenished.

Farmers across the South reported hundreds of thousands of swine dying from hog cholera in every year of the war. In November 1864, for example, Walter Waightstill Lenoir, a lawyer and farmer in North Carolina recently returned from service in the Confederate Army, noticed that one of his hogs was ill. Drowsy and inactive, the pig had stopped eating and drinking. Its back was arched, its tail and ears drooped, and after a few days of listless wandering it began to vomit violently. Every time it approached the feeding trough it squealed and suddenly backed away, its muscles convulsing as its eyes rolled back in its head. The sick hog staggered among the herd for a few more days, increasingly emaciated, until it would only lie on the ground grunting weakly. After it died, two more hogs showed similar symptoms. The next week, Lenoir wrote to his sister that he had lost eight of his thirteen hogs to the disease, and that those that survived were "of little value."[64] Other farmers in Lenoir's county in North Carolina reported even higher mortality rates among their herds. Although no one could pinpoint the disease's mode of introduction or how it spread, it impacted almost every farm. Lenoir, in particular, feared for his ability to sustain agricultural operations the following season because of the sudden lack of meat rations for his slaves, although he noted bitterly that at least his poverty might dissuade any approaching Yankees from raiding his farm. There was little stock left to steal.[65] Indeed, the hog cholera epizootics so drastically reduced the ability of farmers like Lenoir to maintain self-sufficient food production that one historian has argued hog cholera hurt the Confederacy more than all other diseases experienced by humans and animals alike.[66]

The collapse of the Confederacy and the cessation of military operations did little to halt the hog cholera epidemics. Outbreaks continued on a semiannual basis, setting back the expansion of swine herds in every state. Farmers in Alabama, for instance, suffered waves of infection almost every year between 1862 and 1880. In 1867, a report from Calhoun County announced that a rash of cases had carried away one-third of the local swine. Three years later, a more widespread infection claimed a considerable number of hogs in Dallas and Lawrence counties—50 percent and 25 percent losses, respectively—and there were smaller mortalities in Tallapoosa, Marshall, DeKalb, Calhoun, Clarke, Jefferson, and Etowah Counties.[67] During these Reconstruction-era epidemics, market relations rather than army movements determined where and how the infection spread. Buying infected animals from breeders and the use of the "garbage feeding" method (including small portions of carcass in slop) spread the infection, as did the simple act of moving hogs from market to market. Because the virus could stay active in sterilized water and warm, moist soil for months, any secretion from an infected hog might eventually affect others. By 1887, federal regulations were amended to prohibit animals infected with hog cholera from being admitted at "any point of interstate trade," particularly to stockyards, creating a new class of inspectors trained to help control the contagious disease and instituting new "segregated" plans for slaughterhouses.[68]

During the war, the various "cures" advertised for the disease proved wildly divergent. Newspapers and agricultural publications typically placed notices of hog cholera's appearance in an area alongside testimonials of successful methods for eradicating it. Some farmers swore that mixing strychnine into hog feed killed the infection; others promised that a diet of raw turnips kept it at bay. An 1864 report in the Alabama-based *Linden Jeffersonian* declared, "The most successful remedy tried there [Marengo County] has been red pepper cut or beat up and mixed with the feed of the hogs."[69] One breeder attested that he gave his pigs plenty of wood ashes to eat, and when they seemed sick, he shoved a corn cob covered in pine tar down their throats. Another common experiment among farmers appeared to be to withhold water from their hogs for various lengths of time. A "Dr. James" wrote to the *Southern Cultivator* in 1862, testifying that after losing a hundred pigs to the disease, he kept the rest without water for three weeks. According to James, no additional hogs died.[70] Predictably, these methods failed to alleviate the ravages of the disease.

In the 1870s, what had been random and disparate prescriptions for treating the disease began to have a common theme: livestock in the South were not cared for properly, leading to recurrent outbreaks of hog cholera. Advocates of penning stock claimed that the practice of free-range husbandry weakened the animals' constitutions, making the disease deadlier. In 1867, a USDA report chastised southern farmers for giving their stock "no barns or shelter whatever." Since hog cholera was "a serious problem everywhere, with no foreseeable cure, increasing the cost of living for people in the South," reforming southern stock-raising was an "urgent necessity."[71] A Bureau of Animal Industry report claimed that only in places where farmers were "neglectful" of their stock and forced them to fend for themselves without proper food or shelter was hog cholera truly a danger.[72] A bulletin published by the agricultural experiment station at Auburn, Alabama, for example, maintained that hog cholera did not spread as quickly in districts where livestock were legally required to be penned, and in some cases, the disease had been "checked or stopped at the border line between stock-law and non-stock-law districts."[73] In other words, free-range husbandry exacerbated the spread of hog cholera; hogs given "proper attention" did not contract the disease as often as those allowed to "run at large."

The appearance and spread of hog cholera provided a useful rhetorical tool for those who advocated the repeal of fence laws, but considerable numbers of southern farmers in upland or mountainous areas continued to use the open range to provide food and forage for their hogs. They contended that before "improved" breeds of hogs arrived from the North and the West, all hogs were happy and healthy making their own beds in the woods. Actually, these traditionalists were right: penning stock only gave the virus better access to new hosts.[74] Farmers could replace dying or dead hogs, but putting them in the same pen would only cause another outbreak. Allowing hogs to range for even part of the year on common lands or in woodland decreased their risk of contracting the disease or, at the very least, reduced the risk that *other* hogs would catch it.

Regardless, the appearance of hog cholera reinforced a long-standing critique of free-range animal husbandry during a crucial time of transition in southern agriculture, simultaneously reducing the ability of yeomen farmers to remain self-sufficient in livestock production and eliminating a key reason for shifting cultivation—to keep woodland for stock. The movement to restrict common lands in the latter half of the nineteenth century emerged from a range of motivations regarding race and labor relations, but stock raisers had legitimate biological reasons for concern, which added "medical science" to the matrix of arguments against free-range animal husbandry. Nimrod Porter, for instance, began penning his hogs after swine belonging to a neighbor, Mr. Rankin, died of hog cholera while ranging in Porter's woodlot. Hoping to forestall the spread of the disease to his own herd, Porter paid several laborers to build a large pen for his hogs and haul corn daily to the trough.[75]

These changes to the yeoman South's livestock economy had a significant impact on the region's consumption of commercial fertilizers. Whether in the Black Belt, the Piedmont, or more mountainous areas, the economic logic of maintaining (and allowing access to) common spaces collapsed during Reconstruction in myriad ways: the reduction of livestock numbers from the war, changing labor relations, soldiers' and railroads' destruction of woodlands, and the increasing popularity of stock laws in the wake of epizootics. As livestock populations shrank or failed to rebound after the war, the use of animal manure to improve soil-nutrient deficiencies became less common, even in places where stock-raising had been a significant part of the agricultural economy before 1860.[76] The result was an increasing reliance on commercial fertilizers, especially in North Carolina, South Carolina, and Georgia, where thinner, more heavily degraded soils in areas that were heavily trafficked during the Civil War struggled to remain profitable in cash-crop cultivation.

The South experienced a "fertilizer boom" during the Reconstruction years. At this point, guano was not the only commercial fertilizer available. Phosphate rock resources were discovered in several southern states in the late 1860s, helping to expand the commercial fertilizer market and infuse eastern soils with phosphorus—a nutrient often absent from both animal manure and guano. For a time in the late nineteenth century, South Carolina, Florida, and Tennessee enjoyed substantial revenue from phosphate mining. Historian Timothy Johnson notes that the proximity of phosphate deposits to already fragile and long-cultivated soils was a boon to farmers in the states along the eastern seaboard. Because phosphate was not suitable for all soils, farmers looked to the evolving "global economy in plant nutrients" to make up for the deficiencies in other substances. That global network, which had spawned the international demand for guano earlier in the century, thrived on German exports of potash beginning in the 1860s. Phosphates worked best on highly acidic soils with a finely ground texture because of its low solubility, but potassium was a critical nutrient that was often absent in southern soils. Adding potash and phosphates to the soil helped reduce farmers' need to burn trees.[77]

The application of fertilizers did increase yields, particularly for cotton. Yet the proliferation of chemically compounded fertilizers did not help yeomen farmers or laborers increase their profits or achieve self-sufficiency. The *Southern Planter* complained that cotton cultivation consumed all the best fertilizers while farmers put corn, wheat, and other food crops on the poorest soils without manure so that "home production" never exceeded demand.[78] A Georgia farmer wrote to the editor of the *Southern Farm and Home*, arguing, "Without fertilizers we could not compete with the West in making cotton and our lands would have to be abandoned, and . . . every practical man knows that there is no money in grain and stock farms in the South." Indeed, the bales per acre yielded in Georgia and the Carolinas were only a fraction of the output in Mississippi or east Texas—even using the best commercial fertilizers—and Georgia spent over twice as much on fertilizers per year as other cotton-growing states. The 1880 census estimated that planters used fertilizers on 70 percent to 80 percent of the crops grown in the Piedmont, and accompanying reports claimed that without guano or other compounds, most of those soils would not produce crops at all.[79]

Although the liberal application of fertilizers to keep land in cultivation instead of continuously shifting to new ground was a hallmark of the ideal farm, the result was not the healthy, prosperous agricultural landscape that anyone expected. Instead, as a USDA report stated in 1870, "in but few sections of the [region] has agriculture made any progress within the last ten years; almost everywhere, in fact, it has actually retrograded." The "spirit of improvement" the agency hoped for had been overshadowed by the need to simply make a living. Thus, "fertilizers have indeed been used freely, but rather with a view to speedy returns than ultimate improvement. No systematic rotation has been practiced; no course of amelioration steadily pursued." The loss of livestock and the decline of shifting cultivation reduced farmers' ability to circumvent environmental limitations. A man from Massachusetts who moved to Mississippi after the war said it more succinctly: "The [agriculture] business was not lucrative," he lamented, "and I doubt whether any considerable number of the northern men who went south immediately after the war, taking with them hundreds of thousands of dollars in the aggregate, to engage in *planting cotton* were successful financially. They planted their money."[80]

William Gibbs McAdoo's case provides an excellent example. Owner of a farm near Milledgeville, Georgia, on the southern edge of the Piedmont, McAdoo was a native of East Tennessee who had fought in the Mexican-American War and served as attorney general for the Knoxville district of his home state until 1860. His second wife, Mary Floyd, was the daughter of a wealthy man who had rice-planting interests in the area around Savannah, Georgia. In 1857, McAdoo began to split his time between his farm in central Georgia, his wife's rice lands on the coast, and his position in Tennessee. Upon the outbreak of the Civil War, he and his wife moved to Milledgeville permanently. Their circumstances appear to have been significantly reduced during the war.[81] There were strict natural limits on cultivation on his land—the topsoil was thin and acidic, lacked calcium and phosphorous, and was highly erosive—but his system of crop cultivation had seemed to work well before the war reached his part of Georgia, in 1864. In addition to a very basic rotation of cultivars, McAdoo opened new lands and manured his fields. His letters do not mention guano, so the manure more than likely came from livestock.[82] His wartime letters discussed the reduction in livestock due to impressment and raiding, but in 1865, McAdoo made plans to plant more cotton than he ever had before because of its high market price. He also decided to keep his livestock numbers low, assuming that buying meat would be cheaper and easier than trying to access livestock in the postwar South. He wrote, "I shall devote myself to cotton planting chiefly and rely on buying corn in Tennessee, or in the North Western States, in the coming Fall. I shall also have to buy my pork or bacon abroad, as I am not raising enough hogs."[83]

Despite complaints of drought in 1866, the crop rotations in previous years meant that McAdoo's land produced enough cotton to make its continuing production a rational choice. When he stopped planting grains and raising livestock to focus on cotton, however, the nutrient composition of the clay-heavy Piedmont soils on his farm constrained yields. Still, he planted cotton the next year and the year after that. Instead of raising more livestock and collecting their manure, he used what little credit he had to obtain fertilizers. However, McAdoo's yields decreased at the same time cotton prices fell to half their 1866 price; his initial policy of "planting cotton to buy provisions" was no longer sustainable and his degraded Piedmont lands needed more fertilizer than McAdoo could afford.[84] He did not mention new ground, for he could not command the labor to clear it. He continued to plant cotton because he had no other choice: in order to make his land produce anything, he needed fertilizers, and in order to buy fertilizers, he had to plant cotton. The result was failure and, according to his letters, extreme poverty. "I am on the verge of bankruptcy and ruin," McAdoo lamented. "It is no exaggeration to say that I cannot command means to *clothe* my family comfortably the coming winter. . . . Long since we became too poor to eat *meat*. . . . I hope this will not last always."[85]

Like McAdoo, other small farmers became increasingly bound to cash crops and, eventually, cotton, by their need for commercial fertilizer and provisions due to a lack of livestock. Charles Nordhoff, referring to the North Carolina Piedmont, estimated that "a large part of planters are heavily in debt" because they "have here a much poorer soil, and have to spend some money for manure." P. B. Monk of Dooly County, Georgia, referred to the gap between the outlay for fertilizers and the profits of the harvest when he wrote, "We have a good crop, but after expenses the margin must be small with present prices. . . . Much complaint among those who bought guano."[86] The records of factorage L. J. Guilmartin and Co. hint at the debt accrued by the farmers who relied on commercial fertilizers. A farmer named George Eliston tried to explain that he could not hand over all of his cotton to pay his outstanding balance with them because he was "involved for manures," which consumed a part of the lien on his crop. The debt collector for the company, J. L. Johnson, frequently reported that farmers with delinquent bills were "defaulters for phosphate." One farmer vented, "In every direction is heard complaint of the heavy 'guano bills' to be paid out of the cotton crop, leaving nothing for next year."[87]

The war's reduction in livestock populations and the further shrinking of herds in the conflict's immediate aftermath significantly affected the self-sufficiency of yeoman farmers. Southern farmers found it easier to forgo livestock raising, which consumed laborers' time and placed a strain on grain resources, and to instead just pledge cash crops to buy fertilizer. Although the recurrence of hog cholera increased the momentum for adopting a practice of penning livestock instead of letting them roam freely, the effort increased the incidence of disease among hogs, the animal most commonly kept by southern farmers. The region's long-standing "nakedness of livestock" worsened, darkening farmers' prospects and entangling them in a wearisome cycle of debt that proved difficult to escape.

Before the Civil War, northern farming and its free-labor system occupied the fringes of the global agricultural system, but the Union victory made them the standard by default. Yet intensive agriculture in the postwar South formed a kind of "deformed analogue" to the ideal farming operation, for several reasons. Previous land-use practices masked the limitations of continuous production facing farmers, so that after a few decent harvests, cotton production actually increased risk for the cultivator instead of reducing it. Livestock, the keystone species of the intensive system, were becoming less common on farms.[88] Financial constraints meant that many southerners could not replenish the stock they had lost during the war, and disease helped to keep livestock populations from rebounding to their prewar levels. Farmers increasingly had to rely on commercial fertilizers to improve their soils, particularly once the temporarily buoyed postwar cotton yields declined.

Ultimately, continuous operations marked by penned livestock and fertilizer-laced fields worsened the long-standing vulnerabilities of soil-nutrient deficiencies and a lack of self-sufficiency in meat production. Farmers desperately bought provisions and fertilizers at a loss, never able to save enough money to buy and keep livestock. The elimination of key tenets of the extensive land-use regime, such as free-range animal husbandry and shifting cultivation, burdened smaller farmers with additional expenses. By 1870 in some places, and 1875 in others, it was clear that there were limits to the ability of the southern environment to fulfill planters' hopes for a quick return to prosperity. Given the region's heavy rainfall; long, hot summers; and older, acidic soils, the replacement of extensive practices with intensive practices impaired self-sufficiency, crop rotation, soil-nutrient balance, and, by extension, the economic security of farmers. Far from representing the "dawn of a bright and happy day," the New South was a "poorer South."[89]

This proved especially, and tragically, true for ex-slaves. During the war, self-emancipation, impressment, and eventual legal freedom siphoned labor from cotton farms. Crucial land-maintenance tasks began to break down, and land abandonment due to a lack of labor was widespread—and ecologically significant. The environmental implications of these events bled into the postwar period as a large, landless class of black farmers swelled the ranks of cotton producers. Processes of intensification appeared on larger plantations, where environmental constraints not only exposed freedpeople to the vicissitudes of cotton production, but also added to the burdens of racial prejudice, violence, and economic insecurity. The difficulties of operating within the southern environment amid the efforts to restrict the economic opportunities for blacks undermined efforts to realize fully their freedom.

4

Accelerating Change

It is conceded that the industry of the negro race has become greatly relaxed and demoralized, the natural consequences of which is an unsettled and roving disposition, a desire to avoid steady work, and a disposition to pick up a precarious existence by pretended hunting of wild game.

—General Assembly of North Carolina,
1865–1866 session

Southern Alabama did not resemble the "desolate South" John T. Trowbridge had expected. A contributor to the *New York Tribune* and *Atlantic Monthly*, the northern journalist set out, in August of 1865, to document the devastation wrought by "the Great Rebellion." In Virginia, Trowbridge vividly described the "desolate tracts of perforated and broken trees, robbed of their timber to build mazes of breastworks that cut up the fields with tangled lines of "bristling abatis." He reveled in the eerie atmosphere of storied plantations in Georgia, now "ploughed with the furrows of devastation." The lack of farming implements and stock, he surmised, meant that formerly wealthy planters might experience famine for the first time.[1] In the mountains of southeastern Tennessee, Trowbridge visited the sites of famed military clashes at Lookout Mountain and Missionary Ridge, declaring that the battles' imprint on the countryside approximated "the footprints of a Titan on the march." For months, he detailed every farm wiped clean of its fences, every clump of woods dotted with soldiers' graves, every bridge burned. "Wounded," he called the region. But the Black Belt of Alabama seemed untouched by the forces of destruction Trowbridge sought to dramatize for his curious readers. Steaming slowly upriver from Mobile to Selma, his prose conveyed a peaceful, prosperous agricultural landscape. His eyes took in the "pleasantly wooded bluffs and elevated plantations," where blackbirds crowded the branches of the sycamore trees along the shore. Homes appeared well-built, and Trowbridge was surprised to see that every farm had standing cotton gins and slave quarters. In Trowbridge's eyes, this part of the country had managed to escape the wounds of war.[2]

Alabama received comparatively few pages in the journalist's voluminous dispatches—there was too little "desolation" for his purposes. Yet the planters he interviewed along the Alabama River echoed the same sense of despair that Virginians and Georgians wore almost proudly. Farmers from Dallas, Wilcox, Pickens, and other counties in Alabama's cotton belt lamented to Trowbridge the enormous sums they lost in the war, their difficulty in feeding their families, and the lack of hope they held for the future. "Three hundred and fifty thousand dollars in gold wouldn't cover my losses," a Mr. G. bemoaned to the journalist. "I never can feel towards this government like I once did. I got started to leave the country; I swore I wouldn't live under a government that would treat me this way." Other "Yankee-haters" agreed: "The country is ruined." Unlike their counterparts in states heavily trod by armies, however, these planters referred not to fields spoiled by battle or the loss of livestock to foraging. Rather, they blamed the emancipation of the region's four million slaves for the destruction of the South, their fortunes, and the land itself. One planter bluntly concluded, "The prosperity of our people passed away with the institution of slavery."[3]

Despite concern over physical damage from military operations, emancipation proved to be the most far-reaching wartime financial injury. Across the region, property in slaves was valued between three and six billion dollars in 1860; in the Cotton Belt, slaves constituted almost half the total wealth of each state. Thus, the ripple effects of emancipation due to the forfeiture of those investments, as well as the subsequent reduction in slaveholders' spending, cost the economy of both the North and the South more than can be directly documented. Market linkages, banking, and methods of credit all changed drastically after slavery's end.[4] Social structure, too, transformed. Emancipation threatened centuries of sociocultural assumptions regarding the innate inferiority of the African American. Especially in areas isolated from Union occupation, the realities of emancipation took weeks and months to materialize. Some assumed that slaves' freedom was a temporary by-product of Union soldiers' presence and would expire after they moved on; others believed the federal government would re-establish a form of bound labor after the surrender. As planters recognized the approaching end of slavery, they worked their slaves harder, punished them more violently for smaller infractions, and even continued selling them through the end date of the war.[5] They were determined that "freedom" would not alter emancipated slaves' lives. Refusing to admit that the end of the Confederacy meant the end of slavery, a contemporary commented, "the dethroned lords of the lash [clung] to the shadow of slavery like a death grasp."[6]

Nevertheless, chattel slavery fitfully yielded to contract-based arrangements. Blacks across the cotton South challenged planters' assumptions regarding the impermanence of emancipation and defied former masters' efforts to reassert ownership. Because freedom was not "gifted, fully realized, at the moment of emancipation," ex-slaves used direct confrontation, subtle acts of resistance, and the exercise of physical independence to make their own freedom. They rejected "slavery's hours and slavery's pace," and women, in particular, sought to reduce the hours spent in the field in order to spend more time in their own households.[7] Yet the contract labor system also had significant effects on the environment, and the ecology of emancipation forced the evolution of the postwar cotton economy.

This chapter argues that emancipation accelerated the breakdown of the southern agricultural system during the transition years between 1865 and 1875. Whereas the ecological regime of slavery had reinforced the extensive land-use practices of shifting cultivation and free-range husbandry, the end of slavery weakened them. One way it did this was by reducing the amount of time dedicated to land maintenance (the upkeep and clearance of the land), especially in the cotton-growing regions of the lower South. Ex-slaves expected freedom to completely transform every aspect of their lives, and for many, that meant either forgoing agricultural labor altogether or working their own land however they chose. Doing the same labor under the same master (now landlord) on the same terms was not the desired transformation. As a result, ex-slaves also used contract negotiations and sharecropping arrangements to avoid working in centrally directed gangs. Understandably, freedpeople preferred to direct their own labor on an individual plot of land, and the eventual proliferation of share-based or tenant contracts encouraged the physical reorganization of plantations.

The combination of these two progressive alterations to labor relations lessened the practicality of prewar land-use practices, tightening natural limits on cotton production and reducing blacks' access to the South's internal provisioning economy. The cessation or even reduced frequency of doing land maintenance on farms exacerbated erosion, flooding, and crops' susceptibility to drought. The redivision of plantations and farms to accommodate tenant and sharecropper plots made shifting cultivation more difficult and eliminated common spaces for free-range animal husbandry. As the logic for maintaining reserve woodland crumbled, planters began to close off laborers' opportunities to support themselves through subsistence practices. These effects were not immediately apparent, and they occurred amid larger and more long-term changes in land use. They serve as an example, however, of how the efforts of freedpeople to achieve a modicum of autonomy in day-to-day agricultural operations—and the actions of whites to maintain control—drastically altered southern land-use practices. Ultimately, the social, political, and economic upheavals of emancipation had ecological consequences, magnifying the financial burdens facing both white and black farmers.

John Gray Allen's neighbors in Marengo County, Alabama, called him "Squire" because he was a man who always had plenty of money. As with the other Black Belt planters encountered by Trowbridge, the Civil War had swept away Allen's investments in slaves and Confederate bonds, but thanks to a ruthlessness that belied the stereotypical "planter paternalism," Allen managed to finance his postwar cotton crops and even to expand his local authority. Using his long-standing connections with merchants, Allen acquired other farmers' debts and then collected their landholdings as they went bankrupt. He also divided his own substantial property into a home farm and several renters' tracts.[8] A white farmer named W. L. Walston rented one of Allen's lands, called "Lunson Place," for cash. As was common in such arrangements, part of Walston's rent included the maintenance of the property's fences, wells, and ditches. In the autumn of that year, Allen received a panicked letter from Lunson Place. Walston had hired several ex-slaves to work as field hands, and as picking slowed, he ordered them to split rails for fence repair. They split a hundred rails, but then refused to do any more. The laborers demanded additional wages to complete the task or, at least, wanted provisions advanced to them free of charge. Afraid Allen would blame him for the poor state of the farm and charge him additional rent, Walston asked the "Squire" for advice. How could he convince his laborers to fence land? "There is more to do than I thaught there would be," he pleaded, "and I would like to hear from you."[9]

The steadfast refusal of Walston's hired laborers to perform tasks such as fence repair without additional wages was not an isolated labor dispute. After emancipation, contradictory ideas of "free labor" between landowners and ex-slaves made land maintenance and the day-to-day autonomy of workers the subject of frequent clashes. Just as in British Guiana, East Africa, Jamaica, Brazil, and other postemancipation societies around the globe, "the process of defining, categorizing, and selecting forms of tenure was the result of contention between planters, who hoped to reinstate large-scale and centralized gang-system labor, and freedmen and poor whites, who valued economic autonomy."[10] As a result, disputes over land maintenance work became, in the words of historian Frederick Cooper, "questions not just of marginal utility, but of class power."[11] Contract arrangements that required laborers to do work not directly related to the crop—fence repair, ditching, clearing new land—generally failed to satisfy ex-slaves' expectations of freedom. However, the agricultural regime that had been common before emancipation depended on maintenance work to sustain crop yields. Along with shifting cultivation and free-range animal husbandry, land maintenance helped white farmers postpone the effects of what was ultimately unsustainable environmental change. Consequently, freedpeople's efforts to reshape working conditions on farms like Walston's affected the land in ways that constricted the possibilities for profitable cotton farming.

The introduction of labor contracts on postemancipation cotton plantations provides the most accessible window into the ways black laborers' actions
altered land-use practices over time. Contract arrangements between landlords
and laborers changed in response to fluctuating understandings of what was
meant by "freedom" and "free labor," as well as the agency of freedpeople, the
ebb and flow of the labor supply, and the efforts of the Freedmen's Bureau. It
was initially uncertain as to what forms of agricultural tenure would develop,
thus early contracts contained a dizzying array of terms, many of which sought
to reestablish the conditions of slavery. White southerners found it "annoying
and humiliating to be told what they must or should do with the negroes" by
northern officials; whites also thought it inconceivable that they should enter
into negotiation with men and women who—only a few months earlier—had
been their property.[12] The following exchange recorded between a planter and a
correspondent for the Boston-based paper, the *Liberator*, captures the incredu-
lousness with which whites might have approached the topic of emancipation,
and the way they viewed the shift as a temporary state of affairs, rather than the
law of the land.

> "I am a planter," said he, "or, rather, I was a planter before the war. My
> plantation is in Georgia, south of Savannah, not far from Darien. I have
> 4000 acres of land and about ninety negroes. I was well off, I assure you.
> But what am I now? My slaves are all gone; I am sure they are. Whether
> my house is still standing I do not know, but I am sure everything about
> my plantation is gone to wreck and ruin."
>
> "Well, what are you going to do when you get home?"
>
> "Do? I don't know, sir, no more than the man in the moon. May be
> some of my negroes, when they hear that I have come home, will come
> back to me. They were always faithful to me. I treated them well; lost
> but one in four years by death, of congestive fever."
>
> "Well, then, if some of them come back to you, you will make
> contracts with them, give them fair wages, and go to work again, will
> you not?"
>
> He looked surprised. "How so? Make contracts with them?"
>
> "Well," said I, "you know slavery is abolished, and if you want the
> negroes to work for you at all, you will have to make agreements with
> them, as with free laborers."
>
> "Yes," said he, "I have heard of this. I know that's the intention. But,
> now, really, do you think this is a settled thing? Now, niggers won't work
> when they are not obliged to. A free nigger is never good for any thing.
> I know the thing won't work. No Southern man expects it will. No use
> trying."[13]

The paper's account, regardless of the writer's motives, vividly illustrates how difficult it proved to be to convince southern whites to adopt "free labor" ideology. For their part, many northern officials believed ex-slaves should be made to work. Freedpeople would only become full citizens by learning self-sufficiency, and agents' liberal notions of "industry" and "moral improvement" reinforced the reality that farms needed a settled labor force in order to resuscitate southern agricultural production.[14] Both northern and southern whites, therefore, had an interest in making contract labor a system in which free blacks worked on farms under strict supervision.

As a result, labor contracts from 1865 and 1866—even those approved by the Freedmen's Bureau—closely resembled antebellum master-slave relations. They explicitly restricted ex-slaves' movements and activities, included clauses related to behavior and comportment, and laid out fines for "impudence." This proved true even outside the cotton South, where smaller populations of African American laborers resided and landowners were more accustomed to contracting with white laborers.[15] A contract in Brownsville, Tennessee, stipulated that employees could not receive visits during working hours, were expected to labor on evenings and weekends (but only a half day on Sundays), and were not allowed to engage in conversations during working hours. A contract from Alabama gave the landowner the right to physically chastise a freedwoman and her children if they disobeyed orders.[16] Almost universally, contracts stipulated that ex-slaves could not leave the farm or field without permission. One bureau agent in Georgia reported that local freedmen believed that if they left their plantations, they would be sold into slavery.[17] Even the language used to write the early contracts illustrated how closely ex-slaveowners hoped free labor would hew to the rhythms of slave life: freedpeople "firmly bound" themselves to landlords, promised to labor on the farms "unconditionally," would do "whatever is directed" to "endeavor to promote [the landlords'] interests," and were even forced to call their landlords "Master." Freedmen's Bureau agents proved reluctant or unprepared to suggest alternative contract terms and worked only to ensure that agreements provided laborers with "the necessaries of life."[18]

These documents also explicitly preserved antebellum land-use practices. Planters expected freedmen to perform land maintenance tasks during slow periods in the agricultural calendar and assumed their day-to-day operations would be centrally directed. Contracts therefore often included clauses related to work beyond cultivating the crop—the traditional slack-time tasks of the prewar era. Many agreements dictated that laborers clear new ground, maintain ditches, repair fences, and tend stock; some of the lengthier and more explicit examples mentioned cutting and hauling wood for the landlord's use, planting trees, collecting manure, and removing stumps.[19] Former governor Joseph Brown's contract with his freedmen in central Georgia directed his laborers to

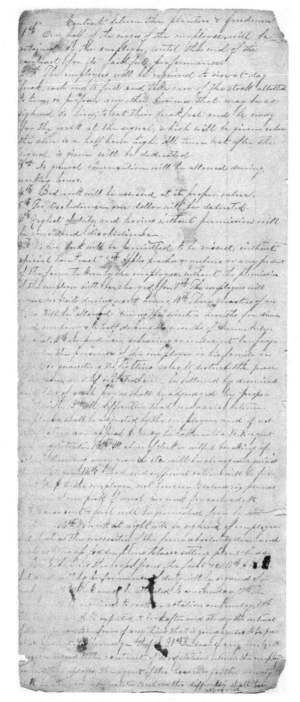

Figure 4.1 Excerpt from the daybook of Fanny Taliaferro showing the contract between Planters and Freedmen, 1866. Fanny Taliaferro was a schoolteacher in Brownsville, Tennessee, and included this contract in her records. It states that freedpeople on the plantation must rise at dawn, perform certain chores before breakfast, are not allowed to own stock, cannot appropriate any fruits they may tend, and will be fined for poor work or lost time. Visits and movements are also restricted. Fanny Taliaferro Daybook, Tennessee Historical Society Collection, Tennessee State Library and Archives. ID# 33975.

"take good care of horses, cattle and other stock, to work in the garden, cut and haul wood, make fires, wait on the table and do any work they are put at." The ex-slaves who signed on with B. F. Duncan of Tennessee, "agree[d] to attend to stock etc. on place and when [they] are not at work in crop to do anything on farm that is to be done." One of the most common ways landlords indicated laborers' responsibility for maintenance work was by stating employees should "do all necessary work in keeping up the farm."[20]

The belief that freedpeople would work at the direction of the landlord also meant that the initial contracts usually applied to a group of freedpeople rather than to individuals. Especially on cotton farms, a group contract meant collective labor—that is, the gang labor system of slave-based cotton farming. One example, dated 1866, from the plantation records of James Boykin of Dallas County, Alabama, reads: "James Boykin agrees to hire the following named Freedmen . . . to work in squads of not more than fifteen hands, such squads to work such land as they may draw or may be allotted to it by said employer."[21] Under such arrangements, planters or overseers closely supervised labor, imposed a system of deductions for infractions, and paid laborers in wages or shares of the crop at the end of the year according to their "value" as workers. Most contracts stipulated that laborers were legally bound to perform whatever task they were assigned. A planter from Issaquena County, Mississippi, declared that as long as laborers worked in groups as they had "in former years," they performed work "finely" and efficiently: "I divide my hands into six companies, with a foreman at the head of each one. I have succeeded in getting a great many rails split and almost my entire fencing repaired." Although centrally directed labor forces made the various jobs of the plantation easier to accomplish, these group contracts and the method of imposing fines or deductions to withhold wages prompted one observer to write, "Although it is admitted that [the freedman] has ceased to be the property of a master, it is not admitted that he has a right to become his own master."[22]

For many freedpeople, these arrangements too closely resembled slavery. Black laborers resented being under the direction of an overseer or foreman, and they refused to spend evenings or "slack time" performing work not related to the crop. Almost immediately, issues of land maintenance became points of contention in the agricultural contracts required by the Freedman's Bureau. Who should ditch the land? When should fences be repaired? How much fuel wood could be consumed by laborers? Who was responsible for the manuring of fields? Did contract laborers have an obligation to work on weekends or during the evenings? When did the agricultural year begin and end? These practical questions took on new meaning during a time of rapidly shifting race and class relations. Unlike their counterparts in sugar- and rice-growing areas, freedpeople in cotton districts did not work a crop immediately and urgently under the threat of collapsing levees or ruined canals. In those coastal crop regions, land maintenance was the foundation of farm labor. On cotton farms, it was deemed extra work. As a result, social and economic concerns often overshadowed the environmental utility of these practices with significant consequences for crop yields.[23]

Freedmen's Bureau and government agency correspondence indicates that black laborers actively protested slack-time work. A South Carolina planter grumbled that due to the "unconquerable indolence" of his laborers, none of his fences had been repaired or cleared of overgrowth. If he tried to burn new ground, the excess vegetation along enclosure lines would ignite, damaging the crops. In Augusta, Georgia, a cotton farmer complained his freedmen were "not willing to cut and haul wood," even if it meant they went without fuel for their own fires.[24] These were common grievances, for white planters insisted that neither their land nor their laborers were as productive as they had been under the hallowed days of slavery, regardless of their yields or profits. For instance, the Cotton Planters' Association of Mississippi claimed that on 393 plantations surveyed, free field hands performed only 65 percent of the work they did before the war. John Horry Dent's characterization of his workers was typical: he drew a chart in his diary comparing the behavior of slaves and freedpeople. The slave was "contented," "obedient," and "industrious," whereas the freedman was "wandering," "insolent," and "soured." Even Federal authorities reported that planters "have but little control or direction" over laborers, and that ex-slaves "have only worked as suited themselves."[25] Clashes over working conditions often became violent. When Berry Smith, an ex-slave in Scott County, Mississippi, confronted his former master about his contract terms, "Marse Bob" simply replied, "If you don't go to work, Nigger, you gwine a-git whupped." Only by the lash, the argument went, would the black man work. Farmers in Fayette County, Tennessee reported to the newly formed USDA that without the whip, it was "an utter impossibility to force the negro to comply with his contract." Some planters discharged workers without giving them notice or compensation; others would use the denial of rations or medical assistance as a way to ensure work discipline.[26]

Despite the ever-present threat of violence or expulsion, freedpeople resisted these coercive contract arrangements. Although a wide range of disputes regarding compensation, punishment, freedom of movement, and living arrangements also complicated contract negotiations, ex-slaves were determined to reduce the oversight of their labor and to only do the work for which they were contracted—cultivating the crop. They employed strategies they had developed during slavery, such as working slowly, damaging crops, or breaking tools, but emancipation also emboldened many to simply disregard their landlords' orders. Shade Richards, an ex-slave from Georgia, remembered giving his ex-master "a lot of mouthin'" until he altered their share agreement. Above all, freed slaves exercised their physical independence in order to secure more satisfactory labor arrangements. A Union soldier who tried his hand at cotton planting after the war wrote from Maury County, Texas, that "hands are so scarce that if they are offended in any way (and they are very sensitive), they leave at once."[27]

Planters flooded the Freedmen's Bureau with complaints of "vagabond" freedmen who broke contracts midseason; some letters mention ex-slaves who left farms for nearby cities, only to return and demand different working conditions. W. W. Woodruff, a cotton planter in southwest Georgia, begged the Federal authorities to adopt measures to keep freedpeople "where they are." "The intention of nearly all the freedman in the section that I live in is to quit at Christmas" and look for better contracts "up the Country," he wrote. A Texas justice of the peace related similar conditions in his state, declaring that black laborers were not concerned with how much they were paid; rather, they sought working conditions where they felt "free."[28] As historian Barbara Fields explains, the failure of land redistribution in the South preserved planters' economic advantage, but "the intense battles fought to preserve some rights (task organization of work and garden plots) and dispense with some duties (ditching, fencing, and other ancillary or menial functions) carried over from slavery served notice that the freedmen would not be pushovers."[29]

The records of planters whose early contracts with freedmen dictated they perform significant slack-time work showed higher incidences of labor turnover. Ex-slaves contested planters' understandings of "necessary" and demanded extra pay for tasks not enumerated in their agreements. Joseph Brown's freedman, whose contract is detailed above, left his employment after four months. John Elliott hired an ex-slave named McCoy in January; McCoy fled Elliott's farm before breakfast one morning in early February. Nelson Clayton, in the Black Belt of Alabama, hired several of his former slaves in 1866. Although they knew their wages would be docked if they left before December, many of his field hands departed midseason. Judy, an ex-slave with two children to support, stayed seven months and twenty days. Simon and Silvy, a couple who had both been purchased by Clayton when they were children, abandoned Clayton's farm after eight months and six days. A. H. Thomas stayed almost the whole year—ten months—but left after a dispute over evening work.[30] While it was not uncommon for ex-slaves to return and stay for years with their former masters, even a temporary absence could provide leverage in the next year's contract negotiations.[31]

Over time, freedpeople's resistance to contracts that were reminiscent of their bondage conditions precipitated a noticeable shift in labor relations. By the late 1860s, share-based and tenant forms of agricultural tenure were becoming more common than gang or squad labor, which typically paid wages. Although Freedmen's Bureau agents and northern officials initially expected wage labor to be the norm, it failed in the cotton South for several reasons. Freedpeople equated a wage laborer with being a "hireling," a "virtual automaton, devoid of volition and unquestioningly obedient," and wished for a system of compensation that provided them with more decision-making power.[32] Another drawback was that wages varied wildly across the cotton-growing regions, and the larger, less-damaged plantations to the west offered the highest monthly rates. The subsequent destabilization of labor forces in states such as Georgia and North Carolina due to outmigration sent planters into a panic regarding an impending "labor shortage." Formerly mixed-farming areas in upper Georgia, North Carolina, and Tennessee found it difficult to compete for workers with wage agreements. Of course, wage labor ultimately failed because very few people had any cash. Ex-slaves distrusted a system in which the very existence of their wages was in doubt and abandoned employers who failed to pay them, regardless of the time of year or the length of their contract.[33] For all parties involved, then, the antebellum systems of sharecropping and tenancy promised to standardize expectations for contract terms, create more stable and autonomous work forces, and solve the shortage of cash.

Sharecropping thus emerged as a "compromise" between cash-poor landlords and property-poor laborers. Croppers worked for a fixed share of the crop, usually one-fourth or one-third; the landlord provided all other supplies. The more property or food a sharecropper had access to, the larger his share of the crop. Planters settled sharecropper accounts for supplies, animals, tools, food, and other items at the end of the year, a strategy that induced employees to stay through the completion of cotton picking (so they might receive their share). A portion of black southerners with more property or capital at their disposal obtained the status of renters, or tenant farmers, who ran agricultural operations with minimal assistance from the landlord in terms of rations, clothing, and work animals. Renters occupied the highest level in the social hierarchy among agricultural laborers, and wage workers the lowest. Economic mobility was possible, but only in small increments. Evans Warrior of Dallas County, Alabama, was in Arkansas with his master during the war, but he returned to Alabama and worked on shares "till [he] got able to rent. Paid five or six dollars a acre. Made some money." Warrior never owned land, but he considered himself financially successful in that he was a cash renter, not a sharecropper or wage laborer. Although share-based labor agreements were deeply flawed, they did solve a number of problems evident in the early contracts, including the expectation of uncompensated land maintenance and the organization of workers.[34]

Between 1865 and the 1870s, share-based contracts less frequently assumed that slack-time tasks were part of crop cultivation. For these tasks, landlords had to pay additional wages or apply a credit to a laborer's account. Contracts that vaguely stated laborers would "do all necessary repairs about the place" became significantly less frequent, unless the value of that work was included as "rent" for a piece of land.[35] Throughout the cotton South, the timeline of these trans- formations varied from place to place, but a survey of almost forty plantations in seven states reveals a general pattern. Large "business" plantations—such as those in Mississippi with hundreds of laborers—had adjusted contract language by 1870. Smaller landholdings altered arrangements in the mid-1870s, especially in longer-cultivated areas such as Georgia.[36] William Wallace White, a farmer in central North Carolina, began paying laborers extra wages for maintenance work around 1873. In his monthly diary, he ceased to discuss land maintenance as a group effort among his "hands" and began delineating the daily wages he paid for each task. For instance, in early April 1873, White paid his tenant Lewis Davis seventy-five cents per day to ditch White's home fields. Federal policies reinforced these changes. During the late 1860s, the Internal Revenue Service ceased to offer a tax deduction to farmers who ditched their land, arguing that it was a "permanent improvement" and not related to the immediate crop.[37] Land- maintenance work became increasingly sporadic either because laborers refused to perform it or landlords were reluctant to pay for it.

Similarly, by the 1870s, family or individual contracts replaced the group con- tracts of the immediate postwar period. A Mississippi cotton farmer observed as early as 1869 that "from laborers great numbers of the negroes have been trans- formed into tenantry."[38] On John Allen's properties in Alabama, contracts once signed by groups of thirteen to ninety laborers had, by the mid-1870s, become differentiated by the employees' status. Some contracts applied to single men hired as field hands on wages or shares; others were with one renter and his family. Henry Laurens Pinckney listed forty-two field hands in his 1866 jour- nal and arranged them by gangs. Several years later, Pinckney began individual and family accounts. Almost every one of the thirteen hired hands had a family of dependents working with them, presumably on separate plots. Freedmen's Bureau employees also noted the shift away from group contracts, and many of them celebrated it. The head of the bureau office in Mobile, Alabama, thought that a group of forty or fifty hands masked individual idleness. It was better for contracts to be attached to individual families to prevent sloth and waste.[39]

This, too, had a noticeable effect on how frequently land maintenance was performed. Although working on an individual plot of land better fit with expec- tations of free labor, this progressive trend chipped away at landowners' abil- ity to keep up with enormously important maintenance tasks. On individual plots, tenants and sharecroppers might have performed these jobs, but on a plantation-wide level, they became more infrequent. Two Boston-based cotton brokers listed the reduction in "necessary repairs" as one of the main drawbacks of sharecropping. The system encouraged industry among freedpeople by giv- ing them "pride" in the crop, but it also created a "great difficulty in carrying on

Figure 4.2 Group of freedpeople on their way to the cotton field, South Carolina. Gang labor arrangements did not resemble most ex-slaves' ideas of what freedom would entail. Prints and Photographs Division, Library of Congress. LC-DIG-stereo-1s03948.

the general work of the farm." Laborers drifted into idleness "for a large part of the year"; landowners became indifferent to the state of their lands, and farms' productivity suffered.[40]

Other contemporary sources reflected the same evolution in the views of land maintenance seen in planters' records. Articles about plantation management in agricultural journals, for instance, documented the changing rhythms of "upkeep" work through the 1860s and 1870s due to fractious labor arrangements. In 1866 and 1867, contributors to these publications concerned themselves with extracting labor from allegedly idle ex-slaves. By the end of the decade, writers were complaining that land maintenance was too costly to perform. In 1869, for instance, the *Southern Planter* lamented that ditching was more expensive than buying fertilizers, and a journal out of Tarboro, North Carolina, the *Reconstructed Farmer*, chastised farmers for taking shortcuts with ditching to avoid paying laborers more money. An article discussing agriculture in Hancock County, Georgia, made similar claims regarding shifting cultivation: "Old fields nearly exhausted will now bring more per acre than rich wood land, because it is cheaper to buy fertilizers and make cotton on them than to clear new land without slave labor." By 1876, ditching was considered an extravagance. A *Southern Planter* review of the recently published book *How to Make a Farm Pay* sneered at its author's suggestion that ditching fields would improve a farm's crop production. The reviewer quipped: "When I accumulate a million and a half [dollars], I shall try to practice its precepts."[41]

This reduction in land maintenance reflected the new reality of the cotton economy, as well as the ability of freed slaves to better control their own labor. However, these changes had severe and unintended ecological consequences. One of the most obvious physical signs of changing contract terms was increased erosion. Labor disputes over clearing new land proved key in this regard, for planters often balked at the cost of practicing shifting cultivation under tenant arrangements. A cotton farmer in southern Alabama turned down an offer to purchase a new plot because he was loath to advance the money to clear it. It is foolish to "talk about putting money into land now," he declared, when "scarcely a planter can command the labour to clear the land he already has!" A contributor to the Georgia-based *Southern Farm and Home* grumbled, "Labor is too expensive to clear land to any extent, but we have not the money to move."[42]

Yet part of the reason shifting cultivation persisted for so long was that the root systems of trees or other secondary vegetation were essential for keeping topsoil in place on fields and on slopes. Once farmers removed that protective vegetation, soils eroded rapidly and destructively, creating serious soil-nutrient imbalances, gullies, and other markers of degraded land. A planter in the mid-nineteenth century noted how easily the Cotton Belt soils eroded, writing, "The land was rich when first cleared of hardwood, but was unproductive after less than twenty years of intensive cultivation. . . . There could be no certainty of what would come of one's children if the soil continued to leach and wash." A Freedman's Bureau agent, R. A. Wilson, noted the onset of this trend as early as 1868 in Marengo County, Alabama. "Men who are free will not clear land," he wrote, ". . . while the breadth of land annually thrown out of cultivation is about the same as formerly." He warned that both land and laborer suffered from the resulting damage to the physical landscape. "The county itself seems to be fast retrograding," he reported, for recent agricultural trends made it "difficult to sustain livelihoods."[43]

Planters' records and agricultural publications discussed the growing crisis of soil quality on cotton lands with regularity, but reduced land maintenance had other effects unrelated to erosion. Ditches, it turned out, played an important role in preventing the dreaded cotton caterpillar from reaching stands of the crop. Known to cotton planters in the United States since 1793, the cotton caterpillar was sometimes called the cotton worm or, incorrectly, the army worm. Before the boll weevil made its appearance, it was the most harmful, visible pest to cotton plants. Damage to crops usually began in June, and by July, entire fields could be completely defoliated. In the 1870s, the USDA discovered that the cotton caterpillar could be poisoned using arsenic-based compounds such as Paris green. Until then, the only moderately effective methods of keeping the worms at bay were crop rotation and ditching; the former removed the worms' host, while the latter acted as a physical brake on the pest's advance.[44]

It is unclear whether planters were aware of the connection between ditching and the damage of the cotton caterpillar, but the pest proved particularly virulent between 1864 and 1869—years when wartime damage and labor contract disputes converged to cause a decline in ditching. A Plantation Bureau employee wrote that the "unexpected appearance of the cotton worm" destroyed the 1864 crop in Louisiana. In 1867, a farmer from Valdosta, Georgia said his crop will "not come up to expectations" because of the caterpillars, and in 1868, James Jenkins Gillette of the Freedman's Bureau wrote that the destruction of crops by the worm caused "enough misery to expiate . . . the national crimes" of the South.[45] The true tragedy of the caterpillar's appearance, of course, was that ex-slaves, who rightly wished to be paid for extra plantation work, refused to spend time away from their own crops or families to ditch a landlord's field. At the end of the year, low cotton yields due to the worm's defoliation of the plants reduced them to the "necessity of begging."[46]

The changed circumstances of land maintenance accelerated both ecological change and the intensification of cotton production that so drastically affected postwar farmers' livelihoods and land. Certainly, other factors were at play in how the land responded to cotton production: extreme weather events, soil type, access to fertilizers, and previous land use. Nonetheless, disputes over arranging and paying for land maintenance encouraged landlords to let their fences rot just a little longer or to allow ditches to fill up, contributing to ongoing problems of soil erosion and crop damage by livestock. More autonomous labor forces disrupted shifting cultivation, forcing both white and black tenants to invest in expensive fertilizers. Although cotton outputs continued to climb during this period, over time, new land-use patterns diminished natural productivity of the landscape and undermined farmers' efforts to secure economic independence through sharecropping and tenancy. Meanwhile, other aspects of emancipation contributed to a political assault on the cotton South's internal provisioning economy and decreased ex-slaves' access to the network of common lands that were once so integral to the southern agricultural system.

The Bennett farm lay just a few miles east of Lunson Place in an area known as Prairie Bluff, Alabama, in Wilcox County. A substantial property, albeit not a large one by Black Belt standards, the farm belonged to a war widow, Elizabeth Bennett, who employed her son, John E. Bennett, as "agent."[47] He handled the laborers' contracts, the provisioning of the farm, and the sale of their cotton. In the winter of 1867, a dispute between the Bennetts and their workers attracted the attention of the Freedmen's Bureau office in nearby Selma and brought agent D. J. Fraser to the place. The case against the Bennetts included complaints they charged for lost time, required an advance for rations, and frequently assigned group-maintenance tasks away from laborers' individual plots. What infuriated the freedmen most, however, and brought the matter to Fraser's desk, was Bennett's treatment of the fences. Before the war, the farm had unbroken range for the livestock along the edges of the property. Once John divided the land into plots for hired laborers, the fencing around each new crop field left only pockets of woodland between the home farm, where Bennett worked, and his laborers' lands. According to Fraser, Bennett "had the fence taken from part of the corn field and refuses to let the hands repair the fence so that his [Bennett's] stock may run on it and have the benefit of both halves [of the farm]." In other words, Bennett had turned his laborers' semiprivate cornfields into a commons where his own livestock could forage. Bennett's excuse was that his mother's land lacked the timber for such extensive fencing. Perhaps the demands of fortifying nearby Selma during the war had increased the pressure on Bennett timber supplies. Regardless, Fraser concluded that Bennett was "determined to act unfair and dishonest." He asked his superiors at the bureau, "Now how are the Freedmen to get their rights?"[48]

The Bennett case was part of a broader postwar pattern of conflict over the region's practice of free-range animal husbandry—whether access to common space was a "right," as Fraser called it, or a privilege. Antebellum agricultural reformers decried free-range animal husbandry as a waste of productive land and valuable timber. Consequently, the practice had suffered waves of localized attacks during the 1840s and 1850s. Those assaults on subsistence practices typically occurred in densely populated rural areas with longer histories of cultivation, such as Virginia, and they failed more often than they succeeded. After 1865, political interest in reversing the centuries-old practice spread to the cotton South.[49] Like John E. Bennett, contemporaries often cited the war as the impetus for replacing fence laws in cotton-growing regions with stock laws. As one Farmer's Assembly concluded, in 1867, free-range animal husbandry may have been "adapted to the wants of the community" before the war, but it "cannot be so now under such a total change of circumstances."[50] Planters claimed that because of widespread foraging and impressment, there were no longer enough livestock to necessitate expensive crop fences. Further, the conflict's large-scale erasure of the South's existing railroads and industrial enterprises sparked a postwar boom in extractive industries, placing further pressure on the region's timber resources. For this reason, the postwar assault on the southern range is sometimes depicted as an ideological battle between preindustrial republican farmers who believed in "cooperative principles" and an "agrarian bourgeoisie" promoting the free market values of an increasingly industrialized region.[51]

In reality, the efforts to close the open range in certain areas of the deep cotton South were far more tied to labor relations and planters' efforts to control ex-slaves. Emancipation broadened the appeal of restricting common lands in two ways. First, the process of contract negotiation helped to decentralize agricultural operations by encouraging share-based individual arrangements, which both reduced land maintenance and required the redivision of plantation lands. As is seen in the case of John Bennett, the creation of tenant plots made free-range animal husbandry less feasible by chipping away at number of common spaces. Clashes over fence repair and other land-maintenance tasks reinforced this trend. Under contract labor, the cutting and hauling of fence rails was simply more troublesome and the ongoing decline of shifting cultivation undermined the need for reserve woodland. Second, the restriction of common lands acted as a method of racial control. Landlords endeavored to maximize their cultivated acreage and increase laborers' dependency on the plantation for supplies, so they actively discouraged the customary rights to common lands and garden plots that were prevalent during the antebellum period. This explains why the opening salvos of the decades-long fight to close the open range began in the Mississippi Valley and the Black Belt, areas largely isolated from wartime military operations and known for their high densities of large cotton plantations and slaves. Black and white agency, working toward the conflicting goals of freedom and control, converged to bring about the gradual closing of the open range in the plantation belt. Thus the shift away from free-range animal husbandry in cotton plantation counties during the 1870s proved to be another way that emancipation accelerated the breakdown of extensive land use, with disastrous consequences for both the land and livelihoods.

Free-range animal husbandry, along with shifting cultivation, was a foundational element in the system, allowing southerners to circumvent environmental limitations on stock-raising.[52] Croplands were usually very large, particularly in the Old Southwest, and enclosing them with fencing strong enough to keep out roaming livestock required significant investments in labor, time, money, and timber. Nevertheless, several features of southern agriculture at the time made the system a logical one. The hardwood trees requisite for the open-range system were plentiful, so both natural forage and fencing materials were abundant. Stock numbers were much higher across the cotton South, although livestock-raising was more common outside the large plantation districts. The common lands created by free-range animal husbandry also played a vital role in the area's agricultural economy and ecology. Not only did they act as reserves for future cultivation, they also provided spaces for subsistence. Slaves could sometimes keep livestock or garden plots in unfenced lands, saving planters money on fodder for penned stock and rations for slaves. Poorer whites, too, used them for keeping livestock, as well as for hunting and foraging grounds.

War and emancipation radically altered the circumstances that made these practices a rational use of land, particularly in areas with high-number densities of ex-slaves. Communities across the cotton South began to challenge the fence laws almost immediately after the conflict had ended. In Hinds County, Mississippi, where 70 percent of the population was black, citizens passed an act in late 1865 to restrict open range to protect farmers "in those sections where the fencing and timber has been destroyed by the late war."[53] The next year, Mississippi extended the act's provisions to seven other counties. The Alabama state legislature passed acts between 1866 and 1868 to allow certain Black Belt counties to prohibit "animals running at large" within "stock law districts." By the 1870s, the calls to repeal the fence laws had rippled outward from the Black Belt to other cotton plantation areas. In 1872, a group of cotton planters met in the city of Griffin, Georgia, "looking for a thorough change in regard to the fence laws" because "the planting interest is the source of all material wealth" and the open range placed a burden on the land and finances of that interest.[54] That same year, the Georgia legislature passed a local-option law, a measure to allow each respective county to decide whether or not to keep fence laws.[55]

As the language of the Hinds County's fence-law repeal indicates, the most commonly cited reasons for passing stock laws or similar provisions were material concerns over the loss of livestock and the acceleration in woodland clearance that had taken place during the war. Although that was true in many areas, wartime damage to fences, timber, and livestock does not explain the rise of stock-law districts in the Black Belt, where military operations had been few. Why would planters, such as John Gray Allen of Marengo County, Alabama, support stock laws? His plantation had retained a majority of its stock during the war, suffered no Union raids, and though it was subject to the typical impressment and tax-in-kind, had easily survived those policies. Allen is even on record as continuing free-range animal husbandry into the 1870s. A brief feud broke out between Allen and his neighbor, John Ryall, over the behavior of Allen's stock. Cows from Allen's plantation had a habit of breaking through the fences Ryall built around his pasture. "Dear Sir, Your stock are still annoying me very much," Ryall wrote to Allen. "I do not like to complain so constantly but I need my pastures and need them badly." The grasses were not easy to cultivate, and the presence of Allen's cows doubled the pressure on the struggling pasture. Ryall pleaded with his neighbor to either confine his stock or fence a portion of unimproved land. "Do try to do something with them . . . they are doing me a great deal of damage."[56]

In some areas, it was the complications over land use arising from emancipation rather than wartime damage or even animal disease, which caused so many cotton planters like John Gray Allen to support the restriction of open range over time. Allen was a large landowner who employed a considerable number of black field hands, white and black tenants, and later, convicts on lease from the state of Alabama.[57] As he divided and redivided his properties to accommodate increasingly decentralized labor arrangements, Allen decreased his use of open grazing. In short, the evolution of southern tenancy contributed to the end of free-range animal husbandry in some areas by decentralizing laborers' living spaces and reducing farmers' use of shifting cultivation.

As methods of dividing and compensating labor evolved, so, too, did ways of organizing land. Across the cotton South, the more autonomous labor forces of the postemancipation period necessitated the spatial transformation of landholdings from a patchwork of fallowing old fields, woodland, and cultivated acreage directed from a central residential area to a series of individual farms that remained relatively static in their boundaries. The alteration was not immediate, for the contract arrangements of the coalescing free-labor regime exhibited startling variety in the first five years or so after the Civil War.[58] In general, however, black agency during contract negotiations altered how landlords measured an employee's work on the crop, redefined the tasks that constituted "all necessary work," and necessitated a change in the way farms looked. The ability to live and work on an individual plot of land was a "geographical expression of freedom" for many ex-slaves, and as black laborers pressed to work more independently, cotton plantations gradually fragmented. Robert Somers, a British writer who traveled the South during 1870 and 1871, noted this trend, remarking on the changing plantations in northern Alabama. "It was usual in slavery times to concentrate the 'quarters' . . . near the homestead. But under free contract, by which the negro field-hand has become a sharer of the crop . . . it is found convenient to spread him . . . more about, near his work."[59]

Larger properties usually consisted of home farms and tenant tracts. The landlord grew his own crops on the home farm, usually with wage laborers. Any reserve woodland was part of the home farm. Tenant tracts were usually twenty to fifty acres, although plots could be as small as three acres and as large as a hundred acres. William Stickney of southern Alabama recorded that one of his renters worked two hundred acres, which the tenant then further subdivided so that he could pay laborers in shares. A planter in central Virginia who flirted with cotton cultivation carved three renters' plots from a 150-acre section of his plantation, using the rest for his own crops. A South Carolina planter's wife, describing the division of her husband's land, wrote that surveyors delineated plots by how many mules it took to work them—one, two, three, or four—and that one-mule parcels were the most popular.[60]

The breakup of large plantations can be seen in census data, which shows the rapid growth in the number of farms in the South during the postwar period.

Across the region there were twice as many farms in 1880 as there were in 1860, despite an average population growth of only 39 percent. These figures represented not the number of farms owned, but the number of farms operated. A tenant plot within a larger landholding was listed as a separate farm. For instance, in 1860, South Carolina had 33,171 farms. In 1880, it had 93,328. Other cotton-growing states saw similarly dramatic increases, though antebellum patterns of settlement affected the rate of farm division. Tennessee, a more densely settled area with smaller average farm acreages, had less land to subdivide and saw a smaller increase in the number of farms during the postwar period. In contrast, Mississippi had large swaths of open land in 1860 and a greater number of sprawling cotton plantations. As more land came under cultivation and massive plantations divided again and again, the number of farms surged 175 percent between the end of the war and 1880. North Carolina experienced a 135 percent jump in the number of farms reported; Alabama's data indicated an astonishing 171 percent increase. Georgia's agricultural landscape comprised 138,026 farms in 1880, compared to the 53,897 farms recorded twenty years earlier.[61]

One of the most famous examples of this process is that of the Barrow Plantation in Oglethorpe County, Georgia. The altered internal geography of the plantation made the practice of shifting cultivation highly impractical, invalidating a key reason for continuing free-range husbandry. The antebellum plantation possessed a center of operations from which labor could be directed and cultivation could spread outward. As the plantation's operator, David Barrow Jr., told *Scribner's Monthly,* postwar farms' layouts contrasted sharply with the days when slaves had been "under the absolute rule of an overseer ... who directed the laborers each as to their work." After a brief period during which Barrow attempted to continue the overseer system, he divided the plantation into halves, each worked by a squad of freedmen. Eventually, "family-sized" tenant farms constituted the bulk of Barrow's acreage. Barrow himself cultivated a 120-acre home farm with two hired hands—judging by his reported cotton yields for 1880, he had clearly reserved the best land for his own crop.[62] Regardless, the 1881 map makes it clear that there was no easy way to "shift" tenants' acreage without running into or overlapping with another plot. Entirely new tenant farms could be carved from the woodland still evident on the edges of the Barrow plantation, but no longer would the boundaries of cultivated acreage move continuously as a few acres were added to a field every two or three years and a few more were allowed to act as grazing land.

Anecdotal evidence supports the growing impracticality of shifting cultivation on plantations such as Barrow's, but the trend is difficult to discern in the census records. During the immediate postwar period, southerners still cultivated around 30 percent of the land they owned. According to calculations made from the 1880 census, the percentage of improved acres in farms in a sample of cotton-growing states was only narrowly higher. Alabama improved 34 percent of the acreage in farms; Arkansas, 30 percent; Georgia, 32 percent; Louisiana, 33 percent; and Mississippi, 33 percent. Between 1860 and 1880, then, these states all saw an increase in the percentage of improved acreage in farms, but only between 1 percent and 6 percent. So it seems that shifting cultivation was still an option—there was plenty of land within farms to clear—and yet the archival records mention it less frequently, soil erosion continued to skyrocket, and fertilizer use climbed. Many planters whose records detailed how slaves cleared new ground every year before the war only mention one, perhaps two, instances of "clearing new ground" between 1866 and 1880. Some planters stopped recording it altogether.[63]

There are several reasons for the reduction in shifting cultivation despite the existence of large tracts of unimproved land. Census records were inconsistent in the categorization of "unimproved" land between 1860 and 1880: in 1860, all uncultivated areas in a farm were listed as "unimproved"; whereas in 1870 and 1880, the Census Bureau distinguished between woodland and "other" unimproved land in farms. It is possible that the acceleration of woodland clearance due to the wartime military operations created larger percentages of "other" unimproved land within farms that were not valuable as reserves for shifting cultivation. For instance, William Syndor Thomson of Marietta, Georgia, bragged to his father in 1867 that he had just purchased a twenty-acre plot of land, "well-located" and "very desirable." He was able to buy it at a reduced price because all of the timber on it was cut in 1862 and thus would "cost a good deal to put it into the condition I intend to have it"—presumably he needed to clear stumps and add fertilizer to jumpstart production, rather than simply girdling, felling, and burning the trees.[64]

A range of factors, then, beyond the loss of woodland and the increase in animal diseases, converged to make the maintenance of common lands less important and widened the appeal of stock laws in the cotton South during this period. More decentralized labor forces and farm operations made shifting cultivation more impractical due to the rearrangement of plantations. Large acreages of reserve woodland once used for clearing new ground suddenly made more sense as additional tenant plots. The contract negotiations over land maintenance reinforced these developments. In a letter to General Davis Tillson of the Freedmen's Bureau, a cotton planter named L. C. Warren from Louisville, Georgia, explicitly related changing labor relations to mounting concerns over livestock-raising in cotton districts. Warren described widespread support for agreements with laborers based on shares, primarily because it reduced the fiduciary responsibility of the planters in poor crop years. However, the Georgia planter felt laborers' ideas about having "no obligation to do anything but work the crops and gather them" hurt the integrity of cotton farming. "If the [contract] system is

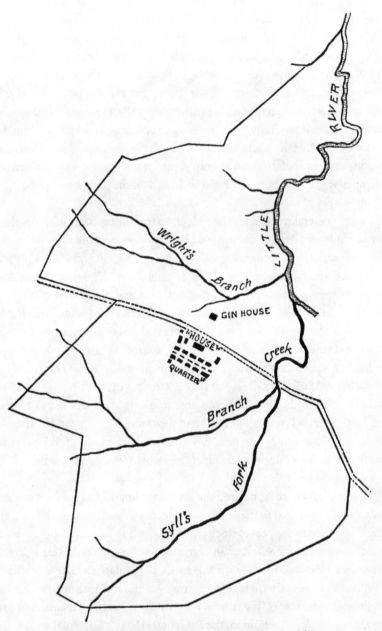

A GEORGIA PLANTATION AS IT WAS IN 1860.

Figure 4.3 Map of the Barrow Plantation 1860, Oglethorpe County, Georgia. These maps, taken from *Scribner's Monthly,* are frequently reproduced because of how they clearly demonstrate the break between antebellum and postbellum plantation division; the latter emphasized individual plots over the centralized operations of the former. Courtesy of Cornell University Library, Making of America Digital Collection.

A GEORGIA PLANTATION AS IT IS IN 1881.
* Negroes who lived on this plantation when slaves.

Figure 4.4 Map of the Barrow Plantation 1881, Oglethorpe County, Georgia. Courtesy of Cornell University Library, Making of America Digital Collection.

Table 4.1 **Type of Land in Farms, 1870**

	Acres Improved	Acres Unimproved	Percentage Improved	Change 1860–1870
Alabama	5,062,204	9,898,974	34%	+1%
Arkansas	1,859,821	5,737,475	24%	+3%
Georgia	6,831,856	16,816,085	29%	−1%
Louisiana	2,045,640	4,980,177	29%	NO CHANGE
Mississippi	4,209,146	8,911,967	32%	NO CHANGE
North Carolina	5,258,742	14,576,668	27%	NO CHANGE
South Carolina	3,010,539	9,094,741	25%	−3%
Tennessee	6,843,278	12,737,936	35%	+2%
Texas	2,964,836	15,431,687	16%	+6%

Note: Percentage increase or decrease of improved land from 1860 to 1870 and the percentage of improved land in farms were calculated by author. "Unimproved" land in farms for the 1870 census was divided into "woodland" and "other." This table combines the two categories, so that all land in farms classified as "unimproved" is listed above. Data source: Table III, "Productions of Agriculture for the Years 1870, 1860, and 1850," in Statistics of Agriculture, Compiled from the Original Returns of the Ninth Census June 1, 1870 (Washington, DC: GPO, 1872), 81, 86, available from the USDA at http://agcensus.mannlib.cornell.edu/AgCensus/censusParts.do?year=1870

to be carried out for many years, we shall necessarily be compelled, to abandon altogether Cattle & hog raising, else our Crops will be destroyed for the want of sufficient fencing to protect the Crops."[65] For the farmers who might still support free-range animal husbandry for their own herds, the altered circumstances of paying workers to clear new ground or fence repair made stock laws more appealing.

For other planters, the restriction of free-range animal husbandry was a means by which they could maintain control of laborers despite the free labor system. Traditionally, woodland held in reserve for future shifting cultivation served as open range on which poor whites and ex-slaves gathered, hunted, or raised food to supplement their incomes and diets. Freed slaves, especially, showed a preference during the immediate postwar period for occupying or renting former provision grounds, abandoned land, and other uncultivated spaces to grow food crops and raise a few livestock rather than work in cotton, sugar, tobacco, or rice. In Dinwiddie County, Virginia, for instance, twenty black families lived in the winter huts the Federal army built and then abandoned on the former property of Job Talmadge. They cultivated small crops of corn and other foods to make the land "entirely self-supporting."[66] Near New Bern, North Carolina, forty freedmen lived and worked 225 acres of the abandoned plantation of J. S. Rhen. Cotton had been the principal crop, but the ex-slaves only grew corn and garden crops. Troops cut all 244 acres of Rhen's woodland, so the livestock the Freedmen's Bureau report mentioned probably grazed on other people's land.[67] Planters feared that easy access to subsistence agriculture undermined what they deemed necessary for efficient plantation work: a dependent labor force with few to no options for alternative employment. Thus, these early stock laws passed more easily because planters sought to reassert control over the lives of freed slaves by eliminating the traditional internal provisioning economy.

Planters' restriction of subsistence spaces and practices as a method of racial control manifested itself in two ways. The first was the use of contracts to transform antebellum-era "rights" into privileges. It became increasingly common for employers to prohibit the keeping of livestock, discontinue the use of garden plots, or require that livestock "be penned and fed at the workers' expense rather than allowed to forage in woods, swamps, or other uncultivated acreage." In South Carolina, articles of agreement allowed laborers to keep hogs in pens, as long as no family possessed more than two. No other animals were acceptable. In Mississippi, a group contract signed for 1867 stated that "laborers will not be allowed to keep horses, mules, stock, hogs, or cows, except by separate, and special permission, and only then during good behaviour."[68] Landowners often used contracts to shape "free" labor in ways that benefited them, even as ex-slaves actively resisted those terms. For instance, landlords increasingly linked rations to the individuals who were specifically under contract (i.e., the male head of household) in order to encourage that individual's dependents to work as well. Allen Cleveland, a freedman working for Tennessean Andrew Payne, testified to the Freedman's Bureau regarding a confrontation over whether Cleveland's wife would work in the field. Payne allegedly threatened Cleveland and his wife with a rock, screaming, "if [she] didn't work they shouldn't eat his provisions."[69]

At the same time, counties attached serious criminal charges to the previously common practice of keeping of livestock in unimproved and unenclosed lands. During the antebellum period, slaves tended stock for themselves or their masters in the expanses between the cultivated fields of the plantation and occasionally appropriated an animal from the master's herd. Planters frequently complained of their "thieving" slaves, but it was not a "crime" dealt with outside of the plantation. After emancipation, however, freedpeople continued to approach wandering stock in the same way.[70] "Since my last report crime has increased very much among the freedpeople, and is principally confined to hog stealing," one South Carolina Bureau agent reported. Another item in Bureau correspondence, this one from Alabama, stated, "petit larceny seems to be rapidly increasing. Shoats and poultry seem to be mainly in quest and they are disappearing beyond precedent." The same report emerged from Mississippi, with a Bureau agent declaring

that "in some cases difficulty is occasioned by some Freedmen killing and appro-
priating to their own use, hogs, and fowls, the property of their employers."[71]
A contributor to the *Southern Cultivator* whined that since the war, "each negro
[has been] almost crazy for a long range rifle" to hunt others' livestock on the
range, and a magazine called the *Carolina Farmer* warned agriculturalists in that
state: "Thieves are numerous and ready to pounce upon anything which may be
taken and converted into money. The horse in your stable is not safe. Your cattle
and hogs in the range are less so!"[72] Planters claimed that freedpeople pilfered
livestock to keep from working; bureau agents largely assumed that the "crimes"
occurred as a result of destitution among blacks.

L. M. Hobbs, a reverend asked to travel around the Florida panhandle to
"explain to the colored people their situation," noted that the general dearth of
livestock keeping and its impact on meat rations escalated conflicts over ex-slaves'
"hog stealing." In his testimony to the Joint Committee on Reconstruction, he
related an incident during which a planter's supposed scarcity of livestock gave
him an excuse to withhold rations from his laborers, provoking a criminal dispute couched in conflicting ideas over freedpeoples' rights to the products of the
plantation:

> One of the planters . . . came [to me] with three negroes whom he
> charged with stealing hogs from his place. I asked the negroes if they
> had taken the hogs; they said they had. I asked what they had done with
> them; they said they had killed them and made meat of them. I said,
> "Do you not think it wrong to steal hogs?" "Well, no; [we] did not think
> it wrong to kill Massa Chairs's hogs." "Why not?" "Because [we] were
> working for him, and he did not give [us] any meat."[73]

The punishments attached to livestock crimes such as the killing of Mr. Chairs's
hogs became steeper over time, and the frequency of larceny convictions
increased. For stealing a hog from his landlord in 1866, a judge fined Henry
Smith, a freed slave, $10 "plus costs" (presumably the price of the animal) and
imprisoned him for thirty days. The *Montgomery Weekly Advertiser* mocked
Smith in its report, saying that he might have "jest cooked a little pig," but he had
been "caught and cornered 'jess' stealing." In the 1870s, however, Mississippi's
"pig law" classified the theft of any cattle or swine as grand larceny; conviction
carried a maximum penalty of five years in the penitentiary. In North Carolina,
the number of larceny convictions jumped 60 percent between 1868 and 1869.[74]

Stereotypes about "thieving negroes" were so pervasive that agricultural
publications began to incorporate them into their arguments for stock laws.
Magazines and journals throughout the South shifted their rhetoric toward the
longtime cause of eliminating free-range animal husbandry. Before emancipation,

agricultural reformers had appealed to practical concerns, such as the scarcity of timber or the cost of fences, to evidence farmers' need to pen their stock. During the late 1860s, articles about fencing, animal care, and agricultural practices subtly (and occasionally not so subtly) exploited whites' insecurities about the sanctity and safety of their property, drawing on inchoate fear about black thieves to make a stronger case for closing the open range. "Senex," a contributor to an 1870 issue of the *Southern Planter*, wrote, "It may be objected that stock raising is likely to be a failure on account of our thieveth freedmen. Perhaps in some sections they steal more stock . . . than they did when they were slaves . . . but if we all fall into the habits of farming, and live better, they will behave better."[75] Senex, making the distinction between "farming" and "planting" that characterized antebellum reform debates, argued that better "farming" practices, such as penning livestock, increasing herd sizes, and creating fewer feral breeds, would not only improve the farm and the farmer's self-sufficiency but also ameliorate the conditions of laborers. Of course, the push to pen livestock and eliminate free-range animal husbandry decreased most poor southerners' self-sufficiency, which, in certain plantation districts, was precisely the point. The *Reconstructed Farmer* put it more bluntly: it would be better to "stall feed" livestock, so that "we shall lose none by thieves. The most reckless freedman would not [be] likely to risk his precious carcass within gun-shot range."[76]

The combination of fewer common spaces, geographical restrictions on free-range animal husbandry, and higher penalties for "thieving" were all part of planters' efforts to control laborers' food supply. The result was that sharecroppers and tenants bought provisions from planters and merchants, who sold them bacon, corn, and flour often imported from the Midwest. Whereas it was once understood that masters would provide their slaves with rations, after the initial postwar period, more and more employers found ways to shift the financial burden of obtaining food to the laborer. Bureau agents in several states reported that "planters generally keep a stock of goods and provisions on hand for sale. Upon these they make a large profit and in many cases they will bring the negro in debt to them at the end of the year, because the Negro must buy something to supply the deficiency in ration."[77] While the demand for foodstuffs helped fuel the expansion of agriculture in the western regions of the United States, the practice of planting staples and buying provisions initiated a cycle of dependency between laborer on landlord, landlord on merchant, and the South on other regions. Any rations, fertilizers, or clothing the sharecropper obtained from the landlord or the landlord's creditor was deducted from the cropper's share. If the landlord said there was no share to give the cropper at the end of the year, the sharecropper could not challenge him.[78]

Had the common land system functioned as it had before the Civil War, blacks would have had access to subsistence resources to offset the economic effects of the worsening ecological conditions on their cultivated lands. They could have appropriated or bought livestock, allowed them to range in the woods, traded their meat for provisions or goods, and perhaps eventually purchased land. Changes in land use eliminated that option. The growing impracticality of free-range animal husbandry and shifting cultivation in the tenant system lessened support for these spaces. Of course, common land and subsistence practices, especially in relation to fishing rights, had long been under attack in the more populous northeastern states; and by the late antebellum period, changing demography, the early pangs of industrialization, and a growing shortage of fresh lands generated similar movements in Virginia. In fact, part of the "doctrine of improvement" promoted by agricultural reformers such as Edmund Ruffin included the elimination of common spaces, such as millponds and swamps, ostensibly to create a more ordered landscape but also to consolidate elites' landholdings and control over natural resources. Early calls for fence law repeals fit within this narrative, as well.[79] So the displacement of poor southerners from subsistence practices was part a decades-long process that began during the antebellum period and was by no means limited to the expanding cotton belt. However, the most transformative effects of the "disappearing commons" could only be seen after changing labor relations threatened the ability of farmers to engage in extensive land-use practices on a large scale.[80]

The closing of the open range was a reflection of and response to the increasing irrelevance of the antebellum extensive agricultural regime in the face of environmental alterations made by war and emancipation.[81] For some farmers, practical concerns, including a lack of timber or the presence of disease, made range land less practical; for others, the cause proved to be the decline in livestock-raising and the physical reorganization of plantations. Regardless, the breakdown in land maintenance and the decline in stock-raising rippled outward to gradually corrode the boundaries of the agro-ecological map of the Old South. The foothills of the Appalachians, the "piney woods," the marshes of Louisiana, the sand hills of Georgia, and other areas where farmers once scratched out an existence were inexorably drawn into the staple crop market. The connection between the ecological aspects of intensification and farmers' poverty was most obvious in the so-called new cotton areas, where the introduction of intensive agriculture coincided with a measurable (and often immediate) drop in farmers' self-sufficiency in food production and a corresponding increase in their levels of debt. The subsequent dislocation of laborers and small farmers from subsistence practices and their transition into truly intensive agriculture not only had serious environmental consequences, but also contributed to the cycle of debt and poverty in the postwar period.

For ex-slaves, the environmental consequences of new land-use patterns represented a tragic irony. The small pieces of autonomy black laborers carved out after the war threatened their long-term economic independence by necessitating that they invest in fertilizers, improved implements, and other inputs that were often out of reach for tenants or sharecroppers. As one freedmen lamented, " '[W]hen we make our crops they takes it away from us . . . we labor from one end of a year to another one & we then goes of[f] with nothing.' "[82] The subsequent poverty of tenants converged with race-based critiques of blacks' ability to independently manage farms. In *The Souls of Black Folk*, W. E. B. Du Bois hinted at the interplay between black autonomy, race relations, and land use:

> [Blacks] cannot see why they should take unusual pains to make the white man's land better. . . . On the other hand, the white landowner argues that any attempt to improve these laborers by . . . higher wages . . . or land of their own, would be sure to result in failure. He shows his Northern visitor the scarred and wretched land; the ruined mansions, the worn-out soil and mortgaged acres, and says, This is Negro freedom![83]

Contemporaries recognized the environmental costs of emancipation, but often blamed the degradation of the land or any decline in productivity on the "wandering," "insolent," and "soured" nature of the free black laborer. As Du Bois observed, nineteenth-century whites accused freedpeople of being careless in cultivating their land. A planter in Washington County, Georgia, argued that it was "better by far" to allow land to lie fallow than rent it out, because tenancy "means to sap all the Life out of . . . land . . . and everything else."[84] When lawyer and former Confederate senator Joseph Daniel Pope toured the plantations of South Carolina to report on the state of cotton cultivation for the local Federal authorities, he characterized the once-productive plantations as wastelands disfigured by "crops miserable beyond description." He noted with disgust that little had been done to protect the land from the constant threats of the summer growing season and remarked that "choked up" ditches and overgrown fields marred the landscape. Rotting, unrepaired fences failed to shield crops from the few remaining livestock, and in many places, the exhausted soil resembled "drift sand blown about by the winds." It would not be long, he warned, before the islands were "an unfruitful jungle fit for the habitation of wild beasts and savages only."[85] Although Pope blamed lazy and inattentive freedpeople for the degraded state of the plantation, his remarks reflected the reality that altered labor arrangements had a physical impact on the land. Worsening ecological conditions, rather than unwise cultivation on the part of the tenant, caused the "scarred and wretched" appearance of these farms.

The removal of land maintenance from contracts and the redivision of plantations to support more autonomous labor forces placed stricter physical limits on agricultural outputs. The older land-use methods had allowed southern farmers to circumvent the environmental limitations of their region without requiring investment in expensive inputs (other than labor). This does not mean that slavery was "good" for the environment, nor should it imply that slave-owning cotton planters practiced agriculture in a sustainable way. It is only when compared to the postwar system—intensively cultivated cotton monoculture using commercial fertilizers and little land maintenance—does the ecological importance of antebellum extensive land use become clear. More static cultivation increased erosion, necessitated investment in expensive fertilizers, and reduced self-sufficiency among tenants. These trends added to the already weighty obstacles to black southerners' economic independence. Legal restrictions and crop lien legislation perpetuated poverty and debt; violence and racial bias kept resources out of black hands; and changing market structures exacerbated the inaccessibility of credit. Ecological forces magnified these hallmarks of the postwar cotton economy and contributed to ex-slaves' failure to achieve economic independence.

5

Facing Limits

King Cotton looks from his window
Toward the westering sun,
And he marks with an anguished horror
That his race is almost run.
His form is thin and shrunken,
His check is pale and wan,
And the lines of care on his furrowed brow
Are dread to look upon.

—Horatio Alger Jr., "King Cotton" (1875)

William Wallace White was, first and foremost, a tobacco farmer. He had other concerns, of course. A fairly religious man, Methodist camp meetings dotted White's social calendar, and he served as justice of the peace, officiating marriages and overseeing the small claims suits of his county.[1] But it was the tens of thousands of "hills" cradling his tobacco seedlings each spring that dominated his diary entries, the months of tedious attention to the number of weeds in his rows or the temperature of his tobacco barn fires. A member of the "Nutbush community" of North Carolina planters who drew their livelihoods from the loamy, loosely textured soils along stream beds in Warren and Granville Counties, White owned a place he called Holly Hill. Throughout the 1850s, he planted tobacco, peaches, corn, oats, sweet potatoes, watermelons, and Irish potatoes, renting slaves to supplement the work of his white farm hands. After 1865, White continued his traditional crop regime with a number of hired workers. Most of them were not tenants or sharecroppers, but rather wage laborers who came and went for a few cents a day, anonymously appearing in White's detailed farm diary during the peak months of the tobacco growing and curing seasons.[2]

In the spring of 1873, however, cotton made an unheralded appearance in White's planting schedules. Amid the descriptions of the seasonal tasks associated with tobacco and corn, he unexpectedly noted: "We are having fine growing weather, cotton planted May 1, coming up."[3] What drove White to suddenly invest in cotton? Was he concerned for his finances amid the economic chaos of the early 1870s? Or was the price of cotton too tempting? White's diaries remain curiously silent on the subject. What is clear, however, is that this planting anomaly required other changes to White's decades-long agricultural routine. He did not pay his workers to clear new ground for his cotton experiment. Instead, he chose an old field—a plot of land that had once grown tobacco and, later, corn, until finally weeds and sassafras overran the beds. He did not apply his usual fertilizer combination of ashes and compost to the crop; instead, White purchased eight bags of expensive Peruvian guano. He penned his hogs more and grazed them less, since he needed more ground for cotton cultivation. White began trading the crop as payment for debts or as an advance on the commercial fertilizers on which he increasingly depended. Although the planter never discussed cotton in his diary the way he did his tobacco plants, White and his tenants grew cotton every season after 1873. Tobacco may have been his interest, but cotton was a necessity.[4]

Between 1866 and 1880, cotton's hold on the economies and ecologies of the South escaped its prewar boundaries and invaded regions once dedicated to other cash crops or subsistence agriculture. This period has been called one of "cotton fever," a veritable epidemic of cultivation in response to high post-surrender prices in which all farmers with or without land, regardless of region, plunged into wealth-maximizing, market-dominated agriculture.[5] Robert Somers, in his 1871 travelogue of the southern states, noted the onset of this vogue, describing corn fields replanted in cotton, subsistence farmers struggling to plant the crop in the deadenings of the forests where girdled and dying trees had not yet been cleared, and the capitulation of planters in other industries, such as rice or sugar, to experiment in cotton. Somers depicted William Wallace White's home state as oddly enthusiastic about the crop, despite being at the northern edge of the region suitable for its cultivation. North Carolina's cotton crop was 20 percent larger in 1872 than it had been the previous year, and other states saw similar increases. The USDA reported that, as a whole, southern states averaged 16 percent more cotton in 1872 than in 1871, and saw a 13 percent jump in the number of acres devoted to the crop.[6] Cotton's upward trajectory continued through the 1880s.

The expansion of King Cotton's fiefdom brought further changes in land use and an increasing lack of self-sufficiency, especially among poorer southerners. Like William Wallace White, farmers more frequently penned livestock, continuous cultivation became more common, and fertilizer replaced shifting cultivation. Reliance on imports of foodstuffs skyrocketed. Rates of crop rotation decreased, and rates of livestock disease went up. Elsewhere in Somers's

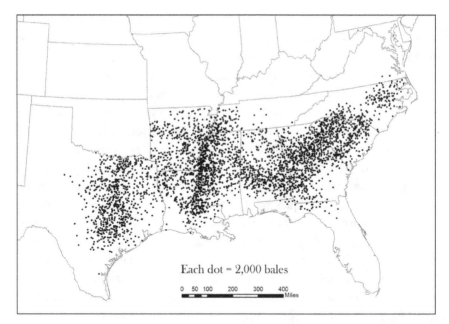

Each dot = 2,000 bales

Figure 5.1 Cotton production, 1890. Map prepared by Michael Austin Mohlenbrok and Jennifer Rahn, Department of Geography, Samford University. Data courtesy of IPUMS National Historical Geographic Information System: Version 12.0 [Database]. University of Minnesota. 2017. http://doi.org/10.18128/D050.V12.0.

travelogue, he writes that "very little livestock is seen on the plantations or about the farmhouses" and remarked on the practice of farmers to adjust their cotton-corn ratios according to the cheapness of grain from the Midwest. Other observers noted how the doctrine of "planting cotton to buy provisions"—generally associated with planters during the late antebellum period—had spread to other classes, as well. "So long as we find it necessary to procure our provisions from the West, even so long will we find it to be impossible to save not only money, but will be often without 'hog and hominy,'" the *Tuscaloosa Independent Monitor* declared.[7] Even in "the Isolated South," where market integration was minimal before 1870, the spread of railroads, mining, and timbering ensured that no part of the region remained untouched by cash-crop integration. Historian Bradley Bond explains, "Where antebellum ideals had espoused the virtues of . . . self-sufficient production within the market economy . . . creating a [New] South of plantations, factories, and railroads required a degree of interconnectedness with the market economy that antebellum citizens, despite their desire for the rewards of the market, had not known."[8]

What caused such a fundamental shift in attitudes toward the doctrine of self-sufficiency in marginal farming areas known for their relative crop diversity or subsistence agriculture before the war? Why did poor southerners, in particular, grow staples at the expense of everything else? It was understandable for farmers to plant cotton when prices were at their peak in 1865 and 1866, but it was not in the immediate interests of individuals to depend on one plant for an income while they were also reducing the acreage dedicated to foodstuffs.

The economics of "cotton fever" stemmed from changes in the ways that southerners negotiated with nature. Ecological processes ensured that cotton production worsened the problems of wartime material loss and financial vulnerability, ensnaring growers in a feedback loop of degrading ecologies. Contrary to the theories of the day, it was not southern farmers' failure to adopt intensive agriculture that caused economic stagnation, but their inability to continue extensive land-use techniques amid wartime debt, constraints on capital, and postwar shifts in market relations. As a result, cotton growers were less insulated from the vicissitudes of agriculture and lacked the luxury of spreading economic risk out over multiple harvests. Ultimately, changes to the natural environment during the decades following the Civil War acted as an important catalyst in the restricting economic opportunity for southern farmers. As one government agent flatly stated, "Nothing pays but cotton, and cotton does not pay."[9]

Just as important as the causes of "cotton fever" are its consequences. This chapter surveys the ecological implications of cotton's spread. The natural characteristics of southern soils and antebellum farming practices contributed to a significant amount of soil erosion and nutrient depletion across the region. Along with this legacy, the Civil War's removal of livestock and provisions, the spread of continuous cultivation, and the subsequent elimination of subsistence practices further reduced farmers' ability to restore the soils they had. The resulting ecological and economic displacement spurred a wave of inter- and intra-regional migration, but expansion as it existed in the antebellum era was far less feasible. In previous decades, displaced farmers had colonized the edges of newly acquired territory, where extensive land use carved farms from frontiers. But the ecological refugees of the postwar cotton belt escaped up the slopes of mountains and into swamps, increasing the number of improved acres but doing little for their livelihoods. Eventually, it was those fleeing the older South of cotton and debt who peopled the "New" South of industry and railroads.

Around the time William Wallace White was converting old fields to cotton production, the *Reconstructed Farmer* celebrated the explosive output of North Carolina's cotton lands. The editors noted that all the figures regarding improved acres, total bales produced, yields, and even weather forecasts pointed to a particularly profitable year for North Carolina's cotton farmers. In fact, increased investment in fertilizers meant that yields in 1872 might surpass even those of the fabled cotton lands of the Old Southwest. The rich soils of Alabama's Black Belt only managed 165 pounds of "white gold" per acre, whereas the publication recorded an average of 175 pounds in the Tar Heel state. "A remarkably favorable season," the editors concluded.[10] Of course, what the *Reconstructed Farmer* did not mention was that North Carolina's corn crops had fallen below average—just as they had the previous year—a dangerous trend that augured a shortage of fodder for livestock and meal for laborers. The publication's optimistic presentation of the figures also obscured the physical effects of "Cottondom." Just a few years later, the *Hand-book of North Carolina*'s "General Sketch" of the state warned against buying cotton lands because of their past usage and present appearance. The publication contrasted the eastern section of the state, where the fields once worked by slaves had been temporarily destroyed by war and now served as parcels on which sharecroppers could grow cotton, to the beauteous, "bold and even rugged" aspect of the mountainous counties along the state's western edge. Hay and pasture crops were rare in the North Carolina's eastern half, making livestock expensive, whereas "clover and other grasses clothe the hills" of the west. The streams of the east "are dyed to a sable hue" by the erosion of decaying soils, but the mountain streams are "as clear and pure as they flowed from their fountains." Although the *Hand-book* did not explicitly blame cotton farmers for the degradation of the landscape, the Sketch's authors clearly recognized that the record number of bales highlighted by the *Reconstructed Farmer* had, over time, resulted in a distinctively despoiled agricultural landscape.[11]

The jump in production numbers reported in the *Reconstructed Farmer* continued to soar, and not just in North Carolina. Factors' records provide evidence of the noticeable shift toward cotton monoculture. Whereas the crops bartered with or sold to factorages were of startling variety during the 1865–1870 planting seasons—farmers traded everything from corn and potatoes to wax and deer hides--after that time, the items planters and farmers mentioned became less and less varied. By the mid-1870s, most correspondence related to one thing: cotton. Farmers pledged cotton for food, they pledged cotton for cash advances, they pledged cotton for fertilizers. J. L. Johnson, a debt collector for a factorage in Georgia, declared, "There is no money in this country until cotton is sold."[12] Most of the letters to cotton factors during the 1870s are farmers' desperate pleas for provisions for their families or their laborers. I. A. Grennet of southern Georgia, for instance, sent all of the cotton he had made for the year 1874 to secure enough guano to start the next crop and 200 pounds of bacon to feed his hands—there was nothing left to settle any debts and he had not raised enough corn to trade. "*You have now every pound of cotton* I made," Grennet anxiously declared. "Most keenly do I feel falling so much behind it can't be helped. You must bear kindly with me *all will be right in the end.*"[13]

The increasing attention given to cotton production among farmers of all classes was not limited to the small corner of Georgia in which I. A. Grennet farmed. Over the course of the Reconstruction period, the Old South boundaries of the regions devoted to rice, sugar, tobacco, grains, stock, and other crops blurred as cotton production expanded. In the decade between 1880 and 1890 alone, the acreage devoted to cotton in Georgia increased by 28 percent, in Mississippi by 37 percent, in Alabama by 18 percent, in South Carolina by 45 percent, in Louisiana by 46 percent, in North Carolina by 28 percent, and in Arkansas by 63 percent.[14] Although the southern edge of the cotton belt held steady because of the profitability of sugar cane and, to some extent, of rice, the northern limits of the cotton-growing region continued to slide and shift in the decades following the Civil War. By the dawn of the New South period, cotton production across the region had far surpassed the boom years of the late ante-bellum period, and more farmers than ever cultivated it. The postwar Cotton Kingdom brightly outshone its antebellum predecessor.

Several economic and legal factors championed King Cotton's reconstitution of its power after the Confederate defeat, luring farmers toward the crop. Cotton commanded a considerably higher price on the international market at the close of the war than it had at the time of secession. Whereas "good" or "middling" cotton sold for from 8 cents to 11 cents per pound in 1860, those same bales of cotton were worth between 50 cents and 83 cents per pound in 1865. "Never since the world began," proclaimed the *Richmond Republic* in January of 1866, "did agriculture offer such rich rewards to labor as the agriculture of the cotton and tobacco States of the South does at this time." Never was agriculture so promising, never had its profits been so certain. All available resources should be funneled into the production of cotton, the *Republic* argued, for the high price of cotton meant that any farmer could recover his prewar wealth. Henry Warren, a native of Massachusetts, admitted that it was the editorials filling the columns of the *New York Tribune* and other papers that were reporting on the "fabulous sums of money to be made growing cotton in the sunny south" that inspired him to quit his post as a teacher and move to Mississippi.[15]

Table 5.1 **U.S. Cotton Prices**

Year	Price (per lb) in New York	Year	Price (per lb) in New York
1860	11 cents	1869	29 cents
1864	$1.01	1870	24 cents
1865	83 cents	1873	18 cents
1866	43 cents	1875	15 cents
1867	32 cents	1877	11 cents
1868	25 cents	1879	10 cents

Source: Prices from M. B. Hammond, *The Cotton Industry* (New York: MacMillan Company, 1897), reprinted in Wright, "Cotton Competition and the Post-Bellum Recovery of the American South," 611.

Prices were indeed high in the late 1860s, although the price of cotton dropped precipitously through the 1870s. The value of cotton in 1866 was half that of 1865; by 1870, the best quality cotton sold for twenty-four cents per pound. Anecdotal evidence suggests planters averaged between twenty and twenty-two cents per pound during the winter of 1870. As farmers devoted more acreage to the crop, a market glut forced down prices. Too much supply and not enough demand meant that by 1879, cotton was fetching just ten cents per pound. Poor-quality cotton (of which there was plenty) sold for as little as five or six cents. But as prices dropped, farmers, particularly small farmers and black tenants, con-tinued to expand production, eschewing grain or food crops for an all-cotton approach. Even the cultivation of corn—the true "king" of southern crops in terms of the acreage devoted to it—declined as cotton hardened its grip on the region. By 1890, the South was making more cotton than ever, but farmers were poorer and not as productive in terms of bales produced per capita.[16]

The slavish devotion to the crop amid falling prices has been explained by financial and legal constraints, linking the cycle of poverty and dependency associated with tenancy and sharecropping to debt, lack of capital, and, later, crop lien laws.[17] During the antebellum period, it was common for cotton plant-ers to exist in a complex web of credit and debt involving factors, merchants, and neighbors—bankruptcy was rarer because slaves provided both collateral and currency. The war swept away the credit system and sources of cash of the Old South, leaving only farmers' debts behind. A large portion of the South's wealth evaporated without compensation during emancipation. Lands, too, depreciated in value. The state auditor for North Carolina, for instance, recorded a steep drop in land values in William Wallace White's county during the same year he began to plant cotton. Similar examples come from all over the South. In Tuscaloosa, Alabama, Robert Jemison, Jr. saw "no escape from utter Bankruptcy and ruin." His property, worth over $200,000 before the war (including slaves), was worth less than $20,000. Even if he sold off everything, he could not pay the full amount owed to his creditors from before and during the war. In East Feliciana Parish, Louisiana, a planter named Henry Marston faced multiple creditors at the same time: his prewar factor siphoned the profits from Marston's cotton crop to pay old debts, a neighbor hounded Marston for the money owed for mules, and Marston still owed money from the purchase of his plantation, Ashland, in the 1850s.[18] Thus, explanations for how and why land practices and crop mixes changed during the postwar period concentrate on the specter of debt and the lack of capital. One historian summarizes the consensus, writing, "The effects of wartime debt, currency collapse, and physical destruction aggra-vated the planters' traditional dependence on credit," the acute need for which "eventually forced the South into a greater dependence on one-crop cultiva-tion than had been the case during the regime of slavery."[19] Cotton was the only feasible way for farmers to escape their debts, merchants required it as payment, and landlords insisted on its cultivation.

This narrative of southern agriculture overlooks the environmental processes that underpinned these fundamental reorientations of economic and legal systems in the Reconstruction South. The antebellum land-use regime conditioned farmers to expect relatively profitable crop production without expensive inputs because shifting cultivation and expansion mitigated decreasing yields. But war and emancipation intensified production and eliminated (on many lands) key practices that made farming profitable.[20] The division of plantations or farms increased continuous cultivation and decreased land maintenance, as did the collapse of shifting cultivation due to woodland clearance or timbering. Livestock shortages and changing fence laws reduced rates of stock-raising, particularly among landless farmers, reinforcing their reliance on fertilizers. The methods used to provide subsistence in the South, such as hunting, foraging, keeping livestock on common lands, and maintaining small garden plots on the edges of the plantation, were increasingly seen as privileges to be paid for rather than rights to common spaces. Because of the money farmers owed for fertilizers to replace lost nutrients, the loss of just one crop to livestock or floods could mean bankruptcy or the forfeiture of lands and property.

In short, farmers required the methods of extensive agriculture to stay afloat, but existed in an increasingly intensive system. The desire of both planters and tenants to maximize acreage in favor of cash crops was, at first, economically rational, when prices were high and yields favorable due to the positive effects of wartime crop conversion. However, continuous cultivation without access to new land or rotating crops caused soil erosion rates to skyrocket and levels of soil nutrients to suffer. The increasing expense of feeding livestock amid the repeal of fence laws across the region, as well as the spread of infectious animal diseases, harmed small farmers' self-sufficiency and removed the option of using animal manure instead of commercial fertilizers. So farmers had to plant cotton to pay for the provisions, livestock, fertilizers, and other necessities needed to plant cotton. This cycle ensnared planters, but those most affected by the disconnect between environmental conditions and agricultural possibilities were "plain folk" and newly freed blacks who were figuratively chained to degrading lands without the capital to move on or the autonomy to improve them. Those who lacked the capital to invest in constant infusions of fertilizers, raise new breeds of stock, or pay for new land once the old soil had washed away often failed to make any money at the end of each year's crop.[21]

The records of laborers and tenants on Nimrod Porter's Tennessee farm illustrate the human dimensions of this conflict between ecologies and economics. Richard Trotter appeared on Porter's farm in the last spring of the Civil War, declaring that his mistress was dead and that he needed somewhere to work and someone to take him on. According to the census, Trotter was about twenty years old at the time, having been born around 1845 in Missouri. Porter took the freed slave in; since most of Porter's male slaves spent their time working on fortifications, the farmer could use the man's labor. After the surrender, only Trotter stayed on Porter's farm. On July 24, 1865, Porter recorded in his diary: "All hands have quit and went to find work to do except Rich. He agrees to stay with me and I will pay his wages." For two years, Rich "knocked about the place," performing tasks for cash. He hauled feed, rebuilt fences, kept neighbors' stock out of Porter's fields, and sowed crops. In 1867, Trotter married Louisa Martin, and the ex-slave became his own head of household on a plot he rented for half shares from Nimrod Porter.[22]

By this time, Porter's crop regime centered on cotton, rather than the mixed-crop approach he took before the conflict. Trotter planted enough of that particular crop that he hired additional help at picking time each year, and Porter received half the proceeds of Trotter's sale of cotton (which Porter handled, of course). By the early 1870s, the ex-slave's growing family required ever-larger supplies of bacon, meal, cloth, and other items not provided through their own farming efforts or their agreement with the Tennessee planter. Since Porter no longer ranged hogs, he did not allow tenants to graze animals either. Porter did not mention garden plots for his laborers, and so presumably, Trotter planted cotton and corn on the same land every year while Porter provided the security for his tenant's advances from nearby merchants. By the time of Nimrod Porter's death, Trotter was hopelessly in the red. Despite taking on extra jobs throughout the year, hauling feed, or tending penned hogs for Porter, Trotter's cotton sales could not cover what he owed for cash advances or foodstuffs.[23] The clash between prewar and postwar land-use systems conspired to keep economic security for many farmers, both white and black, out of reach.

This gap between intensive use and the natural context of southern faming was apparent as early as 1865, particularly to those moving to the South from elsewhere. For northern emigrants and businessmen, the postwar South loomed as a new frontier, a place previously closed off by the abhorrent institution of slavery, ready to be settled, exploited, and remade. Northern men looking to enter the "get rich quick scheme of planting cotton" flooded the Treasury Department with requests for abandoned lands in the South after 1863, hoping to rent better lands at better prices than were available to them in New England or the Old Northwest. Two lawyers from New York, W. W. Mitchell and Charles T. Ames, noticed the emigration of such men and decided to form a real estate company to buy up land around Atlanta and Macon, Georgia, to lease to northerners. Mitchell, especially, got caught up in plantation fever and planned to purchase twelve thousand acres of farmland for his own use.[24] He assumed that he would cultivate over 50 percent of it and use the rest for barns, stables, and pastures.

Mitchell theorized his laborers would receive hundreds of dollars a year in wages, and the profit from his "improved" cotton would more than pay for their work.[25] Mitchell's experiment failed because he did not consider how the northern farming style would work within the constraints of southern institutions, traditional land use, or environment. At the time—even without the chaos of the war—most southerners only cultivated 30 percent of the land they owned and had very few grounds that would have been recognizable as pastures to the northern eye. These conditions matched the land's capacity and the soil and climate conditions common to the South. How could laborers earn hundreds of dollars per year, when payments for fertilizer, stock, fencing, barns, seed, and other requirements of the "northern system" chipped away at Mitchell's profits? E. T. Wright, a New Englander who attempted to run a South Carolina plantation after the war, remarked that northern-style agriculture "can be managed much more easy in the lecture room or an editors sanctorum . . . than in the field practically here."[26]

As W. W. Mitchell and others discovered, production of cotton ran up against several environmental limits, most significantly soil-nutrient deficiencies. The soils of many lands throughout the expanding cotton belt, which were intensely weathered and contained relatively low levels of organic matter, could not support the removal of the same nutrients year after year without either burning vegetation or the purchase of fertilizer. Studies performed on the "Old Rotation" plot at the Auburn University Agricultural Experiment Station showed that with late nineteenth-century fertilizers and no crop rotation, cotton and corn yields continued to decrease every year due to the buildup of disease and pests in the soil, as well as chemical imbalances.[27] If a farmer planted cotton every year, but only applied nitrogen-rich fertilizer, then after a few years, declining phosphorous, calcium, magnesium, and potassium levels would harm crop productivity or, more likely, the quality of the lint and the plant's ability to withstand drought. One of the cheapest, most effective ways to address these issues was the intercropping of corn and peas in order to add nitrogen and plant biomass to the soil. However, landlords began to dictate more continuous staple crop production at the expense of prewar soil improvement techniques in order to ensure that, as planter Adrian Sebastian Van de Graaff insisted, "there will be something to show for [the tenant's] rent."[28]

The southern climate also limited continuous planting, for row crops suffered in the region's heavy rains. Without erosion control measures, the rapid loss of topsoil streaked fields with deep gullies and exposed the dense earth beneath the surface layer. Subsoils contained "tenacious" clay devoid of nutrients needed for plant growth and unable to retain moisture properly. Instead of trickling down through the topsoil, rain pooled atop the clay and created standing water in fields. If heavy rainfall gave way to temporary drought, as it often did in the latter half of the southern summer, the same clayey earth cracked open as the unabsorbed moisture disappeared in the sun's heat. Neither flooding nor "baking" in the sun was beneficial to cotton stands; subsoil planting promoted a variety of rusts, or fungal diseases, as well as stunted growth. Sources noted flooding on farms that "poisoned the fields with stagnant water" and made the soil "actually sterile," as well as soils that "baked" and cracked when rain levels were low. For these reasons, soil scientists have called the focus on continuous cultivation in tenancy and sharecropping arrangements "generally disastrous."[29] By 1880, the rates of erosion on cotton farms prompted Eugene Hilgard to write, "One of the principal reasons for abandoning lands . . . was the washes and gullies" that created a barren and unfruitful agricultural landscape.[30]

A lack of field maintenance or shifting cultivation amid continuous planting further eroded the profitability of the soil. If fields were not ditched regularly, the topsoil dumped its nutrients into nearby waterways. The sediment washing from farms filled streams and rivers with the "detritus" of cultivation, obliterating shoals, altering river currents, creating narrower channels, and making flooding more frequent. "Many of the navigable streams in Georgia are rapidly becoming little more than shallow creeks," a newspaper reported. "Every year . . . the soil of the cultivated lands more easily finds its way into the channels."[31] Of course, soil was not the only material washing from farms into waterways. A contributor to the *Southern Cultivator* begged his fellow farmers to pay for better ditches because of the loss of fertilizer through washing. "By thorough drainage we can save our uplands from the inevitable gully," he maintained. "Without it, concentrated fertilizers . . . will only find their way to the nearest creek." The *Southern Planter* suggested in 1869 that though ditching was expensive under the "free" labor system, "it seems to us that a portion of our money might be more profitably invested in that way" than in fertilizers to replace eroded nutrients or even risk the loss of crops to flooding.[32]

Erosion thus became an acute symptom of the failing southern land-use system. The accelerated exhaustion of the land since the war was obvious to observers, particularly on the thinner soils and steeper slopes of the southern Piedmont, where continuous staple cultivation caused a noticeable spike in erosive land use during this period. The appearance of sharecropper and tenant farms was "a miserable panorama of . . . rain-gullied fields . . . dirt, poverty, disease, drudgery, and monotony that stretches for a thousand miles across the cotton belt."[33] Scholars have since reached similar conclusions regarding agricultural methods in this particular region. Discussing the Carolina Piedmont, soil scientists Daniel Richter and Daniel Markowitz found that before 1860, shifting cultivation had returned almost enough nitrogen to the soil to meet crops' needs. By 1870, that was no longer true.[34] Continuous planting without investing in land maintenance or having the ability to move to new ground resulted in the acceleration of erosion, the proliferation of gullies, and the exposure of relatively infertile subsoils. In the cotton-growing interiors of North Carolina, South Carolina, and Georgia, historical geographer Stanley Trimble calculated that rates of soil erosion rose between 70 percent and 120 percent between 1860 and 1880 as farmers planted clean-cut rows of cotton or corn year after year.[35]

The decline in shifting cultivation practices and the increase in soil erosion produced a system that became an archetype of decay and agricultural irresponsibility, one that led to a more insidious, destructive form of land abandonment across the South. Before, and in many cases, during the Civil War, land abandonment was often equated with a long fallow, but this was not true on the cotton farms of the postwar period. One soil scientist commented, "Several million acres of land in the rolling parts of the Southeast that formerly produced good cotton have been forced out of production because of severe erosion; most of it is either so infertile as to be practically worthless for further cultivation or so badly dissected with gullies that plowing is a physical impossibility."[36] Because the lands in question were "infertile" at the time of desertion, no secondary vegetation sprouted. Thus soil erosion accelerated. Continuous cultivation followed by a much more permanent form of land abandonment helps explain how the percentage of improved acres in farms did not increase significantly in the cotton belt between 1860 and 1880; and yet the number of farms doubled, tripled, and quadrupled in some states during the same period. [37] Intensive cultivation of cotton, then, sometimes resulted in a type of land abandonment that prevented that land from being renewed for later use.

Ongoing environmental degradation was a primary driver of farmers' reduced productivity and caused a measurable decline in yields, despite growers' mounting debts to the fertilizer industry. In Alabama, farms produced an average of 144 pounds per acre of cotton between 1870 and 1875. In the years between 1876 and 1880, cotton crops averaged 136.4 pounds per acre. From 1881 to 1886, however, cotton lands realized only 122.8 pounds per acre.[38] The declines proved more drastic on older plantation lands. In Tennessee, farmers needed to plant a little over two acres in the crop to make a bale of cotton in 1879. A decade later, cultivators required four acres to produce a bale. Only Texas and Arkansas—relatively recent additions to the South's cotton empire—maintained decent yields. This was true not only for cotton but for corn as well. The staple crop of the southern diet was just as sensitive as cotton to soil-nutrient deficiencies and erosion, and the yields per acre of corn in states across the South also spiraled downward during this period. In 1869, South Carolinians averaged 11.6 bushels per acre, while in 1875, they made 10.2 bushels per acre. Some states experienced more dramatic drops in corn yields. Alabama grew 15 bushels to the acre in 1869; in 1875, farms only yielded 12.6 bushels. Louisiana farmers produced only 15.5 bushels per acre in 1875, whereas they managed 25 bushels in 1869.[39]

The reasons cotton farmers were less self-sufficient in foodstuffs and sharecroppers were so poor has been a topic of debate in southern history for decades. In *One Kind of Freedom*, economic historians Roger Ransom and Richard Sutch argued that it was the lender who dictated the overproduction of cotton in order to "drive the farmer into increased dependence upon purchased supplies," resulting in a glut on the market. In a response to their work, Gavin Wright contended that southern poverty was not due to an overproduction of cotton or the predatory practices of lenders, but "the determinants of population growth, the obstacles to Southern industrialization, and the course of migration to Northern jobs."[40]

Attention to the environment offers a simpler explanation. In an intensive agricultural system, the southern landscape required too many inputs to remain profitable year after year. Combined with the war's removal of agricultural resources, the acceleration of environmental change between 1860 and 1880 undermined yields and gave farmers very little choice in what crops they could plant in order to carry on profitable agricultural operations. Diversification, though it would have been ideal, would not have paid for the supplies required to maintain production on a continuously cultivated tenant plot, especially as the common spaces needed for subsistence practices disappeared. As livestock-raising declined in the wake of the war and repeal of the fence laws, pork, beef, milk, and butter locally produced in the cotton states cost more than that produced in the agricultural regions of the Midwest.[41]

The entanglement of continuous cultivation, environmental degradation, and poverty is vividly illustrated in the artwork and photographs of the New South period. The photograph "Home of the Cotton Picker" depicts muddy, eroded land struggling to produce cotton around a sharecropper's cabin. But the cotton stalks are weak and underdeveloped, unable to support the bolls that are almost dripping off the plant. The staple is growing right up to the porch of the house, and there is no visible garden or other area for food crops. A Virginia rail fence runs behind the property barring the "picker" from a sparsely wooded space that could be used to range animals.

A more famous image is the mural "The Cotton Load Is Too Heavy," painted by John Augustus Walker, which exemplified the linkages between the environmental conditions of cotton farms and the economic burden of a lack of self-sufficiency. In the mural, the crop fields are not fenced, indicating that either no stock exists to threaten the crops or the farm is located in a stock-law district. The land is denuded of trees and topsoil, and red-clay gullies transect the hillsides. The only crop being grown is cotton, picked by several wage laborers, and

Figure 5.2 "Home of the Cotton Picker," 1880. This photograph taken by William Henry Jackson captures the visual result of the cotton-based tenancy system. Jackson took the photograph in either Louisiana or Mississippi. Detroit Publishing Company Photograph Collection, Prints and Photographs Division, Library of Congress. LC-DIG-det-4a27008.

a sharecropper is on the road leading to the farm, returning from town with peas, corn meal, and lard in his buggy.

Whereas even antebellum plantations usually grew their own peas, had plenty of corn on hand, and could manufacture their own lard from their animals stocks, by the time of this scenario, the farmer was planting cotton to buy even the most basic provisions so that he could feed his family long enough to get the next cotton crop harvested. As one desperate farmer pleaded with a merchant in 1874: "I have sent you every pound of cotton I made . . . Now are you going to help me along once more or cast me off? If the former send 200 lb of bacon, ½ sides, ½ shoulders. I think 150 to 200 will carry me along." Shrinking incomes in the region led to a more monotonous and less balanced diet as imported meat was less healthy. At least one historian points to the "cotton burden" as the beginning of the South's long struggle with heart disease and obesity.[42]

Both census and anecdotal evidence corroborates the reduction in self-sufficiency on yeoman and tenant farms. In the account books of Charles King, the grandson of one of the wealthiest men in Perry County, Alabama, the lists of items his laborers purchased shifted over time. In the 1870s, tenants bought a diverse mix of foodstuffs and luxury items, such as tobacco or whiskey. By the 1880s, tenants were only buying peas, corn, and bacon.[43] In a study conducted on the Georgia Piedmont, historian J. William Harris found that the cotton-to-corn ratio was the most unbalanced on tenant farms, specifically on black tenant farms. On an antebellum plantation with 250 acres in cultivation, the cotton-to-corn ratio was twenty-seven acres of cotton to every ten acres of corn, whereas on small black-operated tenant farms in 1879, the ratio was fifty-eight acres of cotton to every ten acres of corn.[44] Maximizing cotton acreage at the expense of corn eliminated the primary source of fodder for livestock (further weakening the logic for keeping animals) and forced farmers to rely on planters for a product that formed the backbone of the southern diet. J. H. Norwood, a contributor to the *Southern Planter* throughout the 1870s, summarized the process: "Figures show the fact to be that we have not only made money in raising cotton since the war, but that we have made immense sums of it. What has become of it? We have spent it buying mules, corn, meat, hay, agricultural implements, wagons, fertilizers, and almost everything else we consume."[45]

The "new" system contrasted negatively with what many farmers had known before. Thomas Maguire, a Georgia cotton farmer, fondly remembered the agriculture of his county in the 1850s as a "self-feeding and a self-sustaining one." Since that time, raising cotton to buy supplies had replaced farming methods in which agriculturalists raised provisions and livestock so that cotton could be a source of profit. "We have to bow in humble submission to king cotton," he concluded. "We borrow money that we may make more cotton and less home supplies."[46] Even Henry Grady, the famous promoter of commerce and industry in the New South, lectured his fellow southerners on the absurdity of planting cash crops in such a bountiful natural environment only to allow merchants far from home to confiscate the profits of their cultivation. "To raise cotton and send its princely revenues to the west for supplies, and to the east for usury, would be misfortune if soil and climate forced such a curse. When both invite independence, to remain in slavery is a crime."[47]

Along with upended expectations for the type of farming that was possible in the region came changes in the social structures of agricultural communities. The inside covers of two crumbling plantation account books from the 1890s contain a list of instructions for handling sharecroppers and tenants, one entitled "Suggestions," and the other, "Policy." The writer Adrian Sebastian Van de Graaff was a judge who had married into a wealthy cotton-planting family in Tuscaloosa. As Van de Graaff collected the accumulated wisdom of his father-in-law—who had run the plantation since the 1870s—the judge-turned-planter recorded this advice in the margins of his ledgers.[48] At the time, Van de Graaff had over thirty tenants, most of whom were on fixed share or cash rentals for land plots ranging in size from three to a hundred acres, as well as nine laborers who received a monthly cash wage. Some of the "Suggestions" indicated that Van de Graaff's father-in-law had told him to "try to get collected up as soon as possible after the first of November" and to "look to the collection of white tenant rents especially (they are the hardest to get)," but the "Policy" is very telling:

> Advance as little as practicable.
> Never coddle a tenant . . .
> Don't try to raise stock.
> Employees in our debt are paid half and credited half.
> Try to make every man cultivate some cotton so that there will be
>   something to show for his rent.[49]

The advice Van de Graaff inherited from previous managers of his planta-tion demonstrates just how great the transformation of the southern plan-tation had been since the Civil War. Although the conflict barely disrupted the makeup of the antebellum planter elite—those who were wealthy and had considerable landholdings before the war were often still comparatively well-off afterward—the persistence of the planter class did not mean that the plantation complex remained unchanged after the initial upheavals of eman-cipation.[50] For instance, landlords fearful of a labor shortage after the war encouraged tenants' dependency on the plantation for income, but by the late nineteenth century, the profitability of the agricultural system had decayed so greatly, and the cycle of debt in which most tenants or smaller farmers found themselves seemed so permanent that planters wanted to "advance as little as practicable."[51] Furthermore, the advice to forgo raising stock and to "make every man cultivate a little cotton" illustrates how planters' ideas regarding the end goals of agriculture had diverged from the antebellum ideal. No longer did planters even pretend to want the "self-sufficient" farm or to create "independ-ence" from northern or Midwestern markets forces, as some had professed to in the days after the Civil War. Clearly, the choices being made by farmers, such as William Gibbs McAdoo of Georgia or James Washington Matthews of Tennessee, to raise a cash crop at the expense of stock-raising or the produc-tion of food crops in 1866 or 1867 had persisted to become the norm across the region.

Ultimately, environmental limits help to explain why, once prices dropped, farmers could not get out of cotton production and why cotton farms appeared so degraded. Planters could often ill afford the implements, seed, or provisions promised to tenants; tenants often could not afford food or rent when their share of the crop failed to pay off the advances made to them throughout the year. The inability of the region's soils to support continuous cultivation without the use of costly fertilizers, the subsequent increase in soil erosion on tenant farms and the decrease in yields, the lapse in crop rotation that would have cheaply ameliorated the problem, and the worsening lack of self-sufficiency reinforced debt. The intensification of agriculture in the antebellum plantation belts created a tide of cash-crop refugees who shifted the geography of the South during the postwar period. Unlike expansion in the antebellum period, some of those who migrated did not go west. Rather, they put land previously considered unsuitable for cash-crop production into cultivation, carrying with them a destructive, intensive system.

William Wallace White's diaries obliquely refer to "unrest" among black laborers in his area during the late 1860s and 1870s. Farmers across the region used similar language to describe the renegotiation of social and economic boundaries following emancipation. What White called "unrest" others labeled an "exodus," for thousands of freedpeople left the seaboard states of North Carolina, South Carolina, and Georgia during these years in pursuit of land and opportunities farther west.[52] North Carolina's Freedmen's Bureau transported ex-slaves in family groups and gangs of male laborers in an effort to reduce destitution and dependence on the government. The owners of the cotton factorage, Watt and Phingy, wrote to the bureau requesting transportation for three hundred freedmen and their families. One of the partners in the firm, Jasper Watt, owned a cotton plantation in Greenwood, Mississippi and needed field hands. Watt promised to pay the freedpeople based on contracts approved by the North Carolina bureau, provide one schoolteacher for the laborers' children, hold a weekly reading of the Gospel, and "tolerate no harsh treatment" by his overseer. Although Watt and Phingy had yet to recruit any ex-slaves, they were confident that three hundred black families would be willing to uproot their lives and travel hundreds of miles to plant cotton. They were right. As Phingy pointed out, "the lands are so poor" where the freedmen live, they "will realize almost nothing for their year's work" if they fail to move to a state with a more robust cotton economy. The environment, he implied, could not support profitable agriculture. "Many [freedmen] are satisfied of this fact and are willing and anxious to go west."[53]

The exodus of ex-slaves seen in the "Records Related to Transportation" of the North Carolina Freedmen's Bureau was arguably a continuation of the demographic upheaval of the war years. During the conflict, over 500,000 enslaved men, women, and children fled to Union lines, attached themselves to army trains, or congregated on the edge of Federal encampments in a desperate attempt to transform the horrors of armed conflict into the chance of freedom. Most of these self-emancipated slaves streamed into what were known as "contraband camps." These settlements were, at their core, refugee camps.[54] Like the modern-day refugees from war-ravaged Syria or drought-stricken Somalia, these slaves fled their homes searching for a way to survive amid escalating violence, food scarcities, and the absence of medical care.

The movement and migration of ex-slaves did not end in 1865, although historians cease to use the label "refugee" after that point. At the close of the war, thousands of blacks swelled the class of seminomadic southerners who bounced from farm to farm, seeking higher wages, larger shares, or better opportunities to purchase land. Poor whites experienced the same issues of economic displacement and moved almost as often, but most contemporaries commented on the novel sight of emancipated slaves crowding the roads. L. W. Walsh, a Freedmen's Bureau agent in South Carolina, reported in 1867 that "so many freedpeople have left for the west, that people are becoming alarmed. . . . Large numbers have left for Florida, Mississippi, and Arkansas, more would do so had they the means of transportation."[55] Farmers raised similar concerns in North Carolina and Georgia. Referring to the bygone practice in the upper South of planters selling slaves to planters in the lower South, S. W. Ficklin wrote to a friend in the Black Belt of Alabama, complaining, "We are losing the negro laborers going south faster than in our better days."[56] Turner Whitfield, a white farmer in a region of Mississippi that was rapidly filling up with large plantations worked by black sharecroppers, declared in 1875 that he was moving to Florida, as were many of his peers. "A great many persons are leaving this place, a few have left, and large numbers are going to leave. . . . I think all the white people will have to leave this country and give it up to the negroes." Those who recognized the centrality of black labor to southern farms on the east coast, however, lamented the loss of potential workers in such numbers. A Colonel Smith, one of the largest landholders in North Carolina, complained, "If they leave us, I don't see how we're going to get along." [57]

Histories of the postwar period emphasize more hopeful motivations for migration from rural spaces: the exercise of the newfound "right to move" after being freed, reuniting with family members or children following the surrender, the improvement of material prospects through the abandonment of war-torn areas, and the opening of public lands through the Homestead Act, which attracted aspiring farmers. However, the ability of older lands to support economic independence amid the decline of extensive land use also motivated these migrations. Just as the freedpeople willing to travel to Watt's Mississippi plantation doubted the capacity of the "poor lands" of North Carolina to provide them with a decent livelihood, so, too, did thousands of other farmers and laborers view the older, more fragile agricultural landscapes of the antebellum plantation belt as quagmires of poverty and debt. Environmental limits on profitable cultivation acted in conjunction with a series of "push" and "pull" factors to redraw the agricultural map of the South. This was not the mirror image of antebellum expansion seen across the divide of the Civil War, for there were fewer places east of the Mississippi River where extensive land-use practices could be practiced. Rather than the diffusion of extensive agricultural practices along the outer edges of the continually moving border between frontier and settlement, postbellum expansion often brought intensive agricultural practices to already settled areas that had been previously isolated or ignored.

Ex-slaves' newfound freedom of movement and the development of a "rudimentary free market" based on black labor proved to be a significant driver of internal migration in the immediate postwar years. As journalist Whitelaw Reid discovered after visiting a Louisiana sugar plantation in 1866, all the ex-slaves "knew they were perfectly free to go away if they wished," and some did.[58] For most of those who decided to move it was the opportunity for better wages that pulled them out of Virginia, Georgia, Alabama, and the Carolinas to places further south or west—the Mississippi Delta region, Louisiana, Kentucky, and the cotton plantations of west Tennessee. John Van Hook, an ex-slave originally from Franklin, North Carolina, recalled the excitement and hope as his fellow slaves decided whether they wanted to stay at home, chase better wages, or pursue nonagricultural labor elsewhere. "Lots of the darkies left after they heard about folks getting rich working on the railroads in Tennessee and about the high wages that were being paid on those big plantations in Mississippi," Van Hook recalled. He stayed in North Carolina for several years, but eventually went southwest to Georgia. Of course, thousands also applied to the bureau for transportation to be reunited with families torn apart by war and slavery, and so applications by freedmen reflect both personal and professional concerns.[59]

Migration was often a multiyear, multistate process. Planters complained of "emigration agents," who distributed pamphlets to freedpeople or actively recruited them to leave their landlords for higher wages on massive cotton or sugar plantations. Van Hook remembered these men who would show up and "stir trouble." He said, "Some of those labor agents were powerful smart about stretching the truth, but those folks that believed them and left home found out that it's pretty much the same the world over."[60] Obtaining the capital or transportation needed to move was still daunting, however, and the internal migration of black laborers was not so much a rushing current as a noticeable trickle. One historian estimates that approximately twenty thousand freedpeople migrated from their homes to places within and outside of the South before 1880.[61] Regardless, white landlords complained of labor shortages due to "negro emigration." A white farmer of Marietta, Georgia, just north of Atlanta, complained that he could not find laborers willing to pick for him. "Money is scarce" so "the negroes all seem to be leaving here, attracted I have no doubt by the high wages offered on the Mississippi." As the geography of agriculture (and money) shifted in the postwar South, blacks followed opportunity from place to place, their movement accelerating during economic downturns. Jake Walker, for instance, stayed on his home plantation in Alabama after being freed, but only for three or four years. Around 1870, he moved to Mississippi, where he worked on shares on a cotton plantation until 1876, when he cast off once more. He landed in Arkansas, remaking himself as a carpenter.[62]

Institutional and legislative initiatives influenced migration, both white and black, as much as individual labor recruiters or family locations. Designed in part to help emancipated slaves and the white farmers dispossessed by the war to achieve economic security through land ownership, the Homestead Act and Southern Homestead Act passed by the US Congress made government or "public" land inexpensive and, on paper, easy to obtain. The Homestead Act of 1862 allowed access to 160-acre sections, with the title granted on the condition that the individual cultivate the land for five years; the Southern Homestead Act of 1866 allowed both whites and blacks to take possession of 80- or 160-acre tracts for just five dollars.[63] However, very few claimants in the South took advantage of the acts. This was largely a problem of geography and capital. Poorer southerners looking to move were concentrated in the older plantation states, and Virginia, North and South Carolina, Georgia, and Tennessee contained no public lands available for settlement. Further limiting homesteaders' options were the scarcity of money and lack of cheap transportation to reach the public lands of Arkansas, Texas, Florida, and Mississippi.

The Freedmen's Bureau set up transportation offices to help facilitate blacks' migration, but its efforts ironically reinforced the restriction of black economic opportunity. The bureau did not focus on aiding family units to establish new lives or land ownership, but particularly after 1866, contracted with large groups of freedmen to travel together at Bureau expense to places such as Watt's Greenwood, Mississippi plantation. The records of the Transportation Bureau of North Carolina, for instance, are organized not by the names of freedpeople who wished to move, but by the names of planters in Texas, Mississippi, west Tennessee, and Louisiana who requested groups of laborers ranging in size from twenty-five to three hundred people.[64] This policy fit nicely with planters' ideas about the black laborers' role in the agricultural landscape. Records indicate that the goal of the office was to empty freedmen's colonies and contraband camps as quickly as possible to reduce the amounts of rations the government issued to freed blacks and to prevent additional outbreaks of smallpox and the other contagious diseases that ravaged the camps. Grand ideas of an independent peasant class of black farmers yielded to immediate budgetary and public-health concerns.[65] The misguided and inadequate efforts of the bureau to resettle ex-slaves caused one North Carolina bureau agent to blame the institution for the fact that "nothing had been accomplished" under the Homestead Act.[66] However, the exercise of freed slaves' "right to move" constituted not only a response to social and political upheaval in the South but also to environmental change.

Intensive cotton cultivation played a significant role in pushing both black and white farmers and laborers out of the plantation centers and into their periphery. Because poorer southerners were increasingly barred from using common spaces to raise livestock and tenancy chained them to degrading soils without the ability to clear new ground, they typically sought better opportunities in more sparsely settled areas in their vicinity. Areas with high densities of slaves in 1860 continued to be centers of the black population after the war, but by 1890, African Americans had dispersed in large numbers to areas bordering the plantation belt, where slaves generally had not lived: north-central Alabama, the piney woods of southern Georgia, and east Tennessee. The Wiregrass region of Georgia, for example, attracted migrants from the less prosperous areas of the Georgia cotton belt. Up to the 1870s and 1880s, the farmers in the Wiregrass had retained the broad outlines of the antebellum subsistence system, but the ravages of hog cholera, woodland clearance by timber companies, and the influx of migrants from areas where intensive cotton cultivation was the norm undermined the continuation of traditional practices, erasing and remaking both the social and agricultural landscape of the area.[67]

The out-migration of southerners from rural spaces in the postbellum South both illuminates the results of ecological shifts in the cotton belt and helps to explain why southern cities achieved such rapid growth during this period. In particular, population trends demonstrate that the number of blacks in the urban or industrial areas of the South increased significantly between 1860 and 1880. The black population of Nashville jumped 15 percent in those decades; Atlanta saw a 24 percent increase. The large population of African Americans in north-central Alabama, for instance, stemmed from the spectacularly rapid development of limestone, iron ore, and coal mines around the recently established city of Birmingham, a center of iron and steel production after 1871. Alabama cotton planter John Parrish lost many of his potential laborers to Birmingham; although he complained the town was filling up with "idle negroes," ex-slaves saw the boom town differently: "freedom was freer" in a city. Foreign immigration to the South was relatively small during this period, and so it was the availability of cheap labor due to the migration of blacks and whites from cotton areas that helped cities such as Birmingham and Atlanta experience rapid population growth.

Another draw was the railroad and timbering booms that transformed the region after the war. Railroad, logging, and mining work all offered relatively decent wages to black southerners. Frank Magwood, an ex-slave originally from South Carolina, rejected the rural existence of his much-older parents following the war. He went to work for the railroad at age twenty-one, re-settling in North Carolina, and then later moved to Georgia to labor for the Stone Mountain Rock Quarry. Although an errant dynamite cap at the quarry sent him back to the farm as a sharecropper, he fondly recalled the feeling of

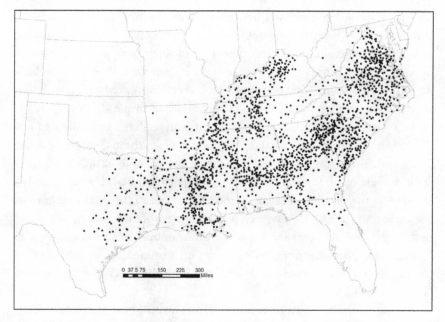

Figure 5.3 Slave population in the South, 1860. Map prepared by Michael Austin
Mohlenbrok and Jennifer Rahn, Department of Geography, Samford University. Data
courtesy of IPUMS National Historical Geographic Information System: Version 12.0
[Database]. University of Minnesota, 2017.

liberty to choose his own occupation. "I thought I was the only man then.
I was so strong." The reasons for black migration during this period, then,
encompassed a wide range of motivations, from the growth of nonagricultural industries and the opening of public lands for homesteading to the
intensification of cotton cultivation in more newly settled areas. Just as in
other plantation societies around the world, the existence of industrial (or
proto-industrial) employment increasingly absorbed the surplus labor created by postemancipation economic shifts and rising birth rates among the
freed population.[68]

Although whites migrated for many of the same reasons blacks did, contemporaries viewed these as separate trends. In fact, observers almost always characterized blacks' movement as "labor unrest" and painted whites as victims of
the war's devastation and destruction of property. Hardship was only reserved
for whites. Discussing the war's effects on the agricultural landscape and the
disastrous consequences for the white "laboring classes," Willoughby Newton,
president of the South Carolina Agricultural Society, wrote, "I doubt not it has
driven from Virginia hundreds, nay, thousands of deserving young men, who
have left their homes in sorrow and despair, as flying from a life of poverty and
servitude."[69] A late nineteenth-century historian contended that the "adverse

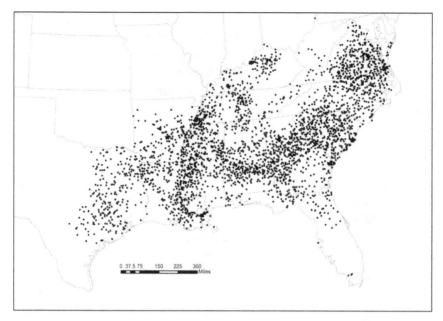

Figure 5.4 African American population in the South, 1890. Map prepared by Michael Austin Mohlenbrok and Jennifer Rahn, Department of Geography, Samford University. Data Courtesy of IPUMS National Historical Geographic Information System: Version 12.0 [Database]. University of Minnesota, 2017.

circumstances" of trying to cultivate a crop without implements, labor, livestock, or money after the war caused "many young [southerners], who despaired of success at home . . . to [move] out where prospects seemed brighter."[70] He did not refer to the ex-slaves who were also attempting to sustain agricultural operations without resources.

The quest of the Alston family of South Carolina for postwar prosperity corroborates nineteenth-century descriptions of the reasons for white migration, but it also shows how postwar movement fit within the narrative of changing land-use and environmental conditions. Southern elites in antebellum times, the Alstons owned extensive tracts of land within multiple plantations along the coastline of South Carolina and regularly entertained such guests as George Washington, General LaFayette, and Aaron Burr, whose daughter, Theodosia, married into the family. When Jacob Motte Alston came of age in the 1840s, he received his own plantation, Woodburne, from his parents and eighty-seven slaves to plant rice on its 1,300 acres.[71] During the war, his slaves left and the rice lands fell into disrepair. Unable to afford to hire field hands on the scrapings he gathered from his law practice, Alston wrote, "My last hope had left me. Urged by [my] uncle to go to Alabama, I did so not knowing what I did." Alston speculated in cotton to raise the capital to buy fertilizers, seed, implements, and wage laborers to establish a cotton farm in Alabama. He never made enough money to buy land in that state, however, and the rent agreement he had with a local landowner proved onerous. "After five years I had lost the little I had saved from a fine fortune," Alston lamented. He moved back to South Carolina to try "inland" rice planting, but a few years later he moved his family to a little farm outside Marietta, Georgia.[72] Despite Alston's protestations of poverty, he was better off after the war than most.

The intensification of land use, combined with accelerated soil erosion and lack of livestock, did make it more difficult for farmers to achieve economic security. As a result, the patterns of environmental change correlate with the patterns of internal migration. The central parts of the Carolinas and Georgia, which had high densities of slaves in 1860 and some of the highest production levels of cotton and tobacco, actually saw a decline in soil erosion between 1870 and 1880 due to out-migration. Although the best lands were heavily fertilized, the already-eroded soils could not support the intensification of cash-crop production in these areas.[73] As a result, despite increasing amounts of land in cultivation, states with more-eroded and heavily used soils were falling behind the production levels of the newer lands in the states farther west. Eugene Hilgard, a geologist who traveled the cotton states for the 1880 census, described this phenomenon in Troup County, Georgia, writing, "Cotton production has greatly decreased within the last few years in this immediate section in spite of the reclaiming of old pine lands and the increased introduction and use of various commercial fertilizers."[74] This meant that the profits of the planters, and the shares and wages of tenants or sharecroppers, were lower in the older areas as well. The US Department of Agriculture's Crop Reports for the 1890s show that the levels of cotton grown per acre in Georgia were 30 percent less than those in Louisiana or Mississippi; North Carolina and South Carolina performed slightly better, but they were no match for Arkansas or Oklahoma.[75]

Geographer Stanley Trimble mapped the rates of land abandonment in the southern Piedmont between Georgia and Virginia and concluded that the areas with the heaviest rates of soil erosion in the period between 1840 and 1860 saw the greatest amounts of land abandonment between 1860 and 1880. Trimble acknowledges the part Civil War military operations played in this trend— soil erosion was highest in the densely settled parts of Virginia, central South Carolina, and central Georgia, which had experienced battles and raids on a larger scale than elsewhere in the South, leading to higher than average rates of land abandonment between 1860 and 1870. After 1870, natural conditions, such as intense rainfall and thinner soils, intersected with altered land-use patterns to create circumstances in which these areas hemorrhaged farmers as a result of decreasing crop productivity and a shrinking base of natural resources. Land abandonment rates skyrocketed. The *Chicago Herald* reported in 1885 that the eastern states were "fast returning to [their] primeval condition." The young men had gone to more promising parts of the South, and the only people left were "old and sad." The report hints at large-scale reforestation due to land abandonment, as well as the continuing decline of livestock herds in the area, noting, "Deer browse where cattle fed and the oak and pine cover great plantations."[76]

However, looking at the agricultural census records state by state shows that between 1870 and 1890 the number of improved acres actually rose in states where Trimble records significant land abandonment.[77] This can be explained very simply: crop production continued to expand and intensify in Georgia and the Carolinas but in places previously considered unsuitable for cultivation or isolated from staple crop agriculture. Upland areas of northern Georgia, for instance, where the Appalachians taper off into a deeply sloping region of thin, rocky soils, experienced a rapid increase in cotton production between 1870 and 1880. In fact, by 1879, the density of cotton farms in the hills of extreme north Georgia matched that of the central part of the state—a wealthy cotton region during the late antebellum period. As the older plantation areas degraded into "worn-out lands" only made productive by expensive fertilizers, some farmers moved upward, onto sparsely populated slopes or mountains, not westward.[78]

Transferring intensive agricultural techniques from the lowlands to the uplands resulted in a considerable amount of environmental damage, threatening yields after only a few years of cultivation.[79] Farming on steeper slopes risked greater rates of soil erosion; once the root systems of hardwood trees were replaced with crop rows, topsoil rapidly washed away. Commercial fertilizers helped to make these lands productive in the short term, but at an enormous cost. The postwar statistics showing rapid expansion of agricultural lands in the South are sometimes questionable, since many of the "new" lands were only able to produce crops for two or three years before being retired or abandoned due to severe erosion. In the central portions of North Carolina, South Carolina, and Georgia, areas with the highest levels of "erosive land use" before the war, soil erosion continued to escalate, primarily because of the intensification of cotton cultivation. But upland areas—those sections that bordered the Piedmont and the Ridge and Valley complex, places previously isolated from the cotton market—experienced a shocking 120 percent increase in soil erosion during this period as farmers cleared slopes to bring more land into cultivation.[80]

The use of intensive agriculture on upland slopes made farming too expensive to be profitable, perpetuating the cycle of clearance and abandonment. Historian John Solomon Otto summarizes the problem of the "intensive" system in degraded areas: "Instead of purchasing costly fertilizers to restore worn-out soils, and instead of raising expensive fodder to sustain enclosed livestock, agriculturalists migrated to the public land states, where they could

raise crops on new soils and graze stock on unfenced lands . . . If it barely paid
to raise cotton in the Carolinas, then it was wise to dispose of worn out soils at
any price and remove to new lands."[81] Indeed, sparsely settled Arkansas, southern Missouri, and east Texas remained outlets for the type of extensive agriculture southerners had typically carried with them to their new homes, and
descriptions of agricultural techniques used in those locations consistently
resemble the antebellum extensive system. For instance, Charles Nordhoff's
descriptions of 1870s Arkansas might have been pulled from a 1850s agricultural journal:

> Arkansas, as viewed from a railroad car, is not a charming country to
> a Northern eye. It seems to contain a good deal of thin and worthless
> land, and where you meet with cultivation the farms have a ragged
> and uncombed look, the farm buildings are usually of poor character,
> and very high fences show that stock is allowed to run wild. Fields are
> oftenest full of stumps; and in the cotton region 'deadenings,' or fields
> with girdled and decaying trees standing upon them, give the land-
> scape a melancholy aspect. But, after all, it is useful for a Northern man
> to remember that dead trees and stumps are more economical than
> a cleaner culture where labor is scarce, and that the Arkansas farmer
> does not need as solid a house as his countryman in New York or
> Massachusetts.[82]

As was seen in the Wiregrass region of Georgia, the tide of poor farmers arriving in places like Arkansas helped to quickly transform the land-use practices
of those states. By the 1880s, regionwide economic and environmental circumstances had shifted so greatly that the antebellum extensive land-use regime was
not practical on a large scale or for long periods of time.

Thus, the movement of southerners during this period continued to follow
roughly the same routes toward the south and west as in the antebellum period,
but the Civil War substantially altered the opportunities for "expansion" as it
had once existed. Many southern farmers or laborers, regardless of race, moved
not from plantation to frontier, but from plantation to plantation, plantation to
upland, or interior to periphery. Freedpeople emigrated from cotton farms in
North Carolina to plantations in Mississippi or Louisiana, hoping for higher
wages. Yeoman farmers, increasingly shut out of cultivable areas by environmental change and the intensification of cotton monoculture, moved into the piney
woods or into the Appalachian foothills, bringing cash-crop agriculture and all
it entailed. Because the Civil War prevented the South from acquiring new territory, most expansion during the postwar period further intensified land use
in already settled areas. Cotton plantations in the Mississippi Valley got larger,

tobacco production in the Black Patch of Tennessee and Kentucky accelerated, and land use in Georgia and Alabama continued to intensify. Only a few havens of extensive agriculture remained, and by the end of the century, even farmers in the sparsely settled and thickly forested areas of Arkansas or Florida had largely abandoned the tenets of the antebellum system because of altered economic, agricultural, and environmental circumstances.

In 1874, a US Department of Agriculture agent reviewed the methods used to grow cotton in the South. Instead of growing cotton continuously using fertilizer, the document suggested, southern farmers should revive "old practices" such as intercropping corn and peas or burning vegetation to restore the soil. Agricultural reformers before the war had also suggested crop rotation and encouraged using legumes to improve soil productivity, but the context in which the USDA agent now suggested it implied that the use of the "new" practices of continuous or intensive cultivation of cotton at the expense of "old" practices in which planters and farmers constantly shifted cultivation and used carefully planned rotations was becoming suspect.[83] A generation after agricultural reformers and USDA agents had touted continuous cultivation of cotton as the way to improve the condition of poor whites and freedpeople in the South after the war, the system had clearly done the opposite.

By the 1880s, the South was producing more cotton than ever before. Yet rates of debt and tenancy escalated, and poor farmers were less self-sufficient in food production. That trend continued. Twenty years later, the region was the nation's "problem child." Rural areas, in particular, were perceived as socially and economically backward, and stereotypes depicted southern cotton farmers as lazy, diseased, and ignorant. Herman Clarence Nixon, in his famous study of the rural South *Forty Acres and a Steel Mule*, called the cotton economy "the middle ages without the cathedrals." Agricultural scientists and journals indicted cotton growers for their irresponsible, ruinous approach to land management. Stark black-and-white photographs of the "southern sharecropper" during the first decades of the twentieth century showed barefooted men following primitive plows across eroded fields, and families of scarcely dressed "pickers" wandering the bare yards of tenant shacks. Both white and black agriculturalists "seemed a throwback to eighteenth-century vagrants." Hookworm and pellagra, illiteracy and malnutrition—these were the conditions associated with southern cotton farming until after World War II.[84]

Blame for the stagnation of the rural economy has focused primarily on merchants, crop lien laws, and cotton prices. Yet as the 1874 USDA report indicated, there had been a fundamental shift in the way farmers approached agriculture that resulted in an incongruity between environmental limitations and land use. Natural characteristics of the soils of the South, along with antebellum farming

practices, contributed to a significant amount of soil erosion and nutrient depletion in the old plantation areas. With this legacy, the Civil War's removal of livestock and provisions, the spread of continuous cultivation, and the subsequent
elimination of subsistence practices further reduced farmers' ability to restore
the soils they had or effectively prevented them from attempting a system of
crop diversification that would have alleviated the issues of food self-sufficiency.
The resulting economic displacement spurred a tide of refugees from the cotton
belt who made the New South "new."

Conclusion

In 1880, southern agricultural output finally surpassed prewar benchmarks. Farmers were dedicating more acreage to cotton than ever before, ginning a record 5,756,000 bales. Rates of land development and "improvement" were up, and investment in the railroad, timber, and mining industries boomed. Cities across the South pulsed with activity. Richmond and Atlanta, flattened in the war, were busy rebuilding and even expanding; Birmingham and other new towns rapidly materialized from clustered industrial enterprises. The increasing number of rail lines and logging roads radiating out from these municipalities acted as advance guards for cotton's spread, allowing the constitution of new kingdoms in previously unconquered lands. The scattered farms along the Mississippi Delta coalesced into a major center of cotton production as railroads pushed into the formerly inaccessible interior of the area's swamps, bringing with them the labor to drain the land and the capital to build new levees. Although the South of 1880 undoubtedly "bore the signs of the preceding twenty years," as historian Edward Ayers writes, observers were hopeful for a "New South" in the region, knitted together by cotton and the Democratic Party.[1]

The South's ostensible recovery after the downfall of the Confederacy has caused the Civil War and Reconstruction periods to be seen as a "momentary, though massive interference" in the remarkably continuous course of southern civilization from the Old South to the New. The seminal events of the 1860s and 1870s had the potential to cripple the planter class, transform race relations, and subsume agriculture to industry, but they did not. Two scholars apply the words of British political economist John Stuart Mill to describe the South's postwar rebound: "An enemy lays waste to a country by fire and sword, and destroys or carries away nearly all the moveable wealth existing in it; all the inhabitants are ruined, and yet in a few years after, everything is much as it was before."[2] Freedom for slaves failed to end their economic bondage; planters and merchants continued to exercise political and economic power; and King Cotton not only kept his crown but expanded his realm. Even Henry Grady, the voice of the industrializing South of the late nineteenth century, wrote, "The New South is simply the Old South under new conditions."[3] Environmental historians have also characterized the Civil War as a devastating but brief interruption, agreeing that the environmental damage of the conflict was "temporary, and arguably, not very significant at all."[4] It did not break the hold of the plantation on the South, it did not reduce the power of cash crops, and it did not halt the exploitation of land on a massive scale.

During the last decade of the nineteenth century, however, a series of financial and ecological calamities threatened the pillars of the embryonic New South, reversing observers' expectations for the region's recovery. The spread of cotton capitalism along newly laid railroad lines into previously yeoman-dominated areas caused the number of landowning farmers to spiral downward. Anger mounted in these upland and piney woods counties, as farmers blamed "middlemen," such as merchants and railroad companies for the problems associated with cotton farming.[5] The Panic of 1893 caused crop prices to plummet, tightening the grip of debt and tenancy on the region. In 1894, the South's cotton farmers outpaced all previous production records by over two million bales, yet sales were a net fifty million dollars less than they would have been a decade earlier. The distrust that built up over the course of the 1880s regarding agricultural conditions—and the politicians, bankers, and merchants who provided neither sympathy nor aid—grew into outright protest after 1890. "We have reached the stage where slow, reasoned arguments cannot any longer affect us, neither the ties of partisanship or political loyalty," wrote one bitter farmer suffering from financial insecurity. "It is a question of bread and meat, and we are ready to fight."[6] The resulting southern Populist movement, while ultimately ephemeral, emerged to address the matrix of producers' economic concerns, threatening long-trusted Democratic leaders. Agitating for local, regional, and national policy changes that would help protect growers from the creditors and the railroad men, Populists drew on decades of concern about the shape and structure of the southern rural economy.

Ecological catastrophes compounded economic and political woes, affecting agricultural land use. The Mississippi River surged past the reconstructed levees at least three times during the 1890s, submerging much of the lower Mississippi Valley. Drought seared many of the newest cotton-growing lands of Texas, Louisiana, Arkansas, and Mississippi in 1896. And in 1892, a new threat appeared from Mexico: the boll weevil. The pest, a small winged beetle with a "pronounced" snout and a penchant for cotton leaves, first appeared in Texas. By 1922, the weevil's range stretched across the former Confederacy. Insecticides and quarantines proved ineffective in halting the pest's advance, so farmers did what they could to limit the damage—they experimented with different varieties of cotton, put fields into corn until the pest moved on, and hoped for weather unfavorable to the weevil's life cycle. Theodore Roosevelt called the spread of the insect "the wave of evil," for by munching on the cotton plant, the pest ate away at the region's levers of economic strength, its systems of labor and racial control, and the prospects of the South's politically powerful. While it is true that even the boll weevil could not rein in the region's addiction to cotton—farmers ginned more "white gold" in 1921 than in 1892—crop losses devastated a number of local economies, affected land values, and arguably spurred demographic shifts in the African American population at the opening of the Great Migration.[7]

The boll weevil's progress across the region is widely accepted as a moment when the region's environment famously shaped the economy—when a nonhuman agent determined human decisions regarding crop mixes, land use, financial prospects, and, of course, whether to stay in the South. As historian James Giesen demonstrates, the weevil's place at the intersection of environment, race, and labor was just as clear, for it endangered planters' control over their largely black labor forces and the sanctity of the socioeconomic hierarchy that had been in place since emancipation. But the South had experienced a similar episode of environmental and economic upheaval four decades earlier, during a period most often associated with the politics of the people who worked the land rather than with the land itself. In many ways, the events of the 1860s and 1870s presaged the agro-economic upheavals of the 1890s and set the stage for the region's stagnating rural economy as it existed through World War II. The inability of southern farmers to revert to the environmental status quo of the prewar period helped to stoke the resentments that much later would congeal in the Populist movement, and created the conditions of the cotton South as they existed upon the boll weevil's arrival.

This book has made a case for revisiting the place of the Civil War and emancipation within the larger trajectory of southern agriculture. Climate and soil conditions in what became the cotton South precluded northern-style commercial farming—a system based on a mixed-crop regime based on grains, livestock-raising, and dairying that was relatively well adapted to continuous cultivation. Under a different set of land-use practices, however, southern agricultural production had flourished. The widespread adoption of methods such as shifting cultivation, free-range animal husbandry, specific forms of crop rotation, and the use of slave labor in land maintenance allowed farmers to circumvent the environmental limitations of their region. The climate and terrain were particularly suited to a series of highly valuable commodity crops, and great herds of swine, cattle, and even sheep grazed in and among farms, and in some areas, stock-raising was the cornerstone of the agricultural economy.

This is not to say that southern farmers before 1861 were paragons of agricultural responsibility. The pace of environmental change was, in many areas, unsustainable. Soil, timber, and wildlife resources throughout the South had suffered enormously during the century of cultivation before the Civil War. In fact, wealthy, white planters in the South dubbed "agricultural reformers" feared that the rate at which southerners were exhausting the natural landscape would lead to an ecological crisis that would undermine the region's most central institution: slavery. But because farmers were able to expand their agricultural system along an almost continuously moving frontier, the environmental collapse of southern farming never fully materialized. Still, extensive land-use practices would only keep agriculture profitable for so long. Farmers needed fresh soils, large tracts of wooded land, and a labor force to carve new fields from old forests. Expansion was crucial to the system's success. Thinking about the environmental and agricultural utility inherent in the expansion of slavery and the extensive land-use system it supported illuminates the practical considerations that fueled the debates over the restriction of slavery during the secession crisis of the late antebellum period.

The war drastically altered the rhythms of southern agricultural life and livelihood by accelerating prewar environmental change, removing necessary resources and labor, and preventing expansion. Battles and the construction of defense works noticeably increased soil erosion and woodland clearance. Land abandonment due to occupation, lack of labor, or confiscation was more widespread and provided a multiyear fallow for hundreds of thousands of acres, temporarily suspending human alterations to the land. The foraging and impressment of livestock, slaves, and materials by the armies also had a diffuse impact, touching most farms in some way during the conflict. The environmental context in which antebellum southern agriculture developed made the region particularly vulnerable to standard military practices. At the macro level, it helps to explain why the South was affected so dramatically by the Civil War and why assumptions regarding the "destructiveness" of the conflict have persisted.

Ironically, ecological processes made the South's agricultural landscape occasionally a "natural enemy" to the Confederates and "natural ally" to the Union.[8] The proliferation of free-range animal husbandry in the South meant that livestock ranging in woodland were easier for soldiers to steal, and if a field's fences were destroyed, what livestock remained had full access to farmers' cropland, reducing the food available for the Confederates but providing food for the Union livestock. The reliance of southerners on national and international markets for agricultural necessities magnified the impact of Union troop movements and the blockade of southern ports. The resulting shortages of livestock and guano negatively impacted the South's crop yields during its desperate scramble to produce foodstuffs. The methods farmers had used during the antebellum period to solve issues of soil fertility—shifting cultivation, the burning of trees, or simply moving somewhere else—were no longer feasible due to the consumption of wood by troops and the loss of labor through conscription and slave emancipation. Military operations thus exacerbated existing weaknesses in the southern system, with significant implications for both Union and Confederate logistics and supply. On many levels, then, the Civil War proved to be a profoundly environmental event, one that not only transformed how Americans thought about nature and their place in it but also shifted the possibilities for human use of the land.[9]

During the war, the South's timberlands, farms, livestock, and men had been cut, neglected, stolen, and killed. Slavery, the cultural and economic underpinning of southern society, had ended, leaving many white southerners with little hope for their financial recovery. Agricultural reformers in the South, as well as government officials working with the newly established Freedmen's Bureau and the US Department of Agriculture, viewed the end of the war differently: they saw emancipation and the supposed collapse of the plantation system as a chance to remake the South into a region of small, free-labor-based, self-sufficient farms worked by prosperous white and black yeoman no longer in thrall to the power of the southern planter. However, social and economic shifts intersected with environmental change in ways that undermined the rehabilitation of labor relations on plantations. The decentralization of the labor force that allowed freedpeople more autonomy in their day-to-day work required redividing the land to support tenant and sharecropper plots. The physical reorganization of both labor forces and plantations encouraged continuous cultivation at the expense of antebellum-era subsistence practices and caused a lapse in important land-maintenance tasks that increased flooding and accelerated the spread of the cotton caterpillar.

By 1870 in some places and 1880 in others, the cracks in the extensive land-use regime had widened considerably, shattering the foundational practices southerners had once used to adapt their agricultural system to the environmental conditions in which they lived and worked. As cotton cultivation spread and intensive farming methods took hold, both smaller farms and larger plantations suffered. For instance, the wartime focus on food crops buoyed cotton yields during the period of cotton fever immediately after the end of the conflict. Drought and labor difficulties caused widespread complaints of failed harvests, but crop rotations and land abandonment during the war meant that the harvests of 1866–1868 were not as bad as they could have been. Unfortunately, these temporarily high cotton yields—like the temporarily high cotton prices of the time—encouraged farmers to prioritize cotton over raising livestock or planting foodstuffs. Another irony of this period was the introduction of animal diseases that spread more easily when livestock were penned. Hog cholera and the reduction in livestock during the conflict increased farmers' reliance on newly available commercial fertilizers and weakened the economic logic for free-range husbandry. Although fertilization and continuous cultivation were key elements of agricultural reform during the antebellum era, it was clear that in the environmental context of the South, these "reforms" merely worsened the problems of soil erosion, soil-nutrient deficiencies, and land abandonment.

The decline of shifting cultivation, free-range animal husbandry, crop rotations, and basic land maintenance threatened the ability of large landholders to continue to drive local economies and eliminated options for subsistence farming that would have poorer farmers be more self-sufficient. Thus, replacing extensive land-use practices with more intensive, continuous cultivation went hand-in-hand with the economic dislocation of sharecroppers and tenants, poor whites and poor blacks. Expansion as it had existed before the war was no longer possible owing to issues of geography, lack of capital, and, most importantly, the absence of slavery, so farmers seeking new opportunities generally sought out areas that were once considered unsuited to cash-crop cultivation. The patterns of postwar migration shifted the boundaries of the ecological South, carrying intensive cash-crop agriculture into areas where subsistence agriculture had once predominated.

Even without the war, white southern farmers would eventually have squandered the ability of the region's landscape to support extensive agriculture. But the conflict ensured that outcome sooner rather than later by altering how southern farmers perceived, exploited, and profited from the natural environment. War and emancipation unmasked environmental limits and constraints already in place, the effects of which had long been forestalled during the antebellum era by territorial expansion and the use of slave labor to create and maintain agricultural landscapes. Accelerated soil erosion, woodland clearance, and land abandonment, as well as emancipation's magnification of environmental change, helped to shape the development of the postwar economy. Far from being inevitable, the expansion of cotton production, the rise of sharecropping, and the assault on the open range across all areas of the South was the result of thousands of individual responses to tightening natural constraints on farming, the disappearance of agricultural resources, and ecological vulnerability during two decades of chaotic reshuffling. As a result, both black and white southern farmers often found themselves unable to "redeem" their lands and fortunes. In the unforgiving soils of the Cotton Kingdom, the ecological legacies of the Civil War eroded the promise of the New South.

NOTES

Introduction

1. Entry dated September 20, 1863, Nimrod Porter Journals, MF 229, Tennessee State Library and Archives, Nashville, Tennessee (hereafter TSLA).
2. Entries dated December 18, 1861, November 7, 1862, September 25, 1865, May 26, 1867, April 20, 1868, and October 19, 1868, Nimrod Porter Journals, TSLA.
3. The 1850 Federal Slave Schedules list Nimrod as owning 31 slaves. By 1860, he presides over a household with up to 44 slaves, some of whom are listed as belonging to Porter's two sons. Both sons are recorded as dependents in Porter's household in the 1860 Census, and Porter's diary lists rations of cloth for 38 slaves on August 19, 1863. 1850 Federal Census—Slave Schedules, District 5, Maury, Tennessee, M432, National Archives and Records Administration (hereafter NARA); 1860 US Census, Population Schedules, District 9, Maury, Tennessee, M653, roll 1264, NARA; 1860 US Federal Census—Slave Schedules, District 6, Dyer, Tennessee, M653, NARA.
4. See, for instance, entries dated March 30, 1857; March 1861; December 3, 1861; November 7, 1862; and May 22, 1863, Nimrod Porter Journals, TSLA. According to the 1860 US Federal Census, Porter owned 10 horses, 12 mules, around 40 cows, 60 sheep, and 200 pigs.
5. Entries dated January 8, January 13, April 9, June 26, July 14, and October 20, 1863; October 13, November 26, December 1, and December 24, 1864; February 18, March 18, May 26, and June 6–9, 1865, Nimrod Porter Journals, TSLA.
6. Example entries include November 4 and December 16, 1865; April 28, August 24, November 29, and December 24, 1866; March 11, April 1, June 28, October 12, November 15, August 19, November 23, and December 25, 1868; January 4, January 30, February 10, May 22, September 27, and November 16, 1869; and January 10 and January 13, 1870, Nimrod Porter Journals, TSLA.
7. The majority of historians characterize antebellum southern farmers, and particularly small-scale farmers, as "safety-first," a phrase taken from Gavin Wright and Howard Kunreuther, "Cotton, Corn, and Risk in the Nineteenth Century," *Journal of Economic History* 35, no. 3 (September 1975): 529–530. For a dissenting view, see James Oakes, *The Ruling Race: A History of American Slaveholders* (New York: Alfred A. Knopf, 1982). One of the songs attributed to Joel Chandler Harris's character "Uncle Remus" has a line: "Oh, Dixie Land is the land of cotton / That's why Dixie's now forgotten." "Uncle Remus," *American Elevator and Grain Trade*, April 15, 1892, 335.
8. Stephen Berry, "The Future of Civil War Studies: Predictions," available from *Journal of the Civil War Era* at http://journalofthecivilwarera.org/wp-content/uploads/2012/02/Final-Berry.pdf (accessed June 28, 2017).
9. Jack Temple Kirby, *Mockingbird Song: Ecological Landscapes of the South* (Chapel Hill: University of North Carolina Press, 2006), xiv.

10. Lynn Nelson, *Pharsalia: An Environmental Biography of a Southern Plantation, 1780–1880* (Athens: University of Georgia Press, 2007), 13–14, quote on 13. For more theoretical discussion of how agroecological systems work, and how that should affect environmental historians' view of them, see Donald Worster, "Transformations of the Earth: Toward an Agroecological Perspective in History," *Journal of American History* 76, no. 1 (March 1990): 1087–1106; Paul Sutter, "The World with Us: The State of American Environmental History," *Journal of American History* 100, no. 1 (June 2013): 94–119; Mart A. Stewart, "If John Muir Had Been an Agrarian: American Environmental History West and South," *Environment and History* 11 (2005): 139–162.

11. Michael Ritter, *The Physical Environment: An Introduction to Physical Geography,* http://www.earthonlinemedia.com/ebooks/tpe_3e/title_page.html (accessed January 13, 2017); Alfred Cowdrey, *This Land, This South: An Environmental History* (Lexington: University Press of Kentucky, 1983), 3; Stanley Trimble, *Man-Induced Soil Erosion on the Southern Piedmont, 1700–1970* (Ankeny, IA: Soil Conservation Society of America, 1974); and Louis Thompson, *Soils and Soil Fertility,* 2nd ed. (New York: McGraw-Hill, 1957), 3.

12. Julius Rubin, "The Limits of Agricultural Progress in the Nineteenth-Century South," *Agricultural History* 49, no. 2 (April 1975): 364–366.

13. Other scholars have discussed one or more of these practices at length and established how the South's climate and soils influenced their development. In addition to Julius Rubin's work, see John Majewski, *Modernizing a Slave Economy: The Economic Vision of the Confederate Nation* (Chapel Hill: University of North Carolina Press, 2009); and Paul Sutter, *Let Us Now Praise Famous Gullies: Providence Canyon and the Soils of the South* (Athens: University of Georgia Press, 2015).

14. See, for example, *Southern Farm and Home,* May 1871, 13.

15. For instance, Roger Ransom and Richard Sutch famously calculated the monetary costs of reduced labor inputs from newly freed slaves who rejected "slavery's hours and slavery's pace," slowing the work of crop production. Quote from William Cohen, *At Freedom's Edge: Black Mobility and the Southern White Quest for Racial Control, 1861–1915* (Baton Rouge: Louisiana State University Press, 1991), 14. Other works referenced include Stephen DeCanio, *Agriculture in the Postbellum South: The Economics of Production and Supply* (Cambridge, MA: Harvard University Press, 1975); Roger L. Ransom and Richard Sutch, *One Kind of Freedom: The Economic Consequences of Emancipation* (Cambridge: Cambridge University Press, 1977); and Jay R. Mandle, *The Roots of Black Poverty: The Southern Plantation Economy after the Civil War* (Durham, NC: Duke University Press, 1978).

16. Quote from title of chap. 1, Eric Foner, *Reconstruction: America's Unfinished Revolution* (New York: Oxford University Press, 1988); Joseph D. Reid Jr., "Sharecropping as an Understandable Market Response: The Postbellum South," *Journal of Economic History* 33, no. 1 (March 1973): 106–130; Gavin Wright, *The Political Economy of the Cotton South* (New York: W. W. Norton, 1978); and Richard Holcombe Kilbourne, *Debt, Investment, Slaves: Credit Relations in East Feliciana Parish, Louisiana, 1825–1885* (Tuscaloosa: University of Alabama Press, 1995).

17. See Jonathan Weiner, *Social Origins of the New South: Alabama, 1860–1885* (Baton Rouge: Louisiana State University Press, 1978); Michael Wayne, *The Reshaping of Plantation Society: The Natchez District, 1860–80* (Baton Rouge: Louisiana State University Press, 1983); James Cobb, *Away Down South: A History of Southern Identity* (New York: Oxford University Press, 2005); Mark Wetherington, *Plain Folk's Fight: The Civil War and Reconstruction in Piney Woods Georgia* (Chapel Hill: University of North Carolina Press, 2009); and Steven Hahn, *The Roots of Southern Populism Yeoman Farmers and the Transformation of the Georgia Upcountry, 1850–1890* (New York: Oxford University Press, 1983).

18. Foner, *Reconstruction;* Julie Saville, *The Work of Reconstruction: From Slave to Wage Laborer in South Carolina, 1860–1870* (Cambridge: Cambridge University Press, 1994); J. William Harris, *Deep Souths: Delta, Piedmont, and Sea Island Society in the Age of Segregation* (Baltimore, MD: Johns Hopkins University Press, 2001); John Rodrigue, *Reconstruction in the Cane Fields: From Slavery to Free Labor in Louisiana's Sugar Parishes, 1862–1880* (Baton Rouge: Louisiana State University Press, 2001); and Susan O'Donovan, *Becoming Free in the Cotton South* (Cambridge, MA: Harvard University Press, 2010).

19. Considerable scholarly interest in both the environmental aspects of the Civil War, on the one hand, and the natural dynamics of land use in 1890s and beyond, on the other, has yet to be bridged in a monograph-length work. The exceptions to the broader trend in environmental history to skip from 1865 to 1890 include Mart Stewart, *"What Nature Suffers to Groe": Life, Labor, and Landscape on the Georgia Coast, 1680–1920* (Athens: University of Georgia Press, 1996); Jack Temple Kirby, *Poquosin: A Study of Rural Landscape and Society* (Chapel Hill: University of North Carolina Press, 1995); Mikko Saikku, *This Delta, This Land: An Environmental History of the Yazoo-Mississippi Floodplain* (Athens: University of Georgia Press, 2005); Drew Swanson, *A Golden Weed: Tobacco and Environment in the Piedmont South* (New Haven, CT: Yale University Press, 2015); and Timothy Johnson, "Reconstructing the Soil: Emancipation and the Roots of Chemical-Dependent Fertilizer Agriculture in America," in *The Blue, the Gray, and the Green: Toward an Environmental History of the Civil War*, ed. Brian Allen Drake (Athens: University of Georgia Press, 2015), 191–206.

20. See James C. Giesen, *Boll Weevil Blues: Cotton, Myth, and Power in the American South* (Chicago: University of Chicago Press, 2011).

21. Cowdrey, *This Land, This South*, 8.

22. A. B. Hulbert, *Soil: Its Influence on the History of the United States* (New York: Russell and Russell, 1930), 6–7.

23. Christian Parenti, *Tropic of Chaos: Climate Change and the New Geography of Violence* (New York: Nation Books, 2011), 7, 9.

24. Historian Paul Sutter highlighted the importance of such work when he mused "that we cannot understand the Civil War without paying detailed attention to the history of farming in the nineteenth-century America, and that we cannot understand the trajectory of agriculture in US history without attending to the legacies of the Civil War." Paul Sutter, "Waving the Muddy Shirt," in Drake, *The Blue, the Gray*, 231. Lisa Brady's work does reflect on the possible connections between the environmental destruction of the American Civil War and the establishment of the nation's national park system. Lisa Brady, *War upon the Land: Military Strategy and the Transformation of Southern Landscapes during the American Civil War* (Athens: University of Georgia Press, 2012). Other works mentioned include Jack Temple Kirby, "The American Civil War: An Environmental View," in *Nature Transformed: The Environment in American History*, Teacher Serve, National Humanities Center website, http://nationalhumanitiescenter.org/tserve/nattrans/ntuseland/essays/amcwar.htm (accessed June 1, 2017); Mark Fiege, "Gettysburg and the Organic Nature of the American Civil War," in *Natural Enemy, Natural Ally: Toward an Environmental History of Warfare*, ed. Edmund Russell and Richard Tucker (Corvallis: Oregon State University Press, 2004), 93–109; Fiege, *The Republic of Nature: An Environmental History of the United States* (Seattle: University of Washington Press, 2012), chap. 5; Ted Steinberg, *Down to Earth: Nature's Role in American History* (New York: Oxford University Press, 2011), 89–98; and Megan Kate Nelson, *Ruin Nation: Destruction and the American Civil War* (Athens: University of Georgia Press, 2012). Kathryn Shively Meier's work takes the opposite approach to Brady and Nelson by examining the impact of the environment on common soldiers' efforts to prevent illness in the context of two Virginia campaigns. Kathryn Shively Meier, *Nature's Civil War: Common Soldiers and the Environment in 1862 Virginia* (Chapel Hill: University of North Carolina Press, 2013). Similar work includes Andrew McIlwaine Bell, *Mosquito Soldiers: Malaria, Yellow Fever, and the Course of the American Civil War* (Baton Rouge: Louisiana State University Press, 2010).

Chapter 1

1. List of slaves dated 1854 and entries for Pounds of Cotton Picked, dated September 4, 1860, Joseph M. Jaynes Plantation Journals, *Records of Ante-Bellum Southern Plantations* (hereafter *RASP*), Series F, pt. 2, reel 1, Rare Books and Manuscripts Special Collections, Duke University (hereafter RBMSC). Jayne's plantation was home to between 29 and 34 slaves in the period between 1854 and 1861.

2. For information about Joseph M. Jayne and his father, see County Tax Rolls, Personal, Rankin County (1855), Series 1202, Mississippi Department of Archives and History (MDAH), 14; County Tax Rolls, Land, Rankin County (1855), Series 1202, MDAH, 8; US General Land

Office Records; listing in 1880 Federal Census; Front Matter, Joseph M. Jaynes Plantation Journals, *RASP*, Series F, pt. 2, reel 1, RBMSC. Many scholars refer to Jayne as "Jaynes" due to a typographical error in the printed finding aid accompanying the microfilmed copies of his plantation journals. However, census records, state and local tax lists, land purchase entries, newspapers, and military service dispatches of the time all cite Jayne as "Jayne." For more on his land and its ecology, see Landris T. Lee Jr., "State Study 151 and 236: Yazoo Clay Investigation," Mississippi Department of Transportation and the US Army Engineer Research and Development Center, 2012; William A. Cole Sr., Roger W. Smith, Mary Louise Spann, and Delmer C. Stamps, *Soil Survey of Rankin County, Mississippi* (Washington, DC: US Department of Agriculture, 1987), http://www.nrcs.usda.gov/Internet/FSE_MANUSCRIPTS/mississippi/rankinMS1987/ms_rankin.pdf (accessed February 26, 2017); Louis Moran, David Pettry, Richard Switzer et al., "Soils of Native Prairie Remnants in the Jackson Prairie Region of Mississippi," *Mississippi Agricultural and Forestry Experiment Station Bulletin* 1067 (June 1997).

3. Quote from Fiege, *Republic of Nature*, 104. Although long-staple cotton was immensely profitable, producing the silky strands growers desired required a climate that did not get frost for most of the year and prolonged exposure to ocean breezes. Drew A. Swanson, *Remaking Wormsloe Plantation: The Environmental History of a Lowcountry Landscape* (Athens: University of Georgia Press, 2012), 61–65; Steinberg, *Down to Earth*, 83.

4. US Census Records, 1830 and 1860; Edward Baptist, *The Half Has Never Been Told: Slavery and the Making of American Capitalism* (New York: Basic Books, 2014), 117–121; Alan L. Olmstead and Paul W. Rhode, "Biological Innovation and Productivity Growth in the Antebellum Cotton Economy," *Journal of Economic History*, 68, no. 4 (December 2008): 1123–1171. Baptist and the Olmstead and Rhode team have dramatically differing opinions as to the source of the antebellum South's increasing productivity in the production of raw cotton. Baptist views the speed-up to be the result of violence and a torture-based incentive he calls the "pushing system," whereas Olmstead and Rhode emphasize the biological revolutions taking place in terms of plant breeds.

5. First quote in "Cause and Care of Hard Times," *Southwestern Baptist*, March 29, 1855; second in letter dated November 22, 1860, from Borden and Buck to the Allen Family, box 250, folder 12, Allen Family Papers I, William S. Hoole Special Collections Library, University of Alabama (hereafter WSHSC). There were two significant pauses in the general profitability of cotton before the Civil War: the Panic of 1837 and a slump due to overproduction in the mid-1840s. For information on cotton prices, see William Cooper Jr. and Thomas Terrill, *The American South: A History*, 2nd ed. (New York: McGraw-Hill, 1996), 181; Joseph Reidy, *From Slavery to Agrarian Capitalism in the Cotton Plantation South: Central Georgia, 1800–1880* (Chapel Hill: University of North Carolina Press, 1995), 29. On the global nature of cotton production and its relation to European textile industries, see Sven Beckert, *Empire of Cotton: A Global History* (New York: Alfred A. Knopf, 2014); and Edmund Russell, *Evolutionary History: Uniting History and Biology to Understand Life on Earth* (Cambridge: Cambridge University Press, 2011), chap. 9.

6. The staple regions of the South were so distinct that if a historian were to sample the counties that produced 98 percent of the cotton crop in 1860, he or she would exclude 96 percent of the rice crop, 75 percent of the sugar cane crop, and 98 percent of the tobacco crop. The sample of cotton counties is known as the "Parker-Gallman sample," as introduced and discussed in Wright, *Political Economy of the Cotton South*, 17–18, esp. fn. 13; Sam Bowers Hilliard, *Atlas of Antebellum Southern Agriculture* (Baton Rouge: Louisiana State University Press, 1984), 6; Cooper and Terrill, *American South*, 173, 183–184.

7. Slaves in the Low Country built a hydraulic grid to house the rice fields, leveling quarter-acre squares of ground, building embankments around them, and connecting them to rivers. The centrality of engineering nature through human labor such as that Bartram witnessed led one South Carolina planter to call a good rice plantation "a huge hydraulic machine," with "the whole apparatus of levels, floodgates, trunks, canals, banks and ditches . . . requiring skill and unity of purpose to keep in order." Cooper and Terrill, *American South*, 176; Stewart, *"What Nature Suffers to Groe"*, 90–91, 98–99, quote on 98.

8. Laurence Walker, *The Southern Forest: A Chronicle* (Austin: University of Texas Press, 1991), 6–9, 11–13; Saikku, *This Delta, This Land*, 40–46; Cooper and Terrill, *American South*, 177;

Peter Sharpe, "Sugar Cane: Past and Present," *Ethnobotanical Leaflets*, Southern Illinois University Carbondale, http://opensiuc.lib.siu.edu/cgi/viewcontent.cgi?article=1388&con text=ebl&sei-redir=1 (accessed June 1, 2017); and Roderick A. McDonald, *The Economy and Material Culture of Slaves: Goods and Chattels on the Sugar Plantations of Jamaica and Louisiana* (Baton Rouge: Louisiana State University Press, 1993), 2–3.

9. B. W. Arnold Jr., *History of the Tobacco Industry in Virginia from 1860 to 1894* (Baltimore, MD: Johns Hopkins Press, 1897), 19; Richard Jones, *Dinwiddie County: Carrefour of the Commonwealth* (Richmond, VA: Whittet and Shepperson, 1976), 46–47; Timothy Silver, "Learning to Live with Nature: Colonial Historians and the Southern Environment," *Journal of Southern History* 73, no. 3 (August 2007): 546; Alan Kulikoff, *Tobacco and Slaves: The Development of Southern Cultures in the Chesapeake, 1680–1800* (Chapel Hill: University of North Carolina Press, 1986), 141; David Orwig and Marc Abrams, "Land-Use History (1720–1992), Composition, and Dynamics of Oak-Pine Forests within the Piedmont and Coastal Plain of Northern Virginia," *Canadian Journal of Forest Research* 24 (1992): 1217.

10. For surveys of these changes, see David W. Miller, *The Taking of American Indian Lands in the Southeast: A History of Territorial Cessions and Forced Relocations, 1607–1840* (Jefferson, NC: McFarland, 2011); and Walter Hart Blumenthal, *American Indians Dispossessed* (New York: Arno Press, 1975). For an explanation of how Indian removal impacted the trajectory of the cotton South in general, see Adam Rothman, *Slave Country: American Expansion and the Origins of the Deep South* (Cambridge, MA: Harvard University Press, 2005). For an example of these changes in one county (Wilcox) in Alabama, see Clinton McCarthy, *The Reins of Power: Racial Change and Challenge in a Southern County* (Tallahassee, FL: Sentry Press, 1999).

11. Quote from Frederick Law Olmsted, *A Journey through Texas; Or, a Saddle-Trip on the Southwestern Frontier* (Lincoln: University of Nebraska Press, 2004), 101. Statistics adapted from US Census Bureau records as reported in Brooks Blevins, *Cattle in the Cotton Fields: A History of Cattle Raising in Alabama* (Tuscaloosa: University of Alabama Press, 1998), 26. Percentages determined by the author for Covington and Conecuh Counties in Alabama. For slaveholding and average farm size, see Frank Owsley, *The Plain Folk of the Old South* (Baton Rouge: Louisiana State University Press, 1949), 181–189.

12. Cowdrey, *This Land, This South*, 5.

13. James Petersen, Dorothy Sack, and Robert Gabler, *Physical Geography*, 10th ed. (New York: Cengage Learning, 2011), 259; M. C. Peel, B. L. Finlayson, and T. A. McMahon, "Updated World Map of the Köppen-Geiger Climate Classification," *Hydrology and Earth System Sciences Discussions* 4 (2007): 439–443.

14. Ritter, *Physical Environment*; quote from Cowdrey, *This Land, This South*, 3. "Gully-washer" originated as a colloquial term to describe the intense summer storms that opened rivulets of washing soil in crop fields, but it so befitted the impact of heavy rainfall on soil that it has since been adopted by scientists. See Timothy Beach and Philip Gersmehl, "Soil Erosion, T Values, and Sustainability: A Review and Exercise," *Journal of Geography* 92, no. 1 (January–February 1993): 16–22.

15. Cowdrey, *This Land, This South*, 2–3; Thompson, *Soils and Soil Fertility*, 3; Beach and Gersmehl, "Soil Erosion, T Values, and Sustainability." It is the character of southern soils that scholars such as Paul Sutter point to when explaining the persistence of extensive land-use practices in the region. See Sutter, *Let Us Now Praise Famous Gullies*, 158–161. The United States north of Ohio was covered in glaciers during the last Ice Age; as they retreated, they deposited layers of minerals over the earth. In addition, wind-blown loess from the tops of glaciers carried the same minerals and deposited them. Areas of the United States where agriculture is performed on loess soils include the Palouse in Washington, the Midwestern prairies, and the eastern bluffs of the Mississippi River. See Michael Singer and Donald Munns, *Soils: An Introduction* (New York: Macmillan, 1991); and Trimble, *Man-Induced Soil Erosion*.

16. See L. D. Wesley, "Les sols résiduels et l'enseignement de la mécanique des sols," Proceedings of the 18th International Conference on Soil Mechanics and Geotechnical Engineering, Paris 2013; A. Vianna da Fonseca et al., "Characterization of a Profile of Residual Soil from Granite . . . " *Geotechnical and Geological Engineering* 24 (2006): 1310–1312; James C. Baker, "Part VI: Soils of Virginia," in *Agronomy Handbook* (Blacksburg, VA: Virginia Tech Cooperative

Extension 2000), 71; Walker, *Southern Forest*, 16–17; C. Mark Cowell, "Historical Change in Vegetation and Disturbance on the Georgia Piedmont," *American Midland Naturalist* 140, no. 1 (July 1998): 78; and Paul Hooper Montgomery, *Erosion and Related Land Use Conditions on the Lloyd Shoals Reservoir Watershed, Georgia* (USDA report, Washington, DC: Government Printing Office, 1940), 6.

17. A. R. Hall, "Early Soil Erosion Control Practices in Virginia" (USDA Miscellaneous Publication no. 256, Washington, DC: Government Printing Office 1937), 5; "Tobacco the Bane of Virginia Husbandry, no. 4," *Southern Planter*, August 1859, 482.

18. H. Jesse Walker and James M. Coleman, "Atlantic and Gulf Coastal Province," in *Geomorphic Systems of North America*, ed. William Graft (Boulder, CO: Geological Society of America, 1987), 65; Alice Simms Jones and E. Gibbes Patton, "Forest, 'Prairie' and Soils in the Black Belt of Sumter County, Alabama, in 1832," *Ecology* 41, no. 1 (January 1966): 75; Roland Harper, "Forests of Alabama," *Geological Survey of Alabama Monographs* 10 (Wetumpka Printing Company, 1943). The label "canebrake" made sense, for an abundance of cane grew wild in the river bottoms and swamps, especially in the western counties. But the use of the term "prairie" in regard to the vegetation at the time of European settlement caused later scholars great confusion. See David Taitt, "The Journal of a Journey through the Creek Country, 1772," in *Travels in the American Colonies*, ed. Newton D. Mereness (New York: Antiquarian Press, 1961), 49-55. Other accounts are mentioned in H. Taylor Rankin and D. E. Davis, "Woody Vegetation in the Black Belt of Montgomery County, Alabama, in 1845–6," *Ecology* 52, no. 4 (July 1971): 716. Because of the types of soil in the area, the density of trees in forest tracts was low compared with that of the more upland areas and interspersed among the forest tracts were grassy expanses. Perennial streams and floodplains contained marshes, swampy thickets, and canebrakes, and rivers were lined with riparian woods. For examples of nineteenth-century sources praising Black Belt fertility, see John Buckner Little, *The History of Butler County, Alabama, 1815–1885* (Elm Street Printing Company, 1885), 16; and B. F. Riley, *Alabama As It Is; Or, the Immigrant's and Capitalist's Guide Book to Alabama* (Atlanta, GA: Constitution Publishing, 1888), 116–117, 121.

19. Walker, *Southern Forest*, 6–9, 11–13; Saikku, *This Delta, This Land*, 40–46; Hilliard, *Atlas of Antebellum Agriculture*, 7; John Solomon Otto, *The Final Frontiers, 1880–1930: Settling the Southern Bottomlands* (Westport, CT: Greenwood Press, 1999), 2; R. T. Avon Burke et al., "Soil Survey of Perry County, Alabama," in *Field Operations of the Bureau of Soils* (USDA report, Washington, DC: Government Printing Office, 1902), 312; R. A. Winston, "Soil Survey of Wilcox County, Alabama" (USDA report, Washington, DC: Government Printing Office, 1918), 10–17; and Howard C. Smith, "Soil Survey of Barbour County, Alabama" (USDA report, Washington, DC: Government Printing Office, 1916), 16–17.

20. Joseph Baldwin, *Flush Times in Alabama and Mississippi* (1853; repr. New York: Sagamore Press, 1957), 60. See Sydney Nathans, *A Mind to Stay: White Plantation, Black Homeland* (Cambridge, MA: Harvard University Press, 2017), for an example of a successful tobacco planter who bought land first in Alabama, and then in Mississippi during this period.

21. Quote from Thomas Perkins Abernethy, *The Formative Period in Alabama, 1815–1828* (Montgomery, AL: Brown Printing Company, 1922), 17–18. See also Daniel Walker Howe, *What Hath God Wrought: The Transformation of America, 1815–1848* (New York: Oxford University Press, 2007), 125; and Lucille Griffith, *Alabama: A Documentary History to 1900* (Tuscaloosa: University of Alabama Press, 1968), 134.

22. Philip Curtin, *The Rise and Fall of the Plantation Complex: Essays in Atlantic History* (Cambridge: Cambridge University Press, 1990); David Brion Davis, *Inhuman Bondage: The Rise and Fall of Slavery in the New World* (New York: Oxford University Press, 2006), 262; and Rothman, *Slave County*. Rothman emphasizes that the global expansion of staple production for core markets depended heavily on the increased use of forced labor, making the emergence of the free-labor ideology in the American North distinctive among Western Hemispheric societies in an early nineteenth-century economic context.

23. Hilliard, *Atlas of Antebellum Southern Agriculture*, 35; and Cooper and Terrill, *American South*, 194. William G. Thomas III and Edward Ayers make a similar point in a project that compared two counties in the same topographic region with similar soils and social makeup, with one exception—one was a slave county, and one was a free county. They concluded that

slavery exerted considerable influence on southern life outside the large cotton plantations, and even in places without a large slave population. William G. Thomas and Edward Ayers, "The Differences Slavery Made: A Close Analysis of Two American Communities," *American Historical Review* 108, no. 5 (December 2003): 1299–1307.

24. Until recently, scholars failed to notice how slaves' interactions with the natural environment within the plantation complex permeated their memories of bondage. Instead, historians saw the South's "peculiar institution" as a way of organizing workers: white Americans forced black Americans to perform tasks not of their choosing and without pay. As Eric Foner writes, "First and foremost, slavery was a system of labor." Eric Foner, *Give Me Liberty: An American History*, vol. 1 (New York: W. W. Norton, 2005), 352. For more on the domestic slave trade, see Baptist, *Half Has Never Been Told*; and Steven Deyle, *Carry Me Back: The Domestic Slave Trade in American Life* (New York: Oxford University Press, 2006).

25. First quote in "To the New Beginner," *American Cotton Planter*, July 1858, 228; second quote in "The American Cotton Planter," *American Cotton Planter*, January 1853, 20–21; third quote from letter dated November 28, 1848, from J. L. Whitten to Edmund Burke, US Commissioner of Patents, *Annual Report of the Commissioner of Patents for 1848* (Washington, DC: Government Printing Office, 1849), 502.

26. First quote in letter dated January 3, 1861, Allen Family Papers I, box 250, folder 11, WSHSC; second in letter dated December 15, 1848, from J. B. De Bow of the Statistical Bureau of Louisiana to Edmund Burke, US Commissioner of Patents; US Congress, *Annual Report of the Commissioner of Patents for 1848*, House Executive Document No. 59, 2nd Sess., 1849 (Washington, DC: Government Printing Office, 1849), 516.

27. The degree to which the antebellum South was self-sufficient in food production occupied a large space in the historical literature of the 1960s and 1970s; historians used plantation records, census data, and estimates of farm production to gauge the extent to which the South relied on interregional trade to compensate for a dearth of locally produced commodities. See the historiographical discussions in William Hutchinson and Samuel Williamson, "The Self-Sufficiency of the Antebellum South: Estimates of Food Supply," *Journal of Economic History* 31, no. 3 (September 1971): 591–593; Earle, "Price of Precocity," 25–31; Robert Gallman, "Self-Sufficiency in the Cotton Economy of the Antebellum South," *Agricultural History* 44 (1970): 24–46; Wright, *Political Economy of the Cotton South*; Douglass C. North, *The Economic Growth of the United States, 1790–1860* (New York: W. W. Norton, 1966); Robert W. Fogel, "A Provisional View of the 'New Economic History,'" *American Economic Review* 54 (May 1964): 377–389; Albert Fishlow, "Antebellum Regional Trade Reconsidered," in *New Views on American Economic Development*, ed. Ralph Andreano (Cambridge, MA: Schenkman, 1965), 187–224.

28. Farm Journal, 1862–1866 (pp. 1–2), Hugh Davis Papers, box 3462, folder 6, WSHSC; and Weymouth T. Jordan, "The Elisha F. King Family Planters of the Alabama Black Belt," *Agricultural History* 19, no. 3 (July 1945): 159.

29. John Inscoe, "Georgia in 1860," *The New Georgia Encyclopedia*, http://www.georgiaencyclopedia.org/articles/history-archaeology/georgia-1860 (accessed April 6, 2016). Small slaveholders, herdsmen, and subsistence farmers were once lumped together into an undifferentiated mass by historians who considered them to be of little importance to the antebellum South because of their isolation from the cash-crop economy. Since the work of Frank Owsley in the mid-twentieth century, however, historians have begun to recognize, not only that the majority of white southerners were plain folk, but also that they were rarely the anticommercial, economically isolated, socially backward frontiersmen they were previously thought to be. Owsley, *Plain Folk of the Old South*; Bradley Bond, "Herders, Farmers, and Markets on the Inner Frontier: The Mississippi Piney Woods, 1850–1860," in *Plain Folk of the South Revisited*, ed. Samuel Hyde Jr. (Baton Rouge: Louisiana State University Press, 1997), 73–99; Wetherington, *Plain Folk's Fight*; Donald Winters, "'Plain Folk' of the Old South Reexamined: Economic Democracy in Tennessee," *Journal of Southern History* 53 (November 1987): 565–586; Harry Watson, "'The Common Rights of Mankind': Subsistence, Shad and Commerce in the Early Republican South," *Journal of American History* 83, no. 1 (June 1996): 13–43.

30. For many years, historians characterized small farmers, or "plain folk," as "disdainful" or suspicious of the market. More recently, however, southern historians have produced more

nuanced descriptions of agricultural production among smaller farmers. See the discussion of this historiography in Bond, "Herders, Farmers, and Markets," 78–79. See also Mary Beth Pudup, "The Limits of Subsistence: Agriculture and Industry in Central Appalachia," *Agricultural History* 64, no. 1 (Winter 1990): 61–92; Paul Escott, "Yeoman Independence and the Market: Social Status and Economic Development in Antebellum North Carolina," *North Carolina Historical Review* 66, no. 3 (July 1989): 275–299; David Weiman, "Farmers and the Market in Antebellum America: A View from the Georgia Upcountry," *Journal of Economic History* 47, no. 3 (September 1987): 639.

31. Philip Racine, ed., *Piedmont Farmer: The Journals of David Golightly Harris, 1855–1870* (Knoxville: University of Tennessee Press, 1990), 2, 4–5; Wright and Kunreuther, "Cotton, Corn, and Risk in the Nineteenth Century," 529–530; Davis, *Where There Are Mountains*, 136–137; and Earle, "Price of Precocity," 26.

32. Rubin, "Limits of Agricultural Progress," 364–366; and Stewart, *"What Nature Suffers to Groe"*, 5.

33. Samuel Wilson, "An Account of the Province of Carolina, in America," in *Narratives of Early Carolina, 1650–1708*, ed. Alexander Salley Jr. (New York: Barnes and Noble, 1959), 169–172, 174, quote on 169–170; letter dated April 30, 1711, from Christen Janzen to unnamed recipients, in *Christoph von Graffenried's Account of the Founding of New Bern*, ed. Vincent H. Todd (Raleigh, NC: Edwards and Broughton Printing Co., 1920), 317–320; *Journal of a Lady of Quality; Being the Narrative of a Journey from Scotland to the West Indies, North Carolina, and Portugal, in the Years 1774 to 1776*, ed. Evangeline Walker Andrews (New Haven, CT: Yale University Press, 1921). Both available electronically through the Documenting the American South Project, http://docsouth.unc.edu/nc/graffenried/menu.html and https://docsouth.unc.edu/nc/schaw/schaw.html(accessed May 30, 2017).

34. Entries dated January 1–7, 24; February 7, 13–16, 20–21; and March 4, 1854, and list of slaves dated January 1860, Joseph M. Jayne Plantation Journals, *RASP* Series F, pt. 2, reel 1, RBMSC.

35. Several scholars have explored the relationship of the environmental conditions in the South and its socioeconomic development during the antebellum period. See Douglas Helms, "Soil and Southern History: Presidential Address to the Agricultural History Society" (prepared by the Agricultural History Society and the Iowa State University Center for Agricultural History, 2000); John Majewski and Viken Tchakerian, "The Environmental Origins of Shifting Cultivation: Climate, Soils, and Disease in the Nineteenth-Century US South," *Agricultural History* 81, no. 4 (Fall 2007): 522–549; Majewski, *Modernizing a Slave Economy*; and Rubin, "Limits of Agricultural Progress."

36. I. E. Lowery, *Life on the Old Plantation in Ante-bellum Days; or, a Story Based on Facts* (Columbia, SC: State Company Printers, 1911), 89–90; J. S. Otto and N. E. Anderson, "Slash-and-Burn Cultivation in the Highlands South: A Problem in Comparative Agricultural History," *Comparative Studies in Society and History* 24, no. 1 (January 1982): 131–133. Examples of farmers noting shifting cultivation include entries for January, February, and March 1843, "Journal of 'Araby' Plantation," Haller Nutt Papers, *RASP*, Series F, pt. 1, reel 1, RBMSC; entries for January and February 1855, "Daybook," Nelson Clayton Papers, box 1, folder 68, WSHSC; diary entry dated February 1860 (p. 21), William Wallace White Diaries, Southern Historical Collection, University of North Carolina at Chapel Hill (hereafter SHC); Time Book January 1851 (pp. 144–145), Plantation Records, vol. 1 (1846–1852), Bayside Plantation Records, box 1, folder 1, SHC.

37. Kirby, *Mockingbird Song*, 99; and John Belton O'Neall, *The Annals of Newberry in Two Parts, Part the First* (Newberry, SC: Aull and Houseal, 1892), 11.

38. See Majewski, *Modernizing the Slave Economy*, 23–24. For further discussion of this subject, see Trimble, *Man-Induced Soil Erosion*, app. C, 155–156.

39. Statistics compiled by the author from the US Census of 1860, Minnesota Population Center, University of Minnesota, National Historical Geographic Information System: Version 11.0, http://www.nhgis.org (accessed June 2, 2017). The drastically lower rural population densities in southern states is cited as one of the reasons for the failure of the South to develop the vibrant internal market economy seen in northern states. Fewer free people meant fewer

consumers, and the high turnover rate of southern farmers because of the practice of shifting cultivation contributed to the lack of "permanent improvements" in the form of town buildings, schools, and other structures.

40. Frederick Law Olmsted, *Cotton Kingdom: A Traveller's Observations on Cotton and Slavery in the American Slave States*, vol. 1 (New York: Mason Brothers, 1861), 12; David Hackett Fischer and James C. Kelly, *Bound Away: Virginia and the Westward Movement* (Charlottesville: University of Virginia Press, 2000); Avery Craven, *Soil Exhaustion as a Factor in the Agricultural History of Virginia and Maryland, 1606–1860* (Urbana: University of Illinois Press, 1926); William Chandler Bagley Jr., *Soil Exhaustion and the Civil War* (Washington, DC: American Council on Public Affairs, 1942).

41. Catherine Keever, "A Retrospective View of Old-Field Succession after 35 Years," *American Midland Naturalist* 110, no. 2 (October 1983): 397, 400; Richard J. Hobbs and Viki A. Cramer, "Why Old Fields? Socioeconomic and Ecological Causes and Consequences of Land Abandonment," in *Old Fields and Restoration of Abandoned Farmland*, ed. Viki A. Cramer and Richard J. Hobbs (Washington, DC: Island Press, 2007), 8–10; and Richard J. Hobbs and Lawrence R. Walker, "Old Field Succession: Development of Concepts," in Cramer and Hobbs, *Old Fields and Restoration*, 25; Henri Grissino-Mayer and David R. Butler, "Effects of Climate on Growth of Shortleaf Pine in Northern Georgia: A Dendroclimatic Study," *Southeastern Geographer* 33, no. 1 (May 1993): 65–81; Daniel Richter and Daniel Markewitz, *Understanding Soil Change: Soil Sustainability over Millennia, Centuries, and Decades* (Cambridge: Cambridge University Press, 2007), 118–119; and Majewski, *Modernizing a Slave Economy*, 35–36.

42. Entry dated November 12, 1843, and entry dated November 5, 1844, "Journal of 'Araby' Plantation," Haller Nutt Papers, *RASP*, Series F, pt. 1, reel 1, RBMSC; Cornelius Cathey, *Agriculture in North Carolina Before the Civil War* (Raleigh: North Carolina Department of Cultural Resources, 1974), 10–11; Steinberg, *Down to Earth*, 105–106; Davis, *Where There Are Mountains*, 76–77; and Virginia DeJohn Anderson, *Creatures of Empire: How Domestic Animals Transformed Early America* (New York: Oxford University Press, 2004), 110, 113–114, 119.

43. Entry dated October 1860, Diary of Capt. William Wallace White, vol. 48, William Wallace White Diaries, SHC; letter dated January 13, 1862, from A. C. Hartgrove to W. W. Lenoir, Series 1.3, Personal Correspondence, 1861–1865, Lenoir Family Papers, SHC; and entry dated March 14, 1860, Journals of David Golightly Harris, in Racine, *Piedmont Farmer*, 128.

44. Supreme Court of Alabama, *Jean v. Sandiford*, January Term, 1864; case records available on *Westlaw*, 39 Ala. 317, 1864 WL 497; and Drew A. Swanson, "Fighting over Fencing: Agricultural Reform and Antebellum Efforts to Close the Virginia Open Range," *Virginia Magazine of History and Biography* 117, no. 2 (2009): 105–106.

45. Thomas Cox et al., *This Well-Wooded Land: Americans and Their Forests from Colonial Times to the Present* (Lincoln: University of Nebraska Press, 1985), 12; and interview with Jesse Rice by Caldwell Sims, WPA Slave Narrative Project, South Carolina Narratives, vol. 14, pt. 4, Manuscript Division, Library of Congress (hereafter LOC).

46. "The Fence Law," *Southern Planter* 8, no. 3, March 1848, 67.

47. Rubin, "Limits of Agricultural Progress," 362–373; and Cowdrey, *This Land, This South*, 77.

48. J. Gray Smith, *Description of Improved Farms in the State of Tennessee in the United States of America, Describing the Number of Acres of Arable, Meadow, Pasture, and Wood Land . . .* (London: C. Mitchell, 1843), microfilm 38, TSLA. See also John Zaborney, *Slaves for Hire: Renting Enslaved Laborers in Antebellum Virginia* (Baton Rouge: Louisiana State University Press, 2012), 12, 17–18, 21–23, 71.

49. Steven Nash, *Reconstruction's Ragged Edge: The Politics of Postwar Life in the Southern Mountains* (Chapel Hill: University of North Carolina Press, 2016), 11; and Martin Crawford, "Mountain Farmers and the Market Economy: Ashe County during the 1850s," *North Carolina Historical Review* 71, no. 4 (October 1994): 430–450.

50. *Thirty Years a Slave, From Bondage to Freedom . . . The Autobiography of Louis Hughes* (Milwaukee, WI: South Side Printing Company, 1897), 27. The Edmund Ruffin Jr. Plantation Journals in the Edmund Ruffin Papers, SHC, provide an excellent example of a planter who combined the records of his slaves in cotton and corn fields.

51. Griffith, *Alabama: A Documentary History to 1900*, 150; *Thirty Years a Slave*, 32–33. See also the John Horry Dent Journals, John Horry Dent Papers, Special Collections and Archives, Auburn University (hereafter SCA); Jordan, "Elisha King Family of Planters"; and Weymouth T. Jordan, *Antebellum Alabama: Town and Country* (Jacksonville: Florida State University Press, 1957), 54–55.

52. *Southern Planter*, August 1854, 225–228.

53. Entry dated November 1855, John Horry Dent Farm Journals, box 1, folder 4, SCA; entries dated February 19, February 27, and March 3, 1857, Francis Terry Leak Papers, Manuscript, vol. 4, folder 11, SHC; entries for January and February 1854 and marginalia dated May 1854 on front inside cover, "Daybook," Nelson Clayton Papers, box 1, folder 68, WSHSC.

54. First quote in *Marion Standard*, April 9, 1909; second in letter dated January 3, 1861, Allen Family Papers I, box 250, folder 11, WSHSC. See also Jordan, "Elisha F. King Family Planters," 153.

55. Statistics compiled by the author from the US Census of 1860, Minnesota Population Center, University of Minnesota, National Historical Geographic Information System: Version 11.0, available at http://www.nhgis.org (accessed June 2, 2017). For descriptions of manuring in Louisiana, see J. D. De Bow's letter to the US Commissioner of Patents in *Annual Report of the U.S. Commissioner of Patents for the Year 1848*, 516. For an example of a farmer who used composted material, see the James Asbury Tait Papers, WSHSC. As discussed earlier, Edmund Ruffin was a proponent of using mineral-based fertilizers, such as marl. A broader discussion is found in Richard Sheridan, "Chemical Fertilizers in Southern Agriculture," *Agricultural History* 53, no. 1 (January 1979): 308.

56. Entries for 1858, 1859, and 1860, James Washington Matthews Journals, TSLA. James Washington Matthews was born in 1799 in North Carolina. Gilbert was one of several children he had on a farm worth almost $13,000 in 1860. US Federal Census for 1860. John Horry Dent wrote that it took a large workforce to keep up his plantation. In 1858, Dent cultivated 761 acres: 205 acres of corn, 456 acres of cotton, 15 acres of potatoes, 15 acres of oats, and 70 of oats. Assuming Dent cultivated the same percentage of his land as other Black Belt farmers, he owned about 2,536 acres.

57. First quote in Davis, *Where There Are Mountains*, 146; second in Majewski, *Modernizing a Slave Economy*, 59.

58. "Democratic Convention of Mississippi," *Oxford Intelligencer*, June 4, 1860.

59. Studies of the debates over the expansion of slavery are part of a larger literature that tries to explain what caused the Civil War, whether it was inevitable, and who supported it and why. Works that represent the evolution and various factions within this literature include Charles Beard and Mary Beard, *The Rise of American Civilization* (New York: Macmillan, 1927); Avery Craven, *The Coming of the Civil War* (Chicago: University of Chicago Press, 1942); Kenneth Stampp, *And the War Came: The North and the Secession Crisis, 1860–61* (Baton Rouge: Louisiana State University Press, 1950); Michael Holt, *The Political Crisis of the 1850s* (New York: Wiley, 1978); William W. Freehling, *The Road to Disunion*, vols. 1 and 2 (New York: Oxford University Press, 1990, 2007); Brian Holden Reid, *The Origins of the American Civil War* (London: Longman, 1996); and Nelson Lankford, *Cry Havoc! The Crooked Road to Civil War, 1861* (New York: Viking, 2007). The most recent works in the field explore the timeline of disunion and its contingency. Excellent historiographical discussions appear in Elizabeth Varon, *Disunion! The Coming of the American Civil War, 1789–1859* (Chapel Hill: University of North Carolina Press, 2008), 1–5; and Edward Ayers, *What Caused the Civil War: Reflections on the South and Southern History* (New York: W. W. Norton, 2005), 112–125. There are scholars who focus on less-traditional aspects of the secession crisis. Christopher Olsen, for instance, details how contemporary ideals of masculinity and honor played out in the secession crisis in *Political Culture and Secession in Mississippi: Masculinity, Honor, and the Anti-party Tradition, 1830–1860* (New York: Oxford University Press, 2000).

60. "Resolutions Adopted by the Convention," in the minutes of the Southern Convention at Savannah, reprinted in *De Bow's Review* 22, no. 1, January 1857, 101.

61. "A View of the Agricultural Conditions of the Lower Counties of Maryland, No. 1," *American Farmer*, June 25, 1819, 95. Discussed and quoted at length in Philip Herrington, "The

Exceptional Plantation: Slavery, Agricultural Reform, and the Creation of an American Landscape" (PhD diss., University of Virginia, 2012), 32.

62. Letter dated October 27, 1847, from J. W. Whitten to Edmund Burke, US Commissioner of Patents, in US Congress, *The Annual Report of the Commissioner of Patents for 1847*, House Executive Document No. 54, 1st Sess., 1848 (Washington, DC: Government Printing Office, 1848), 386.

63. Letter dated January 25, 1849, from J. Balestier to Edmund Burke, US Commissioner of Patents, in US Congress, *The Annual Report of the Commissioner of Patents for 1848*, House Executive Document No. 59, 2nd Sess., 1849 (Washington, DC: Government Printing Office, 1849), 521.

64. First quote in J. H. Norwood, "Can the South Afford to Produce Cotton at Present Prices, and Buy Her Supplies Abroad?" *Southern Planter*, October 1876; second in "The Pine Forests of the South," *De Bow's Review* 27, no. 6, December 1859, 722.

65. James Kirke Paulding, quoted in Saikku, *This Delta, This Land*, 108; *Marion Standard*, April 9, 1909.

66. Quote from Saikku, *This Delta, This Land*, 106; Trimble, *Man-Induced Soil Erosion*, 61; Fiege, *Nature's Republic*, 106.

67. First quote in Joseph Holt Ingraham, *The South-West, by a Yankee* (New York: Harper, 1835), 86; second in Trimble, *Man-Induced Soil Erosion*, 57. See also Arthur R. Hall, "Terracing in the Southern Piedmont," *Agricultural History* 23, no. 2 (April 1949): 97.

68. "The Enclosure System of Virginia," *Southern Planter*, August 1852, 231; "Fences," *Alabama Baptist*, April 5, 1845; and "Enclosure System of Virginia," 233.

69. Frederick Law Olmsted, *A Journey in the Seaboard Slave States* (New York: Dix and Edwards, 1856), 89.

70. Letter dated March 23, 1858, from David Headrick to Alexander Frank, and letter dated May 17, 1858, from John Frank to Alexander Frank, box 1, Alexander Frank Papers, RBMSC.

71. First quote in Craven, *Soil Exhaustion as a Factor*, 58–59; second in Oakes, *Ruling Race*, 77–78.

72. First quote in Bagley, *Soil Exhaustion and the Civil War*, 72; second in Carville Earle, "The Myth of the Southern Soil Miner: Macrohistory, Agricultural Innovation, and Environmental Change," in *The Ends of the Earth: Perspectives on Modern Environmental History*, ed. Donald Worster (Cambridge: Cambridge University Press, 1988), 176.

73. Roy Donohue, *Soils: An Introduction to Soils and Plant Growth*, 2nd ed. (New York: Prentice-Hall, 1965), 110; W. T. Pettigrew, W. R. Meredith, H. A. Bruns, and S. R. Stetina, "Effects of a Short-Term Corn Rotation on Cotton Dry Matter Partitioning, Lint Yield, and Fiber Quality Production," *Journal of Cotton Science* 10, no. 3 (2006): 244; Earle, "Price of Precocity," 39–40. The cowpea/corn rotation was adopted after it was discovered in 1838 that leguminous plants fixed nitrogen from the air. For a lengthy contemporary explanation of this crop rotation and its benefits, see "Plantation Economy—Inquiries," *Southern Cultivator*, October 1860, 297–299.

74. Quotation in *American Husbandry: Containing an Account of the Soil, Climate, Production and Agriculture of the British Colonies by an American*, vol. 1 (London: J. Bew, 1775), 229–230; and William Barney, *The Road to Secession: A New Perspective on the Old South* (New York: Praeger, 1972), 7.

75. Adam Wesley Dean, *An Agrarian Republic: Farming, Antislavery Politics, and Nature Parks in the Civil War Era* (Chapel Hill: University of North Carolina Press, 2015), 4–5.

76. Ibid.

77. First quote in "The South and Progress," *DeBow's Review* 26, no. 2, December 1859, 216; second in Edmund Ruffin, "Consequences of Abolition Agitation, No. 5," *De Bow's Review* 23, no. 6, December 1857, 598. See Bagley, *Soil Exhaustion and the Civil War*, 3–8, for a summary of his argument.

78. Willoughby Newton was a tobacco planter in the Tidewater region of Virginia and the president of the Virginia State Agricultural Society during the 1840s. Whitemarsh Benjamin Seabrook was a lawyer and politician from South Carolina whose primary interest was his cotton plantation on Edisto Island. Both men strongly supported southern rights and secession during the late 1850s. See Mitchell Snay, *Fenians, Freedmen, and Southern Whites in the Era of Reconstruction* (Baton Rouge: Louisiana State University Press, 2007), 107–108; and *History*

of the State Agricultural Society of South Carolina (Columbia, SC: R. L. Bryan Company, 1916), 219.

79. Willoughby Newton, *Address before the Virginia State Agricultural Society: Delivered in the Hall of the Houses of Delegates, February 19, 1852,* and Edmund Ruffin, *To the Virginia State Agricultural Society, on the Effects of Domestic Slavery on . . . the Agricultural Population of the Southern States, December 16, 1852,* both in supplement to *Southern Planter,* vol. 12, 1852, 6, 13, 15.

80. First quote in "Plantation Work for July," *American Cotton Planter and Soil of the South,* July 1858, 204–205; second in "On the Cotton Plantation or the Stock Farm," *American Cotton Planter and Soil of the South,* June 1858, 196.

81. "Report of the Inspector of Guano," January 28, 1850, Maryland, House and Senate Documents.

82. "Guano vs. Manure and Marl Compost," *American Cotton Planter,* January 1853, 49. The *American Cotton Planter* merged with *Soil of the South* in 1857 to become *The American Cotton Planter and Soil of the South.*

83. Gregory Cushman, *Guano and the Opening of the Pacific World: A Global Environmental History* (Cambridge: Cambridge University Press, 2013), 53. See, for instance, Plantation Diary, William C. Adams Papers, reel 20, *RASP,* Series F, pt. 4: North Carolina and Virginia Plantations, RBMSC; "Receipts of Captain Elisha King," box 1, folder 1, King Family Papers, WSHSC; and entries for 1862, T. L. Jones Farm Journal, SHC.

84. Steven Stoll, *Larding the Learn Earth: Soil and Society in Nineteenth-Century America* (New York: Hill and Wang, 2003); Emily Pawley, "'The Balance Sheet of Nature:' Calculating the New York Farm, 1820–1860" (PhD diss., University of Pennsylvania, 2011); Bond, "Herders, Farmers, and Markets," 81; Edward Pressen, "How Different Were the Antebellum North and South?," *American Historical Review* 85, no. 5 (1980): 1122–1123; Stanley Engerman, "A Reconsideration of Southern Economic Growth, 1770–1860," *Agricultural History* 49 (1975): 343–361; Lewis Cecil Gray, *History of Agriculture in the Southern United States to 1860,* 2 vols., 1932-1933 (Reprint, Gloucester, MA: Peter Smith, 1958); Percy W. Bidwell and John I. Falconer, *History of Agriculture in the Northern United States, 1620–1860* (Washington, DC: Carnegie Institution of Washington, 1925); Percy W. Bidwell, "Rural Economy in New England at the Beginning of the 19th Century," *Transactions of the Connecticut Academy of Arts and Sciences* 20 (April 1917): 241-399; Paul W. Gates, *The Farmer's Age: Agriculture, 1815–1860* (London: M. E. Sharpe, 1960); and Fiege, *Republic of Nature,* 201.

Chapter 2

1. Note by "JTG" included in letter dated April 8, 1864, from Alonzo Miller to his Father, Diary, Alonzo Miller Papers, Atlanta History Center, Kenan Research Center, Atlanta, Georgia (hereafter AHC). Annotations of this correspondence, transcribed by the National Park Service, identify JTG as Jasper George, Private Co. A, 12th Infantry, referred to as "Jap" in many of Miller's letters. Henry Hamilton Bennett, another, more experienced member of the 12th Wisconsin, blamed the boat, not the river, for the excruciatingly slow pace of the regiment's transport. See entry dated April 2, H. H. Bennett Diaries, vol. 4 (loose paper at back), Wisconsin Historical Society, Madison (hereafter WHS).

2. Letters dated February 25, April 8, and April 22, 1864, Diary, Alonzo Miller Papers, AHC. Annotations on page 14 detail these men's participation (or lack thereof) in military operations in and around Mississippi. Miller and George were part of a group of new recruits who joined the 12th Wisconsin at "Camp Louis" the first week of March 1864. Their arrival is noted by H. H. Bennett. See entry dated March 4, 1864, H. H. Bennett Diaries, vol. 4, WHS.

3. Descriptions of farms taken from letters dated April 22 and May 16, 1864; quotes from letters dated February 25 and April 8, 1864, from Alonzo Miller to his sister and father, Diary, Alonzo Miller Papers, AHC.

4. Letters dated March 8 and April 8, 1864, from Alonzo Miller to his father, Diary, Alonzo Miller Papers, AHC.

5. Phrase used in "Atlanta 'Growing Fast' 60 Years Ago," *Harper's New Monthly Magazine*, December 1879, box 4, folder 1, Jennie Meta Barker Papers, AHC.

6. T. Harry Williams, *Lincoln and His Generals* (New York: Alfred A. Knopf, 1952), 3. The long-standing debate on the degree to which the Civil War "devastated" the South is discussed in Mark E. Neely, *The Civil War and the Limits of Destruction* (Cambridge, MA: Harvard University Press), 199–203. The most important monographs on the environmental impacts of the conflict document the "destruction" of the southern landscape by military operations. Lisa Brady, in particular, contends that these infamous military operations intended to make the South a new "wilderness" by destroying its economic, military, and agricultural foundations. Brady, *War upon the Land*, 3, 10–11.

7. Note dated June 1864, from J. P. George to Mr. Miller, tucked into letter dated June 14, 1864, from Alonzo Miller to his father, and letter dated June 20, 1864, from Alonzo Miller to his sister, Diary, Alonzo Miller Papers, AHC. In April 1864, Sherman ordered all veteran regiments on furlough in the armies of the Ohio, Cumberland, and Tennessee join him in Tennessee. Miller and George's trip up the Mississippi from Vicksburg to Cairo, Illinois, described earlier, was to meet the veterans in their regiment who had been in Wisconsin—Lonnie calls them the "Old Regiment"—and travel with the forces of General Gresham to Clifton, Tennessee. From there the 12th Wisconsin marched through Alabama to Rome, Georgia, finally joining Sherman's forces in Ackworth on June 8, 1864. Thereafter, they acted as part of the Atlanta Campaign. See E. B. Quiner, *The Military History of Wisconsin: Civil and Military Patriotism of the State in the War for the Union* (Chicago: Clarke and Co., 1866), 579–580, for these movements and their participation in the fighting at Kennesaw Mountain. The Atlanta Campaign took place during the spring and summer of 1864 as Confederate forces under Joseph E. Johnston and, later, John B. Hood attempted to keep General William T. Sherman's Union forces from driving south from Chattanooga, Tennessee, to Atlanta, Georgia. Military clashes of this campaign include the Battles of Picket's Mill, Kennesaw Mountain, Pace's Ferry, Atlanta, Lovejoy's Station, and Jonesborough. See Stephen Davis, "The Atlanta Campaign," *The New Georgia Encyclopedia*, available at http://www.georgiaencyclopedia.org/articles/history-archaeology/atlanta-campaign (accessed June 2, 2017).

8. First quote in letter dated August 11, 1864, from Alonzo Miller to his father. For descriptions of the rain, the fighting, and the construction of defenses, see letters dated June 14, July 9, and July 24, 1864. Final quote in letter dated June 20, 1864, from Alonzo Miller to his father, Diary, Alonzo Miller Papers, AHC.

9. Jacob Dolson Cox, *Military Reminiscences of the Civil War*, vol. 1 (New York: C. Scribner's Sons, 1900), 179, quoted in Allen Guelzo, *Fateful Lightning: A New History of the Civil War and Reconstruction* (New York: Oxford University Press, 2012), 144. There were many manuals in circulation at the time about the construction of fortifications; the one most heavily cited for US military training is D. H. Mahan's *A Treatise on Field Fortification* (New York: John Wiley, 1836).

10. J. Watts de Peyster, "From the Rapidan to Appomattox Court-House" (Philadelphia: L. R. Hamersly & Co., 1888), 2.

11. J. P. Hupy and T. Koehler, "Modern Warfare as a Significant Form of Zoogeomorphologic Disturbance upon a Landscape," *Geomorphology* 157–158 (2012): 168–182; and Stephen Demarais et al., "Disturbance Associated with Military Exercises," in *Ecosystems of Disturbed Ground*, ed. Lawrence R. Walker (Amsterdam: Elsevier, 1999), 386.

12. The maps drawn of the works north of the Spotsylvania Court House, for instance, show a pentagonal system of breastworks protecting the Confederate troops. Outside Petersburg, however, Grant famously built a single line of trenches that stretched for thirty miles. See *Atlas to Accompany the Official Records of the Union and Confederate Armies* (Washington, DC: Government Printing Office, 1891), plate 81, https://ehistory.osu.edu/books/official-records/atlas-plates-61-120. For additional descriptions of Grant's defenses outside Petersburg, see A. Wilson Greene, *Civil War Petersburg: Confederate City in the Crucible of War* (Charlottesville: University of Virginia Press, 2006), chap. 8.

13. Letter dated July 9, 1864, from Alonzo Miller to his sister, Diary, Alonzo Miller Papers, AHC. For descriptions of how abatises and chevaux-de-frise were laid out in defense works and the types of materials used to build them, see "Virginia," *The American Annual Cyclopedia and*

Register of Important Events of the Year 1865, vol. 5, ed. D. Appleton (New York: D. Appleton and Co. 1870), 815.

14. First quotes in entries dated May 5, 1864, and February 23, 1865, in *Civil War Notebook of Daniel Chisholm*, ed. W. Springer Menge and J. August Shimrak (New York: Orion, 1989), 12–13, 65; second quote in entry dated October 6, 1863, in J. Franklin Dyer, *The Journals of a Civil War Surgeon*, ed. Michael Chesson (Omaha: University of Nebraska, 2003), 121; third quote in entry dated May 8, 1864, Diary of Charles Robert Walden, box 7, folder 7, Confederate Miscellany Papers, Manuscripts, Archives, and Rare Books Library, Emory University (hereafter MARBL).

15. First and second quotes in entries dated August 13, 1864, and March 19, 1865, War Diary, James A. Congleton Papers, box 1, folder 1, LOC. There are similar descriptions in the entry dated January 30, 1863, H. H. Bennett Diary, vol. 4, WHS. Artist Alfred Waud sketched a group of General U. S. Grant's soldiers "frantically throwing up breastworks" without tools at Cold Harbor, VA, on June 3, 1864. See Waud's illustration in Ron Field, *American Civil War Fortifications*, vol. 2, *Land and Field Fortifications* (New York: Osprey, 2005), 20.

16. Notebook 1, p. 23, Henry T. Bahnson Papers, SHC; report dated June 29, 1865, by General James H. Wilson, in US War Department, *The War of the Rebellion: A Compilation of the Official Records of the Union and Confederate Armies* (Washington, DC: Government Printing Office, 1863–1891), series 1, vol. 49, pt. I, 359. For mention of Wheeler, see entry dated April 11, 1865, War Diary, box 1, folder 1, James A. Congleton Papers, LOC.

17. See Mark Grimsley, *The Hard Hand of War: Union Military Policy toward Southern Civilians* (Cambridge: Cambridge University Press, 1997), 17–22; Gregory J. Ashworth, *War and the City* (New York: Routledge, 1991); and Nelson, *Ruin Nation*, 12–13. As other scholars have noted, the Civil War officers trained at the US Military Academy at West Point knew that warfare was traditionally conducted on two fronts: pitched battle in the field and siege against an enemy's cities.

18. Letter dated May 2, 1865, from Henry W. Hart to his wife, box 1, folder 32, Union Miscellany Papers, MARBL; report dated June 29, 1865, by General James H. Wilson, *OR*, series 1, vol. 49, pt. 1, 360–361; James Pickett Jones, *Yankee Blitzkrieg: Wilson's Raid through Alabama and Georgia* (Lexington: University Press of Kentucky, 1976), 78–81.

19. Interest in the short- and long-term effects of artillery in twentieth-century wars, such as the First World War, the Vietnam War, and recent engagements in the Middle East, is booming, and the Civil War is often discounted. Until the last decade of the nineteenth century, gunpowder was too unstable to allow for the systematic use of highly explosive munitions. Joseph Hupy, "Assessing Landscape Disturbance and Recovery across a WWI Battlefield" (PhD diss., Michigan State University, 2005), 23. Examples of this literature include Eef Meerschman et al., "Geostatistical Assessment of the Impact of WWI on the Spatial Occurrence of Soil Heavy Metals," *Ambio* 40 (2011): 417–424; Joseph Hupy and Randall Schaetzl, "Introducing 'Bombturbation,' A Singular Type of Soil Disturbance and Mixing," *Soil Science* 171, no. 11 (2006): 823–836; Michael D. Chendorain and Lloyd D. Stewart, "Corrosion of Unexploded Ordnance in Soil-Field Results," *Environmental Science and Technology* 39, no. 8 (2005): 2442–2447; and Farouk El-Baz and R. M. Makharita, *The Gulf War and the Environment* (Lausanne: Gordon and Breach Science Publishers, 1994). For examples of long passages dedicated to artillery's impact on the surrounding landscape, see letter dated July 26, 1862, from George Barnsley to Godfrey Barnsley, box 1, folder 8, Godfrey Barnsley Papers, MARBL; and entry dated July 22, 1864, Diary of Henry Stanley, box 1, folder 26, Antebellum and Civil War Collection, AHC. Studies of the environmental consequences of building fortifications do exist for more recent conflicts. See R. Misak, D. Al-Ajmi, and A. Al-Enezi, "War-Induced Soil Degradation, Depletion, and Destruction (The Case of Ground Fortifications in the Terrestrial Environment of Kuwait)," in *Environmental Consequences of War and Aftermath*, eds. T.A. Kassim and D. Barcelo, *Handbook of Environmental Chemistry*, vol. 3U (Berlin: Springer, 2009), 137.

20. See the discussion of the Piedmont in chapter 1, as well as descriptions in Trimble, *Man-Induced Soil Erosion*, chap. 3 and esp. the map on p. 5, for an explanation of the erosivity of rainfall in the southern Piedmont.

21. For more on Atlanta's role as a Confederate industrial site, see Sean Vanatta and Dan Du, "Civil War Industry and Manufacturing," *New Georgia Encyclopedia*, http://www.georgiaencyclopedia.org/articles/history-archaeology/civil-war-industry-and-manufacturing (accessed May 30, 2017); Chad Morgan, *Planters' Progress: Modernizing Confederate Georgia* (Gainesville: University Press of Florida, 2005); and Ralph Benjamin Singer Jr., "Confederate Atlanta" (PhD diss., University of Georgia, 1973).

22. Entry dated July 16, 1864, Diary of Dr. Henry Stanley, Antebellum and Civil War Collection, box 1, folder 26, AHC. For a description of how the Confederate States of America planned Atlanta's defenses, see letter dated August 11, 1863, from J. F. Gilmer to L. P. Grant, box 6, folder 15, L. P. Grant Papers, AHC. The hand-drawn plans for the defenses are in flat file 1.

23. Quote in George Ward Nichols, *The Story of the Great March: From the Diary of a Staff Officer* (New York: Harper & Brothers, 1865), 16. See William T. Sherman, *Memoirs of Gen. William T. Sherman*, vol. 2, pt. 3 (New York: D. Appleton and Co., 1889), map 5, chap. 18, available online at the *Gutenberg Project*, http://www.gutenberg.org/files/4361/old/orig4361-h/p3.htm#ch18 (accessed May 30, 2017). The number of miles of defensive works calculated by author using the distance between landmarks and letters describing the planning of the Atlanta fortifications. See letter dated August 11, 1863, from J. F. Gilmer to L. P. Grant, box 6, folder 15, L. P. Grant Papers, AHC.

24. For an example of these types of records in which the cubic yards of soil displaced to grade the railroad are accounted for, see "Estimate Book for the Engineering Department of the Alabama and Chattanooga Railroad, 1869–1871," Robert Jemison Papers, box 53, folder 3, WSHSC. One historian claims that fifty-five miles of rice banks for a South Carolina plantation displaced over 6.4 million cubic feet of soil. Because of differences in soil, the depth and size of the works versus a rice bank, and so on, it would be imprudent to use that ratio as the basis for a definitive calculation of how much soil 50 miles of works affected. The comparison does, however, help to characterize the scale of the displaced soil. Judith Carney, *Black Rice: The African Origins of Rice Cultivation in the Americas* (Cambridge, MA: Harvard University Press, 2001), 93–94.

25. Menge and Shimrak, *Civil War Notebook of Daniel Chisholm*, 15–16; and Notebook 1, Henry T. Bahnson Papers, SHC, 23.

26. See Menge and Shimrak, *Civil War Notebook of Daniel Chisholm*, 18, 45. For other examples of soldier observations on the clearing of vegetation for breastworks, see letter dated July 21, 1862, from Godfrey Barnsley to his father, box 1, folder 16, Godfrey Barnsley Papers, MARBL; and Henry T. Bahnson Notebooks, SHC. In one map, the cartographers also noted the areas of timber that were felled for use by armies. The areas of cleared woodland are considerable, and from their position—always adjacent to a cultivated field—it appears as if armies felled privately owned timber or range land to build their fortifications or improve their lines of sight. *Atlas to Accompany the Official Records*, plate 40.

27. First quote (and anecdote) in John T. Trowbridge, *The South: A Tour of Its Battle-Fields and Ruined Cities* (New York: Arno Press and the New York Times, 1969), 139; second quote in letter dated December 6, 1864, from "your loving sister AED," box 6, folder 60, Confederate Miscellany Papers, MARBL. See also Trimble, *Man-Induced Soil Erosion*; Misak, Al-Ajmi, and Al-Enezi, "War-Induced Soil Degradation"; and Edward P. F. Rose, "Impact of Military Activities on Local and Regional Geologic Conditions," in *Humans as Geomorphic Agents*, ed. J. Ehlen, W. C. Haneburg, and R. A. Lawson, Reviews in Engineering Geology, vol. 16 (Boulder, CO: Geological Society of America, 2005), 51-66.

28. "Atlanta 'Growing Fast' 60 Years Ago," *Harper's New Monthly Magazine*, December 1879, in box 4, folder 1, Jennie Meta Barker Papers, AHC.

29. Quote from letter dated May 16, 1864, from Alonzo Miller to his father, Diary, Alonzo Miller Papers, AHC.

30. Letters dated May 16 and May 27, 1864, from Alonzo Miller to his family, Diary, Alonzo Miller Papers, AHC.

31. Letters dated May 27 and October 1, 1864, from Alonzo Miller to his parents, Diary, Alonzo Miller Papers, AHC.

32. Both quotes are from Brady, *War upon the Land*, 128–129. See also Ann Norton Greene, *Horses at Work: Harnessing Power in Industrial America* (Cambridge, MA: Harvard University Press, 2008), 121. Greene is referring to the Civil War's use of animal power—horses in particular—as the foremost source of energy, but the phrase can be applied to the cycle of energy initiated and maintained by the armies' appropriation of all natural resources.

33. First quote in James A. Huston, "Logistical Support of Federal Armies in the Field," *Civil War History* 7 (March 1961): 45; second quote in letter dated September 24, 1864, from Josiah Dexter Cotton to his wife, Anne, Josiah Dexter Cotton Papers, LOC.

34. The Confederate Congress established the Quartermaster, Commissary General, Medical, and Ordnance Departments. Subsistence, or Commissary, agents were responsible for feeding troops; quartermaster agents collected supplies, manufactured clothing and shoes, and coordinated transportation (so marshaled horses and mules, etc.) The Confederate Congress made impressment legal on March 26, 1863. The legislation merely recognized a longstanding practice; however, impressment was so publicly reviled that the Congress repealed it a few months later. Notwithstanding this largely political move, impressment continued. Once it became clear that impressment was not working, Confederate commissaries secured supplies through a policy called "tax-in-kind," whereby farmers paid their taxes in agricultural products. If planters failed to produce the "tithe tax," they were fined by being required to provide an additional percent of agricultural goods. Most sources mention impressment over tax-in-kind, but the policies had similar effects: the steady removal of resources from the home front to support those on the battlefield. See "To the Planters of Bibb, Perry, East Greene and Marengo Counties," *Selma Morning Reporter*, June 13, 1864; William Warren Rogers, *Confederate Home Front: Montgomery during the Civil War* (Tuscaloosa: University of Alabama Press, 1999), 47; and Blevins, *Cattle in the Cotton Fields*, 38–39.

35. Letter dated October 25, 1864, from Josiah Dexter Cotton to his wife, Anne, Josiah Dexter Cotton Papers, LOC; and Sherman, *Memoirs*, 2:220. Foraging was not always an easy task. Civilians often (and sometimes violently) fought back. See Halbert Eleazer Paine, *A Wisconsin Yankee in Confederate Bayou Country: The Civil War Reminiscences of a Union General*, ed. Samuel C. Hyde Jr. (Baton Rouge: Louisiana State University Press, 2009), 57–58. The Union Army began the Civil War with a "soft war" or "conciliatory" policy, but that approach too often created issues with supply, especially when military operations necessitated speed and aggressiveness. During late 1862 and 1863, then, the Union Army command adopted a pragmatic approach to supply that included targeted foraging. In a broader military context, foraging was normal—conciliation and "soft war" were not. See Grimsley, *Hard Hand of War*, chap. 4. In most divisions, specific foraging parties, or "bummers," gathered and confiscated the necessary supplies from nearby homes, and they proved very adept at stripping the southern landscape of anything that might prove valuable in the way of foodstuffs.

36. First quote in Petition from the citizens of Newton County, Georgia, to Gov. Joseph E. Brown, dated October 21, 1864, Orr Family Papers, box 1, folder 5, MARBL; second quote in Trowbridge, *South*, 476. See also Special Field Order No. 120, Section VI, D. W. Whittle Papers, box 1, folder 6, LOC.

37. For instances when Union soldiers could not find a farmer's stock and had to rely on slaves to help them, see "The War Record of J. S. Bartlett," J. S. Bartlett Papers, SHC; and Ervin L. Jordan Jr., *Black Confederates and Afro-Yankees in Civil War Virginia* (Charlottesville: University of Virginia Press, 1995), 78.

38. First quote in *OR*, series 1, vol. 16, pt. 1, 495, 358; second and third quotes in Gates, *Agriculture during the Civil War*, 6–7.

39. The definitive work on the progress of US Army policies toward the South is Mark Grimsley, *Hard Hand of War*. See, for instance, entry dated December 18, 1864, Diary, Alonzo Miller Papers, AHC. Miller writes, "One morning our Corps killed one hundred horses rather than to leave them. We picked up a good many on the way—some nice ones, then we killed off our old ones." Historian Lloyd Lewis corroborates this entry and states that it was under General Kilpatrick's order that soldiers killed so many horses. Lewis, *Sherman, Fighting Prophet* (New York: Harcourt and Brace, 1932), 455.

40. Letter dated September 20, 1863, Lemuel Thomas Foote Papers, box 1, folder 1, LOC. Lisa Brady refers to each of these "scorched earth" campaigns as a *chevauchée*, a medieval concept

of warfare that can be summarized as a "massive forage raid." These US Army campaigns were the keystone of the "hard war" policy that characterized the major military operations during 1864 and 1865, which were intended to create a new "wilderness" in the South by destroying its economic foundations as surely as they were destroying its military ones. Brady, *War upon the Land*, 3, 10–11.

41. Burke Davis, *Sherman's March* (New York: Random House, 1980), 25.

42. "War and Defence," *Charleston Mercury*, June 6, 1863. "Make the South a desert" was a phrase Senator Benjamin F. Wade of Ohio used in December 1860. See Charles Royster, *The Destructive War: William Tecumseh Sherman, Stonewall Jackson, and the Americans* (New York: Alfred A. Knopf, 1991), 79–80.

43. First quote in letter dated February 2, 1863, from Mrs. Ashley of Bowling Green, KY, to Mrs. Barker, box 1, folder 10, Habersham Family Papers, LOC; second quote in entry dated January 1, 1866, Edmund Ruffin Jr. Plantation Journal, SHC.

44. The tallies of the agricultural resources destroyed vary according to source; some historians use Sheridan's final report, whereas others use earlier reports referring to a specific location rather than the valley as a whole. Other scholars round up and provide rougher figures. These particular numbers come from Brady, *War upon the Land*, 86.

45. C. Goldin and F. Lewis, "The Economic Cost of the American Civil War: Estimates and Implications," *Journal of Economic History* 35 (1975): 308, 315–316; and Patrick O'Brien, *The Economic Effects of the American Civil War*, prepared for the Economic History Society (Atlantic Highlands, NJ: Humanities Press International, 1988), 46.

46. One of these instances would arguably be the Carolina phase of Sherman's March. See James Wise and John Wise, *On Sherman's Trail: The Civil War's North Carolina Climax* (Charleston, SC: History Press, 1998); and John G. Barrett, *Sherman's March through the Carolinas* (Chapel Hill: University of North Carolina Press, 1956). Another might be Wilson's Raid, which moved through central and southern Alabama during the spring of 1865. See J. P. Jones, *Yankee Blitzkrieg*.

47. In the order listed in the text: Claims No. 8657, 10225, and 18043, Reports of the Commissioner of Claims for 1871, 1872, 1873, and 1874: Disallowed Claims Submitted to Congress, Records of the House of Representatives, Southern Claims Commission, 1871–1880, RG 233, National Archives and Records Administration, Washington, DC (hereafter NARA). The Southern Claims Commission that operated between 1871 and 1873 was set up to allow Union sympathizers in the former Confederacy to apply for reimbursement for their property losses during the war. Southerners from twelve states could make claims, but *only* if they had been loyal to the United States during the war, and *only* if their property had been taken for official use by the US Army. Over 22,000 claims were made, but only 7,000 were approved. However, the claimant lists provide concrete examples of the types of property removed by the army and estimates of cost.

48. "Letters from Bragg's Army," *Charleston Mercury*, November 18, 1863. See also letter dated November 6, 1863, from James P. Ward to his cousin, box 5, Ward Family Papers, LOC.

49. Quote is from diary entry dated October 23 [year unknown], "Civil War Diary of Captain Edward E. Dickerson," Edward E. Dickerson Papers, LOC. For more on "timber cut by troops" notations, see letter dated November 7, 1864, from Alonzo Miller to family, Diary, Alonzo Miller Papers, AHC; "Report Submitted by Capt. Horace James for the months of July–September of 1865," Quarterly Reports of Abandoned or Confiscated Lands, Records of the Assistant Commissioner for the State of North Carolina, Bureau of Refugees, Freedmen, and Abandoned Lands (hereafter BRFAL), M843, roll 36, NARA.

50. Trowbridge, *South*, 479–480; and entry dated July 10, 1862, Lucy Buck Diary, in *Sad Earth, Sweet Heaven: The Diary of Lucy Rebecca Buck*, ed. William Buck (Birmingham: Buck Publishing, 1973), 119.

51. *American Annual Cyclopedia for 1865*, s.v. "Virginia," 814.

52. Letter dated March 11, 1862, from J. B. Merritt to his mother, William H. E. Merritt Papers, box 1, folder 3, RBMSC; and January 19, 1865, from Mason Whiting Tyler to his brother, reprinted in Tyler, *Recollections of the Civil War: With Many Original Diary Entries and Letters Written from the Seat of War* (New York: G. P. Putnam's Sons, 1912), 319. In Missouri, a private in the Arkansas Volunteer Infantry described the commencement of building his

quarters: "The dense forest of mighty oaks and poplars had to be cut, the brush cleared out of the camp 'streets,' a drill ground formed, discipline and drilling kept up." After the area was cleared of its vegetation, the soldiers used the felled trees to build their huts. *The Civil War Memoir of Philip Daingerfield Stephenson*, ed. Nathaniel Cheairs Hughes (Conway, AR: UCA Press, 1995), 25–26.

53. Letter dated November 13, 1863, from Mason Whiting Tyler to his brother, reprinted in Tyler, *Recollections of the Civil War*, 123–124n2.

54. Letter dated January 6, 1865, Mims Family Papers, box 1, folder 11, Birmingham Public Library and Archives, Birmingham, AL (hereafter BPL); entries dated July 14, 1864, and January 15, 1865, Nimrod Porter Journals, TSLA; "An Act to authorize the Impressment of certain Salt Wells, Furnaces and other Property," passed March 8, 1864, Section 4, *Acts of the General Assembly of the State of Virginia, Passed at the Session of 1863–4* (William F. Ritchie Public Printer, 1864), Rare Book Collection, Wilson Library, University of North Carolina Chapel Hill.

55. Letter dated October 30, 1863, box 1, folder 2, and letter dated October 25, 1861, box 1, folder 2, Lemuel Foote Papers, LOC; O. M. Poe Papers, box 1, LOC. Information on Sherman's March and 12th Wisconsin in Quiner, *Military History of Wisconsin*, 579; Robert Preston Brooks, *The Agrarian Revolution in Georgia, 1865–1912* (1914; Westport, CT: Negro Universities Press, 1970), 401n1; and Noah Trudeau, *Southern Storm: Sherman's March to the Sea* (New York: Harper Collins, 2008), 14–17, 532–533.

56. Quote in entry dated August 31, 1864, Diary of Henry Stanley, box 1, folder 26, Antebellum and Civil War Collection, AHC. See also letter dated October 30, 1863, box 1, folder 2, and letter dated October 25, 1861, box 1, folder 2, Lemuel Foote Papers, LOC; letter dated July 21, 1862, box 1, folder 16, Godfrey Barnsley Papers, MARBL.

57. H. Roger Grant, *The Railroad: The Life Story of a Technology* (Westport, CT: Greenwood Publishing Group, 2005), 31; Walker, *Southern Forest*, 103; and Michael Williams, *Americans and Their Forests: A Historical Geography* (Cambridge: Cambridge University Press, 1992), 251–253, 272. See Kirby, "American Civil War," for an example of an environmental historian who brushes over the impact of railroad destruction during the Civil War. As soon as funding could be secured, southern railroads were rebuilt, improved, and expanded.

58. For an example of land descriptions, see diary entries dated May 29 and June 1, 1865, D. W. Whittle Papers, LOC.

59. The predecessor of the Freedmen's Bureau, the Plantation Bureau, oversaw Union-occupied territory in Mississippi and Louisiana after 1863 and frequently restarted cultivation on abandoned plantations using slaves and northern lessees. Letter dated November 13, 1864, from P. E. Beauvais to Captain Stiles, sent from Bayou Du Large, Parish of Terreborne, Incoming Correspondence of the Plantation Bureau, 1863–1865, RG 366, entry 414, box 5, Third Special Agency Records, Records of Civil War Special Agencies of the Treasury Dept., National Archives and Records Administration, College Park, MD (hereafter NARA II).

60. Quote in letter dated September 1, 1865, from A. P. Ketchum to General Saxton, Reports of Conditions and Operations, Records of the Assistant Commissioner for the State of South Carolina, BRFAL, M869, roll 34, NARA. The radius of an army's camp is explained in detail in several memoirs. See, for instance, *Civil War Memoir of Philip Daingerfield Stephenson*, 147.

61. Quote in Brady, *War upon the Land*, 128; United Nations Environment Programme, "Urban Areas," *Global Environment Outlook 3: Past, Present, and Future Perspectives*, United Nations Environment Programme, 2002, available at http://web.unep.org/geo/assessments/global-assessments/global-environment-outlook-3 (accessed June 3, 2017). Mathis Wackernagel et al., "The Ecological Footprint of Cities and Regions: Comparing Resource Availability with Resource Demand," *Environment and Urbanization* 18, no. 1 (April 2006): 104–105. See also William Rees, "Ecological Footprints and Appropriated Carrying Capacity: What Urban Economics Leaves Out," *Environment and Urbanization* 4, no. 2 (October 1992): 121–130.

62. "Urban Areas," *Global Environmental Outlook 3*; Mathis Wackernagel and William Rees, *Our Ecological Footprint: Reducing Human Impact on the Earth* (Gabriola Island, CAN: New Society Publishers, 1996). Of course, there are drastic differences in the footprints of cities around the world. US urban areas consume the most natural resources per capita, while the cities of Haiti and Pakistan consume the least. See table 1 in Wackernagel et al., "Ecological

Footprint of Cities," 108, for comparisons between the ecological deficits created by cities all over the world. The ecological footprint of US cities is 9.7 global hectares per capita; the United Kingdom is 5.4 global hectares per capita; Japan uses 4.3 global hectares per capita; Indonesia uses 1 global hectare per capita; Pakistan uses 0.7 global hectare per capita. In my calculations, I erred on the conservative side, using the Pakistani footprint to estimate the possible needs of an army smaller than either the Army of the Potomac or the Army of Northern Virginia at their height. It should be noted that populations relying on biomass as fuel (such as wood) sometimes impact a greater surface area than those using more modern, more efficient sources of energy. A more up-to-date version of the ecological footprint data, with records dating back to 1961, can be found at http://www.footprintnetwork.org/content/documents/ecological_footprint_nations/ecological_per_capita.html (accessed July 7, 2017).

63. For a general explanation of how cities serve a nodal function for zones of settlement and production, see James H. Johnson, *Urban Geography: An Introductory Analysis*, 2nd ed. (New York: Pergamon Press, 1976), chap. 5. In his environmental history of Chicago, William Cronon famously applied central place theory to explain the city's inextricable connections to its rural hinterlands and the urban area's ability to transform a "natural landscape into a spatial economy." William Cronon, *Nature's Metropolis: Chicago and the Great West* (New York: W. W. Norton, 1991), 46–52, quote on 52. For discussions of Von Thünen's work in relation to agricultural production, see Daniel Block and E. Melanie DuPuis, "Making the Country Work for the City: Von Thünen's Ideas in Geography, Agricultural Economics and the Sociology of Agriculture," *American Journal of Economics and Sociology* 60, no. 1 (January 2001): 79–98; and M. T. Lucas and D. Chhajed, "Applications of Location Analysis in Agriculture: A Survey," *Journal of the Operational Research Society* 55 (2004): 561–578. The various possible models used to describe urban land use, from central place theory to cell automata, are outlined in Jean-Paul Rodrigue, *The Geography of Transport Systems*, 3rd ed. (New York: Routledge, 2013), chap. 6.

64. "Things Worthy of Attention," *Southern Cultivator*, July 1861, 201–203; "Thoughts for the Crisis," *Southern Cultivator*, January 1861, 9–11; John Solomon Otto, *Southern Agriculture during the Civil War Era, 1860–1880* (Westport, CT: Greenwood Press, 1994), 22; and Sam Bowers Hilliard, *Hog Meat and Hoecake: Food Supply in the Old South, 1840–1860* (Carbondale: Southern Illinois University Press, 1972).

65. For a detailed account of how these processes played out on a year-by-year, region-by-region basis in the South, see R. Douglas Hurt, *Agriculture and the Confederacy: Policy, Productivity, and Power in the Civil War South* (Chapel Hill: University of North Carolina Press, 2015).

66. First quote in "Things Worthy of Attention," *Southern Cultivator*, July 1861, 201; second in *Lynchburg Republican*, May 10, 1862, quoted in Gates, *Agriculture and the Civil War*, 16; third quoted in Hurt, *Agriculture and the Confederacy*, 117. Other examples of pleas to planters to plant food crops can be found in "Plant Corn!" *Southern Cultivator*, March 1861, 84–85; and "Plant Provision Crops," *Southern Cultivator*, February 1861, 67.

67. Otto, *Southern Agricultural during the Civil War Era*, 31. Ironically, because the policy of the Confederacy had been to encourage farmers to plant corn instead of cotton during the war, by the last year of the war, Union forces actually encountered more forage crops in many parts of the South than would be expected. Soldier Henry Hitchcock recorded in his diary: "Good farms along the traveled roads, and crops have all been good . . . *for which we are much obliged.*" Diary entry dated November 24, 1864, Henry Hitchcock, *Marching with Sherman: Passages from the Letters and Campaign Diaries of Henry Hitchcock, Major and Assistant Adjutant General of Volunteers, November 1864–May 1865*, ed. M. A. DeWolfe Howe (New York: Bison Books, 1995), 108.

68. Quote in letter dated August 1, 1862, from John Parrish to his brother Henry, Henry Watson Jr. Papers, box 6, folder 3, RBMSC; Paul Evans and Thomas P. Govan, "A Belgian Consul on Conditions in the South in 1860 and 1862," *Journal of Southern History* 3, no. 4 (November 1937): 487. Cotton was *the* principal weapon of southern foreign policy—Britain, for example, imported three-quarters of its cotton from the American South. The Confederacy discouraged southerners from shipping their cotton to foreign ports during the first two years of

the war and destroyed millions of bales in order to create a cotton shortage. The reasoning was that if no cotton got out, then Europe would see how serious the conflict was and intervene in order to obtain raw cotton. See Eugene Dattel, "Cotton and the Civil War," *Mississippi History Now*, website, July 2008, http://mshistorynow.mdah.state.ms.us/articles/291/cotton-and-the-civil-war (accessed January 12, 2017).

69. Letter dated January 28, 1862 from J. A. Wennyss to Henry Watson, Henry Watson Jr. Papers, box 6, folder 3, RBMSC; "Agricultural News," *Southern Cultivator*, August 1864, 126–127. State laws and public opinion also helped decrease the acreage devoted to cotton. Despite the lack of market options, some planters had continued to raise cotton in the hopes they would be able to sell it as soon as the war ended. Every state in the Confederacy (except Texas and Louisiana) eventually passed laws limiting cash-crop planting. There were ways around this, of course, and planters would use back fields or inaccessible parts of their land for planting cotton. See Gates, *Agriculture and the Civil War*, 17, 19; Otto, *Southern Agriculture during the Civil War Era*, 31.

70. "Our Military Resources," *Charleston Mercury*, February 6, 1863. There were 1.8 hogs per person in the Confederacy during 1860, which was plenty, but considering southerners' reliance on the animal, the region needed 2.2 hogs per person to be self-sufficient in pork production. Otto, *Southern Agriculture during the Civil War Era*, 24, 36; Report on Subsistence dated January 1862, from Frank Ruffin to Col. Northrup, *OR*, series 4, vol. 1, 873.

71. "Meat for Working Hands," *Southern Cultivator*, March 1864; Andrew Smith, *Starving the South: How the North Won the Civil War* (New York: St. Martin's Press, 2011), 32–33; Hurt, *Agriculture and the Confederacy*, 103; and William T. Winham, "The Problem of Supply in the Trans-Mississippi Confederacy," *Journal of Southern History* 27, no. 2 (May 1961): 154.

72. The weather compounded the issues created by military operations. A "ruinous drought" marred the harvests of 1860, 1861, and 1862, and the food crops the army so desperately needed "suffered greatly from the torrid heat." Corn crops failed almost entirely in certain areas of Georgia and the Carolinas. In other places, it was heavy spring rains, not summer drought, which harmed the crops. The weather's impact on the availability of provisions not only lessened the amount of food available for soldiers, it also made it difficult for southerners to fatten their stock for slaughter. Short corn crops meant that after contributing to the war effort and feeding their families, farmers often did not have enough left to feed their animals. See entries dated March 1861; June 21, 1861; and August 1, 1863, John Horry Dent Farm Journal, SCA; letter dated January 20, 1861, "A Belgian Consul on Conditions in the South in 1860 and 1862," 480; entries dated April 13, 14, and 21, 1862, in Racine, *Piedmont Farmer*, 242–243; letter dated October 5, 1863, from Nancy Jett to her husband, Richard, Richard Burch Jett Papers, box 1, folder 2, MARBL; and entry dated February 6, 1864, Samuel P. Richards Diary, AHC. The problem of supplying cities like Atlanta with provisions because of short crops in the countryside is discussed in Franklin Garrett, *Atlanta and Environs: A Chronicle of Its People and Events*, vol. 1 (Athens: University of Georgia Press, 1969), chaps. 40, 41, and 42.

73. Quote from Frank Magwood, interviewed by T. Pat Matthews, North Carolina Narratives, vol. 11, pt. 2, Federal Writers' Project, Ex-Slaves Narratives, LOC. See Ella Lonn, *Salt as a Factor in the Confederacy* (Tuscaloosa: University of Alabama Press, 1965); Smith, *Starving the South*, 13–23; and John Keegan, *The American Civil War: A Military History* (New York: Alfred A. Knopf, 2010), 92. For more on southern women and the blockade, see Drew Gilpin Faust, *Mothers of Invention: Women of the Slaveholding South in the American Civil War* (Chapel Hill: University of North Carolina Press, 2004); Mary Elizabeth Massey, *Ersatz in the Confederacy: Shortages and Substitutes on the Southern Homefront* (Columbia: University of South Carolina Press, 1993); and Louise Chipley Slavicek, *Women and the Civil War* (New York: Infobase Publishing, 2009). Other primary-source examples of the South's efforts to get around guano and salt shortages include letter dated March 26, 1863, from Col. J. R. Gilmer to L. P. Grant, box 6, folder 13, L. P. Grant Papers, AHC; Mrs. J. A. Yarbrough, "Substitutes in Wartime Contrasted—1862 and 1942," *Charlotte Observer*, August 30, 1942; "Molasses vs Salt for Beef," *Southern Cultivator*, February 1862, 45; entry dated August 1862, John Horry Dent Farm Journal, SCA; and entry dated May 19, 1862, in Racine, *Piedmont Farmer*, 247.

74. See Charles Ramsdell, *Behind the Lines in the Southern Confederacy* (Baton Rouge: Louisiana State University Press, 1972); Paul Escott, *After Secession: Jefferson Davis and the Failure of Confederate Nationalism* (Baton Rouge: Louisiana State University Press, 1978); George Rable, *Civil Wars: Women and the Crisis of Southern Nationalism* (Urbana: University of Illinois Press, 1989); and Steven Tripp Elliott, *Yankee Town, Southern City: Race and Class Relations in Civil War Lynchburg* (New York: New York University Press, 1997).

75. Figures taken from James McPherson, *Battle Cry of Freedom: The Civil War Era* (New York: Oxford University Press, 1988), 854; National Park Service, "Civil War Facts," National Park Service website, http://www.nps.gov/civilwar/facts.htm (accessed June 3, 2017). According to the "Soldier Statistics," in the *American Civil War Research Database*, available at http://www.civilwardata.com (accessed March 19, 2017), a total of 1,434,856 men served the Confederacy as soldiers or officers. For more on the legal mechanisms through which the Confederacy created a national army, see James Martin, "Civil War Conscription Laws," *In Custodia Legis*, Library of Congress, http://blogs.loc.gov/law/2012/11/civil-war-conscription-laws/ (accessed June 3, 2017). Planters and overseers on larger plantations were oftentimes exempted from army service under the "Twenty Negro Law," passed in October 1862, which ensured the "proper police of the country" by allowing any white owner of more than twenty slaves to stay on the plantation and supervise their work. Nonslaveholders despised the law, but they put up with it because of widespread fears of potential slave insurrections. Keeping white men at home would help maintain race control. See R. Douglas Hurt's explanation of the law and its implications for agriculture in *Agriculture and the Confederacy*, 211–214.

76. Planters' wives left to run the farm while their husbands and sons served in the military often relied on overseers or other local men to help them manage the property. See letter dated December 14, 1865, from Ann Hairston Hairston to her daughter, Bettie, Hairston and Wilson Family Papers, box 1, folder 10, SHC.

77. First quote in Rebecca Scott, *Degrees of Freedom: Louisiana and Cuba after Slavery* (Cambridge, MA: Belknap Press of Harvard University Press, 2005), 34; diary entry dated November 11, 1864, in Hitchcock, *Marching with Sherman*, 55; second quote in letter dated October 20, 1865, from J. Henry Smith to Alexander Stephens, reel 19, vol. 37, Alexander Hamilton Stephens Papers, LOC. The classic work on wartime emancipation is Ira Berlin et al., *Slaves No More: Three Essays on Emancipation and the Civil War* (Cambridge: Cambridge University Press, 1992).

78. Louisiana planter quoted in Scott, *Degrees of Freedom*, 31; letter dated April 2, 1865, from J. C. Norwood to W. W. Lenoir, Lenoir Family Papers, Subseries 1.3, folder 157, SHC. For an example of a contraband cartoon, see *Frank Leslie's Illustrated Newspaper*, March 18, 1865, Prints and Photographs Division, LOC.

79. Bernard Nelson, "Confederate Slave Impressment Legislation, 1861–1865," *Journal of Negro History* 31, no. 4 (October 1946): 393–396; and Edgar Walter, *South Carolina: A History* (Columbia: University of South Carolina Press, 1998), 361. For records of slave impressment in Alabama, see impressment receipt dated August 11, 1862, box 6, folder 3, and letter dated April 1, 1864, from John Parrish to Henry Watson, box 6, folder 5, Henry J. Watson Jr. Papers, RBMSC.

80. Quote in Thavolia Glymph, "Noncombatant Military Laborers in the Civil War," *Organization of American Historians Magazine of History* 26, no. 2 (April 2012): 27; letter dated March 15, 1864, Lenoir Family Papers: Personal Correspondence, SHC. See also Harrison Trexler, "The Opposition of Planters to the Employment of Slaves as Laborers by the Confederacy," *Mississippi Valley Historical Review* 27, no. 2 (September 1940): 211–224. As historian Thavolia Glymph discusses, the debate over slave impressment centered on where, and to whom, slave labor was most valuable. There were those, such as General Robert E. Lee, who wanted thousands of impressed slaves attached to the War Department to work not only as "field engineers," as the Union called them, but in mines and factories as well. To Lee, assigning a detail of healthy white soldiers to perform menial labor wasted their energy and sapped a vital resource from his army. Having white men build defenses or fell trees represented "a diversion from the legitimate duties of a volunteer Soldier," another southerner wrote, especially since there were "negroes and hirelings enough to do the menial labor." Ira Berlin,

Joseph E. Reidy, and Leslie S. Rowland, *Freedom: A Documentary History of Emancipation, 1861–1867*, series 1, vol. 2: *The Black Military Experience* (Cambridge: Cambridge University Press, 1982), 685–686, quote on 789–790. For more on the enlistment of slaves into the Confederate army, see Bruce Levine, *Confederate Emancipation: Southern Plans to Free and Arm Slaves during the Civil War* (New York: Oxford University Press, 2005).

81. Letter dated January 17, 1865, from A. B. Merritt to his brother at Lawrenceville, VA, box 1, folder 3, William H. E. Merritt Papers, RBMSC.

82. In 1861, he planted 489 acres of cotton and 256 acres of corn. In 1863, he planted 500 acres of corn (much of which, he noted, was in fields "for cotton changed to corn"), 120 acres of cotton, and 645 bushels of potatoes. Entries titled "Crop planted for 1861" and "Crop for 1863 (January)," Farm Journals and Account Books, box 1, folders 5 and 6, John Horry Dent Collection, RG 477, SCA.

83. "Plantation Memoranda 1863," Farm Journals 1863, John Horry Dent Collection, box 1, folder 6, RG477, SCA. Although the soils of the physiographic (as opposed to demographic) Black Belt are rich in calcium and were thus considered more fertile than, say, Piedmont soils, Dent's land still consisted of ultisols, the dominant soil order in all areas of the South outside alluvial lands. Ultisols are acidic and lack key nutrients, particularly potassium, and are most commonly found in tropic and humid subtropical regions, such as the southern United States. See Natural Resources Conservation Service, *Soil Taxonomy: A Basic System of Soil Classification*, 2nd ed. (Washington, DC: US Department of Agriculture, 1999), chap. 19, "Ultisols," available at http://www.nrcs.usda.gov/Internet/FSE_DOCUMENTS/nrcs142p2_051232.pdf (accessed June 5, 2017). For a brief description of the symptoms of potassium deficiency as they relate to Dent's crop, see John E. Sawyer, "Potassium Deficiency in Corn," *Integrated Crop Management* 484, no. 15 (2000): 116.

84. For new ground acreage calculations, compare entries titled "Crop Planted for 1861" and "Crop for 1863." Quote from entry titled "A Sinking Ship," dated July 1861, Farm Journals and Account Books, John Horry Dent Collection, box 1, folders 5 and 6, SCA. See the discussion of Dent's use of cotton seed to feed his hogs in Ray Mathis, *John Horry Dent: South Carolina Aristocrat on the Alabama Frontier* (Tuscaloosa: University of Alabama Press), 204, 207.

85. Arthur R. Hall, "Terracing in the Southern Piedmont," *Agricultural History* 23, no. 2 (April 1949): 97. For discussions of general agriculture in these regions, see Jeffrey Kerr-Ritchie, *Freedpeople in the Tobacco South: Virginia, 1860–1900* (Chapel Hill: University of North Carolina Press, 1999); Pete Daniel, *Breaking the Land: The Transformation of Cotton, Tobacco, and Rice Cultures since 1880* (Urbana: University of Illinois Press, 1985); and Alan Kulikoff, *Tobacco and Slaves: The Development of Southern Cultures in the Chesapeake, 1680–1800* (Chapel Hill: University of North Carolina Press, 1986). Several ecologists and historical geographers have spent their careers studying abandoned cropland in the eastern and southeastern United States; much of what scientists know about southern forest succession, leaf litter chemistry, and the effects of cultivation on land restoration has been learned from the large tracts of abandoned land in the South since 1860. An example of this comes from David Orwig and Marc Abrams, "Land-Use History (1720–1992), Composition, and Dynamics of Oak-Pine Forests within the Piedmont and Coastal Plain of Northern Virginia," *Canadian Journal of Forest Research* 24 (1994): 1216–1225, in which the authors study four Civil War battlefields in Fredericksburg and Spotsylvania, Virginia.

86. William Dwight Billings, "The Structure and Development of Old Shortleaf Pine Stands and Certain Associated Properties of the Soil," *Ecological Monographs* 8, no. 3 (July 1938): 494; Hugh Hammond Bennett, *Soil Conservation* (New York: Macmillan, 1939), 232–233; Keever, "Retrospective View," 397, 400; Cramer and Hobbs, *Old Fields and Restoration*, 8–10, 25; and Henri Grissino-Mayer and David R. Butler, "Effects of Climate on Growth of Shortleaf Pine in Northern Georgia: A Dendroclimatic Study," *Southeastern Geographer* 33, no. 1 (May 1993): 65–81.

87. First quote in diary entry dated October 23, year unknown, "Civil War Diary of Captain Edward E. Dickerson," box 1, folder 3, Edward E. Dickerson Papers, LOC; second in Trowbridge, *South*, 225.

88. "Report Submitted by Capt. Horace James for the Months of July, August, and September of 1865," Quarterly Reports of Abandoned or Confiscated Lands, Records Relating to Lands

and Property, Records of the Assistant Commissioner for the State of North Carolina, BRFAL, M843, roll 36, NARA; and Report for St. Bartholomew's Parish, August 1865, Abandoned Land Reports, August 1865–December 1868, M869, roll 33, Records of the Assistant Commissioner for the State of South Carolina, BRFAL, M869, roll 33, NARA. Discussion of how much land might have been taken out of cultivation can be found in R. L. Ransom and R. Sutch, "The Impact of the Civil War and of Emancipation on Southern Agriculture," *Explorations in Economic History* 12 (1975): 1–28.

89. Saikku, *This Delta, This Land*, 115; Carol Harden and Louise Mathews, "Hillslope Runoff, Soil Detachment, and Soil Organic Content Following Reforestation in the Copper Basin, Tennessee, USA," *Australian Geographical Studies* 40, no. 2 (July 2002): 130–142; Keever, "Retrospective View," 397, 400.

90. Gates, *Agriculture and the Civil War*, 111. Sheridan's Shenandoah Valley campaign, in particular, has been blamed for that area's "devastation," sparking a debate among historians regarding not only the scale of the damage but also the motivations for it. Michael Mahon, *The Shenandoah Valley 1861–1865: The Destruction of the Granary of the Confederacy* (Mechanicsburg, PA: Stackpole, 1999) is the best example of a nuanced view of Sheridan's operations, concluding that the destruction was more localized than has previously been depicted.

91. For explanations of how debt and altered credit systems affected planters, see Kilbourne, *Debt, Investment, Slaves*, 110–117; Wayne, *Reshaping of Plantation Society*, 66–68, 77–78; Harold Woodman, *King Cotton and His Retainers: Financing and Marketing the Cotton Crop of the South, 1800–1925* (Columbia: University of South Carolina, 1990). For more on the problems of currency in the wartime and postwar South, see Marc Weidenmier, "Money and Finance in the Confederate States of America," in *EH.Net Encyclopedia*, ed. Robert Whaples, available at http://eh.net/encyclopedia/money-and-finance-in-the-confederate-states-of-america/ (accessed May 24, 2017); Douglas B. Ball, *Financial Failure and Confederate Defeat* (Urbana: University of Illinois Press, 1991); Richard C. K. Burdekin and Marc D. Weidenmier, "Inflation Is Always and Everywhere a Monetary Phenomenon: Richmond vs. Houston in 1864," *American Economic Review* 91, no. 5 (2001): 1621–1630.

Chapter 3

Parts of Chapter 3 appeared in "The Stockman's War: Hog Cholera in Nineteenth-Century Alabama," *Alabama Review* 70, no. 2, Special Issue: The Environment (April 2017): 126–140.

1. Entries dated February 1866, James Washington Matthews Journals, MF 1712, TSLA. James Washington Matthews was born around 1798 or 1799 in Mecklenburg County, North Carolina. By the time of the 1840 census, he lived and owned small amounts of property in Maury County, Tennessee. He married Surrilda Dooley of Tennessee, who bore him a number of children, including James F., Gilbert Dooley, and William, all of whom helped on the farm. James Washington owned three slaves as of 1860: Cherry, recorded as a forty-year-old black woman, and her two children, a girl of twelve and a boy of eight, who may have been named Isham. See 1850 US Census, Population Schedules, District 8, Maury, Tennessee, M432, roll 890, NARA (listed as Jas W Matthews); 1860 US Census, Population Schedules, District 8, Maury, Tennessee, M653, roll 1264, NARA; and 1860 US Federal Census—Slave Schedules, District No. 8, Maury, Tennessee, M653 (listed as JW Matthews).

2. Entries dated 1864, James Washington Matthews Journals; "Middle Tennessee," in J. B. Killebrew, *Tennessee: Its Agricultural and Mineral Wealth* . . . (Nashville: Tavel, Eastman & Howell, 1876), 53–54. While troop movements were common throughout the war in Middle Tennessee, particularly between 1862 and 1864, the major military action recorded in Matthews's neighborhood occurred in November and December 1864 during Lt. Gen. John Bell Hood's Franklin-Nashville Campaign. The Confederates under Hood and Maj. Gen. Nathan Bedford Forrest engaged Union forces under Maj. Gen. John Schofield in November, and one can map troop movements through Matthews's land in December. See "Report of Maj. Gen. Nathan B. Forrest, CSA, commanding cavalry, of operations November 16, 1864—January 23, 1865," dated January 24, 1864, *OR*, series 1, vol. 45, pt. 1, 751–757, particularly

756–757. For the context of the event, see Wiley Sword, *The Confederacy's Last Hurrah: Spring Hill, Franklin, and Nashville* (Lawrence: University Press of Kansas, 1993). A corroborative source regarding how troops of both sides impacted Maury County's farming operations comes from the Nimrod Porter Journals, vol. 1, MF 229, TSLA. See entries dated January 8, 13, and 22, 1863. For information related to the soils around Matthews's farmland, see Killebrew, *Tennessee: Its Agricultural Wealth*, 65–66; and J. H. Agee and J. A. Kerr, *Soil Survey of Maury County, Tennessee*, USDA Bureau of Soils (Washington, DC: Government Printing Office, 1926), 168. Temperature and precipitation averages for the county are available in Agee and Kerr, *Soil Survey of Maury County*, 156.

3. Entries for Spring 1865, James Washington Matthews Journals, mention Gilbert's capture and eventual return home. It is clear Gilbert—the primary farmhand before the war—had to take several months off from manual labor after arriving back home. As for planting, entries dated May 1866 indicate Gilbert had been allotted his own land in his fathers' holdings. The Census of 1870 does not list Gilbert as a property owner, merely as a farmer with no real-estate holdings. Gilbert enlisted in the 3rd Regiment of the Tennessee Infantry (Clack's) in 1862 as a private and had been promoted to corporal by the time of his capture in 1864. Record of G. D. Matthews, National Park Service, Civil War Soldiers and Sailors System, M231, roll 28, available at http://www.itd.nps.gov/cwss (accessed December 22, 2016). He married Laura Ann Ramsey in 1866. The remarks regarding "boys to be had" can be found in entry dated April 2, 1866, James Washington Matthews Journals. The Matthews property holdings included approximately 891 acres, at least before 1860. The valuation of his property declined drastically between 1860 and 1870—whether owing to loss of land or simply depreciation of the land's worth is unknown. See 1860 US Census; 1870 US Census; Warrant Numbers 28210, 28487, 18695, and 20302, Early Tennessee / North Carolina Land Records, 1846–1849, RG 50, TSLA.

4. The economics of Reconstruction for poorer whites has long been considered a lacuna in what is otherwise a vast literature. Many works, however, treat plain folk either as part of a larger story or on a local basis. Some examples include Idus A. Newby, *Plain Folk in the New South: Social Change and Cultural Persistence* (Baton Rouge: Louisiana State University Press, 1989); Nash, *Reconstruction's Ragged Edge*; Jonathan M. Bryant, *How Curious a Land: Conflict and Change in Greene County, Georgia, 1850–1885* (Chapel Hill: University of North Carolina Press, 1996); Victoria Bynum, *The Free State of Jones: Mississippi's Longest Civil War* (Chapel Hill: University of North Carolina Press, 2016); Reidy, *From Slavery to Agrarian Capitalism*; Robert Tracy McKenzie, *One South or Many? Plantation Belt and Upcountry in Civil-War Era Tennessee* (Cambridge: Cambridge University Press, 1994); Robert Tracy McKenzie, "Rediscovering the 'Farmless' Farm Population: The Nineteenth-Century Census and the Postbellum Reorganization of Agriculture in the U.S. South, 1860–1900," *Histoire Sociale* 28 (1995): 501–520; and F. N. Boney, *Southerners All* (Macon, GA: Mercer University Press, 1984), chap. 2.

5. Robert Penn Warren, *The Legacy of the Civil War* (Lincoln: University of Nebraska Press, 1998), 50–51. For more on the economic implications of physical and psychological trauma sustained during the Civil War, see Judkin Browning, "Reverberations of Battle: The Aftermath of Gettysburg on the 24th Michigan and 26th North Carolina Regiments," *Civil War Monitor* 7, no. 2 (Summer 2017): 54–63, 76–77. Primary sources covering the economic circumstances of whites in these areas include "Southern Destitution: Large Public Meeting at Cooper Institute," *New York Times*, November 14, 1865; and "The Poor of North Alabama," *New York Times*, December 8, 1865. The Freedmen's Bureau referred to whites in reduced economic circumstances as "destitute," a nebulous term used as shorthand for anyone who needed additional clothing, food, or supplies to get through the winter of 1865 and beyond. Report dated November 1, 1866, from Davis Tillson to James Johnson, Provisional Governor, Reports on Operations, 1865–1868, Records of the Assistant Commissioner for the State of Georgia BRFAL, M798, roll 32, NARA; Report dated October 14, 1868, submitted by George O'Reilly in Clarke County, Alabama, Reports of Operations from the Subdistricts, September 1865–December 1868, Records of the Assistant Commissioner for the State of Alabama, BRFAL, M809, reel 18, NARA.

6. This figure is suggested by Roger Ransom, "The Economic Consequences of the American Civil War," in *The Political Economy of War and Peace*, ed. M. Wolfson (Norwell, MA: Kluwer

Academic, 1998), 51; letter dated April 8, 1864 from Robert Rutledge to G. R. Rutledge, Rutledge Family letters, TSLA; and Robert Philip Howell Recollections, box 1, folder 1, SHC, 16–18.

7. Quote in "Southern Agriculture," *Report of the Commissioner of Agriculture for the Year 1867*, 412, 415. See also "New Features in Southern Agriculture," *De Bow's Review* 5, no. 2, February 1868, 203; "Notes of Southern Travels," *Southern Planter*, August 1869, 456. See also "Cotton or Grain?," *Southern Cultivator*, March 1866, 52. The USDA was established in 1862 in one of several acts passed by Congress relating to the issues of agriculture and land use, including the Morrill Act and the Homestead Act. President Lincoln referred to the USDA as the "people's Department"—since over half of the nation's population lived and worked on farms, the USDA would be the government arm that most directly affected their lives (at least for white Americans). See Wayne Rasmussen, "Lincoln's Agricultural Legacy," *National Agricultural Library*, USDA, http://www.nal.usda.gov/lincolns-agricultural-legacy (accessed June 16, 2016).

8. Daniel Goodloe, "Resources and Industrial Condition of the Southern States," *Report of the Commissioner of Agriculture for the Year 1865* (Washington, DC: Government Printing Office, 1866), 107; and "Southern Agriculture," *Report of the Commissioner of Agriculture for the Year 1867*, 415.

9. D. Lee, "The Dawn of Day in Southern Agriculture," *Southern Cultivator*, December 1866, 280.

10. See entries dated April 1858; June 30, 1863; December 13, 1863; June 29, 1866; October 11, 1866; January 1868; February 26, 1868; and June 1869, James Washington Matthews Journals, MF 1712, TSLA.

11. See Hahn, *Roots of Southern Populism*, which forms the basis for most textbook descriptions, versus David Weiman, "The Economic Emancipation of the Non-Slaveholding Class: Upcountry Farmers in the Georgia Cotton Economy," *Journal of Economic History* 45, no 1 (1985): 71–93; J. William Harris, "Crop Choices in the Piedmont before and after the Civil War," *Journal of Economic History* 54 (1994): 526–542; and Peter Temin, "Patterns of Cotton Agriculture in Post-Bellum Georgia," *Journal of Economic History* 43, no. 3 (1983): 661–674. Descriptions of Tennessee as an "indifferent" place for cotton are in Trowbridge, *South*, 280.

12. The 1865 cotton harvest was dismal, primarily because most planters tried to plant cotton between the time they realized the war would end and the time that emancipation began to reach non-occupied plantation districts. Furthermore, the seed planters used that year had mostly been bought in 1861 and then stored, decreasing its productivity.

13. Entries dated March and April 1863; entries dated May 1864; entries dated April and December 1865 (quotation), John Nick Barker Diaries, MF 126, TSLA.

14. First quote in letter dated July 4, 1865, from Chaplain James Hawley to Col. Samuel Thomas, Registered letters Received, Office of the Assistant Commissioner for Mississippi, BRFAL, M826, roll 10, NARA; second quote in Henry Ryan, Newberry, SC, interviewed by G. L. Summer, 8/18/37, South Carolina Narratives, vol. 14, pt. 4, Federal Writers' Project, Ex-Slaves Narratives, LOC. Not all places experienced such change, of course. Some planters continued to cultivate cotton, especially in areas that were relatively untouched by military operations, and in tobacco-growing counties along the Virginia–North Carolina border, cash-crop production remained steady during the war because of the high price of tobacco. Swanson, *Golden Weed*, chap. 4; Lee Formwalt, "Planters and Cotton Production as a Cause of Confederate Defeat: Evidence from Southwest Georgia," *Georgia Historical Quarterly* 74 (Summer 1990): 269–276.

15. One of the most famous examples was on the Sea Islands of Georgia, where General Sherman's Special Field Order No. 15 carved out 400,000 acres of the "rank, intricate wilderness" of the coastal plain, confiscated from Confederate slaveholders, to redistribute among former slaves. Although president Andrew Johnson turned the land back over to white owners relatively soon after the war ended, during the intervening period slaves grew corn and rice and food crops for their families on forty-acre plots. See Clarence Mohr, *On the Threshold of Freedom: Masters and Slaves in Civil War Georgia* (Athens: University of Georgia Press, 1986), 99–119; Paul Cimbala, "The Freedmen's Bureau, the Freedmen, and Sherman's Grant in Reconstruction Georgia," *Journal of Southern History* 55 (1989): 597–632; and Eric Foner, *Forever Free: The Story of Emancipation and Reconstruction* (New York: Vintage,

2006), 64–65. The other commonly cited example is the Union occupation of Davis Bend, the Mississippi home of the Confederate president Jefferson Davis. Some of the 10,000 acres of that farm were leased to ex-slaves; on the rest, freedmen worked the land for the US government to produce cotton. At one time, the Davis Bend Colony consisted of 1,750 freedmen who cleared over $160,000 profit on the cotton they produced. Frank Edgar Everett Jr., *Brierfield: Plantation Home of Jefferson Davis* (Oxford: University Press of Mississippi, 1971), 78; and James Wilford Garner, *Reconstruction in Mississippi* (London: Macmillan, 1902), 258.

16. Coahoma County report in Proctor Moses, Report of Lessees and Plantations on Young's Point, June 1864, Records of the Mississippi Freedmen's Department (Pre-Bureau), Office of the Assistant Commissioner, BRFAL, M1914, roll 2, NARA; quote in testimony of John Covode, dated March 3, 1866, *Report of the Joint Committee on Reconstruction*, 116–117. See the discussion of the process whites had to go through to reacquire their land along the coastline, in William McKee Evans, *Ballots and Fence Rails: Reconstruction in the Lower Cape Fear* (Athens: University of Georgia Press, 1966), 53–57.

17. First quotes in Mathis, *John Horry Dent*, 203; Orr speech in "South Carolina," *American Annual Cyclopedia for 1865*, 760. A veteran of both the South Carolina state House of Representatives and the Congressional House of Representatives, Orr was a state's rights advocate before the war and a delegate to the secession convention in 1860. After President Johnson pardoned him for his service in the Confederate Senate and the Confederate Army, Orr defeated Wade Hampton by 667 votes to become the governor of South Carolina in 1865. Orr was also one of three commissioners sent to Washington, DC, to arrange for the Federal surrender of the forts in Charleston Harbor (such as Fort Sumter). See "Orr, James Lawrence," *Biographical Directory of the United States Congress, 1774–Present*, available at http://bioguide.congress.gov/biosearch/biosearch.asp (accessed March 25, 2017).

18. Reels 1 and 2, John Flannery & Co. Records, 1867–1912, RBMSC.

19. See, for instance, "Correspondence dated Sept–Oct 1865," box 52, folder 1250, Cameron Family Papers, SHC; "Financial Receipts," box 1, folder 23, Whitfield Family Papers, WSHSC; "Receipts of Charles King," box 1, folder 8, King Family Papers, WSHSC; labor contract dated August 14, 1865, box 1, folder 5, Orr Family Papers, MARBL; "Plantation Proclamation," box 8, folder 1, Robert Jemison Jr. Papers, WSHSC; and labor contract dated June 30, 1865," box 7, folder 1, Henry J. Watson Jr. Papers, RBMSC.

20. See letter dated July 6, 1865, from J. Myers to Alexander Stephens and letter dated July 18, 1865, from George Bristow to Alexander Stephens, both in Alexander Hamilton Stephens Papers, reel 19, vol. 37, LOC. Alexander Hamilton Stephens was imprisoned for five months following the collapse of the Confederacy—it was during this time that these letters were received. After his release, Georgians elected him to the US Senate in 1866. See Stephens's biographical entry in Chad Morgan, "Alexander Stephens (1812–1883)," *New Georgia Encyclopedia*, http://www.georgiaencyclopedia.org/articles/history-archaeology/alexander-stephens-1812-1883 (accessed June 6, 2017).

21. Letter dated January 1, 1866, from William O. Nixon to his sister, Rebecca, Algernon Sidney Garnett Collection, box 1, folder 12, Special Collections, Samford University, Birmingham, Alabama (hereafter SU); Sharon Knerr, "A New South Plantation: The Nixon-Bragg Lands of Alabama" (master's thesis, Samford University, 1984), 4–7.

22. Kate Hake et al., "Crop Rotation," *Physiology Today: Newsletter of the Cotton Physiology Education Program* 3, no. 1 (October 1991): 2–3; W. T. Pettigrew, W. R. Meredith Jr., H. A. Bruns, and S. R. Stetina, "Effects of a Short-Term Corn Rotation on Cotton Dry Matter Partitioning, Lint Yield, and Fiber Quality Production," *Journal of Cotton Science* 10, no. 3 (2006): 244–246.

23. Quote in letter dated November 30, 1867, William O. Nixon to his sister, Rebecca, Algernon Sidney Garnett Collection, box 1, folder 20, Special Collections, SU; letters dated January 12, February 12, and March 26, 1866, and November 20, 1867, Algernon Sidney Garnett Collection, Special Collections, SU. For a discussion of Nixon's prewar debt, see letter dated March 25, 1866, from William O. Nixon to his sister, Rebecca, box 1, folder 13, and for his problems getting the land to yield what he needs, see letter dated June 17, 1866, William O. Nixon to his sister, Rebecca, box 1, folder 14, both in Algernon Sidney Garnett Collection, Special Collections, SU.

24. A soil scientist in Georgia noted that even the most eroded soils mottled with "gall spots" where the clay subsoil lies exposed could be reclaimed in two to three years by crop rotation, plowing under vegetable matter, and growing legumes. The only exception was the eroded phase of the Cecil clay, found around Athens, which could not support any secondary succession at all. Fertilizer application would produce some crops, but not enough to make a profit. Paul J. Kalisz, "Soil Properties of Steep Appalachian Old Fields," *Ecology* 67, no. 4 (August 1986): 1020–1021; S. P. Hamburg, "Effects of Forest Growth on Soil Nitrogen and Organic Matter Pools following Release from Subsistence Agriculture," in E. L. Stone, ed., *Forest Soils and Treatment Impacts: Proceedings of the Sixth North American Forest Soils Conference, Knoxville, Tennessee, June 1983*, edited by E. L. Stone (University of Tennessee, 1984), 145–158; and William T. Carter Jr., "Reports on the Soils of Georgia Farms," typed draft with comments, Records of the Soil Survey Division, Bureau of Plant Industry, Soils, and Agricultural Engineering, RG 54, NARA II.

25. Donald Zak et al., "Carbon and Nitrogen Cycling during Old-Field Succession: Constraints on Plant and Microbial Biomass," *Biogeochemistry* 11, no. 2 (November 1990): 111–119, esp. 122–126; Jeremy Singer and Phil Bauer, "Crop Rotations for Row Crops," *Soil Quality for Environmental Health*, last modified June 11, 2009, http://soilquality.org/practices/row_crop_rotations.html (accessed June 18, 2017). Mark McKone and David Biesboer discuss how even plants such as goldenrods—an annual weed that only survives the very first stages of succession after abandonment—help fix enough nitrogen in the soil to improve fertility. See Mark J. McKone and David D. Biesboer, "Nitrogen Fixation in Association with the Root Systems of Goldenrods," *Soil Biology and Biochemistry* 18 (1986): 543–545.

26. "Intensive System—Crops of a One-Horse Farm," *Southern Cultivator*, April 1875, 131–132. Duck Creek, North Carolina is located in Onslow County on the southern coast of North Carolina. Its elevation is 20 feet; it receives upward to 40 inches of rainfall per year; and the soils are characterized as nearly level, well-drained, with a sandy-to-loamy subsoil. See W. L. Barnhill, *Soil Survey of Onslow County, North Carolina*, (USDA Soil Conservation Service report, Washington, DC: Government Printing Office, 1992), 2, 7. For statistics on yield per acre, see "Southern Agriculture," *Report of the Commissioner of Agriculture for the Year 1867*, 415–416.

27. Thomas C. Brinley of Sampsonville, Kentucky, manufactured Brinley's plows beginning in the 1850s. It had a polished steel moldboard that was said to "scour clean" all types of soil. It could be sharpened by a blacksmith, making it last longer, and the steel did not adhere to moist or clay soil as did an iron plow, which had a tendency to rust. John Hebron Moore, *The Emergence of the Cotton Kingdom in the Old Southwest: Mississippi, 1770–1860* (Baton Rouge: Louisiana State University Press, 1988), 47–48. The cotton plant's nitrogen requirements during the "flowering" and "fruiting" stages of cotton are quite high, and because the plant deposits that particular nutrient in the boll (the fruit), a deficiency in nitrogen causes small "fruitage." See Ian Rochester et al., "Nutritional Requirements of Cotton during Flowering and Fruiting," in *Flowering and Fruiting in Cotton*, ed. Derek Oosterhuis and J. Tom Cothren, Cotton Foundation Reference Book Series 8 (Cordova, TN: Cotton Foundation, 2012), 34–50.

28. "Plantation Memoranda 1863," Farm Journals 1863, John Horry Dent Collection, box 1, folder 6, RG477, SCA; Natural Resources Conservation Service, *Soil Taxonomy: A Basic System of Soil Classification*, 2nd ed. (US Department of Agriculture, 1999), chap. 19, "Ultisols," http://www.nrcs.usda.gov/Internet/FSE_DOCUMENTS/ nrcs142p2_051232.pdf (accessed June 5, 2017). For a brief description of the symptoms of K deficiency as they relate to Dent's crop, see John E. Sawyer, "Potassium Deficiency in Corn," *Integrated Crop Management* 484, no. 15 (June 26, 2000): 116.

29. James C. Scott, *Against the Grain: A Deep History of the Earliest States* (New Haven, CT: Yale University Press, 2017), 110–111.

30. Heather M. Kelly, "Cotton Disease and Nematode Control," University of Tennessee Extension, 2016, available through the University of Tennessee Institute of Agriculture at http://ag.tennessee.edu (accessed July 20, 2017); Christopher Cumo, "Cotton," *Encyclopedia of Cultivated Plants*, vol. 1, ed. Christopher Cumo (Santa Barbara, CA: ABC-CLIO, 2013), 339.

31. "Biographical Sketch of John Horry Dent," M. B. Wellborn Collection, RG 50, box 1, folder 1, SCA; and Rochester et al., "Nutritional Requirements of Cotton during Flowering and Fruiting," 35, 37, 39, 45. For more in-depth coverage of all aspects of crop rotation, see J. H. Martin, W. H. Leonard, and D. L. Stamp, *Principles of Field Crop Production*, 3rd ed. (New York: Macmillan, 1976), chap. 6. For descriptions of how increased nitrogen availability affects cotton plants, such as that made available by cowpeas, see S. D. Livingston and C. R. Stichler, "Correcting Nitrogen Deficiencies in Cotton with Urea-Based Products," *Texas Agricultural Extension Service*, http://publications.tamu.edu/COTTON/ (accessed June 18, 2017).

32. First quote in letter dated May 19, 1869, from Mary Brodnax to Alexander Stephens, reel 47, vol. 24, Alexander Hamilton Stephens Papers, LOC; letter dated November 6, 1869, from W. Landers to Wood, sent from Greensboro, AL, Samuel O. Wood Papers, *Records of Southern Plantations from Emancipation to the Great Migration* (hereafter *RSPEGM*), Series A, pt. 1: Alabama and South Carolina Plantations, reel 1, RBMSC; second quote in report dated June 30, 1868, Claiborne, Alabama, Reports of Operations from the Subdistricts, Records of the Assistant Commissioner for the State of Alabama, BRFAL, M809, reel 18, NARA; "Cotton Yields per Acre," USDA QuickStats, https://quickstats.nass.usda.gov (accessed March 21, 2017). See also Report of Affairs for Marion District, June 1867, submitted by J. E. Lewis, "Reports on Conditions and Operations, Dec. 1866–May 1868," Records of the Assistant Commissioner for the State of South Carolina, BRFAL, M869, roll 35, NARA.

33. Contract dated October 26, 1868, between Austell and J. A. Stubbs to rent the Latham Farm in Campbell County, Alfred Austell Papers, box 1, folder 17, MSS 29, AHC. See entry dated 1866, William Wallace White Diaries, box 4, vol. 48, SHC; and diary entries dated January 1, 1866 and May 29, 1866, Edmund Ruffin Jr. Plantation Journal, SHC.

34. Wayne, *Reshaping of Plantation Society*, 58. See, for instance, "To the Destitute of Alabama," *Montgomery Weekly Advertiser*, March 5, 1867.

35. "The Situation," *Southern Planter*, March 1867, 126. Some local reports, too, point to decent harvests. See "The Crops in Georgia," *Montgomery Weekly Advertiser*, April 30, 1867.

36. "Address of Prof. J. W. Mallet, Delivered at the August County Fair," *Southern Planter*, November 1869 and December 1869, 695 and 725. "Practical Working of Mr. Gilmer's System of Farming," *Southern Planter*, May 1869, 295–298; "Our Exhausted Lands—How Shall We Restore Them?" *De Bow's Review*, June 1867, 539; "Pastures and Forage Crops," *Southern Cultivator*, December 1866, 282. By the 1890s, scientific advances in genetic manipulation of plants and veterinary medicine, as well as the maturation of the nation's agricultural experiment station complex, had started to revolutionize the way reformers thought about and discussed the future of agricultural operations. Farms were no longer tied to the ethics-based ideology of improvement; instead, science and the beginnings of agricultural industrialization dominated.

37. The *Rural Sun*, June 19, 1873. The *Rural Sun* served as organ for the Tennessee Bureau of Agriculture, promoting immigration, development of timber and mineral resources and industrialization. The newspaper ceased publication in 1879.

38. The valuation of his property declined drastically between 1860 and 1870—whether due to loss of land or simply depreciation of the land's worth is unknown. See 1860 US Census, Population Schedules, District 8, Maury, Tennessee, M653, roll 1264, NARA; 1870 US Census, Population Schedules, District 8, Maury, Tennessee, M593, roll 1547, NARA.

39. "Letter from Amelia County," *Southern Planter*, April 1869, 200. Similar, although blunter, statements regarding the advantages of animal manure for both the farmer and the welfare of the animal can be found in "Stock," *Reconstructed Farmer*, May 1870, 15.

40. "Farm Management of the Southside," *Southern Planter*, November 1875, 599; *Piedmont Farmer*, 261.

41. 1860 Census of Agriculture, US Bureau of the Census; 1870 Census of Agriculture, US Bureau of the Census. Figures compiled by the author.

42. Testimony of Charles Douglas Gray, dated February 7, 1866, *Report of the Joint Committee on Reconstruction at the First Session, Thirty-Ninth Congress*, 68; "The Future Supply and Price of Pork," *Southern Planter*, April 1869, 206–207. The overall reduction of livestock in the region

meant that for years after the war, horses and mules were expensive and hard to obtain. See letter dated October 12, 1864, from Thomas R. Holland to Alexander Stephens, reel 18, vol. 26, Alexander Hamilton Stephens Papers, LOC; Henry Warren, *Reminiscences of a Mississippi Carpet-Bagger* (Holden, MA), 12.

43. Letter dated February 11, 1866, from G. P. Collins to Paul Cameron, Cameron Family Papers, box 52, folder 1254, SHC. A farmer in Littleton, North Carolina expressed similar sentiments. See letter dated June 18, 1867, from Thomas to Edward Alston Thorne, Edward Alston Thorne Papers, box 1, folder 5, RBMSC.

44. Letter dated March 7, 1866, from William Syndor in Marietta, Georgia, to his father, William Syndor Thomson Papers, box 1, folder 9, MARBL; "The Future Supply and Price of Pork," *Southern Planter*, April 1869, 206–207; letter dated January 15, 1868, from James Jenkins Gillette to his father, sent from Mobile, James Jenkins Gillette Papers, box 1, folder 10, LOC.

45. Quote in letter dated August 20, 1867, from A. J. Youngblood to Guilmartin and Co., sent from Davisboro, GA, John Flannery & Co. Records, 1867–1912, *RSPEGM*, Series A, pt. 3: Georgia and Florida Plantations, reel 1, RBMSC; entry dated January 8, 1866, *Piedmont Farmer*, 402; and Report of the Operations of the Bureau for April 1867, submitted by Col. C. C. Sibley, Macon, GA, Records of the Assistant Commissioner for the State of Georgia, BRFAL, M798, roll 32.

46. Letter dated January 11, 1866, from Ann Hairston to her daughter, Bettie, in Mississippi, Hairston and Wilson Family Papers, box 1, folder 11, SHC. See the list of animal prices in *Report of the Commissioner of Agriculture for the Year 1873* (Washington, DC: Government Printing Office, 1874), 36.

47. Quoted and discussed in Nash, *Reconstruction's Ragged Edge*, 59; entry dated September 25, 1865, Nimrod Porter Journals, TSLA; "Outrageous Attempt at Murder—Horses Stolen," *Weekly Atlanta Intelligencer*, May 9, 1866; and Nathans, *Mind to Stay*, 103. See also Stephen Budiansky, *The Bloody Shirt: Terror after Appomattox* (New York: Viking, 2008).

48. John Stover, *The Railroads of the South, 1865–1900: A Study in Finance and Control* (Chapel Hill: University of North Carolina Press, 1955), 58. See also the discussion in Donald E. Davis, "Uplands: Growing Pains," in *The Southern United States: An Environmental History*, ed. Donald E. Davis et al. (ABC-CLIO, 2006), 156; Williams, *Americans and Their Forests*, 254; Steinberg, *Down to Earth*, 111.

49. Michael Williams writes that railroads were "lines of exploitation," for "mills would be set up at intervals along the line, and the devastation of millions of acres of pine land would follow." Williams, *Americans and Their Forests*, 253. Although wood was traditionally used to build railroad bridges as well, by the 1880s, companies had replaced all the wooden bridges with ones made of Bessemer steel. Crossties continued to be made from timber. For a contemporary explanation of this process, see letter dated July 8, 1887, from Hon. Joseph E. Brown to Governor John B. Gordon, in Reference to the State Road, Joseph E. Brown Papers, MSS 40, box 1, folder 10, AHC.

50. Quote in letter dated October 10, 1870, from M. J. Kenan to Alexander Stephens, sent from Milledgeville, GA, Alexander Hamilton Stephens Papers, reel 29, LOC; calculations in entries for November–December 1869, Estimate Book for the Engineering Dept. of the Alabama and Chattanooga Railroad, 1869–71, Robert Jemison Jr. Papers, box 53, folder 3, WSHSC. The crossties listed come from several different sources in varying amounts. Some are clearly produced by railroad workers, while others come from individuals. Railroads also had to pay landowners for "right of way" through their land, intended as monetary compensation for the property and woodland consumed in the building process. See "Cost of Connecting Track between the Spartanburg and Union RR and Atlanta and Richmond Air Line RR at Spartanburg SC," 1873, Alfred Austell Papers, MSS 29, box 2, folder 2, AHC.

51. For discussions of the origins of commercial logging amidst rapid railroad expansion in the Mississippi Delta and bottomlands, see Otto, *The Final Frontiers, 1880–1930*, 17–23; Saikku, *This Delta, This Land*, 124–126; and Ralph Lutts, "Like Manna from God: The American Chestnut Trade in Southwestern Virginia," *Environmental History* 9, no. 3 (July 2004): 511–513. Lutts discusses the role that chestnut commons played in Virginian life, serving as extra income and food for roaming stock. He also notes that the coming of the railroad did not destroy the trade but allowed counties with access to the railroads to tap into a worldwide

chestnut trade. Sadly, the closing of the commons came not from the exhaustion of the resource but from the chestnut blight.

52. Ronald L. Lewis, *Transforming the Appalachian Countryside: Railroads, Deforestation, and Social Change in West Virginia, 1880–1920* (Chapel Hill: University of North Carolina Press, 1998), 8–10, quote on 47; Wetherington, *Plain Folk's Fight*, 304.

53. "The People of the Country," *Reconstructed Farmer*, April 1871, 357.

54. "Fences and Out-Buildings of the South," *De Bow's Review*, April 1866, 446. See also *Fence Laws* (Worcester, MA: Washburn and Moen Manufacturing Co., 1880).

55. "Fences—No. 1," *Reconstructed Farmer*, August 1869. In 1870, John Gray Allen requested rail timber from a merchant friend, who replied, "[L]umber is rising and I can't keep it from the planters who come along so if you want it you will have to send at once for it." Note dated March 28, 1870, Allen Family Papers I, box 250, folder 11, WSHSC.

56. *Carroll County Times*, September 1, 1882, quoted in Kantor and Kousser, "Common Sense or Commonwealth?," 212. Livestock values declined as drastically as the numbers of livestock during the same decade. The steepest drops in the value of livestock occurred in the following states: Alabama experienced a 39 percent decline; Georgia, 21 percent; Louisiana, 35 percent; Mississippi and North Carolina, 29 percent each; South Carolina, 48 percent; and Virginia, 41 percent. Florida, Kentucky, Maryland, and Tennessee either experienced an increase in the value of their livestock or saw only a slight drop. Table III, "Productions of Agriculture for the Years 1870, 1860, and 1850," in *Statistics of Agriculture, Compiled from the Original Returns of the Ninth Census June 1, 1870* (Washington, DC: Government Printing Office, 1872), 82. The percentage increases or decreases are calculated by the author.

57. For an example of how states made subtle alterations to the liability laws to appease the railroads, see Supreme Court of Alabama, *Mobile and Ohio Railroad Company v. Williams*, December term, 1875, cited in Westlaw as 53 Ala. 595, 1875 WL 1211, as compared to Supreme Court of Alabama, *Alabama Great Southern Railroad Company v. Jones*, December term, 1882, cited in Westlaw as 71 Ala. 487, 1882, WL 1266.

58. G. Terry Sharrer, "The Great Glanders Epizootic, 1861–1866: A Civil War Legacy," *Agricultural History* 69, no. 1 (Winter 1995): 79–97, esp. 87 and 91; and Gregory Whitlock, D. Mark Estes, and Alfredo Torres, "Glanders: Off to the Races with *Burkholderia Mallei*," *FEMS Microbiology letters* 277, no. 2 (2007): 115–122.

59. USDA, *Hog Cholera: Its History, Nature, and Treatment; as Determined by the Inquiries and Investigation of the Bureau of Animal Industry* (Washington, DC: Government Printing Office, 1889), 9; *Times-Daily*, August 28, 1914; *Prescott Evening Courier*, October 27, 1928; *Tuscaloosa News*, July 5, 1958; *Tuscaloosa News*, May 15, 1970; and National Research Council, *Emerging Animal Diseases: Global Markets, Global Safety: Workshop Summary* (Washington, DC: National Academies Press, 2002), 11.

60. As agricultural and veterinarian science gained traction in the state during the 1870s and 1880s with the aid of experiment stations such as the one at Auburn, officials employed this "scientific" approach to farming to justify long-running efforts to exert social and racial control. See Alan Marcus, *Agricultural Science and the Quest for Legitimacy: Farmers, Agricultural Colleges, and Experiment Stations, 1870–1890* (Ames: Iowa State University Press, 1985); and Mark Hersey, *My Work Is That of Conservation: An Environmental Biography of George Washington Carver* (Athens: University of Georgia Press, 2011), chap. 6.

61. A. Lange et al., "Pathogenesis of Classical Swine Fever—Similarities to Viral Haemorrhagic Fevers: A Review," *Berl Much Tierarztl Wochenschr* 124, no. 1–2 (Jan.–Feb. 2011): 36 (in German); V. Moennig, G. Floegel-Niesmann, and I. Greiser-Wilke, "Clinical Signs and Epidemiology of Classical Swine Fever: A Review of New Knowledge," *Veterinary Journal* 165 (2003): 11; Douglas Gregg, "Update on Classical Swine Fever," *Journal of Swine Health and Production* 10, no. 1 (2002): 35; C. A. Lueder, *Hog Cholera: Its Prevention and Control* (US Department of Agriculture and the West Virginia Experiment Station report, Washington, DC: Government Printing Office, 1913), 10.

62. Raymond Russell Birch, *Hog Cholera: Its Nature and Control* (New York: Macmillan Company, 1922), 1; Anna Rovid Spickler, "Classical Swine Fever: Technical Factsheet," *Center for Food Security and Public Health at Iowa State University*, October 17, 2015 (website),

http://www.cfsph.iastate.edu/Factsheets/pdfs/ classical_swine_fever.pdf (accessed April 11, 2016). For a lengthy summary of nineteenth-century instances of mistaken hog cholera reports, see USDA, "Contagious Diseases of Domesticated Animals," Special Report No. 34 (Washington, DC: Government Printing Office, 1881), 143–144.

63. USDA, *Hog Cholera*, 123.

64. Letter dated November 2, 1863, from Major P.W. White at Quincy, Florida, in US War Department, *The War of the Rebellion: A Compilation of the Official Records of the Union and Confederate Armies* (Washington, DC: Government Printing Office, 1863–1891), series 1, vol. 35, pt. 2, 395–396; Letter dated letter dated November 15, 1864, from W. W. Lenoir to his sister, Lenoir Family Papers, Subseries 1.3, folder 155, SHC; Birch, *Hog Cholera: Its Nature and Control*, 36, 38, 40. Walter Waightstill Lenoir entered the Confederate Army as a private in 1861 and, according to his obituary, ranked as a captain in 1862 when he was wounded in the leg at the Battle of Chantilly in Virginia (known to as the Battle of Ox Hill among Confederates). After he recovered, he returned home to Watauga County, NC. James A. Weston, *Services Held in the Chapel of Rest, Yadkin Valley, NC, for the late Capt. Walter Waightstill Lenoir, with Sermon* (New York: E & JB Young, 1890).

65. Letter dated January 15, 1865, from W. W. Lenoir to his mother, Lenoir Family Papers, Subseries 1.3, folder 155, SHC.

66. Gates, *Agriculture and the Civil War*, 90.

67. The USDA Bureau of Animal Industry listed seven major outbreaks in the state between 1862 and 1866, five during the years of Reconstruction, and two additional waves of infection during the 1880s. USDA, *Fourth and Fifth Annual Reports of the Bureau of Animal Industry* (Washington, DC: Government Printing Office, 1889), 188; USDA, *Report of the Commissioner of Agriculture for the Year 1867* (Washington, DC: Government Printing Office, 1868), 99–100; USDA, *Report of the Commissioner of Agriculture for the Year 1870* (Washington, DC: Government Printing Office, 1871), 45; *Birmingham Iron Age*, August 12, 1875; *Birmingham Iron Age*, April 9, 1879; *Weekly Iron Age*, September 10, 1885; *Weekly Age Herald*, February 20, 1889.

68. Birch, *Hog Cholera, Its Nature and Control*, 17–19; USDA, *Rules and Regulations Governing the Operations of the Bureau of Animal Industry* (Washington, DC: Government Printing Office, 1895), 59. Other, more random outbreaks were possibly the result of crows, buzzards, and other scavengers—what scientists called "casual carriers" of the disease—as well as any "spillover" into the wild boar population that went unrecorded and unnoticed. In Europe, classical swine fever is still endemic in the wild boar population, complicating the eradication of the virus in domestic pigs. See Gillermo Risatti and Manuel Borca, "Overview of Classical Swine Fever," Merck Veterinary Manual online, https://www.merckvetmanual.com/generalized-conditions/classical-swine-fever/ (accessed January 2, 2017).

69. *Camden Confederate*, April 20, 1864; "Certain Cure for the Hog Cholera," *Abingdon Virginian*, May 1, 1863. Dr. George Sutton conducted a series of experiments in Dearborn, Indiana, in the 1850s trying various poisons, including strychnine, in hog clop. See "Investigations of Swine Diseases," in USDA, *Hog Cholera*, 14–17.

70. "Hog Cholera," *Memphis Daily Appeal*, May 30, 1876; "Hog Cholera—Cured," *Southern Cultivator*, July and August 1862, 141.

71. "Report of the Statistician," *Report of the Commissioner of Agriculture for the Year 1867*, 96, 98.

72. USDA, *Contagious Diseases of Domesticated Animals*, 304.

73. Appendix, Bulletin No. 22, Agricultural Experiment Station of the Agricultural and Mechanical College, Auburn, AL (Montgomery: Smith, Allred, & Co., 1891), 78–79.

74. USDA, *Fourth and Fifth Annual Reports*, 202, 241, 191; USDA, *Hog Cholera*, 81.

75. Entries dated September 28 and November 15, 1867, Nimrod Porter Journals, TSLA.

76. *Report of the Commissioner of Agriculture for the Year 1870* (Washington, DC: Government Printing Office, 1871), 285.

77. Johnson, "Reconstructing the Soil," 200–201; B. W. Arnold, *The History of the Tobacco Industry of Virginia, 1860 to 1894* (Baltimore, MD: Johns Hopkins University Press, 1897), 24; Robert Mikkelsen and Thomas Bruulsema, "Fertilizer Use for Horticultural Crops in the United States during the 20th Century," *HortTechnology* 15, no. 1 (January–March 2005): 25–26. For a contemporary description of the discovery of phosphate deposits in North Carolina,

see "Commercial Fertilizers," *Bulletin of the North Carolina Department of Agriculture*, March 1886, 2–3.

78. "The Evils of Tobacco Culture," *Southern Planter*, March 1870, 191.

79. "Facts about Fertilizers," *Southern Farm and Home*, November 1870, 21; and Charles Nordhoff, *The Cotton States in the Spring and Summer of 1875* (New York: Burt Franklin, 1876), 107. Nordhoff reports that Georgia Piedmont land averaged between one-third and one-half bale per acre with fertilizer; Mississippi alluvial land averaged three-quarters to one bale per acre, supposedly without fertilizer. For more on the expenditure of each state for fertilizer, see *Report of the Productions of Agriculture Returned in the Tenth Census*, June 1880.

80. First quotes in *Report of the Commissioner of Agriculture for the Year 1870*, 269; second in Warren, *Reminiscences of a Mississippi Carpet-Bagger*, 22.

81. Letters dated March 11, 1865, and May 31, 1865, William Gibbs McAdoo to his mother, container 17, William Gibbs McAdoo Papers, LOC; "Biographical Sketch of William Gibbs McAdoo," dated 1862, container 16, William Gibbs McAdoo Papers, LOC.

82. Letter dated September 20, 1856, from John McAdoo to W. G. McAdoo, container 15; letter dated May 17, 1859 from W. G. McAdoo to F. M. Adams, container 15; and letter dated February 15, 1863, from W. G. McAdoo to his mother, container 17, all in William Gibbs McAdoo Papers, LOC. See "Soil Survey of Baldwin, Jones, and Putnam Counties" (report of the Soil Conservation Service, USDA, 1972), 4. Stanley Trimble's data suggests that Baldwin County (where McAdoo lived) was "severely eroded" by this period; he estimates that by 1900, 30 centimeters of topsoil was gone. Stanley Trimble, *A Volumetric Estimate of Man-Induced Erosion on the Southern Piedmont* (Agricultural Research Service Pub. S40, US Department of Agriculture, Washington, DC, 1975), 142–145.

83. Letter dated February 11, 1866, W. G. McAdoo to his mother, William Gibbs McAdoo Papers, container 17, LOC.

84. Letters dated July 28, 1866; October 27, 1867; November 16, 1867; and October 30, 1868, and the correspondence of January 1869, W. G. McAdoo to his mother, William Gibbs McAdoo Papers, containers 17–18, LOC. This would not be true for all Piedmont soils. In Virginia, especially, where soil erosion was intense before and during the war, crop rotations would not have been enough to restore soils' moisture retention. As a result, the droughts of 1866, 1867, and 1868, which were noticeable but not disastrous in the Black Belt, were much worse in the tobacco-growing areas of Virginia because of the extreme vulnerability of the soils. Jeffrey Kerr-Ritchie, who studies the role of emancipated blacks in postwar tobacco Virginia, argues that climate and emancipation were the primary factors keeping the levels of tobacco produced and the number of improved acres very low through the early 1870s. Kerr-Ritchie, *Freedpeople of the Tobacco South*, 96–99. For more on the timeline of fertilizer development, see Richard Sheridan, "Chemical Fertilizers in Southern Agriculture," *Agricultural History* 53, no. 1, Southern Agriculture Since the Civil War: A Symposium (January 1979): 308–318.

85. Letter dated October 5, 1868, container 18, William Gibbs McAdoo Papers, LOC.

86. First quote in Nordhoff, *Cotton States*, 99; second quote in letter dated October 10, 1870, from P. B. Monk to Alexander Stephens, sent from Byronville, Dooly County, GA, Alexander Hamilton Stephens Papers, reel 29, LOC.

87. First and second quotes in letter dated August 10, 1867, from George Eliston to L. J. Guilmartin and Co., sent from unknown location, and letter dated October 17, 1871, from J. L. Johnson to Guilmartin and Co., sent from Irwinton, GA, John Flannery & Co. Records, 1867–1912, *RSPEGM*, Series A, pt. 3: Georgia and Florida Plantations, reel 1, RBMSC; third quote in "Homemade and Commercial Manures," *Southern Farm and Home*, December 1870, 44–45. There were other, less obvious problems with the increasing reliance on fertilizers, especially guano. Guano contained heavy doses of nitrogen, and its unbalanced nutrient composition meant that after several years in continuous cotton, the depletion of potassium in the soil created a shortage of essential nutrients needed for the development of cotton "fruit," or expansive, fluffy white bolls. In other words, it "stimulated vegetative growth, but did not always increase yields." Mikkelsen and Bruulsema, "Fertilizer Use for Horticultural Crops," 25. In 1869, W. B. Henderson, a planter in Marengo County, Alabama, wrote to his local newspaper asking for better advice regarding fertilizer for cotton lands. Guano had worked for a few years, but his lint yields had steadily decreased, despite his spending more money and

time on the application of the fertilizer. Letter to the Editor from W. B. Henderson, *Selma Morning Times*, September 21, 1869. See also "The Cotton Crop of Georgia," *New York Times*, July 28, 1870, 6.

88. Julie Saville uses the term "deformed analogue" to describe postwar sharecropping's relationship to antebellum tenancy. See Saville, *Work of Reconstruction*, 125.

89. Jack Temple Kirby calls the postwar South a "poorer South," in Kirby, "American Civil War in an Environmental View."

Chapter 4

Parts of Chapter 4 appeared in "Freedom, Economic Autonomy, and Ecological Change in the Cotton South, 1865–1880," *Journal of the Civil War Era* 7, no. 3 (2017): 401–424.

1. Trowbridge, *South*, 15, 125, 198, 464. Trowbridge was only briefly a journalist; his main body of work consisted of novels and children's books. Other examples of journalists' account of the postwar South are John Richard Dennett, *The South As It Is: 1865–1866* (New York: Viking, 1965); and Whitelaw Reid, *After the War: A Southern Tour (May 1, 1865 to May 1, 1866)* (London: Samson Low, Son, & Marston, 1866). "The Great Rebellion" was a name for the Civil War used in the earliest histories of that conflict, published at the same time as Trowbridge's work. See Horace Greeley, *The American Conflict: A History of the Great Rebellion in the United States of America, 1860–'64*, 2 vols. (Hartford: O. D. Case & Co., 1864, 1866).

2. Trowbridge, *South*, 270, 433. For corroboration of Trowbridge's impression that southern Alabama was spared the war's destruction, see letter dated July 26, 1865, from William O_____ at Demopolis, AL, Reports of Operations from the Subdistricts, Records of the Assistant Commissioner for the State of Alabama, BRFAL, M809, reel 18, NARA. The Freedmen's Bureau agent's report covers the same area Trowbridge toured, at approximately the same time.

3. Trowbridge, *South*, , 425–426, 423.

4. Scholars disagree on the monetary value of slaves at the time of emancipation. Patrick O'Brien values them at $3 billion, while James Huston says $4–6 billion. See Patrick O'Brien, *The Economic Effects of the American Civil War* (Atlantic Highlands, NJ: Humanities Press International, 1988), 14, 26; James L. Huston, "Property Rights in Slavery and the Coming of the Civil War," *Journal of Southern History* 65, no. 2 (May 1999): 249–286; R. L. Ransom and R. Sutch, "Growth and Welfare in the American South of the Nineteenth Century," *Explorations in Economic History* 16 (1979): 226.

5. Interview titled "Hongry for pun'kin pie," WPA Slave Narrative Project, Alabama Narratives, vol. 1, LOC; O'Donovan, *Becoming Free in the Cotton South*, 113, 115. O'Donovan points out that especially in places where the war itself had been largely kept at bay—she refers specifically to southwest Georgia, where only impressment and the effects of the blockade brought the war to planters—freedom, too, was kept at bay. See her examples in *Becoming Free*, 114. Also discussed in Leon Litwack, *Been in the Storm So Long: The Aftermath of Slavery* (New York: Vintage, 1980), 115.

6. Lou Falkner Williams, *The Great South Carolina Ku Klux Klan Trials, 1871–1872* (Athens: University of Georgia Press, 1996), 3; report of E. Whittlesley, Assistant Commissioner in the BRFAL, dated February 1866, *Report of the Joint Committee on Reconstruction at the First Session Thirty-Ninth Congress* (Washington, DC: Government Printing Office, 1866), 199.

7. Bruce Baker and Brian Kelly, eds., *After Slavery: Race, Labor, and Citizenship in the Reconstruction South* (Tallahassee: University Press of Florida, 2013), 3; Cohen, *At Freedom's Edge*, 14; letter dated September 13, 1865, from I. A. Pruitt to Brig. General Wager Swayne, Letters Received, Records of the Assistant Commissioner for the State of Alabama, BRFAL, M809, roll 6, NARA; Freedmen's Labor," *Monthly Reports of the Department of Agriculture for the Year 1870* (Washington, DC: Government Printing Office, 1871), 11; Litwack, *Been in the Storm So Long*, 244–245. For examples of the scholarship that intensely examines the emergence of the free-labor system in various regions of the South, see John Rodrigue,

"Labor Militancy and Black Grassroots Political Mobilization in the Louisiana Sugar Regions, 1865–1868," *Journal of Southern History* 67, no. 1 (February 2001): 115–142; Stephen A. West, "'A General Remodeling of Everything': Economy and Race in the Postemancipation South," in *Reconstructions: New Perspectives on the Postbellum United States*, ed. Thomas Brown (New York: Oxford University Press, 2006); Saville, *Work of Reconstruction*; Harris, *Deep Souths*; Rodrigue, *Reconstruction in the Cane Fields*.

8. Note dated January 30, 1872, from M. Rice at Demopolis to Allen at Spring Hill, box 250, folder 11; letter dated March 10, 1881, from J. Lee Terrell of Demopolis, and letter dated December 3, 1883, from Seymour Adams of Linden, both in Allen Family Papers I, box 250, folder 13, WSHSC. By the time of the exchange detailed here, Allen owned at least three farms plus property in the nearest town, with each lot consisting of 300–1800 acres. See Tax Lists, Allen Family Papers I, box 249, folder 7, WSHSC, University of Alabama. For details of Allen's business providing credit for other merchants or buying up debt, see Allen Family Papers I, box 249, folder 9, WSHSC.

9. Letter dated September 22, 1871, from W. L. Walston to J. G. Allen at Spring Hill, Allen Family Papers I, box 250, folder 11, WSHSC.

10. Martin Ruef, *Between Slavery and Capitalism: The Legacy of Emancipation in the American South* (Princeton, NJ: Princeton University Press, 2014), 9. For examples of parallel issues in other postemancipation societies, see Frederick Cooper, *From Slaves to Squatters: Plantation Labor and Agriculture in Zanzibar and Coastal Kenya, 1890–1925* (New Haven, CT: Yale University Press, 1980), 280; Eric Foner, *Nothing but Freedom: Emancipation and Its Legacy* (Baton Rouge: Louisiana State University Press, 1983), 44–45; Rebecca Scott, *Slave Emancipation in Cuba: The Transition to Free Labor, 1860–1899* (Princeton, NJ: Princeton University Press, 1985); and Patrick Bryan, "The Transition of Plantation Agriculture in the Dominican Republic, 1870–1894," *Journal of Caribbean History* 10–11 (1978): 82–105.

11. Cooper, *From Slaves to Squatters*, 280.

12. Letter dated July 4, 1865, from James A. Hawley to Samuel Thomas, Registered Letters Received, Assistant Commissioner for the State of Mississippi, BRFAL, M826, roll 6; O'Donovan, *Becoming Free in the Cotton South*, 113, 115; report of E. Whittlesey, Assistant Commissioner in the BRFAL, dated February 1866, *Report of the Joint Committee on Reconstruction at the First Session Thirty-Ninth Congress*, pt. 2 (Washington DC: Government Printing Office, 1866), 199. See the discussion of the process of emancipation in Jim Downs, *Sick from Freedom: African-American Illness and Suffering during the Civil War and Reconstruction* (New York: Oxford University Press, 2012), 13–14; and the uncertainty of agricultural tenure in Ruef, *Between Slavery and Capitalism*, 7–10.

13. "Interview with a Planter," *The Liberator*, August 11, 1865.

14. Testimony of Rufus Saxton, dated February 21, 1866, *Report of the Joint Committee on Reconstruction*, pt. 2, 220.

15. Contracts between freedpeople and landowners operated similarly in the Southern Appalachians, where white laborers made up a substantial portion of the workforce and antebellum tenant and sharecropping arrangements were common. See Nash, *Reconstruction's Ragged Edge*, 40–41.

16. Contract dated 1866, Fanny Taliaferro Daybook, Tennessee Historical Society Collection, TSLA; and contract dated January 1866 between Nelson Clayton and Judy, a freedwoman, Nelson Clayton Papers, box 1, folder 40, WSHSC.

17. Report dated November 1, 1866, from Davis Tillson to James Johnson, Reports on Operations, Records of the Assistant Commissioner for the State of Georgia BRFAL, M798, roll 32; testimony of Capt. Alexander Ketchum, February 28, 1866, *Report of the Joint Committee on Reconstruction*, pt. 2, 240.

18. Terms pulled from contract dated 1866 between Allen Harris of Dyer County, TN, and his former slaves, Miscellaneous Freedmen Work Contracts, Records of the Assistant Commissioner for the State of Tennessee, BRFAL, M999, roll 20; contract dated January 9, 1866, between Clark Anderson of Mississippi and Freedmen of Wilkes County, GA, Unbound Miscellaneous Papers, Records of the Assistant Commissioner for the State of Georgia, BRFAL, M798, roll 36; "Report of the Assistant Commissioner of Alabama," October 31, 1866, 39th Congress, 2nd Sess., Senate Ex. Doc., No. 6, 6; report dated January 15, 1866, from

Anderson District, South Carolina, included in General Rufus Sexton's testimony, *Report of the Joint Committee on Reconstruction*, pt. 2, 228. A secondary discussion of Freedmen's Bureau agents' reluctance can be found in Steven Hahn et al., *Land and Labor, 1865*, series 3, vol. 1, of *Freedom: A Documentary History of Emancipation, 1861–1867* (Chapel Hill: University of North Carolina Press, 2008)28.

19. See, for example, contract dated December 23, 1865, between Thomas J. Ross and the Freedmen of Rosstown Plantation, Shelby County, TN, Miscellaneous Freedmen Work Contracts, Records of the Assistant Commissioner for the State of TN, BRFAL, M999, roll 20; and contract dated June 1, 1865, between W. C. Penick and Asbury et al., Autauga County, AL, reprinted in Hahn et al., *Land and Labor, 1865*, 341–343.

20. Contract dated January 12, 1866 in Fulton County, Georgia, between Joseph E. Brown and John Bateman and Neal Bateman, colored freedmen, Joseph E. Brown Papers, box 3, folder 6, MSS 40, AHC; contract dated January 1, 1866, between B. F. Duncan and three freedmen, unknown location, Miscellaneous Freedmen Work Contracts, Records of the Assistant Commissioner for the State of Tennessee, BRFAL, M999, roll 20; contract dated February 23, 1866, between Keating S. Ball and 90 freedmen, Keating Ball Plantation Journal, *RASP*, Series F, pt. 2, reel 4, RBMSC; contract dated December 29, 1865 between Joel Light and Gibson, a freedman, Dyer County, TN, Miscellaneous Freedmen Work Contracts, Records of the Assistant Commissioner for the State of Tennessee, BRFAL, M999, roll 20; and contract dated June 30, 1865, box 7, folder 1, Henry J. Watson Jr. Papers, RBMSC.

21. Contract dated 1866, James Boykin Papers, box 1, folder 7, WSHSC. See the discussion of the group contract in Ralph Schlomowitz, "The Origins of Southern Sharecropping," *Agricultural History* 53, no. 3 (July 1979): 571–572; Foner, *Reconstruction*, 171–173.

22. First quote in F. W. Loring and C. F. Atkinson, *Cotton Culture and the South, Considered with Reference to Emigration* (A. Williams & Co., 1869), 10; second quote in *New Orleans Tribune*, December 18, 1866, 4. For a narrative account of how ex-slaves' value as laborers was determined, see Deposition of Howard Mason, April 8, 1895, Civil War Pension File, 13th USCHA and 121st USCI, RG 15, NARA.

23. Both rice and sugar depended on a complex system of levees, ditches, and canals that acted as a tenuous barrier between the waters of the Mississippi River or the Atlantic Ocean and the valuable cane or rice stands. The conditions of the crop regime along the coastlines and previous years of land use shaped contract negotiations, so that the outcomes were vastly different from those in upland regions. Scott, *Degrees of Freedom*; Rodrigue, *Reconstruction in the Cane Fields*.

24. Letter dated December 1865, from William F. Robert to Q. A. Gilmore, and letter dated December 14, 1865, from Shelton Oliver to Captain Campbell, both reprinted in Hahn et al., *Land and Labor, 1865*, 590, 966.

25. Cotton Planters' Association of Mississippi Circular, reprinted in "Prospects of the Cotton Crop," *De Bow's Review*, November 1866, 531–532; entry dated August 1865, Farm Journals, John Horry Dent Collection, box 1, folder 7, SCA; Report dated September 25, 1867, submitted by Allan Rutherford, sent from Wilmington, NC, Annual Report on Operations, Records of the Assistant Commissioner for the State of North Carolina, BRFAL, M843, roll 22.

26. Quote from Interview with Berry Smith by W. B. Allen, WPA Slave Narrative Project, Mississippi Narratives, vol. 9, LOC; testimony of Madison Newby, February 3, 1866, *Report of the Joint Committee on Reconstruction*, pt. 2, 55; and "Freedmen's Labor," *Monthly Reports of the Department of Agriculture for the Year 1866* (Washington, DC: Government Printing Office, 1867), 348.

27. Interview with Shade Richards by Alberta Minor, WPA Slave Narrative Project, Georgia Narratives, vol. 4, pt. 3, LOC; quote from Maury County, Texas in Loring and Atkinson, *Cotton Culture and the South*, 4. For more on both day-to-day resistance and open defiance among slaves before the Civil War, see John Hope Franklin and Loren Schweninger, *Runaway Slaves: Rebels on the Plantation* (New York: Oxford University Press, 1999), 2–11.

28. Letter dated November 3, 1865, from W. W. Woodruff to General Tilson, Unregistered Letters Received, Records of the Assistant Commissioner for the State of Georgia, BRFAL, M798, roll 24; letter dated December 22, 1865, from Frederick Edward Miller to General E. M. Gregory, reprinted in Hahn et al., *Land and Labor, 1865*, 975; "Price of Labor," *Report*

of the Commissioner of Agriculture for the Year 1867 (Washington, DC: Government Printing Office, 1868), 416–417.

29. Barbara J. Fields, "The Nineteenth-Century American South: History and Theory," *Plantation Society* 2, no. 1 (April 1983): 11.

30. Marginalia on contract dated January 12, 1866, between Joseph Brown and John Bateman, a freedman, Fulton County, Georgia, Joseph E. Brown Papers, box 3, folder 6, AHC; entries for January 29 and February 2, 1870, John K. and William M. Elliott Daybooks, box 1, folder 1, WSHSC; miscellaneous contracts dated January 1866, Nelson Clayton Papers, box 1, folder 40, WSHSC. For the bills of sale for the slaves (later freedpeople) Clayton hired that year, see box 1, folder 39.

31. Letter dated September 22, 1871, from W. L. Walston to J. G. Allen at Spring Hill, Allen Family Papers I, box 250, folder 11, WSHSC. For examples of ex-slaves who stayed with no [reported] periods of absence, see interview with Marshal Butler by Sarah Boyd, WPA Slave Narrative Project, Georgia Narratives, vol. 4, pt. 1; and interview with Marriah Hines by David Hoggard, WPA Slave Narrative Project, Virginia Narratives, vol. 17.

32. Reidy, *From Slavery to Agrarian Capitalism*, 148. See also René Hayden et al., *Land and Labor, 1866–1867*, series 3, vol. 2, of *Freedom: A Documentary History of Emancipation, 1861–1867* (Chapel Hill: University of North Carolina Press, 2013), 35–36.

33. On wage variation, see "Price of Labor," *Report of the Commissioner of Agriculture for the Year 1867*, 416–417; Hayden et al., *Land and Labor, 1866–1867*, 369–370. On the much feared "labor shortage" and the pull of western states with higher wages, see Report for January 1867, submitted by L. W. Walsh from Aiken, SC, Reports of Conditions and Operations, Records of the Assistant Commissioner for the State of South Carolina, BRFAL, M869, roll 35; letter dated February 20, 1870, from S. W. Ficklin at Belmont, VA, to Robert Jemison Jr., Robert Jemison Jr. Papers, box 7, folder 9, WSHSC; Robert Preston Brooks, *The Agrarian Revolution in Georgia, 1865–1912* (1914; repr., Westport. CT: Negro Universities Press, 1970), 407–408.

34. It was not initially clear to observers how this arrangement would eventually allow land-owners and merchants to exploit and even increase levels of debt among their sharecrop-pers. See "Southern Agriculture," *Report of the Commissioner of Agriculture for the Year 1867*, 417; Howard Rabinowitz, *The First New South: 1865–1920* (Arlington Heights, IL: Harlan Davidson, 1992), 10–12; Jay Mandle, "Sharecropping and the Plantation Economy in the United States South," in *Sharecropping and Sharecroppers*, ed. T. J. Byres (New York: Taylor & Francis, 1987), 124; Reidy, *Slavery to Agrarian Capitalism*, 148–151; Interview with Evans Warrior, WPA Slave Narratives Project, Arkansas Narratives, pt. 7, LOC.

35. Letter dated July 6, 1876, from Felix Davis to his nephews in Marion, AL, box 3462, folder 11, Hugh Davis Papers, WSHSC; contract dated April 28, 1875, between Alfred Austell and C. W. Bowen, Alfred Austell Papers, box 1, folder 17, MSS 29, AHC; and account of Bob Hill (freedman) dated 1871, Statement of Cherokee Plantation, Robert Jemison Jr. Papers, box 73, WSHSC.

36. I examined agricultural contracts included in the manuscript collections of thirty-eight farms in Georgia, Tennessee, North Carolina, Mississippi, Alabama, South Carolina, and Arkansas. I derived additional data from records of the Freedmen's Bureau (BRFAL); WPA ex-slave narratives from South Carolina, Georgia, and Mississippi; and monthly USDA reports, which detailed developments in all southern states.

37. Entry dated April 1873, William Wallace White Diary, vol. 48, SHC; "Important to Farmers—Decisions of the Commissioner of Internal Revenue," *Montgomery Weekly Advertiser*, August 28, 1866.

38. Loring and Atkinson, *Cotton Culture and the South*, 5; Charles Flynn Jr., *White Land, Black Labor: Caste and Class in Late Nineteenth-Century Georgia* (Baton Rouge: Louisiana State University Press, 1983), 11–25; Schlomowitz, "Origins of Southern Sharecropping," 571–572; Reidy, *From Slavery to Agrarian Capitalism*, 146–152; and Kerr-Ritchie, *Freedpeople of the Tobacco South*, 64.

39. Labor Contracts, Allen Family Papers, box 249, folder 1, WSHSC; entries for 1870, 1873, and 1876, John K. Elliott and William M. Elliott Daybooks, box 1, folders 1 and 3, WSHSC;

Henry L. Pinckney Plantation Journal, *RASP*, Series F, pt. 2, reel 9, RBMSC; and letter dated January 15, 1868, from James Jenkins Gillette to his parents, sent from Mobile, James Jenkins Gillette Papers, box 1, folder 10, LOC.

40. Loring and Atkinson, *Cotton Culture and the South*, 28–29.

41. "Bottom Lands—Their Condition and Improvements—Ditching and Diking," *Southern Planter*, March 1869, 130–131; "Short-comings in Farming," *Reconstructed Farmer*, May 1870, 3; first quote in "Facts about Fertilizers," *Southern Farm and Home*, November 1870, 21; second quote in *Southern Planter*, March 1876, 196.

42. First quote in letter fragment dated April 1870 from William Stickney at Faundsale to his wife, Louisa, Faunsdale Plantation Papers, box 2, folder 23, BPL; second in "Farm Work for the Month," *Southern Farm and Home*, February 1871, 122.

43. First quote in Arthur Raper and Ira de A. Reid, *Sharecroppers All* (Chapel Hill: University of North Carolina Press, 1941), 6–7; second in report dated October 1868, submitted by R. A. Wilson at Demopolis, Alabama, Reports of Operations from the Subdistricts, Records of the Assistant Commissioner for the State of Alabama, BRFAL, M809, reel 18, SU.

44. W. D. Hunter, "The Cotton Worm or Cotton Caterpillar" (USDA Bureau of Entomology Circular No. 153, May1912), 1–2.

45. Letter dated October 10, 1864, from Thomas Henderson to Capt. Stiles, sent from New Orleans, LA, Incoming Correspondence of the Plantation Bureau, 1863–1865, Third Special Agency Records, Records of Civil War Special Agencies of the Treasury Dept., RG 366, entry 414, box 5, folder 1, NARA II; letter dated August 21, 1867, from M. G. Ehrlich to John Flannery, sent from Valdosta, GA, John Flannery & Co. Records, 1867–1912, *RSPEGM*, Series A, pt. 3: Georgia and Florida Plantations, reel 1, RBMSC; and letter dated January 15, 1868, from James Jenkins Gillette to his father, James Jenkins Gillette Papers, box 1, folder 10, LOC.

46. One Freedmen's Bureau agent hints at this connection. See report dated September 16, 1867, submitted by Major George Williams at Charleston, SC, Reports of Conditions and Operations, Dec. 1866–May 1868, Records of the Assistant Commissioner for the State of South Carolina, BRFAL, M869, roll 35, NARA.

47. 1860 US Census, Population Schedule, Western Division: Wilcox County, Alabama, M653, roll 26, NARA. The Bennett farm was worth $13,000 in 1860, and the 1860 Slave Schedules indicate that Elizabeth's husband, Bowen, owned a substantial number of slaves before he died (over fifteen). Although there is some discrepancy regarding the year of his birth, the Census records from 1860 and 1870 indicate that John would have been only nineteen or twenty at the time of the dispute. Prairie Bluff was a river town in Wilcox County "born of a booster's dream of profit," possessing a cotton slide from the bluff to the river below that made it a popular place for river barges. By the 1840s, however, market linkages were drawing business away from Prairie Bluff toward Camden, Cahaba, and other better-situated towns. By the 1880s, Prairie Bluff was only a cotton slide and a sign, a ghost town. See Harvey Jackson, *Rivers of History: Life on the Coosa, Tallapoosa, Cahaba, and Alabama* (Tuscaloosa: University of Alabama Press, 1995): 65–66.

48. Letter dated December 4, 1867, from D. J. Fraser to the Freedmen's Bureau office at Selma, Alabama, letters Received, Records of the Assistant Commissioner for the State of Alabama, BRFAL, M1900, reel 30, Special Collections, SU. It is not known how many freedpeople the Bennetts employed on their property, nor indeed the percentage of their prewar property being farmed by the late 1860s.

49. Although several southern states did not become officially "closed-range" until the mid-twentieth century, political interest in the subject peaked between the 1870s and 1890s. Tennessee officially became a closed-range state in 1947, Alabama in 1951, Georgia in 1955, and Mississippi in 1978. J. Crawford King Jr., "The Closing of the Southern Range: An Exploratory Study," *Journal of Southern History* 48, no. 1 (February 1982): 54.

50. "Report to the Farmer's Assembly on the Law of Enclosures," *Southern Planter*, March 1867, 96.

51. Hahn, *Roots of Southern Populism*. This is not to say that Hahn ignores economic considerations. Instead, he situates the material concerns over fencing and the importance of common property rights for poor or yeoman farmers' agricultural self-sufficiency within a framework

of social relations dominated by kinship and reciprocity rather than the marketplace. See also Hahn, "Hunting, Fishing, and Foraging: Common Rights and Class Relations in the Postbellum South," *Radical History Review* 26 (1982): 37–64, esp. 42. Other scholars characterize the fight over fencing as more of a conflict between the "haves" and "have nots," more in keeping with the fault lines of the antebellum period. See Forrest McDonald and Grady McWhiney, "The South from Self-Sufficiency to Peonage: An Interpretation," *American Historical Review* 85, no. 5 (December 1980): 1095–1118; Shawn Everett Kantor, *Politics and Property Rights: The Closing of the Open Range in the Postbellum South* (Chicago: University of Chicago Press, 1998); Gilbert Fite, *Cotton Fields No More: Southern Agriculture, 1865–1980* (Lexington: University Press of Kentucky, 1984), chap. 1; and Kirby, *Mockingbird Song*, 129–131. An exchange that helps show the various sides in this debate is Shawn Everett Kantor and J. Morgan Kousser, "Common Sense or Commonwealth? The Fence Law and Institutional Change in the Postbellum South," *Journal of Southern History* 59, no. 2 (May 1993): 201–242, and Steven Hahn's response to it, "A Response: Common Cents or Historical Sense?," *Journal of Southern History* 59, no. 2 (May 1993): 243–258. One scholar mentions the racial element of this conflict in the Deep South. See King, "Closing of the Southern Range."

52. In this case, the limitations were a dearth of suitable pasture grasses, acidic soils, and a climate that kept cow milk production low. For a discussion of the difficulties of large-scale stock-raising in the South due to environmental limitations, see Cowdrey, *This Land, This South*, 77; Claire Strom, "Texas Fever and the Dispossession of the Southern Yeoman Farmer," *Journal of Southern History* 66, no. 1 (February 2000): 51–52; and Rubin, "Limits of Agricultural Progress," 364–366.

53. *Laws of the State of Mississippi, 1865–1866* (Jackson: printed for the state of Mississippi, 1866), 199–200, 289–290. Discussed in King, "Closing of the Southern Range," 57; and Hahn, "Hunting, Fishing, and Foraging," 47.

54. Act no. 258, *Acts of the Session of 1866–7 of the General Assembly of Alabama* (Montgomery, AL: Reid and Screws, 1867), 256; *Acts of the General Assembly of the State of Virginia, Passed at the Session 1869–70* (Richmond, VA: James E. Goode, 1870), 544; Resolution number 437, *Acts and Resolutions of the General Assembly of the State of Georgia, Passed at its session in July and August 1872*, vol. 1 (Atlanta, GA: W. A. Hemphill and Co., 1872), 529. At least one city in Virginia tried to pass a stock law in the immediate aftermath of the war—Brunswick Springs, VA, in 1866. It did not pass. See letter dated February 14, 1866, from J. Ravenscroft Jones to W. H. E. Merritt, William H. E. Merritt Papers, box 1, folder 3, RBMSC.

55. Historian Joseph Reidy comments on this legislation as being part of planters' efforts to "[reduce] freedpeople to mudsill status." Reidy, *From Slavery to Agrarian Capitalism*, 222.

56. Letter dated May 29, 1879, from J. Ryall to J. G. Allen, Allen Family Papers I, box 250, folder 11, WSHSC.

57. For more on Allen's arrangements with laborers, see Allen Family Papers I, box 249, folder 1, and box 251, folder 22. The former contains tenant farmer contracts, and the latter, wage labor contracts. Allen relied on convict labor as early as 1885; after Allen's death in 1891, his son, Charles Edward, continued using convicts to work the plantation. Allen's arrangements with the state are typified by the contract dated September 29, 1890, Allen Family Papers I, box 251, folder 21, in which Allen and his son agree to provide prisoner John Carter—convicted of assault—with "good and wholesome food" while Carter works off his court fines and attorney costs. The finances of other members of John Ryall's family are hinted at in letter dated February 21, 1866, from W. S. Ryall to J. G. Allen, Allen Family Papers I, box 250, folder 13. After the exchange described at the beginning of the section, Ryall purchased some of Allen's cattle because Ryall was already feeding them. Letter dated June 1879 from J. Ryall to J. G. Allen, Allen Family Papers I, box 250, folder 11, WSHSC.

58. Flynn, *White Land, Black Labor*, 11–25; Ralph Schlomowitz, "The Origins of Southern Sharecropping," *Agricultural History* 53, no. 3 (July 1979): 571–572; and Hahn et al., *Land and Labor, 1865*, 30–48; Reidy, *From Slavery to Agrarian Capitalism*, 146–152.

59. Charles Aiken, *The Cotton Plantation South since the Civil War* (Baltimore, MD: Johns Hopkins University Press, 1998), 20–21; Robert Somers, *The Southern States since the War, 1870–71* (New York: Macmillan and Co., 1871), 120. This was not true for ex-slaves working on rice or sugar plantations.

60. Letter dated January 20, 1870, from William Stickney at Faunsdale to his wife, Louisa Harrison, Faunsdale Plantation Papers, box 2, folder 23, Archives and Special Collections, BPL; entry dated January 1, 1866, specifically the part referring to Evelynton Plantation, Edmund Ruffin Jr., Plantation Journal, SHC; "Plantations in the South," US Census Bureau, *Thirteenth Census of the United States Taken in the Year 1910: Agriculture* (Washington, DC: Government Printing Office, 1913), 877–878; Mrs. Nicolas Ware Eppes, *The Negro of the Old South: A Bit of Period History* (Chicago: Joseph Branch Pub. Co., 1925), 159.

61. 1860 Census of Agriculture, US Bureau of the Census; and 1880 Census of Agriculture, US Bureau of the Census. Calculations made by the author.

62. Harris, *Deep Souths*, 26–30.

63. Examples of this type of anecdotal evidence in plantation journals include a comparison of entries between 1859 and 1875 in the Elliott Daybooks, WSHSC; Edmund Ruffin Farm Journals, SHC; and the William Wallace White Journals, SHC.

64. Letter dated February 26, 1867, from William Syndor Thomson to his father, William Syndor Thomson Papers, box 1, folder 10, MARBL.

65. Letter dated December 5, 1866, from L. C. Warren to General Davis Tillson, Unregistered Letters Received, Records of the Assistant Commissioner for the State of Georgia, BRFAL, reprinted in Hayden et al., *Land and Labor, 1866–1867*, 459–460.

66. Report for Dinwiddie County dated August 31, 1865, Monthly Reports on Confiscated and Abandoned Lands, August 1865–January 1867, Records of the Assistant Commissioner for the State of Virginia, BRFAL, M1048, roll 50, NARA. See also Proctor Moses, Report of Lessees and Plantations on Young's Point, June 1864, Records of the Mississippi Freedmen's Department (Pre-Bureau), Office of the Assistant Commissioner, BRFAL, M1914, roll 2, NARA; testimony of John Covode dated March 3, 1866, *Report of the Joint Committee on Reconstruction*, 116–117. Secondary discussions include Vernon Burton, "Race and Reconstruction: Edgefield County, South Carolina," *Journal of Social History* 12, no. 1 (1978): 31–56; Reidy, *From Slavery to Agrarian Capitalism*, 150–151; and Hahn, "Hunting, Fishing, and Foraging," 44.

67. Entry for J. S. Rhen property on Trent Road, one mile west of New Bern, Report submitted by Capt. Horace James for the months July, August, and September of 1865, Quarterly Reports of Abandoned or Confiscated Lands, Records Relating to Lands and Property, Records of the Assistant Commissioner for the State of North Carolina, BRFAL, M843, roll 36, NARA.

68. First quote in Hayden et al., *Land and Labor 1866–1867*, 372–373; contract dated February 7, 1866, between Arthur Middleton and Freedmen and Women, Labor Contracts, Records of the Acting Assistant Commissioner for South Carolina, BRFAL, M869, roll 42, NARA; second quote in contract dated February 1866, between Wade Hampton Jr. and Freedpeople of Columbia, SC, Miscellaneous Records, Records of the Assistant Commissioner for the State of Mississippi, M826, roll 37, NARA.

69. Hayden et al., *Land and Labor, 1866–1867*, 421. See also Reidy, *From Slavery to Agrarian Capitalism*, 150–152; Laura Edwards, "The Problem of Dependency: African Americans, Labor Relations, and the Law in the Nineteenth-Century South," *Agricultural History* 72, no. 2 (Spring 1998): 313–340; and Foner, *Nothing but Freedom*, 18.

70. Foner, *Nothing but Freedom*, 58. Tom Okie discusses the same attitude of slaves toward truck crops on the plantation—in this case, peaches. William Thomas Okie, *The Georgia Peach: Culture, Agriculture, and Environment in the American South* (Cambridge: Cambridge University Press, 2017).

71. Report dated May 31, 1868, submitted by Samuel Place in Sumter, SC, Reports of Conditions and Operations, December 1866–May 1868, Records of the Assistant Commissioner for the State of South Carolina, BRFAL, M869, roll 35, NARA; report dated May 22, 1868, submitted by J. A. Gordy in Eutaw, AL, Reports of Operations from the Subdistricts, September 1865–December 1868," Records of the Assistant Commissioner for the State of Alabama, BRFAL, M809, roll 18, NARA; Hayden et al., *Land and Labor, 1866–1867*, 409.

72. "Loss of Livestock," *Carolina Farmer*, August 1869; and "Immigration," *Carolina Farmer*, April 1869, 196.

73. Testimony of Rev. L. M. Hobbs dated February 28, 1866, *Report of the Joint Committee on Reconstruction*, pt. 4, 7–8.

74. "Stole a Pig," *Montgomery Weekly Advertiser*, August 28, 1866; King, "Closing of the Open Range," 57; J. G. de Roulhac Hamilton, *Reconstruction in North Carolina*, Studies in History, Economics, and Public Law 18 (New York: Columbia University, 1914), 419.

75. "Immigration," *Carolina Farmer*, April 1869, RSMBC; "The Evils of Tobacco Culture," *Southern Planter*, February 1870, 192.

76. "Stall-Feeding Stock," *Reconstructed Farmer*, June 1871, 429.

77. Letter dated January 16, 1866, from George Robinson to Bvt. Col. C. Cadle Jr., Unregistered Letters Received, Records of the Assistant Commissioner for the State of Alabama, BRFAL, M809, roll 9; and letter dated December 24, 1865, from William McAdoo to his mother, William Gibbs McAdoo Papers, LOC.

78. "Advance in Corn and Bacon," *Macon Telegraph*, April 28, 1870. This cycle of debt is discussed at length in chapter 5.

79. For more on antebellum efforts to eliminate common spaces or subsistence practices in the South, see Daniel Rood, "Bogs of Death: Slavery, the Brazilian Flour Trade, and the Mystery of Vanishing Millponds in Antebellum Virginia," *Journal of Southern History* 101, no. 1 (June 2014): 20–21; Watson, "'Common Rights of Mankind,'" 13–43; Kirby, *Poquosin*, 130–140, 174. For an overview of the ecological conflicts over rights to waterways and fishing in the antebellum North, see Ted Steinberg, *Nature Incorporated: Industrialization and the Waters of New England* (1991; repr., Cambridge: Cambridge University Press, 2003).

80. Kirby, "American Civil War: An Environmental View"; and Rood, "Bogs of Death," 20.

81. The drastic changes that facilitated the repeal of fence laws and the decline of shifting cultivation in the plantation belt did not affect the uplands, pine belt, or mountainous regions of the South until the late 1870s and 1880s. However, the encroachment of the railroad into these upland regions and the rise of commercial timbering eventually brought the same types of changes seen much earlier in the plantation belt: erosion due to woodland clearance, expanded cash crop production, increased reliance on fertilizers, and the decline of free-range husbandry and shifting cultivation. General descriptions of the postwar transformation of the upland areas of the South, where yeoman, and not planters, predominated, include Hahn, *Roots of Southern Populism*; Mark Wetherington, *The New South Comes to Wiregrass Georgia, 1860–1910* (Knoxville: University of Tennessee Press, 2001); Newby, *Plain Folk of the New South*; and David Weiman, "The Economic Emancipation of the Non-slaveholding Class: Upcountry Farmers in the Georgia Cotton Economy," *Journal of Economic History* 45, no. 1 (March 1985): 71–93.

82. Report dated September 16, 1867, submitted by Major George Williams at Charleston, SC, Reports of Conditions and Operations, December 1866–May 1868, Records of the Assistant Commissioner for the State of South Carolina, BRFAL, M869, roll 35; quoted in Saville, *Work of Reconstruction*, 135.

83. W. E. B. Du Bois, *The Souls of Black Folk: Essays and Sketches* (Chicago: A. C. McClurg and Co., 1908), 155.

84. Entry dated August 1865, Farm Journals, John Horry Dent Collection, box 1, folder 7, SCA; quoted in Harris, *Deep Souths*, 31.

85. Letter dated June 29, 1865, from Joseph Daniel Pope to Major General Q. A. Gillmore, reprinted in Hahn et al., *Land and Labor, 1865*, 103–104.

Chapter 5

1. For examples of White's engagement in the church, see entries dated August 1868, September 1869, and April 1874, William Wallace White Diaries, box 4, vol. 48, SHC. He also claimed a financial interest in the local store, Burwell & White, which provided a portion of his living. His activities as a merchant are also mentioned frequently; examples include entries dated April and May 1866, William Wallace White Diaries, SHC. For evidence of his activities as justice of the peace for Warren County, see Brent Holcomb, *Marriages of Bute and Warren Counties, North Carolina, 1764–1868* (Baltimore, MD: Clearfield and Genealogical Publishing, 1991), 11, 209, 213; and entry dated August 1870, William Wallace White Diaries, SHC.

2. Information about White and his land can be found in 1850 and 1860 US Census Population Schedules, Warren County, North Carolina, M653, roll 916, NARA; US Bureau of Soils, *Soil Survey of Vance County, North Carolina* (Washington, DC: Government Printing Office, 1921), 20–22. White lived in a part of Warren County near Nutbush Creek that became part of Vance County in 1881. The type of planter community in that area is described in US Department of the Interior, National Register of Historic Places Registration Form for "Belvidere," or the Boyd House, dated October 13, 1992, available through the North Carolina State Historic Preservation Office. Belvidere was built by one of White's close friends, William H. Boyd, and White frequently noted the number of slaves Boyd "sent over" to help him strip, worm, plant, or cure tobacco. See entry dated May 1861, William Wallace White Diaries, SHC. For more on the basic process of growing and curing tobacco, see "Tobacco Growing in Maryland," *American Farmer*, February 1849, 257; and "Essay on the Cultivation of Tobacco," *American Farmer*, March 10, 1841, 329.

3. Entry dated May 1873, William Wallace White Diaries, SHC.

4. Entries dated June 1873, September 1875, November 1875, December 1876, and December 1878, William Wallace White Diaries, SHC.

5. Fite, *Cotton Fields No More*, 6–8.

6. Farmers lived in fear of an early frost in both spring and autumn, and Somers likened cotton fields in North Carolina to an English field of daisies because of the stunted height of the plants. Somers, *Southern States Since the War, 1870–71*, 13, 29–30, 48–49; "Cotton," USDA Monthly Reports, November–December 1872 (Washington, DC: Government Printing Office, 1872), 475.

7. Somers, *Southern States since the War, 1870–1871*, 70, 263, 266–267; "Advice," *Tuscaloosa Independent Monitor*, October 16, 1867.

8. Bradley Bond, *Political Culture in the Nineteenth-Century South: Mississippi, 1830–1900* (Baton Rouge: Louisiana State University Press, 1992), 187. The phrase "the Isolated South," and its geographical definitions, comes from Rubin, "Limits of Agricultural Progress," 364.

9. "Report on the Condition of Agriculture," US Department of Agriculture, *Monthly Reports*, February–March 1874 (Washington, DC: Government Printing Office, 1874), 77.

10. "Cotton," *Reconstructed Farmer*, April 1871.

11. USDA, "Monthly Report—December 1873" (Washington, DC: Government Printing Office, 1874); and *Hand-Book of the State of North Carolina, Exhibiting its Resources and Industries* (Raleigh: Ashe & Gatling, 1883), 12–13.

12. Letter dated October 17, 1871, from J. L. Johnson to Guilmartin and Co., sent from Irwinton, GA, John Flannery & Co. Records, 1867–1912, reel 1, RBMSC.

13. Letter dated February 19, 1874, from I. S. Grennet, John Flannery & Co. Records, 1867–1912, reel 2, *RSPEGM*, RBMSC. See also letter dated September 24, 1877, from G. Abhairez to John Flannery and Co., John Flannery & Co. Records, 1867–1912, reel 5, *RSPEGM*, RBMSC.

14. "United States Census: Cotton," *Annual Cyclopedia and Register of Important Events for the Year 1892* (New York: D. Appleton and Co., 1893), 764–765.

15. Gavin Wright, "Cotton Competition and the Post-bellum Recovery of the American South," *Journal of Economic History* 34, no. 3 (September 1974): 611; first quote in "Planting Prospects," *Southern Cultivator*, January 1866, 8; second in Warren, *Reminiscences of a Mississippi Carpet-Bagger*, 11.

16. Letter fragment dated April 1870 from William Stickney to his wife, Louisa, box 2, folder 23, Faunsdale Plantation Papers, BPL; USDA, *Report of the Commissioner of Agriculture for the Year 1867*, xii; USDA, "Report on the Condition of Agriculture," *Monthly Reports*, February–March 1874 (Washington, DC: Government Printing Office, 1874), 77; Harris, "Crop Choices in the Piedmont," 528–532. For a discussion of the historiography of southern economic decline in terms of per capita productivity, see Jeremy Atack and Peter Passell, "The South after the Civil War," in *A New Economic View of American History*, 2nd ed. (New York: W. W. Norton, 1994), 378–385.

17. An excellent exploration of historians' assumptions regarding New South debt and debt peonage can be found in J. Williams Harris, "The Question of Peonage in the History of the New South," in Hyde, *Plain Folk of the South Revisited*, 101–116. For more on lien laws

and the legal underpinnings of debt in this period, see Harold Woodman, *New South, New Law: The Legal Foundations of Credit and Labor Relations in the Postbellum Agricultural South* (Baton Rouge: Louisiana State University Press, 1995), 28–66; Roger Ransom and Richard Sutch, "Debt Peonage in the Cotton South after the Civil War," *Journal of Economic History* 32 (1972): 641–649; Woodman, *King Cotton and His Retainers*.

18. North Carolina State Auditor, *Report of the Comptroller of Public Accounts of North Carolina for the Year ending September 30th, 1867* (Raleigh, NC: W. E. Pell, 1868); North Carolina State Auditor, *Report of the Comptroller of Public Accounts of North Carolina for the Year ending September 30th, 1872* (Raleigh, NC: W. E. Pell, 1873); letter dated May 16, 1867, from Robert Jemison Jr. at Tuscaloosa to his mother, Robert Jemison Jr. Papers, box 1, folder 7, WSHSC; Marston discussed in Kilbourne, *Debt, Investment, Slaves*, 110–112; letter dated February 1868 from Martha to George Hairston, George Hairston Papers, box 1, folder 10, SHC. See also Kenneth Edson St. Clair, "Debtor Relief in North Carolina during Reconstruction," *North Carolina Historical Review* 18, no. 3 (July 1941): 215–235. For contemporary views on the bonds of creditors and debtors in the postwar chaos, see "Creditors and Debtors—Forced Collections," *Montgomery Weekly Advertiser*, August 28, 1866.

19. Fields, "Nineteenth-Century American South," 11.

20. There were exceptions, of course. Some farmers continued to engage in extensive land use, while others intensified *some* practices, but not all. A good example of a farmer who did, in fact, experience many of the same processes identified in chapters 3–5 but managed to range his animals in the woods and, at least once, to clear new ground, is John Elliott of Sumter County, Alabama. His daybooks lay out the various tasks performed on the farm during the 1870s. See the John K. and William Elliott Daybooks, WSHSC.

21. Nelson, *Pharsalia*, chaps. 4–5, illustrate the issue of capital-intensive agriculture in the southern environment as it played out on one plantation.

22. Entries dated March 27, July 24, and August 8, 1865, Nimrod Porter Journals, TSLA; 1880 US Census, Population Schedules, District 8, Maury County, Tennessee, Microfilm Publication T9, roll 1271; County Clerk, Maury County, Tennessee, Marriage Bonds (Colored), Microfilm vol. C1–C3, roll 113, TSLA.

23. Entries dated December 24, 1866; October 12, 1867; January 4, January 30, April 29, September 18, 1869; and January 13, 1870, Nimrod Porter Journals, TSLA.

24. Letter dated September 26, 1865, from W. W. Mitchell to Charles T. Ames, Esq., New South Miscellany Papers, box 1, folder 5, MARBL. Most of the enterprising Yankees who moved to the South, however, did so, not to buy land as Mitchell wished to, but to rent it—they expected that one, maybe two, cotton crops would be enough to reshape their fortunes, so there was no need to resettle permanently. Whitelaw Reid, one of the many northern journalists touring the postwar South, related that a northern lessee on Lake Providence, Louisiana, anticipated making $65,000 in one year working a 1,500-acre plantation. This type of wild expectation of future wealth drove the demand for leased plantations and caused rents to jump in the best cotton districts. In the Natchez District of Mississippi, "fifteen thousand dollars seemed a common rent of a thousand acres of good land." Reid, *After the War*, 415, 480–481. See also Lawrence Powell, *New Masters: Northern Planters during the Civil War and Reconstruction* (New York: Fordham University Press, 1999).

25. Letter dated September 26, 1865, from W. W. Mitchell to Charles T. Ames, Esq., New South Miscellany Papers, box 1, folder 5, MARBL.

26. Letter dated October 6, 1865, from E. T. Wright at Hilton Head to Lieutenant Colonel H. B. Clitz, Letters Received, Department of South Carolina, Records of the US Army Continental Commands, RG 393, quoted in Hahn et al., *Land and Labor, 1865*, 20.

27. The Old Rotation is relevant to tobacco-growing areas, too, because it contains acidic ultisols derived from granitic gneiss, close relatives of soils commonly found throughout the Piedmont. See J. A. Entry, C. C. Mitchell, and C. B. Backman, "Influence of Management Practices on Soil Organic Matter, Microbial Biomass and Cotton Yield in Alabama's 'Old Rotation,'" *Biology and Fertility of Soils* 23, no. 4 (November 1996): 353–358; and Richter and Markewitz, *Understanding Soil Change*, 131–132.

28. Plantation ledger for 1899, box 2, folder 4, in Adrian Sebastian Van de Graaff Papers, WSHSC.

29. Mathis, *John Horry Dent*, 204, 207; *Southern Planter*, February 1852, 55–56; "generally disastrous" comment in Richter and Markewitz, *Understanding Soil Change*, 128; Bennett, *Soil*

Conservation, 217–226; Daniel Richter et al., "Legacies of Agriculture and Forest Regrowth in the Nitrogen of Old-Field Soils," *Forest Ecology and Management* 138 (2000): 246.

30. Eugene Hilgard, *Report on the Cotton Production in the United States*, pt. 2 (Department of the Interior Census Office report, Washington, DC: Government Printing Office, 1884), 509.

31. "Protect Our Streams," *Dublin Post* (Georgia), March 30, 1887.

32. "Drainage of Lands," *Southern Cultivator*, May 1870, 139; "Bottom Lands—Their Condition and Improvements—Ditching and Diking," *Southern Planter*, March 1869, 130–131.

33. Charles Johnson, Edwin Embree, and W. W. Alexander, *The Collapse of Cotton Tenancy: Summary of Field Studies and Statistical Surveys, 1933–1935* (Chapel Hill: University of North Carolina Press, 1935), 14.

34. Richter and Markewitz, *Understanding Soil Change*, 123.

35. Trimble, *Man-Induced Soil Erosion*, 70–78.

36. Bennett, *Soil Conservation*, 223.

37. See "Statistics of Agriculture," *The Report of the Production of Agriculture in the Tenth Census* (Washington, DC: Government Printing Office, 1884), 3–4.

38. Averages calculated by author using statistics in Eddie Wayne Shell, *Evolution of the Alabama Ecosystem* (Montgomery, AL: New South Books, 2013), fig. 8.23.

39. "Tennessee Map of Crop Production, 1892," TSLA; *Report of the Commissioner for Agriculture for the Year 1869* (Washington, DC: Government Printing Office, 1870), 26–28; *Report of the Commissioner for Agriculture for the Year 1875* (Washington, DC: Government Printing Office, 1876), 31.

40. Ransom and Sutch, *One Kind of Freedom*, 161–168, quote on 161; Gavin Wright, "Freedom and the Southern Economy," in *Market Institutions and Economic Progress in the New South, 1865–1900*, ed. Gary Walton and James Shepherd (New York: Academic Press, 1981), 101.

41. Letter dated December 24, 1865, from William McAdoo to his mother, William Gibbs McAdoo Papers, LOC. When drought or other factors reduced crop output in the Midwest, farmers in the cotton belt suffered. The editors of the *Macon Telegraph* were "baffled" at the willingness of local planters to "shell out" cash for western bacon rather than raise corn and buy livestock. "Advance in Corn and Bacon," *Macon Telegraph*, April 28, 1870. Renters, or tenant farmers, had the most property at their disposal, and so could run an agricultural operation with minimal assistance from the landlord in terms of rations, clothing, and work animals. It was the landlord's responsibility to provide the land, a house, and in many cases, fuel. Some tenants rented their lands in cash, but most agreed to pay a stipulated portion of the crop, sometimes one-third but often one-half (called "working halves"). See "Southern Agriculture," *Report of the Commissioner of Agriculture for the Year 1867*, 417; and Rabinowitz, *First New South*, 10–12. Jay Mandle explains how the sharecropping "compromise" emerged and the motivations behind the concessions of each side in the labor arrangement, in "Sharecropping and the Plantation Economy in the United States South," in *Sharecropping and Sharecroppers*, ed. T. J. Byres (New York: Taylor and Francis, 1987), 124.

42. Letter dated February 17, 1874, I. A. Grennet to L. J. Guilmartin & Co., John Flannery & Co. Records, 1867–1912, *RSPEGM*, Series A, pt. 3, RBMSC. Jack Temple Kirby writes that, unlike the range animals of the South, the "pork shipped south from Cincinnati came principally from new breeds such as the Poland China, an enormous porcine balloon on stick-legs, bred for fat." Kirby, "American Civil War: An Environmental View," 7; Cowdrey, *This Land, This South*, 106.

43. This change over time can be seen by comparing the "hands accounts" for the years 1872, 1874, 1882, and 1884. Hands Accounts, Receipts of Charles King, King Family Papers, box 1, folder 8, WSHSC.

44. Harris's sample includes Hart, Glascock, and Taliaferro Counties. Taliaferro was located in the antebellum cotton belt with a high density of slaves in 1860; Glascock was also in the cotton belt, but because of poorer soils, small, white cotton farmers predominated in 1860; and Hart produced very little cotton before the war. He shows that cotton production rose and grain production fell in every county, with the sharpest rises in cotton among poor white farmers in Hart county and black tenant farmers in Taliaferro. Harris, "Crop Choices in the Piedmont," 526–542, ratios cited on 531.

45. J. H. Norwood, "Can the South Afford to Produce Cotton at Present Prices, and Buy Her Supplies Abroad?" *Southern Planter*, October 1876.

46. Document dated 1872, unsigned but in Maguire's handwriting, Thomas Maguire Papers, box 1, folder 5, AHC.

47. Henry Grady, "South and Her Problems," speech at Dallas, TX, October 1887, *New South: Writings and Speeches of Henry Grady*, 30–31.

48. Judge Adrian Sebastian Van de Graaff (also spelled Vandegraaff, Vandegraf, or Vandegraff) was born in 1859 in Sumter County, Alabama, but grew up in California and attended school in California and Connecticut. He graduated from the University of Alabama Law School in 1884 and married the daughter of Andrew Hargrove and Cherokee Mims Jemison Hargrove. Cherokee was the daughter of Robert Jemison Jr., a wealthy planter and railroad entrepreneur. Andrew Hargrove took charge of part of Jemison's planting interest after the war, as Jemison became increasingly consumed with industrial developments in the Tuscaloosa and Birmingham area. Adrian Van de Graaff, then, inherited operations of both Robert Jemison and Andrew Hargrove. See the Guide to the Adrian Sebastian Van de Graaff Papers, MSS 1493, WSHSC.

49. Plantation Account Book, 1898, box 2, folder 3, and Plantation Ledger for 1899, box 2, folder 4, in Adrian Sebastian Van de Graaff Papers, WSHSC.

50. A sample of the works documenting the continuity in the planter class trans–Civil War includes Wayne, *Reshaping of Plantation Society*; Weiner, *Social Origins of the New South*; Dwight Billings, "Class Origins of the 'New South': Planter Persistence and Industry in North Carolina," *American Journal of Sociology* 88 (1982): S52–S85. For a discussion of the same subject from the perspective of economic motivation and development, see Philip Ager, "The Persistence of De Facto Power: Elites and Economic Development in the US South, 1840–1960," European Historical Economics Society Working Paper 38, 2013, http://ideas.repec.org/p/hes/wpaper/0038.html (accessed June 14, 2017).

51. This attitude of planters toward their dependents had shifted considerably since the days of planter "paternalism." On planter paternalism—its origins, manifestations, and representations—see Eugene Genovese and Elizabeth Fox-Genovese, *Fatal Self-Deception: Slaveholding Paternalism in the Old South* (Cambridge: Cambridge University Press, 2011); Allan Gallay, "The Origins of Slaveholders' Paternalism: George Whitefield, the Bryan Family, and the Great Awakening in the South," *Journal of Southern History* 53 (August 1987): 369–394; Susan Tracy, *In the Master's Eye: Representations of Women, Blacks, and Poor Whites in Antebellum Southern Literature* (Amherst: University of Massachusetts Press, 2009); and Rhys Isaac, *The Transformation of Virginia: 1740–1790* (Chapel Hill: University of North Carolina Press, 1982).

52. See "The North Carolina Exodus," *Chicago Tribune*, December 9, 1879.

53. Letter dated November 1866 from Watt and Phingy of Athens, GA, Records Relating to Transportation, Records of the Assistant Commissioner for the State of North Carolina, M843, roll 28, BRFAL, NARA.

54. Chandra Manning, *Troubled Refuge: Struggling for Freedom in the Civil War* (New York: Alfred A. Knopf, 2016), 151. Contraband camps were named for the legal designation of runaway slaves as "contraband" of war, drawing authority from the confiscation acts in order to negate Confederate claims of ownership.

55. Report for January 1867, submitted by L. W. Walsh from Aiken, SC, Reports of Conditions and Operations, December 1866–May 1868, Records of the Assistant Commissioner for the State of South Carolina, M869, roll 35, BRFAL, NARA. Samuel Agnew of Mississippi complained of crowds of blacks' wagons in entry dated October 5, 1869, Samuel Agnew Diary, SHC.

56. Letter dated February 20, 1870, from S. W. Ficklin at Belmont, VA, to Robert Jemison Jr., Robert Jemison Jr. Papers, box 7, folder 9, WSHSC; and Brooks, *Agrarian Revolution in Georgia*, 407–408.

57. Letter dated February 27, 1875, from Turner Whitfield at Columbus, Mississippi, to Bryan Whitfield, Whitfield Family Papers, RG 863, box 6, folder 7, SCA; "The North Carolina Exodus," *Chicago Tribune*, December 9, 1879.

58. Reid, *After the War*, 273; Kerr-Ritchie, *Freedpeople of the Tobacco South*, 64. See also the discussion in Loren Schweninger, "Black Economic Reconstruction in the South," in *The Facts of Reconstruction: Essays in Honor of John Hope Franklin*, ed. Eric Anderson and Alfred Moss Jr. (Baton Rouge: Louisiana State University Press, 1991), 178–179.

59. Interview with John Van Hook dated December 1, 1938, by Sadie Hornsby, WPA, *Slave Narratives: A Folk History of Slavery in the United States from Interviews with Former Slaves,*

Georgia Narratives, pt. 4 (Washington, DC: Federal Writer's Project, 1941). At the time of his interview, Van Hook lived in Athens, Georgia.

60. Interview with Van Hook, WPA, *Slave Narratives*. For more on ex-slaves asking to be transported to live with family members, see "Transportation Requests Received April 20–December 21, 1866," Records of the Assistant Commissioner for the State of Soul Carolina, M869, roll 44, BRFAL, NARA; and "List of Refugees, Their Wants & Conditions for Transporting," Miscellaneous Records June 1865–October 1868, Records of the Assistant Commissioner for the State of Tennessee, M999, roll 34, BRFAL, NARA.

61. Jim Haskins, *The Geography of Hope: Black Exodus from the South after Reconstruction* (Brookfield, CT: Twenty-First Century Books, 1999), 14. Haskins uses the concept of "biblical exodus" to frame his discussion of African American migration, contrasting pre–Civil War black migration (long in planning, careful) with postwar black migration (spontaneous, reaction to violence).

62. Quote in letter dated February 12, 1867, from William Syndor Thomson to his father, William Syndor Thomson Papers, box 1, folder 9, MARBL; interview with Jake Walker by Bernice Bowden, WPA, *Slave Narratives: A Folk History of Slavery in the United States, from Interviews with Former Slaves*, Arkansas Narratives, pt. 7 (Washington, DC: Federal Writer's Project 1941). See also "Exodus from the South," *De Bow's Review*, April/May 1867, 353.

63. This was not the first legislation of its kind—as early as the 1820s, lawmakers opened public domain lands to purchasers, homesteaders, and builders of canals and railroads in an effort to encourage westward expansion. Michael Lanza, "'One of the Most Appreciated Labors of the Bureau': The Freedman's Bureau and the Southern Homestead Act," in *The Freedmen's Bureau and Reconstruction: Reconsiderations*, ed. by Paul Cimbala and Randall Miller (New York: Fordham University Press, 1999), 67; Walker, *Southern Forest*, 39–42.

64. See the Records relating to Transportation, Records of the Assistant Commissioner for the State of North Carolina, M843, roll 28, BRFAL, NARA. The roll introduction describes the goals and shortcomings of the transportation offices.

65. Report dated October 30, 1866, submitted by Stephen Moore, Annual Report on Operations, Records of the Assistant Commissioner for the State of North Carolina, BRFAL, M843, roll 22, NARA. Contraband camps were frequently the sites of disease outbreaks—measles, mumps, cholera, smallpox—and officials had a difficult time controlling the spread of the epidemics both within the camps and once they reached white populations nearby. See Bobby Lovett, "African Americans, Civil War and Aftermath in Arkansas," *Arkansas Historical Quarterly* 54, no. 3 (Autumn 1995): 304–358.

66. Report dated October 1866, submitted by W. Meady, Annual Report on Operations, Records of the Assistant Commissioner for the State of North Carolina, M843, roll 22, BRFAL, NARA. There were many instances when freedmen who obtained homesteads through the act did not successfully complete the five-year settling period, leaving the land available for purchase when the law was repealed. In addition to the obvious capital difficulties, Michael Lanza suggests that homestead lands were "hostile" environments for freed slaves; in Florida, blacks were consistently run off their homesteads by neighboring white farmers. Lanza, "Freedmen's Bureau and the Southern Homestead Act," 67–68.

67. For contemporary discussions of black labor, see "What is NC to do for Labor?" *Reconstructed Farmer*, June 1871; "Exodus from the South," *De Bow's Review*, April–May 1866. White movement in Ann Patton Malone, "Piney Woods Farmers of South Georgia, 1850–1900," *Agricultural History* 60, no. 4 (Autumn 1986): 51–84, esp. 78–79; Wetherington, *Plain Folk's Fight*, 296–300.

68. Letters dated June 19, 1865 and July 30, 1865, box 7, folder 1, Henry Watson, Jr. Papers, RBMSC; Elizabeth Regosin and Donald Shaffer, eds., *Voices of Emancipation: Understanding Slavery, the Civil War, and Reconstruction through the U.S. Pension Bureau Files* (New York: New York University Press, 2008), 83; Frank Magwood, interviewed by T. Pat Matthews, North Carolina Narratives, vol. 11, pt. 2, Federal Writers' Project, Ex-Slaves Narratives, LOC. A survey of black population growth in Nashville, Atlanta, Richmond, Montgomery, and Raleigh between 1860 and 1880 in Howard Rabinowitz, *Race, Ethnicity, and Urbanization: Selected Essays* (Columbia: University of Missouri Press, 1994), 119, table 1. A discussion of how the existence of industrial employment affected Brazil, see John Crocitti, "Landlords and Tenants

in the Wake of Abolition and Ecological Devastation in Brazil's Middle Paraiba Valley," *Agricultural History* 83, no. 2 (Spring 2009): 143–173.

69. Willoughby Newton, "An Essay on the Social and Material Interests of Virginia," *Southern Planter*, May 1869, 281.

70. B. W. Arnold Jr., *History of the Tobacco Industry in Virginia from 1860 to 1894* (Baltimore, MD: Johns Hopkins Press, 1897), 20.

71. Typed Memoir, Alston Family Papers, box 1, folder 1, LOC, 65–66. Jacob Alston recorded the major events of his life up through the 1890s (he died in 1909) in an open letter addressed to his grandson, Motte Alston Read. Jacob was a part of the Alston branch of the Allston-Alston-Smith-Pettigrew-Pettigru family of South Carolina. There is some discrepancy regarding where Jacob planted during the war—his memoir states very simply that his lands fell into disrepair, but records show that Col. Henry Buck purchased Woodburne from Alston in 1858 and renamed it Tip Top. So, the exact location of the lands Alston owned during the war is unknown. See "Woodburne Plantation—Winyah—Horry County," *South Carolina Plantations*, Horry Historical Society, http://south-carolina-plantations.com/horry/woodbourne.html (accessed June 1, 2017). For more on the Allston-Pettigrew branch of the family, see William Kauffman Scarborough, *The Allstons of Chicora Wood: Wealth, Honor, and Gentility in the South Carolina Lowcountry* (Baton Rouge: Louisiana State University Press, 2011).

72. Typed Memoir, Alston Family Papers, box 1, folder 1, LOC, 65–66. See also *Rice Planter and Sportsman: The Recollections of J. Motte Alston, 1821–1909*, ed. Arney Childs (Columbia: University of South Carolina Press, 1999). Childs does not include large portions of the memoir dealing with the postwar period because the focus of the book is on prewar rice planting and planter culture.

73. Trimble, *Man-Induced Soil Erosion*, 70, 73.

74. Eugene Hilgard, *Report on the Cotton Production in the United States*, pt. 2, Department of the Interior, Census Office (Washington, DC: Government Printing Office, 1884), 280.

75. Charles Nordhoff described the lower wages available to tenants and sharecroppers in the seaboard states, as well as made note of the incredible numbers of white farmers leaving Georgia. See Nordhoff, *Cotton States*, 99, 105. For copies of the USDA Crop Reports, see "Crop Reports, 1897–1900," Division of Statistics, Records of the Bureau of Agricultural Economics, RG 83, NARA II.

76. *Chicago Herald*, April 16, 1885; Trimble, *Man-Induced Soil Erosion*, 70–88. Joseph Taylor reports that North Carolina suffered a "Great Migration" in 1879 as both whites and blacks left that state in a "terrible cleaning out." Primarily from Greene, Jones, Lenoir, and Wayne Counties, over three thousand people left North Carolina in just six months of 1879. Taylor does not, however, make the connection between those particular counties and soil conditions. Joseph Taylor, "The Great Migration from North Carolina in 1879," *North Carolina Historical Review* 31, no. 1 (January 1954): 18–33.

77. Between 1870 and 1880, Georgia's number of improved acres increased by 20 percent, North Carolina's by 23 percent, and South Carolina's by 37 percent, but Virginia saw just a 4 percent increase. Between 1880 and 1890, Georgia's number of improved acres increased by 17 percent, North Carolina's by 20 percent, and South Carolina's by 27 percent, although Virginia saw just a 7 percent increase during that period. Calculated by the author using Statistics of Agriculture, Compiled from the Original Returns of the Ninth, Tenth, and Eleventh Censuses.

78. Hahn, *Roots of Southern Populism*, 149–152, esp. the chart on 150.

79. In North Carolina, for instance, acreage devoted to cotton increased by 28 percent between 1879 and 1889, yet the number of bales produced on that land shrank. In the 1870s, North Carolina farmers averaged 0.44 bales per acre; in 1890, they only averaged 0.29 bales per acre. See *Appleton's Annual Cyclopedia of Important Events for 1892*, 765.

80. Trimble, *Man-Induced Soil Erosion*, 78; Carol Harden and Louise Mathews, "Hillslope Runoff, Soil Detachment, and Soil Organic Content Following Reforestation in the Copper Basin, Tennessee, USA," *Australian Geographical Studies* 40, no. 2 (July 2002): 130–142; Carol Harden and P. Delmas Scruggs, "Infiltration on Mountain Slopes: A Comparison of Three Environments," *Geomorphology* 55 (2003): 5–24.

81. Otto, *Southern Agriculture during the Civil War Era*, 110–111, 115.

82. Nordhoff, *Cotton States*, 105.

83. Report for the Month February–March 1874, *Monthly Reports of the US Department of Agriculture for the Year 1874* (Washington, DC: Government Printing Office, 1874), 64, 78.

84. Herman Clarence Nixon, *Forty Acres and Steel Mules* (Chapel Hill: University of North Carolina Press, 1938), 19. See also the photographs throughout the book. Second quote and other discussion from Nancy Isenberg, *White Trash: The 400-Year-Old Untold History of Class in America* (New York: Viking, 2016), 198.

Conclusion

1. Edward L. Ayers, *The Promise of the New South: Life after Reconstruction*, 15th Anniversary ed. (New York: Oxford University Press, 2007), 3; and James C. Giesen, "'The Truth about the Boll Weevil': The Nature of Planter Power in the Mississippi Delta," *Environmental History* 14 (October 2009): 688. The South produced 4.5 million bales of cotton in 1860. See the US Censuses of Agriculture for 1860 and 1880, US Census Bureau, available at http://www.census.gov.

2. Mill, *Principles of Political Economy*, quoted in Ransom and Sutch, "Impact of the Civil War," 2. John Stuart Mill, *Principles of Political Economy, with some Applications to Social Philosophy*, 7th ed. (London: Longmans, Green, 1909), bk. 1, chap. 5, p. 19. First published in 1848.

3. Henry Grady, "The New South," *New York Ledger*, November–December 1889, reprinted in *The New South: Writings and Speeches of Henry Grady* (Savannah: The Beehive Press, 1971), 107. For examples of scholars who emphasize change over continuity, those who think the Civil War revolutionized the South, see C. Vann Woodward, *Origins of the New South, 1877–1913* (Baton Rouge: Louisiana State University Press, 1951); Beard and Beard, *Rise of American Civilization*; W. E. B. Du Bois, *Black Reconstruction in America, 1860–1880* (New York: Simon and Schuster, 1935); Woodman, "How New Was the New South?" A very incomplete sample of those who see continuity over change includes Wayne, *Remaking of Plantation Society*; Robert Higgs, *Competition and Coercion: Blacks in the American Economy, 1865–1914* (Cambridge: Cambridge University Press, 1977); and Douglas Blackmon, *Slavery by Another Name: The Re-enslavement of Black Americans from the Civil War to World War II* (New York: Anchor, 2008). There is a group of scholars who argue that the nineteenth-century South was one marked by continuity *and* change. Howard Rabinowitz summarized this literature by writing, "The New South was new, but not new enough." Eric Foner arguably fits into this category, for although his work stresses the revolutionary changes of Reconstruction, he has to admit that the change failed to last. See Rabinowitz, *First New South*, 186; Eric Foner, "Reconstruction Revisited," *Reviews in American History* 10, no. 4 (December 1982): 82–100; Foner, *Reconstruction*.

4. Kirby, "American Civil War: An Environmental View."

5. Hahn, *Roots of Southern Populism*. See also the essay by Matthew Hild, "Reassessing 'The Roots of Southern Populism,'" *Agricultural History* 82, no. 1 (Winter 2008): 36–42.

6. Woodward, *Origins of the New South*, 269–274, quote on 270.

7. Woodward, 270; Fabian Lange, Alan L. Olmstead, and Paul W. Rhode, "The Impact of the Boll Weevil, 1892–1932," *Journal of Economic History* 69, no. 3 (September 2009): 685–696, Theodore Roosevelt quoted on 685; Giesen, "'Truth about the Boll Weevil'"; Robert Higgs, "The Boll Weevil, the Cotton Economy, and Black Migration: 1910–1930," *Agricultural History* 50, no. 2 (1976): 335–350.

8. Those phrases are a reference to Richard Tucker and Edmund Russell, eds., *Natural Enemy, Natural Ally: Toward an Environmental History of War* (Corvallis: Oregon State University Press, 2004).

9. For more on the broader role of the American Civil War in environmental history as a whole (rather than just of the South), see Nelson, *Ruin Nation*; Brady, *War upon the Land*; and Aaron Sachs's essay, "Stumps in the Wildnerness," in Drake, *The Blue, the Gray*, 96–112.

BIBLIOGRAPHY

Manuscript Collections

Atlanta History Center, Kenan Research Center, Atlanta, Georgia
    Alfred Austell Papers
    Alonzo Miller Papers
    Antebellum and Civil War Collection
    L. P. Grant Papers
    Jennie Meta Barker Papers
    Joseph E. Brown Papers
    Samuel P. Richards Diaries
    Thomas Maguire Papers
Auburn University, Special Collections and Archives, Auburn, Alabama
    John Horry Dent Collection
    M. B. Wellborn Papers
    Tait Family Papers
    Whitfield Family Papers
Birmingham Public Library, Archives and Special Collection, Birmingham, Alabama
    Faunsdale Plantation Papers
    Mims Family Papers
Duke University, Rare Book, Manuscripts, and Special Collections Library, Durham, North Carolina
    Alexander Frank Papers
    Edward Alston Thorne Papers
    Haller Nutt Papers
    Henry Pinckney Plantation Journal
    Henry Watson Jr. Papers
    John Flannery & Co. Records
    Joseph M. Jaynes Plantation Journals
    Keating Ball Plantation Journal
    Samuel O. Wood Papers
    William H. E. Merritt Papers
Emory University, Manuscripts, Archives, and Rare Book Library, Atlanta, Georgia
    Confederate Miscellany Papers
    Godfrey Barnsley Papers
    New South Miscellany Papers
    Orr Family Papers

Richard Burch Jett Papers
William Syndor Thomson Papers
Union Miscellany Papers
Library of Congress, Manuscript Division, Washington, DC
Alexander Hamilton Stephens Papers
Alston Family Papers
D. W. Whittle Papers
Edward E. Dickerson Papers
Edward Frost Papers
Federal Writer's Project, Ex-Slave Narratives
Habersham Family Papers
James A. Congleton Papers
James Jenkins Gillette Papers
Josiah Dexter Cotton Papers
Lemuel Thomas Foote Papers
Montgomery Family Papers
O. M. Poe Papers
Ward Family Papers
William Gibbs McAdoo Papers
Mississippi Department of Archives and History, Jackson, Mississippi
County Tax Rolls, Rankin County
National Archives and Records Administration, Washington, DC
Record Group 15, Records of the Veterans Administration
Record Group 105, Bureau of Refugees, Freedmen, and Abandoned Lands
Record Group 233, Records of the Southern Claims Commission
Record Group 393, Records of the U.S. Army Continental Commands
National Archives and Records Administration, College Park, Maryland
Record Group 54, Bureau of Soils
Record Group 83, Bureau of Agricultural Economics
Record Group 95, United States Forest Service
Record Group 366, Civil War Special Agencies of the Treasury Department
Samford University, Special Collections, Birmingham, Alabama
Algernon Sidney Garnett Collection
Catherine Allen Collection
Minutes of the Alabama Baptist State Convention
Tennessee State Library and Archives, Nashville, TN
Civilian Life during the Civil War Collection
Early Tennessee / North Carolina Land Records
Fanny Taliaferro Daybook
James Webb Smith Donnell Papers
James Washington Matthews Journals
John Nick Barker Diaries
Nimrod Porter Journals
Owsley Charts, Greene County
Reconstruction and the African-American Legacy in Tennessee Collection
Rutledge Family Letters
University of Alabama, W. S. Hoole Library, Tuscaloosa, Alabama
Adrian Sebastian Van de Graaff Papers
Allen Family Papers I
Bird Griffin Papers
Edgar G. Dawson Papers
Francis Terry Leak Papers
Gaius Whitfield Papers
Hugh Davis Papers

James Asbury Tait Papers
James Boykin Papers
John K. and William M. Elliott Daybooks
King Family Papers
Margaret Pearson Sharecropping Agreement
Nelson Clayton Papers
Robert Jemison Papers
Thomas H. Clements Letters
V. M. Elmore Letters
University of North Carolina at Chapel Hill Wilson Library, Southern Historical Collection,
Chapel Hill, North Carolina
Bayside Plantation Records
Cameron Family Papers
Edmund Ruffin Jr. Papers
Elizabeth Seawell Hairston Hairston Papers
George Hairston Papers
Hairston Family Papers
Hairston and Wilson Family Papers
Henry T. Bahnson Papers
J. S. Bartlett Papers
Lenoir Family Papers
L. L. Polk Papers
Peter Hairston Papers
Rare Book Collection
Robert Philip Howell Collection
Samuel Agnew Diary
T. L. Jones Farm Journal
William Wallace White Diaries
Wilson Family Papers
Wisconsin Historical Society, Madison, Wisconsin
H. H. Bennett Diaries

Journals and Newspapers Consulted

The Abingdon Virginian (VA)
The Alabama Baptist (AL)
The American Cotton Planter and Soil of the South (AL)
The American Farmer (MD)
The American Elevator and Grain Trade (CA)
Birmingham Iron-Age (AL)
The Bulletin of the North Carolina Department of Agriculture (NC)
The Camden Confederate (SC)
The Carolina Farmer (SC)
The Charleston Mercury (SC)
The Charlotte Observer (NC)
The Chicago Tribune (IL)
De Bow's Review (LA)
The Dublin Post (GA)
The Elevator (CA)
The Farmer's Register (VA)
Harper's New Monthly Magazine (NY)
The Houston Telegraph (TX)
The Liberator (MA)
The Lynchburg Republican (VA)

The Macon Telegraph (GA)
Marion Standard (AL)
The Memphis Daily Appeal (TN)
The Montgomery Weekly Advertiser (AL)
New Orleans Tribune (LA)
The New York Herald (NY)
The New York Times (NY)
The Oxford Intelligencer (MS)
Prescott Evening Courier (AL)
The Reconstructed Farmer (NC)
The Rural Sun (TN)
The Selma Morning Reporter (AL)
The Selma Morning Times (AL)
Southern Farm and Home (GA)
The Southern Cultivator (GA)
The Southern Planter and Farmer (VA)
The Southwestern Baptist (AL)
The Times-Daily (AL)
Tuscaloosa Independent Monitor (AL)
Tuscaloosa News (AL)
Weekly Iron Age (AL)
The Weekly Atlanta Intelligencer (GA)

Published Primary Sources

Agee, J. H., and J. A. Kerr. *Soil Survey of Maury County, Tennessee.* US Bureau of Soils report. Washington, DC: Government Printing Office, 1926.

Agricultural Experiment Station of the Agricultural and Mechanical College, Auburn, AL Bulletin No. 22. Montgomery: Smith, Allred, & Co., 1891.

Alger, Horatio, Jr. *Grand'ther Baldwin's Thanksgiving and Other Ballads and Poems.* Boston: Loring, Publisher, 1875.

American Husbandry: Containing an Account of the Soil, Climate, Production and Agriculture of the British Colonies by an American. Vol. 1. London: J. Bew, 1775.

Andrews, Evangeline Walker, ed. *Journal of a Lady of Quality; Being the Narrative of a Journey from Scotland to the West Indies, North Carolina, and Portugal, in the Years 1774 to 1776.* New Haven, CT: Yale University Press, 1921.

Appleton, D. *The American Annual Cyclopedia and Register of Important Events of the Year 1865.* Vol. 5. New York: D. Appleton and Co. 1870.

———. *The American Annual Cyclopedia and Register of Important Events of the Year 1892.* Vol. 17. New York: D. Appleton and Co. 1893.

Atkinson, Edward. "The Future Supply of Cotton." *North American Review* 98 (April 1864): 495–498.

Baldwin, Joseph. *Flush Times in Alabama and Mississippi.* 1853. Reprint, New York: Sagamore Press, 1957.

Barnhill, W. L. *Soil Survey of Onslow County, North Carolina.* USDA Soil Conservation report. Washington, DC: Government Printing Office, 1992.

Battle, Cullen A. *Third Alabama! The Civil War Memoir of Brigadier General Cullen Andrews Battle, CSA.* Edited by Brandon H. Beck. Tuscaloosa: University of Alabama Press, 1999.

Birch, Raymond Russell. *Hog Cholera: Its Nature and Control.* New York: Macmillan Company, 1922.

Buck, Lucy Rebecca. *Sad Earth, Sweet Heaven: The Diary of Lucy Rebecca Buck.* Edited by William Buck. Birmingham: Buck Publishing Co., 1973.

Burke, R. T. et al. "Soil Survey of Perry County, Alabama." In *Field Operations of the Bureau of Soils*, 309–323. USDA report. Washington, DC: Government Printing Office, 1902.

Chisholm, Daniel. *Civil War Notebook of Daniel Chisholm*. Edited by W. Springer Menge and J. August Shimrak. New York: Orion, 1989.

Cole, William et al. *Soil Survey of Rankin County, Mississippi*. US Department of Agriculture, 1987. http://www.nrcs.usda.gov/Internet/FSE_MANUSCRIPTS/mississippi/rankinMS1987/ms_rankin.pdf. Accessed February 26, 2016.

Cox, Jacob Dolson. *Military Reminiscences of the Civil War*. Vol. 1. New York: C. Scribner's Sons, 1900.

Dennett, John Richard. *The South As It Is, 1865–1866*. Edited by Henry Christman. New York: Viking, 1965.

Dyer, J. Franklin. *The Journals of a Civil War Surgeon*. Edited by Michael Chesson. Omaha: University of Nebraska, 2003.

Eppes, Mrs. Nicolas Ware. *The Negro of the Old South: A Bit of Period History*. Chicago: Joseph Branch Publishing Co., 1925.

Evans, Paul, and Thomas P. Govan, eds. "A Belgian Consul on Conditions in the South in 1860 and 1862." *Journal of Southern History* 3, no. 4 (November 1937): 478–491.

Fence Laws. Worcester, MA: Washburn and Moen Manufacturing Co., 1880.

Geological Survey of Alabama. *Forests of Alabama*. By Roland Harper. *Geological Survey of Alabama*. Monograph no. 10. Tuscaloosa, AL: Geological Survey of Alabama, 1938.

Geological Survey of Alabama. *Plant Life of Alabama*. By Charles Mohr. *Geological Survey of Alabama*. Monograph no. 5. Tuscaloosa, AL: Geological Survey of Alabama:,1901.

General Assembly of Alabama. *Acts of the Session of 1866–1867 of the General Assembly of Alabama . . .* Montgomery, AL: Reid and Screws, 1867.

General Assembly of Georgia. *Acts and Resolutions of the General Assembly of the State of Georgia, Passed at its session in July and August 1872*. Vol. 1. Atlanta, GA: W. A. Hemphill and Co., 1872.

General Assembly of Maryland. *Report of the Inspector of Guano*. Annapolis, MD, 1850.

General Assembly of Mississippi. *Laws of the State of Mississippi, 1865–1866*. Jackson, MS: Printed for the State of Mississippi, 1866.

General Assembly of Virginia. *Acts of the General Assembly of the State of Virginia, Passed at the Session 1869–1870*. Richmond, VA: James E. Goode, 1870.

Grady, Henry Woodfin. *The New South: Writings and Speeches of Henry Grady*. Savannah, GA: Beehive Press, 1971.

Greeley, Horace. *The American Conflict: A History of the Great Rebellion in the United States of America, 1860–64*. 2 vols. Hartford, CT: O. D. Case and Co., 1864, 1866.

Hague, Parthenia Antoinette. *A Blockaded Family: Life in Southern Alabama during the Civil War*. 1888. Reprint, New York: Applewood, 1995.

Hahn, Steven, Steven S. Miller, Susan E. O'Donovan, and John C. Rodrigue. *Land and Labor, 1865*. Series 3. Vol. 1 of *Freedom: A Documentary History of Emancipation, 1861–1867*. Chapel Hill: University of North Carolina Press, 2008.

Hall, A. R. *Early Soil Erosion Control Practices in Virginia*. USDA Miscellaneous Publication no. 256. Washington, DC: Government Printing Office, 1937.

Hamilton, J. G. de Roulhac. *Reconstruction in North Carolina*. Studies in History, Economics, and Public Law 18. New York: Columbia University, 1914.

Hammond, M. B. *The Cotton Industry*. New York: MacMillan Company, 1897.

Hand-Book of the State of North Carolina, Exhibiting Its Resources and Industries. Raleigh, NC: Ashe & Gatling, 1883.

Harris, David Golightly. *Piedmont Farmer: The Journals of David Golightly Harris, 1855–1870*. Edited by Philip Racine. Knoxville: University of Tennessee Press, 1990.

Hayden, René, Anthony E. Kaye, Kate Masure, Steven F. Miller, Susan E. O'Donovan, Leslie S. Rowland, and Stephen A. West. *Land and Labor, 1866–1867*, Series 3, Vol. 2 of *Freedom: A Documentary History of Emancipation, 1861–1867*. Chapel Hill: University of North Carolina Press, 2013.

Hilgard, Eugene Allen. *Report on Cotton Production in the United States.* US Department of the Interior Census Bureau report. Washington, DC: Government Printing Office, 1884.

Hitchcock, Henry. *Marching with Sherman: Passages from the Letters and Campaign Diaries of Henry Hitchcock, Major and Assistant Adjutant General of Volunteers, November 1864–May 1865.* Edited by M. A. DeWolfe Howe. New York: Bison Books, 1995.

Holcomb, Brent. *Marriages of Bute and Warren Counties, North Carolina, 1764–1868.* Baltimore, MD: Clearfield Company, 1991.

Hughes, Louis. *Thirty Years a Slave, from Bondage to Freedom . . . The Autobiography of Louis Hughes.* Milwaukee, WI: South Side Printing Company, 1897.

Hundley, D. R. *Social Relations of Our Southern States.* New York: Henry B. Price, 1860.

Hunter, W. D. "The Cotton Worm or Cotton Caterpillar." USDA Bureau of Entomology Circular No. 15. Washington, DC: Government Printing Office, May 18, 1912.

Ingraham, Joseph Holt. *The South-West, by a Yankee.* New York: Harper, 1835.

Killebrew, J. B. *Tennessee: Its Agricultural and Mineral Wealth . . .* Nashville: Tavel, Eastman, and Howell, 1876.

King, Edward. *The Great South: A Record of Journeys.* Hartford, CT: American Publishing Co., 1875.

Lee, Landris T. "State Study 151 and 236: Yazoo Clay Investigation." Mississippi Department of Transportation. 2012.

A Letter to the Commanding General of the Fifth Military District, from Col. J. Edmonston, Judge William Hawes Harris and Others . . . Concerning State Reconstruction under the Constitution . . . New Orleans: J. H. Keefe, 1867.

Lettsom, John Coakley. *The Works of John Fothergill, MD.* London: Charles Dilly, 1783.

Little, John Buckner. *The History of Butler County, Alabama, 1815–1885.* Cincinnati, OH: Elm Street Printing Company, 1885.

Lowery, I. E. *Life on the Old Plantation in Ante-bellum Days; or, a Story Based on Facts.* Columbia, SC: State Company Printers, 1911.

Lueder, C. A. *Hog Cholera: Its Prevention and Control.* USDA and the West Virginia Experiment Station report. Washington, DC: Government Printing Office, 1913.

Mahan, D. H. *A Treatise on Field Fortification.* New York: John Wiley, 1836.

Memorial from the Board of Levee Commissioners of the State of Louisiana . . . New Orleans: New Orleans "Times" Book and Job Office, 1866.

Montgomery, Paul Hooper. *Erosion and Related Land Use Conditions on the Lloyd Shoals Reservoir Watershed, Georgia.* USDA report. Washington, DC: Government Printing Office, 1940.

Murray, Charles Augustus. *Travels in North America during the Years 1834, 1835, and 1836 . . .* Vol. 1. London: Richard Bentley, 1839.

National Park Service. Civil War Soldiers and Sailors System. Available at http://www.itd.nps.gov/cwss. Accessed December 22, 2016.

Neese, George. *Three Years in the Confederate Horse Artillery.* New York: Neale Publishing Co., 1911.

Newton, Willoughby. *Address before the Virginia State Agricultural Society: Delivered to the Hall of the Houses of Delegates, February 19, 1852.* Published by the Society. Richmond: Office of the Southern Planter, 1852.

Nichols, George Ward. *The Story of the Great March: From the Diary of a Staff Officer.* Harper & Brothers, 1865.

Nordhoff, Charles. *The Cotton States in the Spring and Summer of 1875.* New York: Burt Franklin, 1876.

North Carolina State Auditor. *Report of the Comptroller of Public Accounts of North Carolina for the Year ending September 30th, 1867.* Raleigh: W. E. Pell, 1868.

North Carolina State Auditor. *Report of the Comptroller of Public Accounts of North Carolina for the Year ending September 30th, 1872.* Raleigh: W. E. Pell, 1873.

Olmsted, Frederick Law. *Cotton Kingdom: A Traveller's Observations on Cotton and Slavery in the American Slave States.* Vol. 1. New York: Mason Brothers, 1961.

———. *A Journey in the Seaboard Slave States.* 1856. Reprint. University of Nebraska Press, 2004.

———. *A Journey through Texas: Or, A Saddle-Trip on the Southwestern Frontier.* Lincoln: University of Nebraska Press, 2004.

O'Neall, John Belton. *The Annals of Newberry in Two Parts, Part the First.* Newberry, SC: Aull and Houseal, 1892.

Paine, Halbert Eleazer. *A Wisconsin Yankee in Confederate Bayou Country: The Civil War Reminiscences of a Union General.* Edited by Samuel C. Hyde Jr. Baton Rouge: Louisiana State University Press, 2009.

Perdue, Charles L., Jr., Thomas E. Barden, and Robert K. Phillips, eds. *Weevils in the Wheat: Interviews with Virginia Ex-Slaves.* Charlottesville: University Press of Virginia, 1976.

Peyster, John Watts de. *From the Rapidan to Appomattox Court-House.* Philadelphia: L. R. Hamersly & Co., 1888.

Quiner, E. B. *The Military History of Wisconsin: Civil and Military Patriotism of the State in the War for the Union.* Chicago: Clarke and Co., 1866.

Reid, Whitelaw. *After the War: A Tour of the Southern States, 1865–1866.* London: S. Low, Son, & Marston, 1866.

Riley, B. F. *Alabama As It Is, or, The Immigrant's and Capitalist's Guide Book to Alabama.* Atlanta, GA: Constitution Publishing, 1888.

Ruffin, Edmund. "An Essay on Calcareous Marls." 5th ed. Richmond, VA: J. W. Randolph, 1852.

———. *Nature's Management: Writings on Landscape and Reform, 1829–1859.* Edited by Jack Temple Kirby. Athens: University of Georgia Press, 2000.

———. *To the Virginia State Agricultural Society, on the Effects of Domestic Slavery on . . . the Agricultural Population of the Southern States, December 16, 1852.* Published by the Society. Richmond: Office of the Southern Planter, 1852.

Sherman, William T. *Memoirs of Gen. William T. Sherman.* New York: D. Appleton and Co., 1889.

Smith, Gustavus W. *The Battle of Seven Pines.* New York: C. G. Crawford, 1891.

Smith, Howard C. *Soil Survey of Barbour County, Alabama.* USDA report. Washington, DC: Government Printing Office, 1916.

Smith, J. Gray. *Description of Improved Farms in the State of Tennessee in the United States of America, Describing the Number of Acres of Arable, Meadow, Pasture, and WoodLand.* London: C. Mitchell, 1943.

Somers, Robert. *The Southern States since the War, 1870–1871.* New York: Macmillan Co., 1871.

Stephenson, Philip Daingerfield. *Civil War Memoir of Philip Daingerfield Stephenson.* Edited by Nathaniel Cheairs Hughes. Conway, AR: UCA Press, 1995.

Taitt, David. "The Journal of a Journey through the Creek Country, 1772." In *Travels in the American Colonies,* edited by Newton D. Mereness, 49–55. New York: Antiquarian Press, 1961.

Todd, Vincent H., ed. *Christoph von Graffenried's Account of the Founding of New Bern.* Raleigh, NC: Edwards and Broughton Printing Co., 1920.

Trowbridge, John T. *The South: A Tour of Its Battlefields and Ruined Cities a Journey Through the Desolted States, and Talks with the People; Being a Description of the Present State of the Present State of the Country, Its Agriculture, Railroads, Business and Finances.* Hartford, CT: L. Stebbins, 1886.

Tyler, Mason Whiting. *Recollections of the Civil War: With Many Original Diary Entries and Letters Written from the Seat of War.* Edited by William S. Tyler. New York: G. P. Putnam's Sons, 1912.

US Bureau of Land Management. General Land Office Records, 1850–1860. Washington, DC: Government Printing Office, 1861.

US Bureau of Soils. *Soil Survey of Vance County, North Carolina.* Washington, DC: Government Printing Office, 1921.

US Census Bureau. US Census of 1830. Washington, DC: Government Printing Office, 1830. Minnesota Population Center. National Historical Geographic Information System: Version 11.0. Minneapolis: University of Minnesota, 2016. http://www.nghis.org. Accessed June 2, 2017.

US Census Bureau. US Census of 1850. Washington, DC: Government Printing Office, 1850. Minnesota Population Center. National Historical Geographic Information System: Version

11.0. Minneapolis: University of Minnesota, 2016. http://www.nghis.org. Accessed June 2, 2017.

US Census Bureau. US Census of 1860. Washington, DC: Government Printing Office, 1860. Minnesota Population Center. National Historical Geographic Information System: Version 11.0. Minneapolis: University of Minnesota, 2016. http://www.nghis.org. Accessed June 2, 2017.

US Census Bureau. US Census of 1870. Washington, DC: Government Printing Office, 1872.

Minnesota Population Center. National Historical Geographic Information System: Version 11.0. Minneapolis: University of Minnesota, 2016. http://www.nhgis.org. Accessed June 2, 2017.

US Census Bureau. US Census of 1880. Washington, DC: Government Printing Office, 1884. http://www.agcensus.usda.gov/Publications/Historical_Publications. Accessed March 25, 2017.

US Census Bureau. US Census of 1890. Washington, DC: Government Printing Office, 1891. http://www.agcensus.usda.gov/Publications/Historical_Publications. Accessed June 20, 2017.

US Census Bureau. "Plantations in the South." US Census of 1910. Washington, DC: Government Printing Office, 1913.

US Census Bureau. *Water Power of the United States*. Part I. Washington, DC: Government Printing Office, 1885.

US Congress. *Report of the Joint Committee on Reconstruction at the First Session Thirty-Ninth Congress*. Washington, DC: Government Printing Office, 1866.

US Department of Agriculture. *Fourth and Fifth Annual Reports of the Bureau of Animal Industry*. Washington, DC: Government Printing Office, 1889.

US Department of Agriculture. *Report of the Commissioner of Agriculture for the Year 1865*. Washington, DC: Government Printing Office, 1866.

US Department of Agriculture. *Report of the Commissioner of Agriculture for the Year 1866*. Washington, DC: Government Printing Office, 1867.

US Department of Agriculture. *Report of the Commissioner of Agriculture for the Year 1867*. Washington, DC: Government Printing Office, 1868.

US Department of Agriculture. *Report of the Commissioner of Agriculture for the Year 1870*. Washington, DC: Government Printing Office, 1871.

US Department of Agriculture. *Report of the Commissioner of Agriculture for the Year 1873*. Washington, DC: Government Printing Office, 1874.

US Department of Agriculture. *Report of the Commissioner of Agriculture on the Operations of the Department for the Year 1875*. Washington, DC: Government Printing Office, 1876.

US Department of Agriculture. *Rules and Regulations Governing the Operations of the Bureau of Animal Industry*. Washington, DC: Government Printing Office, 1895.

US Department of Agriculture. *Monthly Reports*. November–December 1872. Washington, DC: Government Printing Office, 1873.

US Department of Agriculture. *Monthly Reports*. November–December 1873. Washington, DC: Government Printing Office, 1874.

US Department of Agriculture. *Monthly Reports*. February–March 1874. Washington, DC: Government Printing Office, 1874.

US Department of Agriculture. "Contagious Diseases of Domesticated Animals." Special Report No. 34. Washington, DC: Government Printing Office, 1881.

US Department of Agriculture. *Hog Cholera: Its History, Nature, and Treatment*. Washington, DC: Government Printing Office, 1889.

US Department of Agriculture. *Soil Survey of Baldwin, Jones, and Putnam Counties*. Washington, DC: Government Printing Office, 1972.

US Department of Agriculture. *Soil Taxonomy: A Basic System of Soil Classification*, 2nd ed. Natural Resources Conservation Service Handbook no. 436, Washington DC, 1999. http://www.nrcs.usda.gov/Internet/FSE_DOCUMENTS/nrcs142p2_051232.pdf. Accessed June 5, 2017.

US Geological Survey. *Southern Wetland Flora: A Field Guide to Plant Species*. Washington, DC: Government Printing Office, 1999. http://www.npwrc.usgs.gov/resource/plants/floraso/species.htm. Accessed June 13, 2017.

US Department of the Interior. *National Register of Historic Places.* Belvidere Registration Form. North Carolina State Historic Preservation Office, 1992.

US Patent and Trademark Office. *Annual Report for the Commissioner of Patents for the Year 1847.* Washington, DC: Government Printing Office, 1848. https://archive.org/details/ annualreportofco1847unit. Accessed December 6, 2013.

US Patent and Trademark Office. *Annual Report for the Commissioner of Patents for the Year 1848.* Washington, DC: Government Printing Office, 1849. https://archive.org/stream/ annualreportofco1848unit#page/n5/mode/1up. Accessed June 1, 2017.

US War Department. *Atlas to Accompany the Official Records of the Union and Confederate Armies.* Washington, DC: Government Printing Office, 1891. http://ehistory.osu.edu /osu/ sources/. Accessed July 7, 2017.

US War Department. *The War of the Rebellion: A Compilation of the Official Records of the Union and Confederate Armies.* Washington, DC: Government Printing Office, 1863–1891. http:// ehistory.osu.edu/osu/sources/. Accessed February 10, 2017.

Warren, Henry. *Reminiscences of a Mississippi Carpet-Bagger.* Holden, MA: 1914.

Watkins, Sam R. *Col. Aytch: A Confederate Memoir of the Civil War.* New York: Touchstone, 2003.

Weston, James A. *Services Held in the Chapel of Rest, Yadkin Valley, NC, for the late Capt. Walter Waightstill Lenoir, with Sermon.* New York: E & JB Young, 1890.

Wilson, Samuel. "An Account of the Province of Carolina, in America." In *Narratives of Early Carolina, 1650–1708,* edited by Alexander Salley Jr., 161–176. New York: Barnes and Noble, 1959. First published in 1911.

Winston, R. A. *Soil Survey of Wilcox County, Alabama.* USDA report. Washington, DC: Government Printing Office, 1918.

Work, Bertram, ed. *Songs of Henry Clay Work.* New York: J. J. Little & Ives Co. 1920.

Works Progress Administration. *Slave Narratives: A Folk History of Slavery in the United States, from Interviews with Former Slaves.* Washington, DC: Federal Writer's Project, 1941.

Secondary Books, Articles, and Websites

Abernethy, Thomas Perkins. *The Formative Period in Alabama, 1815–1828.* Montgomery: Brown Printing Company, 1922.

Ager, Philip. "The Persistence of de Factor Power: Elites and Economic Development in the U.S. South, 1840–1960." European Historical Economics Society Working Paper 38, 2013 http://ideas.repec.org/p/hes/wpaper/0038.html. Accessed June 14, 2017.

Aiken, Charles. *The Cotton Plantation since the Civil War.* Baltimore, MD: Johns Hopkins University Press, 1998.

Anderson, Virginia DeJohn. *Creatures of Empire: How Domestic Animals Transformed Early America.* New York: Oxford University Press, 2004.

Arnold, B. W., Jr. *History of the Tobacco Industry in Virginia from 1860 to 1894.* Baltimore, MD: Johns Hopkins Press, 1897.

Ashworth, Gregory J. *War and the City.* New York: Routledge, 1991.

Ayers, Edward. *The Promise of the New South: Life after Reconstruction.* 15th Anniversary ed. New York: Oxford University Press, 2007.

———. *What Caused the Civil War: Reflections on the South and Southern History.* New York: W. W. Norton, 2005.

Bagley, William Chandler, Jr. *Soil Exhaustion and the Civil War.* Washington, DC: American Council on Public Affairs, 1942.

Baker, Bruce, and Brian Kelly, eds. *After Slavery: Race, Labor, and Citizenship in the Reconstruction South.* Tallahassee: University Press of Florida, 2013.

Baker, James C. "Part VI: Soils of Virginia." *Agronomy Handbook.* Blacksburg, VA: Virginia Tech Cooperative Association, 2000.

Ball, Douglas B. *Financial Failure and Confederate Defeat.* Urbana: University of Illinois Press, 1991.

Baptist, Edward E. *The Half Has Never Been Told: Slavery and the Making of American Capitalism.* New York: Basic Books, 2014.

Barney, William. *The Road to Secession: A New Perspective on the Old South.* New York: Praeger, 1972.

Barrett, John G. *Sherman's March through the Carolinas.* Chapel Hill: University of North Carolina Press, 1956.

Beach, Timothy, and Philip Gersmehl. "Soil Erosion, T Values, and Sustainability: A Review and Exercise." *Journal of Geography* 92, no. 1 (January–February 1993): 16–22.

Beard, Charles, and Mary Beard. *The Rise of American Civilization.* New York: Macmillan, 1927.

Beckert, Sven. *Empire of Cotton: A Global History.* New York: Alfred A. Knopf, 2014.

Bell, Andrew McIlwaine. *Mosquito Soldiers: Malaria, Yellow Fever, and the Course of the American Civil War.* Baton Rouge: Louisiana State University Press, 2010.

Bennett, Hugh Hammond. *Soils and Agriculture of the Southern States.* New York: MacMillan Company, 1921.

———. *Soil Conservation.* New York: Macmillan, 1939.

Benson, T. Lloyd. "The Plain Folk of Orange: Land, Word, and Society on the Eve of the Civil War." In *The Edge of the South: Life in Nineteenth-Century Virginia,* edited by Edward Ayers and John Willis, 56–78. Charlottesville: University Press, of Virginia, 1991.

Berlin, Ira, Barbara J. Fields, Steven F. Miller, Joseph E. Reidy, and Leslie S. Rowland. *Slaves No More: Three Essays on Emancipation and the Civil War.* Cambridge: Cambridge University Press, 1992.

Berry, Stephen. "The Future of Civil War Studies: Predictions." Available from *Journal of the Civil War Era.* http://journalofthecivilwarera.org/wp-content/uploads/2012/02/Final-Berry.pdf. Accessed June 28, 2017.

———, ed. *Weirding the War: Stories from the Civil War's Ragged Edges.* Athens: University of Georgia Press, 2011.

Bidwell, Percy W. "Rural Economy in New England at the Beginning of the 19th Century." *Transactions of the Connecticut Academy of Arts and Sciences* 20 (April 1916): 241–399.

Bidwell, Percy W. and John I. Falconer, *History of Agriculture in the Northern United States, 1620–1860.* 1925. Reprint, Washington, DC: Carnegie Institution of Washington, 1941.

Billings, Dwight. "Class Origins of the 'New South': Planter Persistence and Industry in North Carolina." *American Journal of Sociology* 88 (1982): S52–S85.

Billings, William Dwight. "The Structure and Development of Old Shortleaf Pine Stands and Certain Associated Properties of the Soil." *Ecological Monographs* 8, no. 3 (July 1938): 437–500.

Blackmon, Douglas. *Slavery by Another Name: The Re-enslavement of Black Americans from the Civil War to World War II.* New York: Anchor, 2009.

Blevins, Brooks. *Cattle in the Cotton Fields: A History of Cattle Raising in Alabama.* Tuscaloosa: University of Alabama Press, 1998.

Block, Daniel, and E. Melanie Du Puis. "Making the Country Work for the City: Von Thünen's Ideas in Geography, Agricultural Economics and Sociology of Agriculture." *American Journal of Economics and Sociology* 60, no. 1 (January 2001): 70–98.

Blumenthal, Walter Hart. *American Indians Dispossessed.* New York: Arno Press, 1975.

Boles, John, and Betsy Johnson, eds. *The Origins of the New South Fifty Years Later: The Continuing Influence of a Historical Classic.* Baton Rouge: Louisiana State University Press, 2003.

Bond, Bradley. "Herders, Farmers, and Markets on the Inner Frontier: The Mississippi Piney Woods, 1850–1860." In *Plain Folk of the South Revisited,* edited by Samuel Hyde Jr., 73–99. Baton Rouge: Louisiana State University Press, 1997.

———. *Political Culture in the Nineteenth-Century South: Mississippi, 1830–1900.* Baton Rouge: Louisiana State University Press, 1992.

Boney, F. N. *Southerners All.* Macon, GA: Mercer University Press, 1984.

Brady, Lisa. *War upon the Land: Military Strategy and the Transformation of Southern Landscapes during the American Civil War.* Athens: University of Georgia Press, 2012.

Brooks, Robert Preston. *The Agrarian Revolution in Georgia, 1865–1912.* Reprint, Westport, CT: Negro Universities Press, 1970. First published in 1914.

Brown, Corrie, and Alfonso Torres. *Foreign Animal Diseases: "The Gray Book"*, 7th ed. Boca Raton, FL: United States Animal Health Association, 1998.

Browning, Judkin. "Reverberations of Battle: The Aftermath of Gettysburg on the 24th Michigan and 26th North Carolina Regiments," *Civil War Monitor* 7, no. 2 (Summer 2017): 56–63, 76–77.

Bryan, Patrick. "The Transition of Plantation Agriculture in the Dominican Republic, 1870–1894," *Journal of Caribbean History* 10–11 (1978): 82–105.

Budiansky, Stephen. *The Bloody Shirt: Terror after Appomattox.* New York: Viking, 2008.

Burdekin, Richard, and Marc D. Weidenmier. "Inflation Is Always and Everywhere a Monetary Phenomenon: Richmond vs. Houston in 1864." *American Economic Review* 91, no. 5 (2001): 1621–1630.

Burton, Vernon. "Race and Reconstruction: Edgefield County, South Carolina." *Journal of Social History* 12, no. 1 (1978): 31–56.

Bynum, Victoria. *The Free State of Jones: Mississippi's Longest Civil War.* Chapel Hill: University of North Carolina Press, 2016.

Cash, W. J. *The Mind of the South.* New York: Alfred A. Knopf, 1941.

Cason, Clarence. *90 Degrees in the Shade.* Chapel Hill: University of North Carolina Press, 1935.

Cathey, Cornelius. *Agriculture in North Carolina before the Civil War.* Raleigh, NC: North Carolina Department of Cultural Resources, 1974.

Chendorain, Michael D., and Lloyd D. Stewart. "Corrosion of Unexploded Ordnance in Soil-Field Results." *Environmental Science and Technology* 39, no. 8 (2005): 2442–2447.

Cimbala, Paul. "The Freedmen's Bureau, the Freedmen, and Sherman's Grant in Reconstruction Georgia." *Journal of Southern History* 55 (1989): 597–632.

Cimbala, Paul, and Randall Miller, eds. *The Freedmen's Bureau and Reconstruction.* New York: Fordham University Press, 1999.

"Civil War Facts," *The Civil War*, National Park Service website. http://www.nps.gov/civilwar/facts.htm. Accessed June 3, 2017.

Cobb, James. *Away Down South: A History of Southern Identity.* New York: Oxford University Press, 2005.

Cohen, Benjamin. *Notes from the Ground: Science, Soil and Society in the American Countryside.* New Haven, CT: Yale University Press, 2009.

Cohen, William. *At Freedom's Edge: Black Mobility and the Southern White Quest for Racial Control, 1861–1915.* Baton Rouge: Louisiana State University Press, 1991.

Conkin, Paul K. "Hot, Humid, and Sad." *Journal of Southern History* 64, no. 1 (February 1998): 3–22.

Cook, Frederick, Larry Brown, and Jack Oliver. "The Southern Appalachians and the Growth of Continents." *Scientific American* 243 (October 1980): 156–168.

Cooper, Frederick. *From Slaves to Squatters: Plantation Labor and Agriculture in Zanzibar and Coastal Kenya, 1890–1925.* New Haven, CT: Yale University Press, 1980.

Cooper, William, Jr., and Thomas Terrill. *The American South: A History.* 2nd ed. New York: McGraw-Hill, 1996.

Coulter, E. Merton. *The Confederate States of America, 1861–1865.* Baton Rouge: Louisiana State University Press, 1950.

Cowdrey, Albert. *This Land, This South: An Environmental History.* Lexington: University Press of Kentucky, 1983.

Cowell, Mark. "Historical Change in Vegetation and Disturbance on the Georgia Piedmont." *American Midland Naturalist* 140, no. 1 (July 1998): 78–89.

Cox, Thomas, Robert S. Maxwell, Phillip Drennon Thomas, and Joseph J. Malone. *This Well-Wooded Land: Americans and Their Forests from Colonial Times to the Present.* Lincoln: University of Nebraska Press, 1985.

Cramer, Viki A., and Richard J. Hobbs, eds. *Old Fields and Restoration of Abandoned Farmland.* Washington, DC: Island Press, 2007.

Craven, Avery. *The Coming of the Civil War.* Chicago: University of Chicago Press, 1942.

———. *Soil Exhaustion as a Factor in the Agricultural History of Virginia and Maryland, 1606–1860.* Urbana: University of Illinois Press, 1926.

Crawford, Martin. "Mountain Farmers and the Market Economy: Ashe Country during the 1850s." *North Carolina Historical Review* 71, no. 4 (October 1994): 430–450.

Crocitti, John J. "Landlords and Tenants in the Wake of Abolition and Ecological Devastation in Brazil's Middle Paraiba Valley." *Agricultural History* 83, no. 2 (Spring 2009): 143–173.

Cronon, William. *Changes in the Land: Indians, Colonists, and the Ecology of New England.* New York: Hill and Wang, 1983.

———. *Nature's Metropolis: Chicago and the Great West.* New York: W. W. Norton, 1991.

Cumo, Christopher. "Cotton." In *Encyclopedia of Cultivated Plants*, vol. 1, edited by Christopher Cumo, 332–341. Santa Barbara, CA: ABC-CLIO, 2013.

Curtin, Philip. *The Rise and Fall of the Plantation Complex: Essays in Atlantic History.* Cambridge: Cambridge University Press, 1990.

Cushman, Gregory. *Guano and the Opening of the Pacific World: A Global Environmental History.* Cambridge: Cambridge University Press, 2013.

Daniel, Pete. *Breaking the Land: The Transformation of Cotton, Tobacco, and Rice Cultures since 1880.* Urbana: University of Illinois, 1985.

Dattel, Eugene. "Cotton and the Civil War." *Mississippi History Now.* Mississippi Historical Society. http://mshistorynow.mdah.state.ms.us/articles/291/cotton-and-the-civil-war. Accessed January 12, 2017.

Davis, Burke. *Sherman's March: The First Full-Length Narrative of General William T. Sherman's Devastating March through Georgia and the Carolinas.* New York: Random House, 1980.

Davis, David Brion. *Inhuman Bondage: The Rise and Fall of Slavery in the New World.* New York: Oxford University Press, 2006.

Davis, Donald E. *Where There Are Mountains: An Environmental History of the Southern Appalachians.* Athens: University of Georgia Press, 2000.

———. "Uplands: Growing Pains." In *The Southern United States: An Environmental History*, edited by Donald E. Davis, 133–155. Santa Barbara, CA: ABC-CLIO, 2006.

Davis, Robert S., Jr. "Selective Memories of Civil War Atlanta." *Georgia Historical Quarterly* 82, no. 4 (Winter 1998): 735–750.

Davis, Stephen. "The Atlanta Campaign." *The New Georgia Encyclopedia.* http://www.georgiaencyclopedia.org/articles/history-archaeology/atlanta-campaign. Accessed June 2, 2017.

Dean, Adam Wesley. *An Agrarian Republic: Farming, Antislavery Politics, and Nature Parks in the Civil War Era.* Chapel Hill: University of North Carolina Press, 2015.

Dean, Warren. *With Broadax and Firebrand: The Destruction of the Brazilian Atlantic Forest.* Berkeley: University of California Press, 1995.

DeCanio, Stephen. *Agriculture in the Postbellum South: The Economics of Production and Supply.* Cambridge, MA: Harvard University Press, 1975.

Demarais, Stephen, D. J. Tazik, P. J. Guertin, and E. E. Jorgensen. "Disturbance Associated with Military Exercises." In *Ecosystems of Disturbed Ground*, edited by Lawrence R. Walker, 385–396. Amsterdam: Elsevier, 1999.

Deyle, Steven. *Carry Me Back: The Domestic Slave Trade in American Life.* New York: Oxford University Press, 2006.

Donohue, Roy. *Soils: An Introduction to Soils and Plant Growth*, 2nd ed. Englewood Cliffs, NJ: Prentice-Hall, 1965.

Dowdey, Clifford. *The Seven Days: The Emergence of Lee.* Boston: Little, Brown, 1964.

Doyle, Peter, and Matthew Bennett. *Fields of Battle: Terrain in Military History.* Dordrecht: Kluwer Academic, 2002.

Du Bois, W. E. B. *Black Reconstruction in America, 1860–1880.* New York: Simon and Schuster, 1935.

———. *The Souls of Black Folk: Essays and Sketches.* Chicago: A. C. McClurg and Co., 1903.

Dunaway, Wilma. *Slavery in the American Mountain South.* Cambridge: Cambridge University Press, 2003.

Earle, Carville. *Geographical Inquiry and American Historical Problems.* Stanford, CA: Stanford University Press, 1992.

———. "The Myth of the Southern Soil Miner: Macrohistory, Agricultural Innovation, and Environmental Change." In *The Ends of the Earth: Perspectives on Modern Environmental History,* edited by Donald Worster, 175–210. Cambridge: Cambridge University Press, 1988.

———. "The Price of Precocity: Technical Choice and Ecological Constraint in the Cotton South, 1840–1890." *Agricultural History* 66, no. 3 (Summer 1992): 25–60.

Edelson, Max. *Plantation Enterprise in Colonial South Carolina.* Cambridge, MA: Harvard University Press, 2006.

Edgar, Walter. *South Carolina: A History.* Columbia: University of South Carolina Press, 1998.

Edwards, Laura. "The Problem of Dependency: African Americans, Labor Relations, and the Law in the Nineteenth-Century South." *Agricultural History* 72, no. 2 (Spring 1998): 313–340.

Ehlen, J., W. C. Haneberg, and R. A. Larson, eds. *Humans as Geological Agents.* Boulder, CO: Geological Society of America, 2005.

El-Baz, Farouk, and R. M. Makharita. *The Gulf War and the Environment.* Lausanne: Gordon and Breach Science Publishers, 1994.

Elliott, Steven Tripp. *Yankee Town, Southern City: Race and Class Relations in Civil War Lynchburg.* New York: New York University Press, 1997.

Engerman, Stanley. "A Reconsideration of Southern Economic Growth, 1770–1860." *Agricultural History* 49 (1975): 343–361.

Entry, J. A., C. C. Mitchell, and C. B. Backman. "Influence of Management Practices on Soil Organic Matter, Microbial Biomass and Cotton Yield in Alabama's 'Old Rotation.'" *Biology and Fertility of Soils* 23, no. 4 (November 1996): 353–358.

Escott, Paul. *After Secession: Jefferson Davis and the Failure of Confederate Nationalism.* Baton Rouge: Louisiana State University Press, 1978.

———. "Yeoman Independence and the Market: Social Status and Economic Development in Antebellum North Carolina." *North Carolina Historical Review* 66, no. 3 (July 1989): 275–299.

Evans, William McKee. *Ballots and Fence Rails: Reconstruction in the Lower Cape Fear.* Athens: University of Georgia Press, 1966.

Everett, Frank Edgar, Jr. *Brierfield: Plantation Home of Jefferson Davis.* Oxford: University Press of Mississippi, 1971.

Ezell, John Samuel. *The South Since 1865.* New York: Macmillan, 1963.

Faust, Drew Gilpin. *Mothers of Invention: Women of the Slaveholding South in the American Civil War.* Chapel Hill: University of North Carolina Press, 2004.

Fiege, Mark. "Gettysburg and the Organic Nature of the American Civil War." In *Natural Enemy, Natural Ally: Toward an Environmental History of Warfare,* edited by Edmund Russell and Richard Tucker, 93–109. Corvallis: Oregon State University Press, 2004.

———. *The Republic of Nature: An Environmental History of the United States.* Seattle: University of Washington Press, 2012.

Field, Ron. *American Civil War Fortifications.* Vol. 2: *Land and Field Fortifications.* New York: Osprey, 2005.

Fields, Barbara J. "The Nineteenth-Century American South: History and Theory." *Plantation Society* 2, no. 1 (April 1983): 7–27.

Fischer, David Hackett, and James C. Kelly, *Bound Away: Virginia and the Westward Movement.* Charlottesville: University of Virginia Press, 2000.

Fishlow, Albert. "Antebellum Regional Trade Reconsidered." *American Economic Review* 54 (1964). Reprinted in *New Views on American Economic Development,* edited by Ralph Andreano, 187-224. Cambridge, MA: Schenkman Publishing, 1965.

Fite, Gilbert. *Cotton Fields No More: Southern Agriculture, 1865–1980.* Lexington: University of Kentucky Press, 1984.

Fleming, Walter. *Civil War and Reconstruction in Alabama*. New York: Macmillan, 1905.

Flynn, Charles, Jr. *White Land, Black Labor: Caste and Class in Late Nineteenth-Century Georgia*. Baton Rouge: Louisiana State University Press, 1983.

Fogel, Robert W. "A Provisional View of the 'New Economic History." *American Economic Review* 54 (May 1964): 377-389.

Foner, Eric. *Forever Free: The Story of Emancipation and Reconstruction*. New York: Vintage, 2006.

———. *Give Me Liberty: An American History*. Vol. 1. New York: W. W. Norton, 2005.

———. *Nothing but Freedom: Emancipation and Its Legacy*. Baton Rouge: Louisiana State University Press, 1983.

———. *Reconstruction: America's Unfinished Revolution*. New York: Oxford University Press, 1988.

———. *A Short History of Reconstruction, 1863–1877*. New York: Harper & Row, 1990.

Fonseca, A. Vianna da, J. Carvalho, C. Ferreira, J. A. Santos, F. Almeida, E. Pereira, J. Feliciano, J. Grade, and A. Oliveira. "Characteriziation of a Profile of Residual Soil from Granite Combining Geological, Geophysical and Mechanical Testing Techniques." *Geotechnical and Geological Engineering* 24 (2006): 1310–1312.

Ford, Lacy. "Rednecks and Merchants: Economic Development and Social Tensions in the South Carolina Upcountry, 1865–1900," *Journal of American History* 71 (1984): 294–318.

Formwalt, Lee. "Planters and Cotton Production as a Cause of Confederate Defeat: Evidence from Southwest Georgia." *Georgia Historical Quarterly* 74 (Summer 1990): 269–276.

Forret, Jeff. *Race Relations on the Margins: Slaves and Poor Whites in the Antebellum Countryside*. Baton Rouge: Louisiana State University Press, 2006.

Franklin, John Hope, and Loren Schweninger. *Runaway Slaves: Rebels on the Plantation*. New York: Oxford University Press, 1999.

Freehling, William W. *The Road to Disunion*. 2 vols. New York: Oxford University Press, 1990, 2007.

Gallay, Allan. *The Formation of a Planter Elite: Jonathan Bryan and the Southern Colonial Frontier*. 1989. Reprint, Athens: University of Georgia Press, 2007.

———. "The Origins of Slaveholders' Paternalism: George Whitfield, the Bryan Family, and the Great Awakening in the South." *Journal of Southern History* 53 (August 1987): 369–394.

Gallman, Robert. "Self-Sufficiency in the Cotton Economy of the Antebellum South." *Agricultural History* 44 (1970): 5–23.

Garner, James Wilford. *Reconstruction in Mississippi*. London: Macmillan, 1902.

Garrett, Franklin. *Atlanta and Environs: A Chronicle of Its People and Events*. Vol. 1. Athens: University of Georgia Press, 1969.

Gates, Paul. *Agriculture and the Civil War*. New York: Alfred A. Knopf, 1965.

———. *The Farmer's Age: Agriculture 1815–1860*. Economic History of the United States 3. London: M. E. Sharpe, 1960.

Genovese, Eugene, and Elizabeth Fox-Genovese. *Fatal Self-Deception: Slaveholding Paternalism in the Old South*. Cambridge: Cambridge University Press, 2011.

Giesen, James C. *Boll Weevil Blues: Cotton, Myth, and Power in the American South*. Chicago: University of Chicago Press, 2011.

———. "'The Truth about the Boll Weevil': The Nature of Planter Power in the Mississippi Delta." *Environmental History* 14 (October 2009): 683–704.

Glymph, Thavolia. "Noncombatant Military Laborers in the Civil War." *Organization of American Historians Magazine of History* 26, no. 2 (April 2012): 25–29.

Goldin, C., and F. Lewis. "The Economic Cost of the American Civil War: Estimates and Implications." *Journal of Economic History* 35 (1975): 299–326.

Gorman, Hugh. *The Story of N: A Social History of the Nitrogen Cycle and the Challenge of Sustainability*. New Brunswick, NJ: Rutgers University Press, 2013.

Grant, H. Roger. *The Railroad: The Life Story of a Technology*. Westport, CT: Greenwood, 2005.

Gray, Lewis Cecil. *History of Agriculture in the Southern United States to 1860*. 2 vols. 1932, 1933. Reprint, Gloucester, MA: Peter Smith, 1958.

Greene, A. Wilson. *Civil War Petersburg: Confederate City in the Crucible of War*. Charlottesville: University of Virginia Press, 2006.

Greene, Ann Norton. *Horses at Work: Harnessing Power in Industrial America.* Cambridge, MA: Harvard University Press, 2008.

Gregg, Douglas. "Update on Classical Swine Fever." *Journal of Swine Health and Production* 10, no. 1 (2002): 33–38.

Griffith, Lucille. *Alabama: A Documentary History to 1900.* Tuscaloosa: University of Alabama Press, 1968.

Grimsley, Mark. *The Hard Hand of War: Union Military Policy toward Southern Civilians.* Cambridge: Cambridge University Press, 1997.

Grissino-Mayer, Henri, and David R. Butler. "Effects of Climate on Growth of Shortleaf Pine in Northern Georgia: A Dendroclimatic Study." *Southeastern Geographer* 33, no. 1 (May 1993): 65–81.

Guelzo, Allen. *Fateful Lightning: A New History of the Civil War and Reconstruction.* New York: Oxford University Press, 2012.

Guiccione, M. J., and D. L. Zachary. "Geologic History of the Southeastern United States and Its Effects on Soils of the Region." *Southern Cooperative Series Bulletin* 395 (January 2000). http://soilphysics.okstate.edu/S257/book/geology/index.html. Accessed July 6, 2017.

Hahn, Steven. "Hunting, Fishing, and Foraging: Common Rights and Class Relations in the Postbellum South." *Radical History Review* 26 (1982): 37–64.

———. *A Nation under Our Feet: Black Political Struggles in the Rural South from Slavery to the Great Migration.* Cambridge, MA: Harvard University Press, 2003.

———. "A Response: Common Cents or Historical Sense?" *Journal of Southern History* 59, no. 2 (May 1993): 243–258.

———. *The Roots of Southern Populism: Yeoman Farmers and the Transformation of the Georgia Upcountry, 1850–1890.* New York: Oxford University Press, 1993.

Hake, Kate, Don Blasingame, Charles Burmester, Peter B. Goodell, and Charles Stichler. "Crop Rotation." *Physiology Today: Newsletter of the Cotton Physiology Education Program* 3, no. 1 (October 1991): 1–4.

Hall, Arthur R. "Terracing in the Southern Piedmont." *Agricultural History* 23, no. 2 (April 1949): 96–109.

Hamburg, S. P. "Effects of Forest Growth on Soil Nitrogen and Organic Matter Pools Following Release from Subsistence Agriculture." In *Forest Soils and Treatment Impacts: Proceedings of the Sixth North American Forest Soils Conference, University of Tennessee, Knoxville, June 1983,* edited by E. L. Stone. University of Tennessee, 1984, 145–158.

Harden, Carol, and Louise Mathews. "Hillslope Runoff, Soil Detachment, and Soil Organic Content Following Reforestation in the Copper Basin, Tennessee, USA." *Australian Geographical Studies* 40, no. 2 (July 2002): 130–142.

Harden, Carol, and P. Delmas Scruggs. "Infiltration on Mountain Slopes: A Comparison of Three Environments." *Geomorphology* 55 (2003): 5–24.

Harris, J. William. "Crop Choices in the Piedmont before and after the Civil War." *Journal of Economic History* 54, no. 3 (September 1994): 526–542.

———. *Deep Souths: Delta, Piedmont, and Sea Island Society in the Age of Segregation.* Baltimore, MD: Johns Hopkins University Press, 2001.

———. "The Question of Peonage in the History of the New South." In *Plain Folk of the South Revisited,* edited by Samuel C. HydeJr., 100–128. Baton Rouge: Louisiana State University Press, 1997.

Haskins, Jim. *The Geography of Hope: Black Exodus from the South after Reconstruction.* Brookfield, CT: Twenty-First Century Books, 1999.

Helms, Douglas. "Soil and Southern History: Presidential Address to the Agricultural History Society." Prepared by the Agricultural History Society and the Iowa State University Center for Agricultural History, 2000.

Heitmann, John Alfred. *The Modernization of the Louisiana Sugar Industry, 1830–1910.* Baton Rouge: Louisiana State University Press, 1987.

Hersey, Mark D. *My Work Is That of Conservation: An Environmental Biography of George Washington Carver.* Athens: University of Georgia Press, 2011.

Higgs, Robert. "The Boll Weevil, the Cotton Economy, and Black Migration: 1910–1930." *Agricultural History* 50, no. 2 (1976): 335–350.

Hilliard, Sam Bowers. *Atlas of Antebellum Southern Agriculture.* Baton Rouge: Louisiana State University Press, 1984.

———. *Hog Meat and Hoecake: Food Supply in the Old South, 1840–1860.* Carbondale: Southern Illinois University Press, 1972.

History of the State Agricultural Society of South Carolina. Columbia, SC: R. L. Bryan Company, 1916.

Holt, Michael. *The Political Crisis of the 1850s.* New York: Wiley, 1978.

Holt, Sharon. "Making Freedom Pay: Freedpeople Working for Themselves, North Carolina, 1865–1900." *Journal of Southern History* 60 (1994): 229–262.

Howe, Daniel Walker. *What Hath God Wrought: The Transformation of America, 1815–1848.* New York: Oxford University Press, 2007.

Hupy, Joseph, and Randall Schaetzl. "Introducing 'Bombturbation,' A Singular Type of Soil Disturbance and Mixing." *Soil Science* 171, no. 11 (2006): 823–836.

Hupy, Joseph, and T. Koehler. "Modern Warfare as a Significant Form of Zoogeomorphologic Disturbance upon a Landscape." *Geomorphology* 157–158 (2012): 169–182.

Hurt, R. Douglas. *Agriculture and the Confederacy: Policy, Productivity, and Power in the Civil War South.* Chapel Hill: University of North Carolina Press, 2015.

Huston, James A. "Logistical Support of Federal Armies in the Field." *Civil War History* 7 (March 1961): 36–47.

Huston, James L. "Property Rights in Slavery and the Coming of the Civil War." *Journal of Southern History* 65, no. 2 (May 1999): 249–286.

Hutchinson, William, and Samuel Williamson. "The Self-Sufficiency of the Antebellum South: Estimates of Food Supply." *Journal of Economic History* 31, no. 3 (September 1971): 591–612.

Inscoe, John. "Georgia in 1860." *The New Georgia Encyclopedia.* Last modified June 6, 2017. http://www.georgiaencyclopedia.org/articles/history-archaeology/georgia-1860. Accessed April 6, 2016.

Jackson, Harvey. *Rivers of History: Life on the Coosa, Tallapoosa, Cahaba, and Alabama.* Tuscaloosa: University of Alabama Press, 1995.

Johnson, Bethany L. "Introduction: C. Vann Woodward and the Reconstruction of the New South." In *Origins of the New South Fifty Years Later: The Continuing Influence of a Historical Classic,* edited by John B. Boles and Bethany L. Johnson, 1–20. Baton Rouge: Louisiana State University Press, 2003.

Johnson, Charles, Edwin Embree, and W. W. Alexander. *The Collapse of Cotton Tenancy: Summary of Field Studies and Statistical Surveys, 1933–1935.* Chapel Hill: University of North Carolina Press, 1935.

Johnson, James H. *Urban Geography: An Introductory Analysis.* 2nd ed. New York: Pergamon Press, 1976.

Johnson, Timothy. "Reconstructing the Soil: Emancipation and the Roots of Chemical-Dependent Agriculture in America." In *The Blue, the Gray, and the Green: Toward an Environmental History of the Civil War,* edited by Brian Allen Drake, 191–208. Athens: University of Georgia Press, 2015.

Johnson, Walter. *River of Dark Dreams: Slavery and Empire in the Cotton Kingdom.* Cambridge, MA: Belknap Press of Harvard University Press, 2013.

Jones, Alice Simms, and E. Gibbes Patton. "Forest, 'Prairie' and Soils in the Black Belt of Sumter County, Alabama, in 1832." *Ecology* 41, no. 1 (January 1966): 75–80.

Jones, James Pickett. *Yankee Blitzkrieg: Wilson's Raid through Alabama and Georgia.* Lexington: University Press of Kentucky, 1976.

Jones, Richard. *Dinwiddie County: Carrefour of the Commonwealth.* Richmond, VA: Whittet and Shepperson, 1976.

Jordan, Weymouth T. *Antebellum Alabama: Town and Country.* Jacksonville: Florida State University, 1957.

―――. "The Elisha F. King Family Planters of the Alabama Black Belt." *Agricultural History* 19, no. 3 (July 1945): 152–162.

―――. "The Rules of an Alabama Black Belt Plantation, 1848–1862." *Agricultural History* 18, no. 1 (January 1944): 53–64.

Lankford, Nelson. *Cry Havoc! The Crooked Road to Civil War, 1861.* New York: Viking, 2007.

Lovett, Bobby. "African Americans, Civil War and Aftermath in Arkansas." *Arkansas Historical Quarterly* 54, no. 3 (Autumn 1995): 304–358.

Kalisz, Paul J. "Soil Properties of Steep Appalachian Old Fields." *Ecology* 67, no. 4 (August 1986): 1011–1023.

Kantor, Shawn Everett. *Politics and Property Rights: The Closing of the Open Range in the Postbellum South.* Chicago: University of Chicago Press, 1998.

Kantor, Shawn Everett, and J. Morgan Kousser. "Common Sense or Commonwealth? The Fence Law and Institutional Change in the Postbellum South." *Journal of Southern History* 59, no. 2 (May 1993): 201–242.

Keegan, John. *The American Civil War: A Military History.* New York: Alfred A. Knopf, 2010.

Keever, Catherine. "A Retrospective View of Old-Field Succession after 35 Years." *American Midland Naturalist* 110, no. 2 (October 1983): 397–404.

Kelly, Heather M. "Cotton Disease and Nematode Control." Prepared for the University of Tennessee Extension Service, 2016. https://ag.tennessee.edu. Accessed July 20, 2017.

Kerr-Ritchie, Jeffrey. *Freedpeople of the Tobacco South: Virginia, 1860–1900.* Chapel Hill: University of North Carolina Press, 1999.

Kilbourne, Richard Holcombe, Jr. *Debt, Investment, Slaves: Credit Relations in East Feliciana Parish, Louisiana, 1825–1885.* Tuscaloosa: University of Alabama Press, 1995.

King, J. Crawford, Jr. "The Closing of the Southern Range: An Exploratory Study." *Journal of Southern History* 48, no. 1 (February 1982): 53–70.

Kirby, Jack Temple. "The American Civil War: An Environmental View." In *Nature Transformed: The Environment in American History.* Teacher Serve. National Humanities Center website, 2001. http://nationalhumanitiescenter.org/tserve/nattrans/ntuseland/essays/amcwar.htm. Accessed June 1, 2017.

―――. *Mockingbird Song: Ecological Landscapes of the South.* Chapel Hill: University of North Carolina Press, 2006.

―――. *Poquosin: A Study of Rural Landscape and Society.* Chapel Hill: University of North Carolina Press, 1995.

Kulikoff, Alan. *Tobacco and Slaves: The Development of Southern Cultures in the Chesapeake, 1680–1800.* Chapel Hill: University of North Carolina Press, 1986.

Lal, Brij V., Doug Munro, and Edward D. Beechert, eds. *Plantation Workers: Resistance and Accommodation.* Honolulu: University of Hawaii Press, 1993.

Lange, A. et al. "Pathogenesis of Classical Swine Fever—Similarities to Viral Haemorrhagic Fevers: A Review." *Berl Much Tierarztl Wochenschr* 124, no. 1–2 (Jan–Feb 2011): 36–47.

Lange, Fabian, Alan L. Olmstead, and Paul W. Rhode. "The Impact of the Boll Weevil: 1892–1932." *Journal of Economic History* 69, no. 3 (September 2009): 685–718.

Leopold, Luna. "River Channel Change with Time: An Example." Address as retiring president of the Geological Society of America. *Geological Society of American Bulletin* 84 (June 1973): 1845–1860.

Levine, Bruce. *Confederate Emancipation: Southern Plans to Freed and Arm Slaves during the Civil War.* New York: Oxford University Press, 2005.

Lewis, Lloyd. *Sherman, Fighting Prophet.* New York: Harcourt and Brace, 1932.

Lewis, Ronald L. *Transforming the Appalachian Countryside: Railroads, Deforestation, and Social Change in West Virginia, 1880–1920.* Chapel Hill: University of North Carolina Press, 1998.

Litwack, Leon. *Been in the Storm So Long: The Aftermath of Slavery.* New York: Vintage, 1980.

Livingston, S. D., and C. R. Stichler. "Correcting Nitrogen Deficiencies in Cotton with Urea-Based Products." *Texas Agricultural Extension Service*. http://publications.tamu.edu/COTTON. Accessed June 18, 2017.

Lonn, Ella. *Salt as a Factor in the Confederacy*. Tuscaloosa: University of Alabama Press, 1965.

Lucas, M. T., and D. Chhajed. "Applications of Location Analysis in Agriculture: A Survey." *Journal of the Operational Research Society* 55 (2004): 561–578.

Lutts, Ralph. "Like Manna from God: The American Chestnut Trade in Southwestern Virginia." *Environmental History* 9, no. 3 (July 2004): 497–525.

Mahon, Michael. *The Shenandoah Valley 1861–1865: The Destruction of the Granary of the Confederacy*. Mechanicsburg, PA: Stackpole, 1999.

Majewski, John. *Modernizing a Slave Economy: The Economic Vision of the Confederate Nation*. Chapel Hill: University of North Carolina Press, 2009.

Majewski, John, and Viken Tchakerian. "The Environmental Origins of Shifting Cultivation: Climate, Soils, and Disease in the Nineteenth-Century U.S. South. *Agricultural History* 81, no. 4 (Fall 2007): 522–549.

Malone, Ann Patton. "Piney Woods Farmers of South Georgia, 1850–1900: Jeffersonian Yeomen in an Age of Expanding Commercialism." *Agricultural History* 60, no. 4 (Autumn 1986): 51–84.

Mandle, Jay R. "The Re-establishment of the Plantation Economy in the South, 1865–1910." *Review of Black Political Economy* 3, no. 2 (1973): 68–88.

———. *The Roots of Black Poverty: The Southern Plantation Economy after the Civil War*. Durham, NC: Duke University Press, 1977.

———."Sharecropping and the Plantation Economy in the United States South." In *Sharecropping and Sharecroppers*, edited by T. J. Byres, 120–129. New York: Taylor and Francis, 1987.

Manning, Chandra. *Troubled Refuge: Struggling for Freedom in the Civil War*. New York: Alfred A. Knopf, 2016.

Marcus, Alan. *Agricultural Science and the Quest for Legitimacy: Farmers, Agricultural Colleges, and Experiment Stations, 1870–1890*. Ames: Iowa State University Press, 1985.

Marler, Scott. "Two Kinds of Freedom: Mercantile Development and Labor Systems in Louisiana Cotton and Sugar Parishes during Reconstruction." *Agricultural History* 85 (Spring 2011): 225–251.

Martin, J. H., W. H. Leonard, and D. L. Stamp. *Principles of Field Crop Production*. 3rd ed. New York: Macmillan, 1976.

Martin, James. "Civil War Conscription Laws." *In Custodia Legis*. Library of Congress. http://blogs.loc.gov/law/2012/11/civil-war-conscription-laws/. Accessed June 3, 2017.

Massey, Mary Elizabeth. *Ersatz in the Confederacy: Shortages and Substitutes on the Southern Homefront*. Columbia: University of South Carolina Press, 1993.

Mathis, Ray. *John Horry Dent: South Carolina Aristocrat on the Alabama Frontier*. Tuscaloosa: University of Alabama Press, 1979.

McCarthy, Clinton. *The Reins of Power: Racial Change and Challenge in a Southern County*. Tallahassee: Sentry Press, 1999.

McDonald, Forrest, and Grady McWhiney. "The South from Self-Sufficiency to Peonage: An Interpretation." *American Historical Review* 85, no. 5 (December 1980): 1095–1118.

McDonald, Roderick A. *The Economy and Material Culture of Slaves: Goods and Chattels on the Sugar Plantations of Jamaica and Louisiana*. Baton Rouge: Louisiana State University Press, 1993.

McKenzie, Robert. *One South or Many? Plantation Belt and Upcountry in Civil War–Era Tennessee*. Cambridge: Cambridge University Press, 1994.

———. "Rediscovering the 'Farmless' Farm Population: The Nineteenth-Century Census and the Postbellum Reorganization of Agriculture in the U.S. South, 1860–1900." *Histoire Sociale* 28 (1995): 501–520.

McKone, M. J. and D. D. Biesboer. "Nitrogen Fixation in Association with the Root Systems of Goldenrods." *Soil Biology and Biochemistry* 18 (1986): 543–545.

McMillan, Malcolm C. *The Alabama Confederate Reader*. Tuscaloosa: University of Alabama Press, 1969.

McPherson, James M. *Battle Cry of Freedom: The Civil War Era*. New York: Oxford University Press, 1988.

Meerschman, Eef, Liesbet Cockx, Mohammad Monirul Islam, Fun Meeuws, and Marc Van Meirvenne. "Geostatistical Assessment of the Impact of WWI on the Spatial Occurrence of Soil Heavy Metals." *Ambio* 40 (2011): 417–424.

Meier, Kathryn Shively. *Nature's Civil War: Common Soldiers and the Environment in 1862 Virginia*. Chapel Hill: University of North Carolina Press, 2013.

Meirvenne, M. Van, T. Meklit, S. Verstraete, M. De Boever, and F. Tack. "Could Shelling in the First World War Have Increased Copper Concentrations in the Soil around Ypres?" *European Journal of Soil Science* 59 (2008): 372–379.

Menard, Russell. "Colonial America's Mestizo Agriculture." In *The Economy of Early America: Historical Perspectives and New Directions*, edited by Cathy Matson, 107–123. Philadelphia: Pennsylvania State University Press, 2011.

Merchant, Carolyn, ed. *Major Problems in American Environmental History*. Lexington, MA: D. C. Heath, 1993.

Mikkelsen, Robert, and Bruulsema, Thomas. "Fertilizer Use for Horticultural Crops in the U.S. during the 20th Century." *HortTechnology* 15, no. 1 (January–March 2005): 24–30.

Miller, David W. *The Taking of American Indian Lands in the Southeast: A History of Territorial Cessions and Forced Relocations, 1607–1840*. Jefferson, NC: McFarland, 2011.

Miller, Henry M. "Transforming a 'Splendid and Delightsome Land': Colonists and Ecological Change in the Chesapeake, 1607–1820." *Journal of the Washington Academy of Sciences* 76, no. 3 (September 1986): 173–187.

Miller, Steven. 'Plantation Labor Organization and Slave Life on the Cotton Frontier." In *Cultivation and Culture: Labor and the Shaping of Slave Life in the Americas,* edited by Ira Berlin and Philip Morgan, 155–169. Charlottesville: University Press of Virginia, 1993.

Misak, R., D. Al-Ajmi, and A. Al-Enezi. "War-Induced Soil Degradation, Depletion, and Destruction (The Case of Ground Fortifications in the Terrestrial Environment of Kuwait)." In *Environmental Consequences of War and Aftermath*, edited by T. A. Kassim and D. Barcelo, 125–139. Handbook of Environmental Chemistry. Vol. 3U. Berlin: Springer, 2009.

Moennig, V., G. Floegel-Niesmann, and I. Greiser-Wilke. "Clinical Signs and Epidemiology of Classical Swine Fever: A Review of New Knowledge." *Veterinary Journal* 165 (2003): 11–20.

Mohr, Clarence. *On the Threshold of Freedom: Masters and Slaves in Civil War Georgia*. Athens: University of Georgia Press, 1986.

Moneyhon, Carl. *The Impact of the Civil War and Reconstruction on Arkansas: Persistence in the Midst of Ruin*. Baton Rouge: Louisiana State University Press, 1994.

———. *Texas after the Civil War: The Struggle of Reconstruction*. College Station: Texas A&M University Press, 2004.

Moore, John Hebron. *The Emergence of the Cotton Kingdom in the Old Southwest: Mississippi, 1770–1860*. Baton Rouge: Louisiana State University Press, 1988.

Moran, Louis, David Pettry, and Richard Switzer. "Soils of Native Prairie Remnants in the Jackson Prairie Region of Mississippi." *Mississippi Agricultural and Forestry Experiment State Bulletin* 1067 (June 1997).

Morgan, Chad. "Alexander Stephens (1812–1883)." *New Georgia Encyclopedia*. http://www.georgiaencyclopedia.org/articles/history-archaeology/alexander-stephens-1812-1883. Accessed June 6, 2014.

———. *Planters' Progress: Modernizing Confederate Georgia*. Gainesville: University Press of Florida, 2005.

Morgan, Edmund. *American Slavery, American Freedom: The Ordeal of Colonial Virginia*. New York: W. W. Norton, 1975.

Morgan, Lynda. *Emancipation in Virginia's Tobacco Belt, 1850–1870*. Athens: University of Georgia Press, 1992.

Nash, Steven. *Reconstruction's Ragged Edge: The Politics of Postwar Life in the Southern Mountains*. Chapel Hill: University of North Carolina Press, 2016.

Nathans, Sydney. *A Mind to Stay: White Plantation, Black Homeland.* Cambridge, MA: Harvard University Press, 2017.

National Research Council. *Emerging Animal Diseases: Global Markets, Global Safety: Workshop Summary.* Washington, DC: National Academies Press, 2002.

Neely, Mark. *The Civil War and the Limits of Destruction.* Cambridge: Cambridge University Press, 2007.

Nelson, Lynn. *Pharsalia: An Environmental Biography of a Southern Plantation, 1780–1880.* Athens: University of Georgia Press, 2007.

Nelson, Bernard. "Confederate Slave Impressment Legislation, 1861–1865." *Journal of Negro History* 31, no. 4 (October 1946): 392–410.

Nelson, Megan Kate. *Ruin Nation: Destruction and the American Civil War.* Athens: University of Georgia Press, 2012.

Newby, Idus A. *Plain Folk in the New South: Social Change and Cultural Persistence.* Baton Rouge: Louisiana State University Press, 1989.

North, Douglass C. *The Economic Growth of the United States, 1790–1860.* New York: W. W. Norton, 1966.

O'Brien, Patrick. *The Economic Effects of the American Civil War.* Prepared for the Economic History Society. Atlantic Highlands, NJ: Humanities Press International, 1988.

Oakes, James. *The Ruling Race: A History of American Slaveholders and Slavery.* New York: Alfred A. Knopf, 1982.

O'Donovan, Susan. *Becoming Free in the Cotton South.* Cambridge, MA: Harvard University Press, 2010.

Okie, William Thomas. *The Georgia Peach: Culture, Agriculture, and Environment in the American South.* Cambridge: Cambridge University Press, 2017.

Olmstead, Alan, and Paul W. Rhode. "Biological Innovation and Productivity Growth in the Antebellum Cotton Economy." *Journal of Economic History* 68, no. 4 (December 2008): 1123–1171.

Opie, John. *Nature's Nation: An Environmental History of the United States.* New York: Harcourt Brace, 1998.

"Orr, James Lawrence." *Biographical Directory of the United States Congress, 1774–Present.* Available at http://bioguide.congress.gov/scripts/biodisplay.pl?index=O000104 . Accessed March 25, 2014.

Orwig, David, and Marc Abrams, "Land-Use History (1720–1992), Composition, and Dynamics of Oak-Pine Forests within the Piedmont and Coastal Plain of Northern Virginia." *Canadian Journal of Forest Research* 24 (1992): 1216–1225.

Otto, John Solomon. *The Final Frontiers, 1880–1930: Settling the Southern Bottomlands.* Westport, CT: Greenwood, 1999.

———. *Southern Agriculture during the Civil War Era, 1860–1880.* Contributions in American History. Santa Barbara, CA: Praeger, 1994.

Otto, John Solomon, and N. E. Anderson. "Slash-and-Burn Cultivation in the Highlands South: A Problem in Comparative Agricultural History." *Comparative Studies in Society and History* 24, no. 1 (January 1982): 131–147.

Owsley, Frank. *The Plain Folk of the Old South.* Baton Rouge: Louisiana State University Press, 1949.

Parenti, Christian. *Tropic of Chaos: Climate Change and the New Geography of Violence.* New York: Nation Books, 2011.

Peel, M. C., B. L. Finlayson, and T. A. McMahon. "Updated World Map of the Köppen-Geiger Climate Classification." *Hydrology and Earth System Sciences Discussions* 4 (2007): 439–473.

Petersen, James, Dorothy Sack, and Robert Gabler. *Physical Geography.* 10th ed. New York: Cengage Learning, 2011.

Pettigrew, W. T., W. R. Meredith, H. A. Bruns, and S. R. Stetina. "Effects of a Short-Term Corn Rotation on Cotton Dry Matter Partitioning, Lint Yield, and Fiber Quality Production." *Journal of Cotton Science* 10, no. 3 (2006): 244–251.

Powell, Lawrence. *New Masters: Northern Planters during the Civil War and Reconstruction.* New York: Fordham University Press, 1999.

Pressen, Edward. "How Different Were the Antebellum North and South?" *American Historical Review* 85, no. 5 (1980): 1119-1149.

Pudup, Mary Beth. "The Limits of Subsistence: Agriculture and Industry in Central Appalachia." *Agricultural History* 64, no. 1 (Winter 1990): 61–92.

Rabinowitz, Howard. *The First New South 1865–1920.* Arlington Heights, IL: Harlan Davidson, 2002.

———. *Race, Ethnicity, and Urbanization: Selected Essays.* Columbia: University of Missouri Press, 1994.

Rable, George. *Civil Wars: Women and the Crisis of Southern Nationalism.* Urbana: University of Illinois Press, 1989.

Ramsdell, Charles. *Behind the Lines in the Southern Confederacy.* Baton Rouge: Louisiana State University Press, 1972.

Rankin, H. Taylor, and D. E. Davis, "Woody Vegetation in the Black Belt of Montgomery County, Alabama, in 1845–6." *Ecology* 52, no. 4 (July 1971): 716–719.

Ransom, Roger. "The Economic Consequences of the American Civil War." In *The Political Economy of War and Peace,* edited by Murray Wolfson, 49–74. Norwell, MA: Kluwer Academic, 1998.

Ransom, Roger, and Richard Sutch. "Debt Peonage in the Cotton South after the Civil War." *Journal of Economic History* 32 (1972): 641–669.

———. "Growth and Welfare in the American South of the Nineteenth Century." *Explorations in Economic History* 16 (1979): 207–235.

———. "The Impact of the Civil War and Emancipation on Southern Agriculture." *Explorations in Economic History* 12 (1975): 1–28.

———. *One Kind of Freedom: The Economic Consequences of Emancipation.* 1977. Reprint, Cambridge: Cambridge University Press, 2001.

Raper, Arthur, and Ira de A. Reid. *Sharecroppers All.* Chapel Hill: University of North Carolina Press, 1941.

Rasmussen, Wayne. "Lincoln's Agricultural Legacy." *National Agricultural Library.* USDA. http://www.nal.usda.gov/lincolns-agricultural-legacy. Accessed June 16, 2014.

Rees, William. "Ecological Footprints and Appropriated Carrying Capacity: What Urban Economics Leaves Out." *Environment and Urbanization* 4, no. 2 (October 1992): 121–130.

Reid, Brian Holden. *The Origins of the American Civil War.* London: Longman, 1996.

Reid, Joseph D., Jr. "Sharecropping as an Understandable Market Response: The Postbellum South." *Journal of Economic History* 33, no. 1 (March 1973): 106–130.

Reidy, Joseph. *From Slavery to Agrarian Capitalism in the Cotton Plantation South: Central Georgia, 1800–1880.* Chapel Hill: University of North Carolina Press, 1995.

———. "Obligation and Right: Patterns of Labor, Subsistence, and Exchange in the Cotton Belt in Georgia, 1790–1860." In *Cultivation and Culture: Labor and the Shaping of Slave Life in the Americas,* edited by Ira Berlin and Philip Morgan, 138–154. Charlottesville: University Press of Virginia, 1993.

Regosin, Elizabeth, and Donald Shaffer, eds. *Voices of Emancipation: Understanding Slavery, the Civil War, and Reconstruction through the U.S. Pension Bureau Files.* New York: New York University Press, 2008.

Richter, Daniel, and Daniel Markewitz. *Understanding Soil Change: Soil Sustainability over Millennia, Centuries, and Decades.* Cambridge: Cambridge University Press, 2007.

Richter, Daniel, Daniel Markewitz, Paul R. Heine, Virginia Jin, Jane Raikes, Kun Tain, and Carol G. Wells. "Legacies of Agriculture and Forest Regrowth in the Nitrogen of Old-Field Soils." *Forest Ecology and Management* 138 (2000): 233–248.

Risatti, Gillerno, and Manuel Borca. "Overview of Classical Swine Fever." *Merck Veterinary Manuel.* 2016. https://www.merckvetmanual.com/generalized-conditions/classical-swine-fever. Accessed January 2, 2017.

Ritter, Michael. *The Physical Environment: An Introduction to Physical Geography.* 2006. http://www.earthonlinemedia.com/ebooks/tpe_3e/title_page.html. Accessed July 6, 2013.

Roark, James. "Behind the Lines: Confederate Economy and Society." In *Writing the Civil War: The Quest to Understand,* edited by James M. McPherson and William J. Cooper Jr., 201–227. Columbia: University of South Carolina Press, 1998.

Rochester, Ian, Greg A. Constable, Derrick M. Oosterhuis, and Meredith Errington. "Nutritional Requirements of Cotton during Flowering and Fruiting." In *Flowering and Fruiting in Cotton,* edited by Derek Oosterhuis and J. Tom Cothren, 35–50. Cotton Foundation Reference Book Series 8. Cordova, TN: Cotton Foundation, 2012.

Rodrigue, Jean-Paul. *The Geography of Transport Systems.* 3rd ed. New York: Routledge, 2013.

Rodrigue, John. "Labor Militancy and Black Grassroots Political Mobilization in the Louisiana Sugar Regions, 1865–1868." *Journal of Southern History* 67, no. 1 (February 2001): 115–142.

———. *Reconstruction in the Cane Fields: From Slavery to Free Labor in Louisiana's Sugar Parishes, 1862–1880.* Baton Rouge: Louisiana State University Press, 2001.

Rogers, William Warren. *Confederate Home Front: Montgomery during the Civil War.* Tuscaloosa: University of Alabama Press, 1999.

Rood, Daniel. "Bogs of Death: Slavery, the Brazilian Flour Trade, and the Mystery of Vanishing Millponds in Antebellum Virginia." *Journal of Southern History* 101, no. 1 (June 2014): 19–43.

Rose, E. P. "Impact of Military Activities on Local and Regional Geologic Conditions." In *Humans as Geologic Agents,* edited by J. Ehlen, W.C. Haneburg, and R.A. Lawson, 51–66. Reviews in Engineering Geology. Boulder, CO: Geological Society of America, 2005..

Rostlund, Erhard. "The Myth of a Natural Prairie Belt in Alabama: An Interpretation of Historical Records." *Annals of the Association of American Geographers* 47, no. 4 (December 1957): 392–411.

Rothman, Adam. *Slave Country: American Expansion and the Origins of the Deep South.* Cambridge, MA: Harvard University Press, 2005.

Rothman, Joshua. *Flush Times and Fever Dreams: A Story of Capitalism and Slavery in the Age of Jackson.* Athens: University of Georgia Press, 2012.

Royster, Charles. *The Destructive War: William Tecumseh Sherman, Stonewall Jackson, and the Americans.* New York: Alfred A. Knopf, 1991.

Rubin, Julius. "The Limits of Agricultural Progress in the Nineteenth-Century South." *Agricultural History* 49, no. 2 (April 1975): 362–373.

Ruef, Martin. *Between Slavery and Capitalism: The Legacy of Emancipation in the American South.* Princeton, NJ: Princeton University Press, 2014.

Russell, Edmund. "Evolution and the Environment." In *The Wiley-Blackwell Companion to Global Environmental History,* edited by J. R. McNeill and Erin Stewart Mauldin, 377–393. London: Wiley-Blackwell, 2012.

———. *Evolutionary History: Uniting History and Biology to Understand Life on Earth.* Cambridge: Cambridge University Press, 2011.

Russell, Richard J. *River and Delta Morphology.* Coastal Series Study No. 20. Baton Rouge: Louisiana State University Press, 1967.

Sachs, Aaron. "Stumps in the Wilderness." In *The Blue, the Gray, and the Green: Toward an Environmental History of the Civil War,* edited by Brian Allen Drake, 96–112. Athens: University of Georgia Press, 2015.

Saikku, Mikko. *This Delta, This Land: An Environmental History of the Yazoo-Mississippi Floodplain.* Athens: University of Georgia Press, 2005.

Saville, Julie. *The Work of Reconstruction: From Slave to Wage Laborer in South Carolina, 1860–1870.* Cambridge: Cambridge University Press, 1994.

Sawyer, John E. "Potassium Deficiency in Corn." *Integrated Crop Management* 484, no. 15 (June 26, 2000). http://www.ipm.iastate.edu/ipm/icm/2000/6-26-2000/kdef.html. Accessed March 13, 2014.

Scarborough, William Kauffmann. *The Allstons of Chicora Wood: Wealth, Honor, and Gentility in the South Carolina Lowcountry.* Baton Rouge: Louisiana State University Press, 2011.

Schmitz, Mark D. "Postbellum Developments in the Louisiana Sugar Cane Industry." *Publications of the Business History Conference* 5 (1976): 88–101. http://www.jstor.org/stable/23702782. Accessed January 5, 2014.

Schlomowitz, Ralph. "'Bound' or 'Free'? Black Labor in Cotton and Sugarcane Farming, 1865–1880." *Journal of Southern History* 50, no. 4 (November 1984): 569–571.

Schweninger, Loren. "Black Economic Reconstruction in the South." In *The Facts of Reconstruction: Essays in Honor of John Hope Franklin*, edited by Eric Anderson and Alfred Moss Jr., 167–188. Baton Rouge: Louisiana State University Press, 1991.

Scott, James C. *Against the Grain: A Deep History of the Earliest States.* New Haven, CT: Yale University Press, 2017.

Scott, Rebecca J. *Degrees of Freedom: Louisiana and Cuba after Slavery.* Cambridge, MA: Belknap Press of Harvard University Press, 2005.

———. *Slave Emancipation in Cuba: The Transition to Free Labor, 1860–1899.* Princeton, NJ: Princeton University Press, 1985.

Sharpe, Peter. "Sugar Cane: Past and Present." *Ethnobotanical Leaflets*, Southern Illinois University Carbondale. Last updated October 26, 1998. http://opensiuc.lib.siu.edu/cgi/viewcontent.cgi?article=1388&context=ebl. Accessed July 3, 2017.

Sharrer, G. Terry. "The Great Glanders Epizootic, 1861–1866: A Civil War Legacy." *Agricultural History* 69, no. 1 (Winter 1995): 79–97.

Shell, Eddie Wayne. *Evolution of the Alabama Ecosystem.* Montgomery, AL: New South Books, 2013.

Sheridan, Richard. "Chemical Fertilizers in Southern Agriculture." *Agricultural History* 53, no. 1 (January 1979): 308–318.

Silver, Timothy. *A New Face on the Countryside: Indians, Colonists, and Slaves in South Atlantic Forests, 1500–1800.* Cambridge: Cambridge University Press, 1990.

———. "Learning to Live with Nature: Colonial Historians and the Southern Environment." *Journal of Southern History* 73, no. 3 (August 2007): 539–552.

Simkins, Francis Butler, and Charles Pierce Roland. *A History of the South.* 4th ed. New York: Alfred A. Knopf, 1972.

Singer, Jeremy, and Phil Bauer. "Crop Rotations for Row Crops." *Soil Quality for Environmental Health.* Last modified June 11, 2009. http://soilquality.org/practices/row_crop_rotations.html. Accessed June 18, 2014.

Singer, Michael, and Donald Munns. *Soils: An Introduction.* New York: Macmillan, 1991.

Slavicek, Louise Chipley. *Women and the Civil War.* New York: Infobase Publishing, 2009.

Smiley, David. "History, Central Themes." In *The New Encyclopedia of Southern Culture*, vol. 3: *History*, edited by Charles Reagan Wilson, 126–130. Chapel Hill: University of North Carolina Press, 2006.

Smith, Andrew. *Starving the South: How the North Won the Civil War.* New York: St. Martin's Press, 2011.

Smith, C. Wayne, and J. Tom Cothren, eds. *Cotton: Origin, History, Technology, and Production.* London: John Wiley and Sons, 1999.

Spickler, Anna Rovid. "Classical Swine Fever: Technical Factsheet." Center for Food Security and Public Health at Iowa State University. http://www.cfsph.iastate.edu/Factsheets/pdfs/classical_swine_fever.pdf. Accessed April 11, 2014.

Snay, Michael. *Fenians, Freedmen, and Southern Whites in the Era of Reconstruction.* Baton Rouge: Louisiana State University Press, 2007.

Souvent, P., and S. Pirc. "Pollution Cause by Metallic Fragments Introduced into Soil Because of World War I Activities." *Environmental Geology* 40, no. 3 (2001): 317–323.

St. Clair, Kenneth Edson. "Debtor Relief in North Carolina during Reconstruction." *North Carolina Historical Review* 18, no. 3 (July 1941): 215–235.

Stampp, Kenneth. *And the War Came: The North and the Secession Crisis, 1860–61.* Baton Rouge: Louisiana State University Press, 1950.

Steinberg, Ted. *Down to Earth: Nature's Role in American History.* 3rd ed. New York: Oxford University Press, 2012.

———. "Fertilizing the Tree of Knowledge: Environmental History Comes of Age." *Journal of Interdisciplinary History* 35, no. 2 (Autumn 2004): 265–277.

———. *Nature Incorporated: Industrialization and the Waters of New England.* 1991. Reprint, Cambridge: Cambridge University Press, 2003.

Stewart, Mart A. "If John Muir Had Been an Agrarian: American Environmental History West and South." *Environment and History* 11 (2005): 139–162.

———. "Slavery and the Origins of African American Environmentalism." In *"To Love the Wind and the Rain": African Americans and Environmental History,* edited by Dianne D. Glave and Mark Stoll, 9–20. Pittsburgh, PA: University of Pittsburgh Press, 2006.

———. "Southern Environmental History." In *A Companion to the American South,* edited by John B. Boles, 409–423. Oxford: Blackwell, 2002.

———. *"What Nature Suffers to Groe": Life, Labor, and Landscape on the Georgia Coast, 1680–1920.* Athens: University of Georgia Press, 1996.

———. "'Whether Wast, Deodand, or Stray': Cattle, Culture, and the Environment in Early Georgia." *Agricultural History* 65, no. 3 (Summer 1991): 1–28.

Stoll, Steven. *Larding the Learn Earth: Soil and Society in Nineteenth Century America.* New York: Hill and Wang, 2003.

Stover, John. *The Railroads of the South, 1865–1900: A Study in Finance and Control.* Chapel Hill: University of North Carolina Press, 1955.

Strom, Claire. *Making Catfish Bait out of Government Boys: The Fight against Cattle Ticks and the Transformation of the Yeoman South.* Athens: University of Georgia Press, 2009.

———. "Texas Fever and the Dispossession of the Southern Yeoman Farmer." *Journal of Southern History* 66, no. 1 (February 2000): 49–74.

Sutter, Paul. *Let Us Now Praise Famous Gullies: Providence Canyon and the Soils of the South.* Athens: University of Georgia Press, 2015.

———. "Waving the Muddy Shirt." In *The Blue, the Gray, and the Green: Toward an Environmental History of the Civil War,* edited by Brian Allen Drake, 225–235. Athens: University of Georgia Press, 2015.

———. "The World with Us: The State of American Environmental History." *Journal of American History* 100, no. 1 (June 2013): 94–119.

Sutter, Paul, and Christopher Manganiello, eds. *Environmental History and the American South: A Reader.* Athens: University of Georgia Press, 2009.

Swanson, Drew A. "Fighting over Fencing: Agricultural Reform and Antebellum Efforts to Close the Virginia Open Range." *Virginia Magazine of History and Biography* 117, no. 2 (2009): 104–139.

———. *A Golden Weed: Tobacco and Environment in the Piedmont South.* New Haven, CT: Yale University Press, 2015.

———. *Remaking Wormsloe Plantation: The Environmental History of a Lowcountry Landscape.* Athens: University of Georgia Press, 2012.

Sword, Wiley. *The Confederacy's Last Hurrah: Spring Hill, Franklin, and Nashville.* Lawrence: University Press of Kansas, 1993.

Taylor, Joseph. "The Great Migration from North Carolina in 1879." *North Carolina Historical Review* 31, no. 1 (January 1954): 18–33.

Temin, Peter. "The Post-Bellum Recovery of the South and the Cost of the Civil War." *Journal of Economic History* 36, no. 4 (December 1976): 898–907.

Thomas, William G., and Edward Ayers. "The Differences Slavery Made: A Close Analysis of Two American Communities." *American Historical Review* 108, no. 5 (December 2003): 1299–1307.

Thompson, Louis Milton. *Soils and Soil Fertility.* New York: McGraw-Hill, 1952.

Tracy, Susan. *In the Master's Eye: Representations of Women, Blacks, and Poor Whites in Antebellum Southern Literature.* Amherst: University of Massachusetts Press, 2009.

Trexler, Harrison. "The Opposition of Planters to the Employment of Slaves as Laborers by the Confederacy." *Mississippi Historical Valley Historical Review* 27, no. 2 (September 1940): 211–224.

Trimble, Stanley W. *Man-Induced Soil Erosion on the Southern Piedmont 1700–1790.* Ankeny, IA: Soil and Water Conservation Society, 1974.

Trudeau, Noah Andrew. *Southern Storm: Sherman's March to the Sea.* New York: Harper Collins, 2008.

University of Oregon. "Slave Crops in the American South: 1860." Mapping History. http://mappinghistory.uoregon.edu/english/US/map16.html. Accessed July 6, 2017.

"Urban Areas." *Global Environmental Outlook 3: Past, Present, and Future Perspectives.* United Nations Environment Programme, 2002. http://www.grida.no/publications/other/geo3/?src=/geo/geo3/english/406.htm. Accessed June 3, 2017.

Vale, Lisa. *Four Valiant Years in the Lower Shenandoah Valley, 1861–1865.* Strasburg, VA: Shenandoah, 1968.

Vanatta, Sean, and Dan Du. "Civil War Industry and Manufacturing," *New Georgia Encyclopedia.* http://www.georgiaencyclopedia.org/articles/history-archaeology/civil-war-industry-and-manufacturing. Accessed May 30, 2017.

Varon, Elizabeth. *Disunion! The Coming of the American Civil War, 1789–1859.* Chapel Hill: University of North Carolina Press, 2008.

Wackernagel, Mathis, and William Rees. *Our Ecological Footprint: Reducing Human Impact on the Earth.* Gabriola Island, CAN: New Society, 1996.

Wackernagel, Mathis, Justin Kitzes, Dan Moran, Steven Goldfinger, and Mary Thomas. "The Ecological Footprint of Cities and Regions: Comparing Resource Availability with Resource Demand." *Environment and Urbanization* 18, no. 1 (April 2006): 103–112.

Walker, H. Jesse, and James M. Coleman. "Atlantic and Gulf Coastal Province." In *Geomorphic Systems of North America,* edited by William Graft, 51–110. Boulder, CO: Geological Society of America, 1987.

Walker, Laurence. *The Southern Forest: A Chronicle.* Austin: University of Texas Press, 1991.

Walsh, Lorena. "Plantation Management in the Chesapeake, 1620–1820." *Journal of Economic History* 49, no. 2 (June 1989): 393–406.

Warren, Robert Penn. *The Legacy of the Civil War.* Lincoln: University of Nebraska Press, 1998.

Watson, Fred S. *Coffee Grounds: A History of Coffee County, Alabama, 1841–1970.* Anniston, AL: Higginbotham, 1970.

Watson, Harry. "'The Common Rights of Mankind': Subsistence, Shad and Commerce in the Early Republican South." *Journal of American History* 83, no. 1 (June 1996): 13–43.

Wayne, Michael. *The Reshaping of Plantation Society: The Natchez District, 1860–1880.* Urbana: University of Illinois Press, 1983.

Weidenmier, Marc. "Money and Finance in the Confederate States of America." *EH.Net Encyclopedia.* http://eh.net/encyclopedia/money-and-finance-in-the-confederate-states-of-america/. Accessed May 24, 2014.

Weiman, David. "The Economic Emancipation of the Non-Slaveholding Class: Upcountry Farmers in the Georgia Cotton Economy." *Journal of Economic History* 45, no. 1 (March 1985): 71–93.

———. "Farmers and the Market in Antebellum America: A View from the Georgia Upcountry." *Journal of Economic History* 47, no. 3 (September 1987): 627–647.

Weiner, Jonathan. *Social Origins of the New South: Alabama, 1860–1885.* Baton Rouge: Louisiana State University Press, 1978.

Wells, B. W. "Ecological Problems of the Southeastern United States Coastal Plain." *Botanical Review* 8 (1942): 533–561.

Wesley, L. D. "Les sols résiduals et l'enseignement de la mécanique des sols." Proceedings of the 18th International Conference on Soil Mechanics and Geotechnical Engineering. Paris, 2013.

Wetherington, Mark V. *The New South Comes to Wiregrass Georgia, 1860–1910.* Knoxville: University of Tennessee Press, 2001.

———. *Plain Folk's Fight: The Civil War and Reconstruction in Piney Woods Georgia.* Chapel Hill: University of North Carolina Press, 2009.

West, Stephen A. "'A General Remodeling of Everything': Economy and Race in the Postemancipation South." In *Reconstructions: New Perspectives on the Postbellum United States,* edited by Thomas Brown, 10–39. New York: Oxford University Press, 2006.

White, Marjorie Longnecker. *The Birmingham District: An Industrial History and Guide.* Birmingham, AL: Birmingham Historical Society, 1981.

Whitlock, Gregory, D. Mark Estes, and Alfredo Torres. "Glanders: Off to the Races with *Burkholderia mallei. FEMS Microbiology Letters* 277, no. 2 (2007): 115–122.

Wiley, Bell Irvin. *Life of Johnny Reb: The Common Soldier of the Confederacy.* 1943. Reprint, Baton Rouge: Louisiana State University Press, 2008.

Williams, Lou Falkner. *The Great South Carolina Ku Klux Klan Trials, 1871–1872.* Athens: University of Georgia Press, 1996.

Williams, Michael. *Americans and Their Forests: A Historical Geography.* Cambridge: Cambridge University Press, 1992.

Williams, Phil. "Richmond Plans for Defense." *150* [Special Issue of *RVa News*]. http://rvanews. com/features/richmond-plans-defense/46868. Accessed January 29, 2017.

Williams, T. Harry. *Lincoln and His Generals.* New York: Alfred A. Knopf, 1952.

Wilson, Edmund. *Patriotic Gore: Studies in the Literature of the American Civil War.* New York: Oxford University Press, 1962.

Windham, William T. "The Problem of Supply in the Trans-Mississippi Confederacy." *Journal of Southern History* 27, no. 2 (May 1961): 149–168.

Winters, Donald. "'Plain Folk' of the Old South Reexamined: Economic Democracy in Tennessee." *Journal of Southern History* 53 (November 1987): 565–586.

Winters, Harold. *Battling the Elements: Weather and Terrain in the Conduct of War.* With Gerald E. Galloway Jr., William J. Reynolds, and David W. Rhyne. Baltimore, MD: Johns Hopkins University Press, 1998.

Wise, James, and John Wise. *On Sherman's Trail: The Civil War's North Carolina Climax.* Charleston, SC: History Press, 1998.

Wood, Peter. *Black Majority: Negroes in Colonial South Carolina from 1670 through the Stono Rebellion.* New York: W. W. Norton, 1996.

"Woodburne Plantation—Winyah—Horry County." *South Carolina Plantations.* Horry Historical Society. http://south-carolina-plantations.com/horry/woodbourne.html. Accessed June 1, 2017.

Woodland, Dennis. *Contemporary Plant Systematics.* 3rd ed. Berrien Springs, MI: Andrews University Press, 2000.

Woodman, Harold D. "How New Was the New South?," *Agricultural History* 58, no. 4 (October 1984): 529–545.

———. *King Cotton and His Retainers: Financing and Marketing the Cotton Crop of the South, 1800–1925.* Columbia: University of South Carolina Press, 1990.

———. *New South, New Law: The Legal Foundations of Credit and Labor Relations in the Postbellum Agricultural South.* Baton Rouge: Louisiana State University Press, 1995.

———. "The Reconstruction of the Cotton Plantation in the New South." In *Essays on the Postbellum Southern Economy,* edited by Thavolia Glymph and John J. Kushma, 95–119. College Station: Texas A&M University Press, 1985.

———. "Sequel to Slavery: New History Views the Postbellum South." *Journal of Southern History* 43, no. 4 (November 1977): 523–554.

Woodward, C. Vann. *The Origins of the New South, 1877–1913.* Baton Rouge: Louisiana State University Press, 1951.

Worster, Donald. "Transformations of the Earth: Toward an Agroecological Perspective in History." *Journal of American History* 76, no. 1 (March 1990): 1087–1106.

Wright, Gavin. "Cotton Competition and the Post-Bellum Recovery of the American South." *Journal of Economic History* 34, no. 3 (September 1974): 610–635.

————. "Freedom and the Southern Economy." In *Market Institutions and Economic Progress in the New South, 1865–1900,* edited by Gary Walton and James Shepherd, 85–102. New York: Academic Press, 1981.

————. *Old South, New South: Revolutions in the South Economy since the Civil War.* Baton Rouge: Louisiana State University Press, 1997.

————. *The Political Economy of the Cotton South: Households, Markets, and Wealth in the Nineteenth Century.* New York: W. W. Norton, 1978.

Wright, Gavin, and Howard Kunreuther. "Cotton, Corn, and Risk in the Nineteenth Century." *Journal of Economic History* 35, no. 3 (September 1975): 526–551.

Zaborney, John. *Slaves for Hire: Renting Enslaved Laborers in Antebellum Virginia.* Baton Rouge: Louisiana State University Press, 2012.

Zak, Donald, David F. Grigal, Scott Gleeson, and David Tilman. "Carbon and Nitrogen Cycling during Old-Field Succession: Constraints on Plant and Microbial Biomass." *Biogeochemistry* 11, no. 2 (November 1990): 111–129.

Theses and Dissertations

Bowlby, Elizabeth. "The Role of Atlanta during the Civil War." Master's thesis, Emory University, 1939.

Brady, Lisa. "War upon the Land: Nature and Warfare in the American Civil War." PhD diss., University of Kansas, 2003.

Cochran, James. "James Asbury Tait and His Plantations." Master's thesis, University of Alabama, 1951.

Herrington, Philip Mills. "The Exceptional Plantation: Slavery, Agricultural Reform, and the Creation of an American Landscape." PhD diss., University of Virginia, 2012.

Hupy, Joseph. "Assessing Landscape Disturbance and Recovery Across a WWI Battlefield." PhD diss., Michigan State University, 2005.

Knerr, Sharon. "A New South Plantation: The Nixon-Bragg Lands of Alabama." Master's thesis, Samford University, 1984.

Long, Mark Howard. "Cultivating a New Order: Reconstructing Florida's Postbellum Frontier." PhD diss., Loyola University, 2007.

Pawley, Emily. "'The Balance Sheet of Nature:' Calculating the New York Farm, 1820–1860." PhD diss., University of Pennsylvania, 2011.

Singer, Ralph Benjamin, Jr. "Confederate Atlanta." PhD diss., University of Georgia, 1973.

Swanson, Drew. "Land of the Bright Leaf: Yellow Tobacco, Environment, and Culture along the Border of Virginia and North Carolina." PhD diss., University of Georgia, 2010.

INDEX

CPSIA information can be obtained
at www.ICGtesting.com
Printed in the USA
BVHW080203120222
628033BV00002B/8